SINDH

AND

THE RACES THAT INHABIT THE VALLEY OF THE INDUS

WITH

NOTICES OF THE TOPOGRAPHY AND HISTORY OF PROVINCE

SINDH

AND

THE RACES THAT INHABIT THE VALLEY OF THE INDUS

WITH

NOTICES OF THE TOPOGRAPHY AND

HISTORY OF PROVINCE

RICHARD F. BURTON

GYAN

Published by

GYAN

Gyan Publishing House
5, Ansari Road
Daryaganj, New Delhi-110002
Phone: 011-47034999, 9811692060
E-mail: books@gyanbooks.com

Distribution Network
gyanbooks.com
India, USA, Canada, UK, Australia, France

ISBN : 978-81-212-4019-2 (PB)
First Published, London, 1851

2nd Impression 2020

Printed at: Gyan Press, Delhi.

Sindh and the Races that Inhabit the Valley of the Indus
Author: Richard F. Burton

TO THE

HONOURABLE THE COURT OF DIRECTORS

OF THE

EAST INDIA COMPANY,

THIS ATTEMPT TO DELINEATE

A PROVINCE OF THE EMPIRE OWNING THEIR EXTENDED RULE,

IS,

WITH MUCH RESPECT,

DEDICATED

BY THEIR VERY OBEDIENT SERVANT,

R. F. BURTON,

LIEUTENANT BOMBAY ARMY.

PREFACE.

THE object of the following pages must briefly be explained.

During a residence of five years in Sindh, the author had frequent opportunity to remark, and cause to regret, the want of a single work treating upon the several subjects of the manners and customs, the domestic details, and the religious opinions of the people among, and with whom, he lived. The descriptions of Sindh and its inhabitants hitherto published were found of little use: they are either of too popular a nature, intended to introduce the country to the home reader, or written with the view of imparting a superficial knowledge of the language. Equally unserviceable are the many valuable works composed by residents in Hindostan and the Deccan, on account of the difference of dialects, habits and belief.

This work is offered to the Sindhi student with little hesitation. It contains long descriptions of the studies, religion and ceremonies peculiar to the race inhabiting our newly conquered country, the first specimens of the language, and notices of the literature ever printed, and what is of more consequence, a detailed account of native habits and customs, manners and ceremonies.

It were needless to enlarge upon our duty as a nation "accurately to know the condition of so many of our fellow-subjects in the East." And it would be difficult to supply a better illustration of the popular axiom, "Knowledge is power," than the conduct of Orientals towards those who understand them, compared with their contempt felt, if not expressed, for the ignorant.

The learned Orientalist will find little in the following pages to merit or attract his attention. Much new matter has, it is presumed, been collected by the labour of years. But the splendid mine of Oriental literature has long ceased to enrich all who will take the trouble to rifle its superficial treasures. Labourers must now content themselves with following out the veins that have escaped the notice of those who preceded them. And, generally, the European Orientalist is satisfied with a certain amount of details, as he has little inducement to pursue the subject to its end.

Yet it is hoped these pages will supply a few items to the list of useful details, and correct some grave errors which have hitherto been allowed to pass unnoticed.

For the convenience of the general reader, short sketches of the topography and history of the country have been drawn from the pages of former labourers in the field. The frequent insertion of hard Oriental words, and the occasional introduction of passages in the vernacular language of the province, will, it is hoped, be excused, in consideration of the advantage which may therefrom accrue to the Sindhi and Eastern students. As regards the details of domestic life, the author has striven to the utmost to avoid all unnecessary indelicacy; but in minute descriptions of the manners and customs of a barbarous or semi-civilized race, it is, as every traveller knows, impossible to preserve a work completely pure.

One point remains to be touched upon. The author has sedulously shunned all allusion to the "still vexed" questions concerning the conquest of Sindh, which for some years have been before the public. It was his intention to write a work interesting to the linguist and the ethnographer, not to enlist himself in the ranks of political partisanship.

In conclusion, it may be remarked that the following pages might long have remained in the obscurity of manuscript, had they not been drawn from it by the liberal patronage which the Court of Directors of the Hon. E. I. Company have ever been ready to extend to their servants.

Especially to Lieut.-Colonel Sykes, F.R.S., John Petty Muspratt, Esq., and Professor Horace Hayman Wilson, the gratitude of the author is due for the kind assistance and friendly advice with which they forwarded his views and encouraged his labours.

LONDON, 1*st October*, 1851.

CONTENTS.

HISTORY OF SINDH.

CHAPTER I.

GENERAL APPEARANCE OF SINDH; ITS VALUE AS A MILITARY AND COMMERCIAL POSITION.—SKETCHES OF ITS TOPOGRAPHY AND HISTORY.

THE traveller who visits Sindh after Western India, sees at the first glance that he has entered a new land. The face of the country,—here a vast waste of silt, sand, or arid rock, thinly covered with different species of salsolæ, cactus, and euphorbia; there a thick jungle of tamarisk, mimosa, and acacia, with rare intervals of cultivated ground, intersected by a network of water-courses, canals, and dried-up beds of rivers, first attracts his attention. He observes that the towns are collections of narrow streets and alleys, formed by huts and houses of sun-dried brick, and walls made of Kahgil[1] plastered over a framework of Babul (mimosa) wood, with the high stories, diminutive doors and windows, flat roofs, and numerous ventilators of Central Asia. Not less remarkable are the little Goths or villages, with their cottages of wattle work and matting, surrounded by thorny fences, or low walls of coarsely-made puddle. The forms and features, the complexion and costume of the inhabitants, also appear strange to the Indian tourist.

B

As regards climate, the visitor soon discovers that the want of a monsoon is but poorly supplied by the cloudiness of the summer months, and the heavy dews that fall throughout the year. The extremes of diurnal heat and cold, the burning rays of the sun, and the frequent dust-storms[2] which prevail at certain seasons, are severely felt.

The chief merits which Sindh in its present state possesses, are its capability of improvement, and its value to us as a military and commercial position. The vast heaps of ruins which cover the face of the country, the traces of great and important works, the concurrence of tradition, historians, and travellers, in describing its ancient glories, are so many proofs that the province was not always what it is now. And as its gradual decline may be attributed to internal dissensions and external wars, with their natural result—a thinness of population caused by famine, disease, and consequent emigration—the means of restoring health and vigour to the system are always in our hands. The events of the last three years have proved the value of Sindh as a depot for the material of war, and a base for concentrating forces, establishing reserves, and executing flank movements against the unruly nations to the north and north-east. The advantage already secured to us by its conquest is simply this. Had the Sikhs in the Punjab and Multan, the Affghans in the north, and the fierce, warlike, and bigoted mountaineers to the west, been aided and directed by the Ameers of Sindh,[3] the most disastrous consequences must have ensued. The merits of the province as a commercial position, also, are, to a certain extent, established by the increase of the Cafila trade, and the decline of the harbours along the coast of Mekran and Southern Persia. The once flourishing ports of Sonmeanee, Guadel, Bucker, and others as far as Bunder Abbas, are rapidly becoming of so little value to their native rulers, that eventually we shall find no difficulty in becoming masters of them by purchase or treaty. Nor is it too much to expect, that with this line of guarded outposts, we might easily collect the whole trade of Central Asia, and direct it at our will, by establishing Bombay as the point to which all these widely-diverging rays would tend.

The territory called Sindomana by the Greeks, the Sindhudesha of the ancient Hindoos, the Sind[4] of the Arabian geographers, and the Sindhu of its present inhabitants, is bounded by the Bahawalpur territories on the north, and on the south by the Indian Ocean. Sandy deserts compose its eastern frontier, and on the western rises the rocky range known in Europe by the name of the Hala Mountains. It is situated between the 23rd and 29th degrees of north latitude, and the 67th and 70th parallels of east longitude: its greatest length is about three hundred, and its maximum breadth one hundred and twenty miles.

The river Indus bisects the whole length of the country.

The geography and history of the province in ancient ages are equally obscure. Deserts spring up, cities, ports and towns fall in the space of time which it takes the Indus to shift its bed for a few miles, or a native prince to remove his capital. Except in a few cases, it is vain to speculate on the topography of the country fifty years ago.

Sindh has been divided from time immemorial into three[5] districts:—

1. Lar, or Southern Sindh, comprehending the country south of Hyderabad.

2. Wicholo, or Central Sindh, the district lying immediately around Hyderabad; and,

3. Siro, or Northern Sindh, comprising the provinces of Sehwan, Larkhana, Khairpur, and the tract that separates Sukkur from Cutch Gundava.

Lower Sindh, including the Delta of the Indus, occupies a space of from seventy to eighty English miles in length and breadth. It is a vast plain of silt, thickly covered with tamarisk and camel-thorn, and thinly populated on account of the saltness of the water. The whole of this tract is within the influence of the sea-breeze; but the inundations of the Indus, and the fierce rays of the sun, combine to render the atmosphere essentially insalubrious.

Towards the west of Lar, the country is desert and arid, presenting the appearance of a thin layer of sand, spread over a mass of limestone rock, which, in the vicinity of Gharrah, Tattah, and other places, forms irregular chains of low, abrupt and rugged hills. The coast is particularly dangerous during the prevalence of the south-west monsoon, when a heavy, tumultuous sea is continually running: it abounds in shoals and sandbanks, and each little harbour and roadstead has its bar. In the fine season, it offers few or no difficulties; the soundings are always a sufficient guide to, and the alternate land and sea-breezes that prevail during the cold weather facilitate the operations of, the navigator.

The principal towns in Lar, are Kurrachee and Tattah.

Kurrachee, in ancient times, belonged to the province of Mekran; it was wrested from the chief of Kelat by the Talpur Ameers, and is now the head-quarters of the local government. Its present importance is the result of advantageous position; its cool[6] and comparatively healthy climate rendering it the common sanitarium of Sindh, whilst its port carries on a brisk trade with Persia, Arabia, and Western India. The native town is a miserable collection of wattle huts and mud houses, clustering round the ruined walls of a native fort. To the north and west, where sweet water is found, there are some gardens, well planted with vegetables and fruit trees, but the rest of the neighbouring country is a salt or sandy desert. Kurrachee is rapidly increasing in size and improving in appearance: it now contains about 24,000 inhabitants, and the large military cantonment adds every day population and prosperity to the place.

Tattah has erroneously been supposed to be the ancient Pattala.[7] Under the Moslem dynasties, it was the capital of the Delta, and the most considerable place in Sindh. At one time the Indus washed its walls, bringing to its gates the wealth and traffic which Kurrachee now monopolizes; at present the stream is about three miles distant. Its population, anciently estimated at 280,000, probably does not amount to 7,000 souls; and some migrate every year to towns and districts which suffer less from malaria fever.[8] The town is a squalid mass of ruins, with here and there a lofty brick house or a glittering minaret, the vestiges of old prosperity: it is surrounded by plantations of mangos, which are celebrated for their flavour, and the usual tamarisk jungle. In the vicinity are to be seen ruins of extensive forts, places of Hindoo pilgrimage, and on the Mekli Hills, some beautiful mausolea erected over the remains of great governors and celebrated saints.[9]

The only other localities of any note in Lar, are Garrah, a large village, and once a military cantonment, situated on a creek that runs up from Kurrachee to within twenty-four miles of Tattah; Vikkur, a port on the Hujamri branch of the Indus; and Maghribi, on the eastern arm of the Delta.

In Wicholo, or Central Sindh, stands Hyderabad, which succeeded Tattah as the metropolis of the country. It was built by the Kalora dynasty, upon the ruins of an ancient Hindoo town, which occupied a ridge of limestone hills running parallel with the eastern bank of the Indus. The city, like most native capitals in this part of Asia, consists of a huge mass of huts and houses, bazaars, and mosques, with a fort or citadel of formidable appearance, but of no real value, formerly appropriated to the use of the reigning family. The population has been variously estimated: it is now about equal to that of Kurrachee, but owing to the prevalence of fever and ague, and the decadence caused by the removal of the seat of government, it is gradually decreasing. During the inundation, the Fulailee river, a branch of the main stream, encircles Hyderabad, and flows through beautiful gardens of palm, mimosa, pomegranate, mango, and other trees. A road leads down from the city to the Entrenched Camp on the Indus, the scene of the celebrated attack on the British Agency by the rabble army of the ill-fated ex-rulers of Sindh. On the other side of the river is Kotree, the station of the flotilla: to the westward of Hyderabad are some remarkable monuments and cenotaphs, erected in honour of the Kalora princes and Talpur Ameers.

In Wicholo are also Jarrak, a pretty town built on a ledge of rock which overhangs the Indus; Nasirpur, near Hyderabad, supposed by D'Anville to be the Mansura of the Arabs; Khudabad, an ancient town of more past fame than present prosperity; Mirpur, the capital of a branch of the royal house of Talpur; and further towards the Tharr or Little Desert, Omerkot, the birth-place of the Emperor Akbar, and the desert stronghold of the Hyderabad princes of Sindh.

Advancing up the river, the traveller arrives at the confines of Siro; the first thing that he remarks, is the sensible change of climate. Beyond Hyderabad the sea-breeze is not felt, the consequence of which, during the hot season, is a stagnation of atmosphere, peculiarly distressing. The summer lasts from eight to nine months, with no other break but an occasional cloudiness of sky, or a passing shower: the simoom, or wind of the desert, is a frequent visitor, and the dust-storms, which prevail throughout the province, here increase in violence and frequency. In Siro, rain is considered a blessing, as the evaporation caused by the excessive dryness of the air soon carries off the water which the Indus spreads over the country.

During the cold season, the temperature of Northern is sensibly lower than that of Southern Sindh; and this, combined with the absence of moisture, is probably the reason why it is considered, notwithstanding its intense heat, the healthier of the two districts.

The land of Siro is here rich and productive, there dreary and sterile. Near the Indus are some fine and valuable districts—gardens, plantations, and hunting-grounds: away from it, all is either a howling waste of sand, a rank mass of tamarisk, or a wild heap of rocky mountains. The villages are, generally speaking, composed of huts built with reed-mats stretched across rafters and posts of any procurable wood; and the rude mud-forts, which protect every considerable settlement, give a predatory character to the general appearance of the country.

Northern Sindh contains many cities and towns of ancient and modern celebrity. On the western bank of the Indus lies Sehwan, the Sewistan of the Arabs: its ruined citadel has been supposed to be a relic of Alexander's power, and was, in Akbar's time, the key to the lower province. It is a hot, filthy, and most unwholesome place, remarkable for the rascality of its inhabitants, the mausoleum of its patron saint, Shah-Baz,[10] and the abundance of its beggars, devotees, and courtezans. The population of Sehwan scarcely amounts to 6,000 souls, and the miserably dilapidated appearance of the buildings, proves that its condition is by no means improving. Beyond Sehwan is Larkhana, the chief town of a well-watered and well-cultivated district; and apparently, with the exception of Kurrachee, the most prosperous place in Sindh. A large canal from the river affords it the means of water communication during the floods, and the country is studded with beautiful villages. Crossing the Indus, the traveller arrives at Khairpur, the seat of government and fortified residence of Mir Ali Murad, the only remaining ruler of the Talpur clan. It is a small place, although formerly the capital of Northern Sindh: its population scarcely equals that of Larkhana. The lands around it, though not so well cultivated as those lying on the western bank of the river, are, perhaps, equally fertile. Nearly due north of Khairpur, are Sukkur, Bukkur, and Rohri, all three places of considerable antiquity, and much sacred celebrity among the Sindhis, Hindoo as well as Moslem. Sukkur is a native town and a large European cantonment, built on a range of low, bare, and barren hills, the summits of which are crowned with ruined tombs and mosques: groves of date trees surround the place, and the scenery on the river is much admired. The island of Bukkur, a rocky mass disengaged from both banks by the action of the Indus, which rushes round it with immense velocity, was anciently looked on as the gate of Sindh. Opposite Sukkur is Rohri: several centuries ago it attained a high state of wealth and importance by its commerce, and the circumstance of its possessing a hair of the prophet's beard; the extortions of the Khairpur Ameers, however, soon reduced its fortunes to the lowest ebb. Sukkur and Rohri have been calculated to contain about 12,000 souls each; the number probably is underrated.

Shikarpur, a town twenty-four miles north-west of

Sukkur, is a place of almost Asiatic fame, on account of the mercantile speculations and extensive banking influence of its adventurous natives. It is built on a sultry and dusty plain, capable of being converted by irrigation into a rich and fertile country : a few miles beyond its walls begins a hopeless desert of salt sand. Shikarpur contains about 24,000 inhabitants : its houses and buildings are in a dilapidated condition, and nothing can be more filthy than the state of its narrow streets, and the large bazaar for which the town was once famous. It is now steadily declining: we have considerably reduced the extensive establishment which the occupation of Affghanistan required us to maintain on the high road to Candahar,[11] and its commerce is no longer in its former flourishing condition.

The other towns of note in Lar are, Kusmore, on the bank of the Indus, a port formerly of some consequence, and Subzulcote, a fort about fifty miles above Rohri, on the same side of the river.

The noble Indus is the characteristic geographical feature of Sindh.[12] It is at once the great fertilizer of the country, the medium of transit for merchandise, and the main line of communication for the inhabitants.

The general direction of the "Sweet-water Sea," as it is here termed, is nearly north and south. After rushing through the rocky gap which separates the towns of Bukkur and Rohri, it flows calmly and tranquilly in a south-west direction towards Sehwan, throwing off on its way a great branch, the Narrah, which passes through the Manchar Lake, becomes the Arral, and is received back into its parent stream. Meeting the rocky barrier at Sehwan, the Indus shifts to the south-east as far as Hyderabad, where it again changes to a S.S.W. course till it reaches Tattah. At the latter town the river splits into two streams, the Sata or eastern, and the Bagar or western arms, embraces the Delta, and disembogues itself into the sea through a number of embouchures, large and small.[13]

The inundation of the Indus, caused by the falling of heavy spring showers in the elevated regions traversed by its tributaries, and the snows of the Himalayas dissolved by the intense summer heat, commences about the middle of March, attains its maximum in August, continues alternately to rise and fall till the end of September, when it may be said to have a second flood, and regularly subsides from the beginning of October. During this season the river becomes a foul and turgid stream, abounding in gyratory currents, tremendous rapids, dangerous drift wood, shifting sandbanks, and violent swells, produced by the pressure of stormy winds against the mighty course of the torrent. Numerous channels, natural and artificial, carry off the surplus water, feeding and refilling the lakes and dandhs,[14] whose moisture has evaporated during the cold season. This periodical inundation so far answers the purposes of monsoon rain,[15] that it prevents the ground becoming salt, the inevitable consequence of drought in Sindh.

The native annals of the province are written in three languages, Arabic, Persian, and Sindhi.

The first attempts at a regular history of the country were composed in the learned dialect of the Moslems.

The author of the "Tohfat el Kiram," a well-known chronicle, expressly states that no attention was paid to the subject till about A.D. 1216, when Ali, the son of Ahmed, an inhabitant of Ooch, visited Bukkur, and found an Arabic account of the conquest of Sindh in the possession of one Kazi Ismail, a descendant of the compiler.[16]

The Persian histories of Sindh are very numerous and valueless. The earliest is the work of Ali, the son of Ahmed, above alluded to; and all succeeding authors have copied, word for word, his account of the age preceding and immediately following the Moslem invasion of the province. The other generally read books are,

1. Ferishtah's history, which borrows from the Haj-Nameh, the Khulasat el Hikayat, and the annals of Haji Mohammed Kandahari.[17]

2. The chronicle of Mir Masum of Bukkur, composed in Akbar's time: it is the most popular composition of its kind in Sindh.

3. The Tohfat el Kiram; 4. The Chach Nameh;[18] 5. The Tarikh Tahiri;—general histories of the province.

6. The Beglar Nameh; 7. The Tarkhan Nameh; 8. The Urghun Nameh;—works illustrating the particular portions of the history to which their names point.

The histories, if they may be so called, written in the Sindhi dialect, consist chiefly of stories and traditions of the infidel monarchs who defended, and the Moslem heroes who conquered, the country. They will be noticed in a future chapter.

It has been truly remarked by an acute observer,[19] that the country of Sindh, though traversed by the classic water of the Indus, and trodden by the armies of every invader of Hindustan, produces few monuments of antiquity useful to the historiographer, or interesting to the archæologist. To the native annals we look in vain for any account of the ages which intervened between the inroad of Alexander and the conquest of the country by the generals of the caliphs: except a few names of kings and some puerile legends, all lies shrouded in Cimmerian gloom.

The following is a compendium of Sindhi history :—

Sindh ruled by Hindoos, until conquered by the Moslems, A.D. 711.

Governed by the deputies of the Ommiad Caliphs, A.D. 750.

Governed by the deputies of the Abbasides, till annexed by Mahmud of Ghazni to his dominions in A.D. 1025.

Governed by a Sindhi tribe called the Sumrah, A.D. 1054.

The Sammah Rajputs overthrew the Sumrahs, A.D. 1315.

Conquered by Shah Beg Urghun, prince of Candahar, A.D. 1519.

Invaded by Humayun Padshah, the dethroned monarch of Delhi, A.D. 1543.

The Tarkhans, a family of military adventurers, obtained power, A.D. 1545.

Annexed by Akbar to Delhi, A.D. 1591.

Nur Mohammed, a Sindhi of the Kalora clan, became Subedar or governor under Nadir Shah, the Persian conqueror, in A.D. 1740.

The Kalhora dynasty overthrown by the Talpur Belochis, A.D. 1786.

Sindh conquered by Sir Charles Napier, and annexed to British India by Lord Ellenborough, A.D. 1843.

According to the Moslem historians, a dynasty of five Rahis,[20] who had their capital at Alor,[21] "ruled the lovely land of Sindh in ease and prosperity" for about 140 years. In the seventh century of our era, Rahi Sahasi the Second died without children, and his queen, after causing the death of all the rightful heirs to the sceptre, bestowed it upon her paramour, one Chach, a priestly politician. The Brahman was attacked by the neighbouring Rajput princes, but by much tact, and more treachery, he defeated all his enemies, and firmly seated himself on the usurped throne. His reign lasted forty years; and at his death he was succeeded by his son Dahir.

The fanatics of early Islam, who looked on Sindh as the gateway of India, soon found a pretext for declaring war against its infidel sovereign. The Caliph, Abd el Malik of the Ommiad dynasty, on receiving the intelligence that some of his ships had been plundered by the heathen, took immediate measures to punish the aggressors, and entrusted the command of a large army to one of his lieutenants, Hajjaj bin Yusuf. After some delay in consequence of the death of Abd el Malik, his son and successor, Walid, dispatched in the year 710 Mohammed Kasim, a general only seventeen years old, with 6,000 horse, an equal number of baggage camels, and a large body of infantry, to spread the faith of Mohammed and the desolation of war over the land of the Hindoo.

After capturing Dewal,[22] the principal port of Sindh, and Nirunkot, the stronghold of the southern provinces, and after defeating Dahir's immense army and slaying that sovereign under the walls of Alor, the capital, the youthful conqueror,[23] who appears to have managed the expedition with consummate skill, cruelty, and bravery, in A.D. 711 reported to his master that the highway of India was cleared of all that could oppose the heaven-directed progress of Islam.

For forty years subsequent to this period, Sindh was governed by deputies appointed by the Ommiad caliphs. When the Abbasides rose to power, they expelled the functionaries to whom their predecessors had committed the country, and in lieu of them, established lieutenants of their own. During the three subsequent centuries, the history of the province is a mere list of Hakims or governors, whose uninteresting rule seems scarcely to merit mention.

In A.D. 1025, Mahmud of Ghazni, the mighty Ghazi, or crusader, annexed Sindh to his wide dominions; and his deputies ruled throughout it in his name. Under the later Ghaznivites, a tribe of unknown extraction, called the "men of Sumrah,"[24] who, as influential landholders, had long exercised a kind of authority over certain portions of the country, became sufficiently powerful to declare their independence, and to secure the hereditary government of their native land. They maintained their position, when the descendents of Mahmud fell before the Affghan house of Ghor, in A.D. 1186, numbered a succession of twenty princes, took possession of Cutch and ruled for a period of about 260 years.

The Sammah Rajputs,[25] who are fancifully derived by the native annalists from Shem, the son of Noah, or Jamshid, the apocryphal Persian monarch, under a leader named Abrah, assisted by the forces of Ala el Din, the Delhi emperor, overthrew the power of the Sumrahs, and about the year 1315, became sovereign princes in Cutch and Sindh, converted probably by motives of policy to Islam. Fifteen Jams or chiefs in regular succession ruled the country nominally under the Patthan powers of Hindustan. The early Sammahs were, it would appear, refractory vassals, for one of them was attacked and chastised by Firuz Toghlak, of Delhi, about A.D. 1361.

Baber the Moghul caused, by defeating and slaying Ibrahim Lodi, the downfal of the Patthan dynasty, and established his own power in India about A.D. 1526 Seven years before that time, he had invaded Affghanistan, and driven from Candahar the descendant of its old possessors, Shah Beg Urghun. The latter prince made a descent upon Sindh, and overthrew the Sammah government in the person of Jam Firuz. The conqueror, however, recalled the dethroned chief from Guzerat, and allowed him to govern the districts about Tattah in feudatory subjection to himself. Shah Beg was harassed by the Moghuls, and hated by his new subjects: in A.D. 1521, when Bukkur, his stronghold, fell into the hands of the enemy, and Jam Firuz proved treacherous to him, he died, some say of grief, others by his own hand. His son and successor, Shah Hosain, expelled the Sammah, and retrieved the falling fortunes of his house by storming Multan, and by decisively defeating Rao Kingar, the Cutch prince, who had invaded the southern extremity of the province.

In A.D. 1540, Humayun, the son of Baber, being surprised, defeated, dethroned and succeeded by a celebrated soldier of fortune, Shir Khan Sur, turned towards Sindh, where he hoped his authority might be recognised. He passed into the Urghun territories through Ooch, spent a year and a half, and all his funds, in fruitless negotiations and futile hostilities, and when Shah Hosain advanced to attack him, fled precipitately for his liberty and life.[26] He made a second attempt on Sindh in 1543, but being only partially successful, he was glad to enter into a treaty with the Urghun, and marched towards his native kingdom, leaving that prince in greater authority than before.

Soon after Humayun's restoration, Mirza Isa Tarkhan, the head of a family of military adventurers, who had risen to the government of Tattah, raised the standard of revolt, and Shah Hosain Urghun, the infirm old sovereign of Sindh, died before he could stem the torrent of rebellion. In 1591, the great Akbar determining to recover a province which he considered an ancient fief of the house of Delhi, sent two armies, one to attack Sehwan, the other, *viâ* Omerkot, to distract the attention of Jani Beg, the Tarkhan chief.[27] The latter, after a brave defence, yielded, and was received with distinction by Akbar, who, as was his custom, raised him to a high rank among the nobles of his empire, and permanently annexed the province to the throne of Delhi, by attaching it to Multan and Candahar. The Tarkhans ruled in Sindh until the reign of Shah Jehan, when governors were appointed from Hindustan direct, to farm the revenues and manage the administration of the province.

The Kalora house owed their elevation to one of the causes which, amongst a Moslem people, leads to the highest honours of the state — a reputation for spiritual holiness.

About A.D. 1450, during the sway of the Sammahs, one Adam Shah Kalhora, a religious Sindhi,[28] became the Khalifeh (successor to the saintly rule) of a great devotee, Miyan Mohammed Mehdee, and thus founded a family which eventually ruled the land. His numerous descendants, not content with their eternal, began to improve their temporal prospects by plundering the neighbouring landholders with such vigour, that about the end of the seventeenth century, they became Zemindars of the first class. Their ever increasing power received a check from the Mogul governor of Multan, who routed their forces, and destroyed Din Mohammed, their chief. But the pliant saints, after a year's self-imposed exile to the hills of Kelat, obtained by timely submission an amnesty for all past offences, and under Miyan Nasir Mohammed, the son of Din Mohammed, returned to Sindh, determined to act as before, but with increased circumspection and subtilty.

Miyan Yar Mohammed, who succeeded his father as head of the house in A.D. 1708, thinking that his ambitious views were more likely to be gratified at Delhi than at Tattah, repaired to the Mogul metropolis, and at last obtained from Aurungzeb the gift of a province, and the title of Khuda Yar Khan as the reward of his persevering intrigue. He left two sons, Miyan

Mir Mohammed, and Miyan Daud Khan, to dispute the succession. The former, who appears to have been a brave and politic chief, defeated his rival brother, and in 1717 added to his father's possessions the province of Sehwan, bestowed by Mohammed Shah, of Delhi. He then overthrew and slew Mir Abdallah Khan, the Brahui lord of Kelat, who had invaded the low country, and in A.D. 1738, obtaining the Subedarship of Tattah from his imperial patron, he became the *de facto* ruler of Sindh.

In A.D. 1739, Nadir, the Persian conqueror, by a treaty made with the unfortunate Mohammed Shah, secured to himself all the countries west of the Indus. Eight years afterwards, when the great king fell by the sabre of conspiracy, Ahmed Khan, the Durrani,[29] hereditary chief of the Abdalis, caused himself to be formally declared king of Candahar, and exercised absolute authority over Sindh, as well as the other provinces which had been subjugated by Nadir Shah. Miyan Mir Mohammed, by his irregularity in paying tribute, incurred the displeasure of the Durrani, who after a successful invasion of Hindustan, turned his steps towards the Indus, for the purpose of chastising the unruly vassal. The latter in alarm fled towards the desert, fell sick there, and died. He was succeeded by his son, Murad Yab Khan, who did homage to the suzerain for investiture with the dignity of the family.

In A.D. 1756, Murad Yab Khan was deposed and confined by his nobles, who raised his brother Miyan Attar Khan to the vacant post of dignity. After a few month's reign, the new ruler was in his turn dethroned to make room for a third brother, Miyan Ghulam Shah.

Attar Khan, finding his cause hopeless in Sindh, fled to the court of Kabul, and so exerted himself there, that he procured a royal order for his restoration. Ghulam Shah fled to Joudpur, but shortly afterwards returning with a body of troops, fell upon his brother, and compelled him again to fly the country. The fugitive once more appealed to the Durrani throne, and the king, in order to support an authority which he had himself created, sent him back with a large Affghan army, which drove Ghulam Shah a second time into exile.

The chieftains and landholders of Sindh having advised and caused a division of the country between the two brothers, the Durrani's troops returned to Candahar; upon which, Ghulam Shah, disgusted with his share, one third, again rose up in arms against his brother. The latter fled to the Daudputra country, and placing himself under the protection of Bahadur Khan, began to make preparations for recovering his rights; but Ghulam Shah at once became the offensive party, attacked and slew the protector, and compelled the fugitive to seek an asylum elsewhere. Thus victorious, he returned to Sindh, and by judicious intrigue at the court of Candahar, obtained from Ahmed Shah all the titles, if not the rights, of an independent prince.

Ghulam Shah was eminently successful in his attempts to regulate and secure the prosperity[30] as well as the tranquillity of his dominions. He chastised the Khosas, a predatory tribe in northern Sindh, and defeated the ruler of the Daudputra country, in three or four pitched battles. He made additions to his territory by wresting the districts about Kurrachee from the Brahui people, and attacked Cutch with such violent cruelty,[31] that its prince was happy to make conditions of peace with him on any terms. Ghulam Shah put to death his nephews, whom he had discovered conspiring against his person; but he spared the life of, although he imprisoned, their father, Attar Khan, who, finding submission the only course left him, had ventured upon the perilous experiment of trusting to the tender mercies of an eastern brother. In A.D. 1765, he founded the fort of Hyderabad; and six years afterwards, he died in consequence, say his superstitious countrymen, of the curse of a Fakir, whose hut he had destroyed to make room for his palace.

Ghulam Shah was succeeded by his eldest son, Miyan Sarfaraz Khan, who obtained a confirmatory Firman and an exalted title from the Affghan monarch. He committed the fatal error of murdering the chief of the Talpur Beloch clan, Mir Bahram,[32] and took the equally impolitic step of expelling the Company's factory from Tattah. His violence and tyranny so offended all his subjects, that they conspired against, seized, and confined him, in the fifth year of his reign.

Upon the formal deposition of Sarfaraz, his brother, Miyan Mohammed Khan was raised to the Masnad: after about ten months' rule, being judged incapable of governing, he shared the fate of his predecessor. The chiefs of Sindh, amongst whom the turbulent Belochis, headed by their chief, Mir Fath Khan, now played the leading part, again took council, selected Miyam Sadik Ali Khan, a nephew of Ghulam Shah, to rule over them, dethroned and imprisoned him within the year.

About A.D. 1778, Ghulam Nabi Khan, uncle to the last ruler, by the aid of the Likhi Raja, a powerful Kalora noble, was elevated to the seat of government.

His first act was one of hostility against the Talpurs. Fearing that Mir Bijjar, a son of the murdered Bahram, who, at the time of his father's death, was absent on a pilgrimage to Mecca, would, if permitted to return, punish him for his nephew's crime, he intrigued with the Arabs of Muscat, employing every means in his power to despatch or secure the expected enemy. He failed, however, in the attempt, and paid the forfeit of aggression by losing his life in a battle fought against the Beloch clan, headed by their hereditary chief.

The last of the effete Kalora line was Miyan Abd el Nabi, brother to Ghulam Nabi. This prince began his reign by putting to death the imprisoned Sarfaraz Khan, and all the other near relations who might be dangerous to the permanency of his sway. Relying upon the religious respect claimed by his family, he boldly issued from the fort of Hyderabad, met the victorious Bijjar, and persuaded him and all his men to take an oath of allegiance.

By the good aid of the Belochis and their brave leader, Abd el Nabi defeated and put to flight Izzat Yar Khan, his nephew, who, with Affghan troops and a Firman from the court of Candahar, came down to assert his claim to Sindh. The ungrateful Kalora, influenced, it is supposed, by some jealous fear of his powerful subject, requited his services by treacherously murdering him. He then, with consummate deceit, exonerated himself of any participation in the deed to Mir Abdullah, the son of Mir Bijjar, and Mir Fath Khan, the son of Mir Sobdar, and soon after, persuading them to partake of his hospitality, destroyed them both. The Belochis, furious at this outrage, flew to arms, and headed by Mir Fath Ali Khan, the grandson of Mir Bahram, and his nephew, Sohrab Khan, marched upon Hyderabad. Abd el Nabi in A.D. 1781, fled the country, and thus the dynasty of the Kaloras came to an end.

The Talpur chiefs made a triumphal entry into Hyderabad, and Mir Fath Ali Khan, the head of the house, proceeded to settle himself firmly in his new position, knowing that it was threatened with many a storm. By his too evident anxiety to guard against danger from his own family, he alarmed his nephew Sohrab, and Mir Tharra, the son of Mir Fath Khan, to such an extent, that flying the capital, they seized the towns of Khairpur and Shah Bunder, possessed themselves of the neighbouring districts, remitted part of the revenue to Taymur Shah, and renounced allegiance to their ambitious kinsman. Thus the country was divided into three independent principalities, in which state it continued till conquered by the British army.

From A.D. 1786, may be dated the accession of the Talpurs, as they were about that time confirmed in their sovereignty by Taymur Shah.[33] When the latter died, Zeman Shah, his successor to the throne of Kabul, determined to collect in person the tribute of Sindh, which had been irregularly paid by Mirs Fath Ali, Sohrab and Tharra, and for that purpose he advanced as far as Multan. The three chiefs fled from the northern host, sent penitential excuses and promises of future punctuality; by the friendly intercession of Meer Mohammed, the Wazir, the monarch was prevailed upon to forgive the past, and the fugitives were admitted into the royal presence. When all danger of foreign invasion disappeared, domestic dissensions again threatened the Talpurs. Mir Sohrab proposed that Ghulam Hosain, the son of Abd el Nabi, the dethroned Kalora, should occupy the Masnad, of course to the exclusion of Fath Ali Khan. The latter immediately mustered all his kinsmen and adherents; both parties took the field, and torrents of blood would have been shed, had not the women of the tribe, throwing themselves between the swords of the hostile parties, dissuaded them from fratricidal strife.

The house of Talpur was divided, as has before been said, into three distinct branches, all offshoots of the same stem. The Hyderabad, or Shahdadpur family, ruled in central Sindh. The Mirpur, or Manikani house, descendants from Mir Tharra, reigned over a province called Mirpur, lying to the east of Hyderabad; and the Khairpur, or Sohrabani branch, by the right of descent from Mir Sohrab, governed at Khairpur, in Upper Sindh.

Mir Fath Ali, the head of the Hyderabad house, in order to preserve by union the strength of his family, devised the strange expedient of participating sovereign rank and power with his three younger brothers, Mirs Ghulam Ali, Karam Ali, and Murad Ali, all agreeing to live and reign together as Ameers or lords of Sindh. The real, or apparent unanimity subsisting between these princes, gained for them the appellation of the Char Yar, or "Four Friends," and community of interests made them truly formidable to their enemies. They cruelly persecuted the Kalora tribe, and secured the peace of the country by reducing to absolute obedience all the clans who showed any disposition to rebellion. They enlarged their dominions by recovering Kurrachee and Omerkot, which had been alienated to Kelat and Joudpur by their predecessor, Abd el Nabi, and by every petty art of intrigue sedulously exerted, they became powerful at the court of the Affghan monarch.

Fath Ali died A.D. 1801, leaving his treasure and territory unequally divided[34] between his surviving three brothers, to the exclusion of his infant son, Sobdar; he also made arrangements for state expenses, and for the regular payment of the Kabul tribute.[35] This event occasioned a change in the strictly feudal system of administration: the chiefs governed conjointly, under the title of Ameers, but the senior was invested as Rais, or chief of the family, with a degree of authority which gave a patriarchal character to the government.

In A.D. 1811, Ghulam Ali, the Rais, was killed when hunting; he left a single son, then eighteen years old, Mir Mohammed. The latter prince was, as well as his cousin Sobdar, excluded from all participation in power by their two remaining uncles, who continued for the rest of their lives to rule the country with joint authority. Karam Ali died in A.D. 1828, without issue; Murad Ali was succeeded by his two sons, Mir Mohammed and Nasir Khan.

The government at Hyderabad, up to A.D. 1840, was composed of Mir Mohammed, the Rais, his brother Nasir Khan, and their two cousins, Sobdar and Mir Mohammed.

In A.D. 1839, a treaty formed with the British Government, by substituting foreign for domestic influence, struck a direct blow at the patriarchal office of Rais-ship. Two years afterwards, when Mir Mohammed died, his sons, Mirs Shahdad and Hosain Ali, were allowed to share his possessions, under the guardianship of their uncle Nasir; but the latter prince, though nominally principal Ameer, could exercise no control over his nephews' affairs.

There is little to be noticed in the fortunes or the policy of the Khairpur and Mirpur houses, except that the former, as will presently be explained, threw the country into our hands, and the latter numbered amongst its chieftains the only Ameer whose personal prowess offered any resistance to our arms.

The connection between Sindh and the British Government in India began about A.D. 1758, when the Honourable East India Company obtained from Ghulam Shah, the Kalora, permission to establish a factory and send an agent to Tattah. The most friendly politic relations and a close commercial union subsisted between the two powers, until the year 1775, when they were suddenly and rudely broken off by the unworthy despot, Sarfaraz.

Towards the end of the eighteenth century, the local and home governments resolved to re-establish amicable intercourse, ostensibly for the purpose of trade, in reality to counteract the wide-spreading influence of the Mysore, and the ambitious aims of the Kabul thrones. Fath Ali Khan, the then ruler, gladly entered into the Company's views, restored to them the old Tattah factory, and treated their agent, Mr. Nathan Crow, of the Bombay Civil Service, with honourable distinction. The native traders, however, set on foot a system of intrigues which, combined with motives of policy, ended in the expulsion of the British representation. No attempt was made by our authorities to punish their barbarian insulter; Sindh had been found to offer few or no commercial advantages, and the political horizon was once more bright and clear.

In 1809, the views of Napoleon upon our Indian empire rendered it necessary to send embassies to the crowned heads of Persia, Kabul, and Sindh. The latter court behaved with overweening arrogance, and it was not before a succession of tedious and trying negotiations, that a treaty, bearing date 22nd August, was concluded by Mr. Hankey Smith, under Lord Minto, between the Company and the Talpur Ameers. It provided for "eternal friendship" between the two powers, interchange of friendly embassies, and the exclusion of all foreigners, especially French and Americans, from Sindh.

For some years the bonds of amity remained unimpaired. In A.D. 1825, however, the unprovoked attack upon our ally, the Rajah of Cutch, and the incursions of the Khosahs and other predatory tribes into our territories, caused the assemblage of a British force of demonstration, amounting to 5,000 or 6,000 men, upon the frontier of Sindh. The *causa belli* was at once removed.

In 1830 took place the voyage of Sir Alexander, then Lieutenant Burnes, up the Indus to the court of Runjeet Singh; and his report and accounts of the capabilities of the river, and the advantages to be derived from the countries on and beyond it, induced the British Government to look anxiously for a renewal of friendly intercourse with the Sindh Durbar. Two treaties were ratified and signed, one in '32, the other in '34, by Lord William Bentinck and Mir Murad Ali, the Rais of the Hyderabad house; by them the British Government gained its long-coveted object—permission of passage through Sindh, and the use of the river for their merchants and traders. The conditions required by the Hyderabad court were, that no armed boats should ascend or descend the Indus; that no military stores should be conveyed about the country; that no Englishman should settle in, and that no native trafficker should visit Sindh, without a passport from the resident at the court of Cutch. The tolls and duties were permanently settled; but the high rate charged, combined with the insecurity of travelling, tended to depress commercial enterprise. An Indus Steam Navigation Company was formed in England, and detailed surveys of the coast and river were prepared by scientific officers; still trade did not prosper.

In June 1838, was signed the tripartite treaty between Shah Shuja, Ranjeet Singh, and the British Government. The restoration of the Affghan monarch to his own country was determined upon. In the autumn of the same year, a large British force was despatched from Bengal through Upper Sindh towards the Bolan Pass, and simultaneously troops were ordered up from Bombay under Sir John Keane, commander-in-chief, with orders to land at the mouth of the Indus, and to effect a junction with the main column *viâ* the western bank of the river. This movement was fatal to the native rulers of Sindh. In the early part of 1838, terrified by the threats of the Punjab sovereign, they had availed themselves of the mediatory powers of the British, and in consideration of the service thus rendered to them, they had consented to receive an accredited agent at Hyderabad. Colonel Pottinger, the officer appointed, was directed by the Governor-General, Lord Auckland, to apprise the Talpurs, that contrary to the articles of the treaty between the two powers, the Indus must be used for the passage of military stores. The conduct of the native princes on this occasion seems to have been peculiarly Asiatic;[36] they promised all things, and did nothing but evade acting up to their professions; it was only by extraordinary exertions on the part of the political officers, that carriage for the Bombay column was at length forthcoming. The army with difficulty reached Tattah, when the demeanour of the Sindhian chiefs became so decidedly hostile,[37] that a reserve force was despatched from Bombay and landed at Kurrachee, to co-operate with a detachment of the Bengal army, marching down the river on Hyderabad. Before reaching their capital, Sir John Keane forwarded to the Ameers a memorandum of complaints, and a demand of one lac of rupees (10,000*l.*), to be paid annually by three of the chiefs,[38] in part of the expenses of the 5,000 British troops to be stationed in Sindh. After Sir John Keane's departure, Colonel Pottinger brought another treaty with the seal and signature of Lord Auckland, guaranteeing absolute future independence to the native princes, on condition of their liquidating certain arrears of tribute claimed by Shah Shuja. This the Ameers of Hyderabad[29] agreed to sign, at the same time despatching an envoy to Simlah for the purpose of appealing to the Governor-General against it, and their seals were not affixed to the document till some months after its transmission to them.

The success of the British arms in Affghanistan, and the indefatigable exertions of Major Outram, who had succeeded Colonel Pottinger as political agent at the court of Hyderabad, reconciled the minds of the Ameers and their jealous feudatories to what they at first considered an unjust encroachment upon their most sacred rights.

But the aspect of affairs changed at the close of 1840, when the defeats we had sustained in the Murree Mountains, and the violent outbreaks of fanatic fury in Shal and Kelat, aroused the spirit of independence in the Beloch bosom. The hill tribes in the north of Sindh had been exasperated by the disgrace with which their chiefs, who had submitted to us, were treated by the political agent at Sukkur; and after their irreconcileable hostility had been secured, the heads of clans were set at liberty. Family discord began to agitate the minds of the native princes. Mir Rustam, the Rais of the Khairpur house, was a debauched old man, in a state of dotage; his death was therefore soon to be expected, and three different factions[40] stood arrayed and ready for contest whenever the event might occur. Ali Murad, the ruler's younger brother, who had ostentatiously avoided British connection, then came forward to solicit our good offices in settling certain points at issue between him and the senior Mir. The decision was given in favour of the junior, a crafty, ambitious, and unprincipled man, who now, seeing how much was to be gained by us, suddenly became our warmest adherent.

During the fearful catastrophe which occurred at Kabul, the Sindhis and their chiefs took no part against us, a circumstance generally attributed to the honourable and sagacious line of policy adopted by Major Outram, the resident.

In the autumn of 1842, Sir Charles Napier arrived at Kurrachee, invested with sole authority, military and political, over the territories of the Lower Indus; all former arrangements for their administration being declared null and void. That distinguished soldier, after an interview with the Ameers at Hyderabad, embarked for Sukkur, and despatched an officer, bearing a letter and a new treaty, for the signature of the native princes. As a punishment for their former hostile intentions against us, they were required by Lord Ellenborough to cede in perpetuity the towns of Kurrachee, Tattah, Sukkur, Bukkur, and Rohri, with a strip of land on each bank of the river;[41] to abolish all transit dues throughout the Sindian territories, and to give over to the Khan of Bahawalpur the whole of the country from Rohri northward to Subzulcote. The terms imposed upon the Khairpur branch of the family, were the supercession of the elder Mir (Rustam), and the appointment of the junior and unpopular brother, Ali Murad, to the dignity of the Rais-ship, with a revenue that included one-fourth of the possessions belonging to the other seventeen co-rulers of Upper Sindh. The Ameers twice sent agents to the general, representing the loss of revenue and respect which their acceptance of such propositions would entail upon them; Sir Charles Napier replied, that he acted by the orders of the Governor-General.

Sir Charles Napier allowed the Ameers short time for debate or counsel: a march in the two capitals was intimated in case of delay or evasion in signing the treaty, and a body of troops at once took the field. Mir Rustam Khan fled from Khairpur, towards the desert, whither he was followed by the British general. In the meantime, Major Outram, whose political appointment in Sindh had been abolished, was suddenly recalled from Bombay, and joined Sir Charles Napier at the fortress of Diji. A detached force[42] pursued the flying chief to Imamgarh, a small castle in the eastern desert; finding the place deserted, they blew up the works and retired. Major Outram proceeded alone to the camp of Mir Rustam, and brought the chief's son and nephew into the general's presence, but nothing could now avert the coming storm.

Pursuant to orders, Sir Charles Napier, with a small army of 2,700 men of all arms, marched down the eastern bank of the Indus upon Hyderabad; whilst Major Outram, escorted by the light company of H.M. 22nd regiment, preceded him to the capital. The Ameers, having the excuse of compulsion to oppose to the violent indignation of their Beloch feudatories, on the 14th of February, 1843, formally affixed their seals to the draft treaty, under the delusion entertained, notwithstanding the envoy's open assurances of his inability to make any promises, that their submissive attitude would entitle their representations of Mir Rustam's case to the favourable consideration of the highest authority.

Still Sir Charles Napier had continued to advance, and the assembled clansmen, irritated to the highest pitch, determined to fall upon Major Outram, and those who accompanied him on their return from the fort of Hyderabad. The Ameers, obtaining timely information of the intended attack, re-conducted the British representative in safety to the Agency, under the protection of several of their principal chiefs: and Mir Nasir Khan, feeling that he had lost power over his infuriated subjects, sent messages and letters to Major Outram, warning him of his danger, and entreating him to retire from the vicinity of Hyderabad with the least possible delay.

On the 15th of February, 1843, a dense body of Beloch cavalry and infantry attacked Major Outram in the Agency, a building surrounded by a low wall, on the eastern bank of the river. After a most gallant defence, which lasted for four hours, against overwhelming numbers, the British troops, commanded by Captain Conway, retreated in perfect order, with the loss of only two men, embarked on board the steamers, and started up the Indus to rejoin the general.[43]

On the 17th, took place the celebrated battle of Meeanee, in which Sir Charles Napier and his little army, by admirable conduct and desperate valour, obtained a decisive victory over a vast host of the enemy, strongly posted, and defended by artillery. The principal Ameers of Hyderabad and Khairpur surrendered to the general, who, after taking up a position at the Agency, marched into the capital, and seized the treasures which the fort contained.

War, however, had not ceased in Sindh. Attacks were made in different parts of the country on our detachments, but in every case, the sepoys repulsed them with courage and discipline. On the 24th of March, Sir Charles Napier, reinforced by troops from Sukkur, attacked at the village of Dubba, with his 5,000 men, the 20,000 Belochis whom Sher Mohammed of Mirpur had led into the field. The enemy was completely defeated, their leader fled to the desert, the forts of Omerkot and Mirpur opened their gates, and by this second blow, the tottering throne of the house of Talpur irretrievably fell. The conqueror of Sindh was appointed to govern as well as to command the province which his gallantry had won; and British officers were nominated to collect the revenue and administer justice throughout the newly annexed possession.

The fallen Ameers, consisting of Nasir Khan, and his nephews, Shahdad and Hosain Ali, with Mir Mohammed, and Sobdar[44] of Hyderabad; Mir Rustam Khan, and his nephews, Nasir Khan, and Wali Mohammed of Khairpur, with others, were sent in captivity to Bombay; whence, in 1844, they were removed to Bengal, where a few of them still exist in a kind of state prison, the melancholy spectacle of fallen greatness.

CHAPTER II.

THE ANCIENT COURSE OF THE INDUS. CANAL IRRIGATION UNDER THE NATIVE PRINCES, AND THE PRESENT RULE. SYSTEM OF TAXATION IN THE TIME OF THE AMEERS.

WITH respect to the geographical position of the Indus in remote ages, little remains to be said. The different opinions concerning its course in the days of Alexander, and the various arguments for and against the theory of its ancient channel having been to the eastward of the present bed, have been discussed *usque ad nauseam*.

The natives of Sindh now enter, to a certain extent, into the spirit of the inquiry; and, like true Orientals, do their best to baffle investigation by the strange, ingenious, and complicated lies with which they meet it. At Hyderabad, an old man, when questioned upon the subject, positively assured me that in his father's time the Indus was fordable from the spot where the Entrenched Camp now stands, to Kotree, on the opposite bank of the river. The people[1] abound in stories and traditions, written as well as oral, about the shifting of their favourite stream; and are, besides, disposed to theorize upon the subject. Some, for instance, will declare that the Puran river on the eastern frontier of Sindh was the original bed, and adduce its name ("the ancient") as a proof of the correctness of their assertion. Thence they say it migrated westwards to the channel called the Rain: its next step was to the waterless branch, now known as the Phitto (the "ruined" or "destroyed"), lying to the eastward of, and not far from, Hyderabad. Another move, they assert, brought it into the Fulailee, whence it passed into its present bed.

The best accounts of the first Moslem invasion never fail to give a circumstantial account of the siege and capture of Dewal, or Debal Bunder,[2] by the youthful general of the Caliph. That port was, we are expressly told, situated on the Indus. About the middle of the fourteenth century, Ibn Batuta, a celebrated Arabian traveller, visited our province, and he mentions that both Ooch and Bukkur[3] are built on the banks of the main stream. Lastly, in A.D. 1699, Captain Hamilton found the river about Tattah as nearly as possible where it is now.

It is, therefore, by no means necessary to assume any shifting of the course of the Indus. That the face of the country has materially altered there is little doubt, and to judge from present appearances, the Puran, Narrah, Rain, Phitto, and Fulailee, have all at some time or other been considerable streams, second only to the main body of water. Ever since Sindh was inhabited, the country must have been a network of rivers and canals; some perennial, others dry in the cold weather. If, however, these beds be ancient courses of the Indus, that stream was all but ubiquitous, for in many parts I have met with traces of some considerable channel almost every day's journey.

It is solely to the canal irrigation of Sindh that we must look for the means of ameliorating its present state. Under the native rulers, one great cause of the land's decline was the imperfect system of excavation. The plan adopted was as follows :—Each Ameer had his own separate Pergunnahs (or districts), which he ruled as a prince. He had rude maps, and lists of names of the canals in his land, and the face of the country was of course perfectly familiar to him. As the season[4] for excavation approached, the Kardars (revenue officers) of the several districts were directed to send in their estimates of the work required. This part of the operation was pretty well conducted, and with rough measurements and much practice, they could produce a tolerable approximation to the necessary length, depth, and cubic contents of the excavation required. The calculations were made in the rupee[5] belonging to each district, and the measure used was the Gaz or yard. The latter was an uncertain standard of length, varying in almost every Pergunnah. The number of yards excavated for the rupee depended upon the nature of the soil, the height of the spoil-banks, the distance to which the excavated earth had to be carried, and other such considerations. As instruments were unknown, the survey was an imperfect one; a cotton rope being used to measure the work, and the eye to calculate the rise and fall of the ground. The estimates were sent on to the Ameer, who then issued the necessary orders. Workmen were paid partly in grain, partly in money, for amount of labour done, not by the day. Whenever a Wah[6] (or canal) was finished, benches (called Taki) were left across the bed at short intervals, to serve as marks in ascertaining the length and depth excavated. Finally Ameens (or commissioners) were sent by the Ameer to measure,[7] inspect and report upon the work.

The practical effect of the system was, that the Ryot, or agriculturist, was defrauded by three different sets of superiors.

First, by the Ameer, who wished to collect as much revenue, and to excavate as little, as possible. When his treasury was not full, he could not afford to make advances of money for the public works, but he never failed at harvest time to levy the usual sum by extorting it either from the Ryots, or from the civil officers employed on the canals.

Secondly, by the Kardar, whose object it was to get as much money from the Ameer, and to pay as little as he could to the Ryot. Hence it was that the depth and breadth of the canals gradually diminished to such an extent, that many beds originally named "chaugazo," or "the four-yard-wide," have shrunk to half or one third of their original dimensions. Defrauding the labourers of their hire was a dangerous operation, and required skilful management. The difficulty lay in keeping the exact mean, so as not to compel the workmen to complain in a body against the Kardar. When this occurred, the Ameer would never neglect the opportunity of extorting money from his revenue officer, theoretically, with a view of benefitting the Ryot; practically, to add a few thousand rupees to his own hoards.

Thirdly, by the Ameen, who almost always bought the appointment, and was very poorly paid by the government. His object was to share in the unlawful gains of the Kardar, who, on the other hand, was glad to bribe him to silence.

Thus, the Ryots, besides suffering under statute labour,[8] were compelled to pay their rents and to work for the ruler, without receiving the whole of a mere pittance, at a time of the year when remuneration was necessary. The frequent wars, which allowed the land the benefit of lying fallow, the comparatively small number that subsisted by mere agriculture, and the facility of complaint at court, were the peasant's chief aids. When these failed, his habit was to emigrate,—in other words, to run away; and this he learned to do readily enough, and with considerable effect, as the mutual jealousy of the Ameers made each one chary of driving his vassals into another's districts. The little villages were easily and speedily removed, and terrible as it may sound in England, in Sindh it is very venial "to raze a village to the ground because the crowing of the cocks disturbed the game in the Shikargahs." Most villages could be razed to the ground, transported to the requisite distance, and re-erected in a week, at an expense of probably a couple of rupees per house.

The sins of ignorance committed in the canal department under the Talpurs, were not less than the quantity of roguery displayed. The following were the principal consequences of having no level but the eye, and no measure but a rope.

1st. The water was drawn off from the Indus in

indefinite quantities, and allowed to run down the canal into some pond or marsh at the tail. Such ground was useful for growing paddy, but as the water gradually evaporated, leaving a bed of fetid black mud, thickened with decayed vegetation, and exposed to the rays of an October or November sun, a pestilential miasma was the result. Moreover, it is evident from the compound slope[9] of the country, that the waters derived from the river might in many cases have been returned to it in a purified state. Thus some little would be done towards remedying the evils complained of in the Indus,—shallowness and an over deposit of silt.

2nd. The faulty shape adopted for the canals, and the perseverance displayed in adhering to that form. The banks were perpendicular walls of silt or stiff clay, and when undermined by the water, they readily fell in. The excavated earth was disposed of in an immense and ever-increasing spoil-bank close to the canal, so as to obstruct clearance, and give the workmen as much trouble as possible. No judgment was displayed in choosing a position for the head; no attention to prevent the winding of the channel.

3rd. The main trunks, as the Fulailee, Goonee, and other beds, which, generally speaking, are the courses of dried-up rivers, were rarely, if ever cleaned out, on account of the expense and trouble of such works. The consequence was, that in cold weather they were choked with drifted sand, and every inundation supplied them with an additional coat of silty deposit. The effects of this neglect were severely felt at the tails of those streams. In some cases, as in the Rain river, these beds shrank into mere water-courses; in others, as in the Phitto, they were utterly ruined.

4th. Under the native princes, the canal department suffered much from the curious state of misrule in which the people lived. It is not uncommon to see two, or even three large watercourses, running nearly parallel to each other for probably six or seven miles. The reason of this useless excavation is, that the land to the north might belong to a Rind, that to the south to a Nizamani,[10] and the country at the tail might be Ryot land. Each family would be compelled to dig for its own water, through pride and jealousy of its neighbour; the Ryots were of course left to the mercy of government. Occasionally a Jagirdar of consequence, especially if a Beloch, would throw an embankment across a canal when the water began to sink, in order to retain it for the irrigation of his own lands.[11]

With respect to our management of this important department, the following remarks may be offered.

Money payments should be made as much as possible; and the increase of expense be regarded as an outlay of capital destined to repay itself at some future period. Sindh is an exception to the general rule of our Indian conquests; it came to our hands in an almost exhausted state. Experience in the great Peninsula has taught us, that few states under the British rule pay more than two-thirds of the revenue raised by the native princes. Here, however, the country for the last century has been gradually becoming a desert, and merely requires a liberal expenditure of money to regain its original prosperity.

By substituting, where practicable, a whole instead of the present part payment in money, the canal labourers would be persuaded to leave their homes more than they now do, and they would get through a much greater proportion of work. Nothing can be more unenergetic than the present system of excavation in Sindh. The workman scrapes up the caked deposit of the river with a little hoe, carries it over the high and steep spoil-bank in a flat wicker-work basket, about a foot and a half in diameter, and after each trip, sits down to rest himself for a quarter of an hour. As the warm weather approaches, he refuses to work, except in the mornings and afternoons. Many, if not all, of these defects might be remedied by such simple means as the introduction of dredges on the main trunks, ploughs down the canals, and other improvements which naturally suggest themselves; but the chief point to be considered is an amelioration of the condition of the labourer. It must be recollected that the season of excavation is that during which the peasant must prepare his land for the rise of the river; and as the Khamriya (workmen) are all of this class, some solid advantage must be offered to induce them to quit their fields, and commit the labour of agriculture to the women, children, and the few adults who might be left at home. Finally, by means of money payments, a large body of hardy and vigorous labourers could always be procured from the hills to the west, and among the tribes who inhabit the districts about the Tharr.[12]

The more important works, such as the clearing out of large trunks, and the excavation of considerable canals, should be superintended by Europeans, or, at any rate, by a class of people capable of conducting the work scientifically. To them, too, would be committed the duty of gradually reforming the old beds, so as to obviate the inconvenience and expense now perpetually arising from their defects; and of making such obvious improvements as planting trees along the banks, and preparing the canal for boats when required. An inspection of the levels of the country, and of the position of the present lines, would, I believe, bear me out in the assertion, that their number is at least one third more than required, and therefore injurious to cultivation, as taking away labour and money from the important to the useless works.

All the minor canals and watercourses should be left to the Kardars, as was customary under the rule of the Ameers. At the same time, we might take the most stringent measures to save, on the one hand, the Ryot from being defrauded; and on the other, to prevent government being the loser. This is undoubtedly a difficult undertaking, but if due care and attention were given to the subject, our precautions would not be in vain. The labourer well knows that it is the interest of his rulers to redress his injuries, and part measurements of the work done would generally suffice to secure government from fraud.

The following short sketch of the taxation of Sindh under its former rulers is offered as a specimen of the financial and revenue system of the native princes.

As in all states under Moslem rule, so in Sindh, the money levied from the Ryots by the Ameer may be classed under the two heads of,—

1. The general taxes, which formed the revenue of the state.

2. The partial taxes, which may be considered as a kind of perquisite of the ruler, and served to involve every class and condition in the misfortune of having to pay from one third to one half of their gains towards supporting a government, which plundered under pretext of protecting, and betrayed instead of befriending them.

The former division contained three great items, viz.:—

1. ZEMINDARI, or the land tax; 2. SARSHUMARI, or the poll tax; 3. SAIR, or transit dues.

I. ZEMINDARI was of two kinds; 1. That levied by Jamma, or land rent. 2. That taken in Jins or kind. The former was paid by what was called Dhalka Zamin, or land, on which were grown cotton, tobacco, poppy-seed, indigo, opium, sugar-cane, melons, and other such produce, but not grain. The amount paid per Jarib or Beegah[13] varied from five to eighty rupees per mensem, according to the nature and value of the crop. The tax taken in kind was either farmed out to Ijarehdars, by a deed called a "Patto," which generally lasted for the two harvests, the Rabi and Kharif;[14] or, as was much more usually the case, was taken by the Kardars, who transferred the grain to the Ambardars, or government storekeepers. The latter again either sent it on to the Ameer, sold it to Hindoo traders, or paid it as a salary to public and other servants whose importunities for ready money the prince might think fit to silence by means of an order upon the Ambardar of a particular district.

The rate demanded from the peasant was as variable as the value of the crop, the description of soil,[15] the weather, the inundation, the necessities of the ruler, and a variety of similar considerations could make it. Sometimes land paid Chauthi-patti, or one fourth of the produce; at other times Tri-patti (one-third), Panja-dui (two-fifths), and Nisfa-nisf (one-half), were levied. The actual quantity of produce which the ruler expected was settled every season by an operation called Nazar-did. The Kardar, accompanied by some officer appointed by government, went over the Pergunnah at regular intervals between the sowing and reaping seasons. Reports were duly forwarded to the Ameer, and the latter never failed to require, at the harvest-time, the amount specified by the Kardar.

The portion of the produce belonging to the ruler was collected in one of the three following ways:—In some places, the water-wheels were subject to a tax called Charkhshumari; the Nar, or larger kind, paying annually about forty, and the Hurla, or smaller ones, twenty-four Kasa.[16] When an arrangement was made between the ruler and the Ryot, the latter binding himself beforehand to pay a certain portion, on speculation as it were, the method was called Danehbandi. The usual way, however, was that called Bhatai, or the regular division of the produce after it had been reaped. The heaps were laid out near the several villages, and the government servants proceeded to settle the portion belonging to them. After this, various Abwab, or fees, were deducted by the Ameer, such as the expense of

Pistarah, or carriage, of the grain, and Kahgil, or smearing the granary, together with alms for the village Fakir, the Mulla, and other beggars, and presents to the different officers, as the Kamdar, the Kotwal, the Karawo, or individual who guarded the grain, and the Paimankash (the person who measured or weighed the produce). The residue remained with the happy owner of the soil.

When the ground belonged to a Zemindar, or landholder, the usual plan was for him to divide his share of the produce with the Hari, or peasants, under him. On an average the Zemindar, after defraying all expenses, would retain about one-third of his harvest. In favourable years, from three to four hundred per cent. might be reckoned as the profit derived from an outlay of capital on agriculture. Yet the landholder was almost everywhere a bankrupt. This fact, however, may partially be accounted for by the debauched manners and the extreme idleness and ignorance of this class. As long as the Zemindar could procure his daily bread and dose of Bhang, support a wife or two, and possibly a dancing girl, wear a sword, and ride a horse, he would rarely, if ever, condescend to think or care about his property. The richer class used to keep Karkuns,[17] who managed the accounts as they pleased, the more easily, as probably the master would be unable to read, write, or comprehend a simple sum in arithmetic. Under such circumstances, borrowing money was, of course, the only resource, and the Hindoo traders were generally ready to advance it on such conditions as the following:—For every 100 rs. borrowed, a receipt was signed for rs. 125, or rs. 150, according to circumstances, with eight or ten per cent. interest on the latter sum, and a promise to pay off the debt at the next harvest time. The latter condition could seldom be fulfilled, as the borrower, instead of having any ready money at his disposal, would generally, about the Bhatai season, be in want of the wherewithal to satisfy former creditors. The Zemindar would, therefore, require a new loan at the same exorbitant rate of interest; and the crafty Hindoo might compel him to take the lowest possible price for his grain, and even then make a favour of buying it. The debtor was also expected to be generous in proportion to his rank and wants: a great man could never raise money without gifts of horses and gold-handled swords to the usurer.

The Kardars, under the native princes, were sometimes, though not often, able extensively to defraud their masters of the share of produce belonging to them. It suited, however, the ruler's interest periodically to accuse them of such misdemeanour, and to punish them to prevent its occurrence. Occasionally, a Kardar, whose monthly salary was not more than rs. 200, would be mulcted a sum of rs. 1,200; and such apparently ruinous fines would be at once paid, the more readily, as the official might be sure of being permitted to collect a similar hoard without much opposition.

II. The SARSHUMARI, or poll tax, was farmed out in the several districts to Ijarehdars, or Tahwildars (certain civil officers), who collected the amount, and paid a fixed sum into the treasury. The only races that were subject to it were the Sindhi and Jat tribes;

the Belochis always considered themselves in the service of the head of their clan, and therefore claimed immunity. Great Jagirdars and nobles were often empowered by the terms of their Sanad, or grants, to receive Sarshumari, as well as Zemindari, and other taxes from their Ryots, who in such cases paid nothing to government. Zemindars, public officers and servants, military men, as well as all religious characters, Cazees, Pirs, Pirzadahs, Sayyids, and others were not assessed.

Sarshumari was managed as follows:—Men, women, and children beyond infancy were all taxed, and the head of the family was held responsible for those under him.[18] Moreover, each member of the household was security for the other; the son had to answer for the father, the uncle for the nephew, and so forth. For instance, if a family originally consisting of twenty persons, lost five or six of its number, either by death or emigration, the ruler would always claim the original sum assessed, besides sending to the absentees, to demand their share of them.[19] The poll-tax was eight annas per Fasl, or one rupee per annum, for each person, and ready money was always required. It was soon abolished by Sir Charles Napier, as vexatious and troublesome to the people. Such as it is, however, there is no description of assessment more common throughout this portion of the eastern world: we find it in Affghanistan, Multan, Bhawulpore, Jesulmere, the Punjab, and in many of the country parts of Persia. Its main disadvantage is its liability to be embezzled by the officials through whose hands it passes.

The Hindoos of Sindh, being principally traders and merchants, paid no regular poll tax. Those among them who were employed by the Ameers as Amils, or civil officers, contributed nothing to the state, except in the form of periodical fines.

III. The SAIR, or transit dues on merchandise, was always a ready money impost. If the goods were imported by water, they paid a certain sum, usually about six per cent., on disembarking; if they came by land, the tax was levied at the frontier. They then travelled free till they reached the town where the sale was to take place. A second and heavier sum was there taken, according to a fixed Nerrick or tariff, for each camel-load before opening it, the average being about five Annas per Maund. The sum paid for horses was between three and three and a-half Rupees a head.

These double transit dues were demanded even from the traders who were merely passing through the country, as, for instance, when a Cafila from Affghanistan entered Sindh in order to embark at Kurrachee for Bombay. In certain cases, as when grain and Ghee (clarified butter) were sent from one town to another, Sair was claimed when the sale took place.

In some places, the Sair was managed by Amani;[30] in others it was farmed out to Ijarehdars. The great Seths or merchants had many privileges, the chief being, that of only paying between two and three, when goods belonging to poorer traders were charged five or six, Rupees per cent. A wealthy man in the confidence of the Ameers, or employed by them to execute occasional commissions, was often allowed to sell his merchandise without the delay and trouble caused by having to pay the Sair at once. To some highly-favoured individuals, the rulers remitted one-fifth, and even one-fourth of the transit dues; and this was done the more frequently, as the money in reality came out of the Ijarehdar's pocket.

Besides the Sair, Rahdari, a kind of black mail, was levied by several chiefs; as, for instance, the Jokia, who charged the small sum of from one to three Annas, under the name of Nath ("nosering"), for each camel-load passing through the country.

The partial taxes were extremely numerous, and some of very trifling amount. The following short list of the principal imposts of this description, will show the assiduity, if not the skill, of the native government in equalizing the burden of assessment.

1st. Peshkash i Mahajan. The Hindoo part of the community in Sindh was too considerable and influential to be burthened with the Jeziat-el-Hunud,[21] or tax paid by infidels living under the protection of Islam, as the Koran directs, and governments purely Moslem, Bokhara for instance, still levy. The Banyans, or shopkeepers, preferred to offer their yearly Peshkash (offering), of between five and ten Rupees per annum, only the males paying. Great merchants, and all civil officers,[22] were exempt from this charge.

2nd. Sarshumari Asnafgaran, a poll tax paid by the different trades, such as dyers, carpenters, smiths, masons and others. The average sum contributed by each male adult liable to this tax, was three Rupees per annum.

3rd. Dallali, a tax on Dallals or brokers; each of whom paid to the Ameer a small sum every month for permission to transact business for the caravans and travelling traders. The consequence was, that the broker became indispensable to merchants; for even had the latter tried to dispose of their goods without the aid of the former, whether successfully or not so, still they would have been compelled to pay brokerage.

4th. Hawai. The merchandise saved out of ships sunk or wrecked, became a royal perquisite.

5th. Furui. When camels, goats, or any grazing animals happened to stray into cultivated and assessed ground, the whole flock or herd was sold, and the price appropriated by the ruler. Neither the owner of the animals, nor the proprietor of the land, received any compensation whatever. Cattle found straying, if not immediately claimed, were also confiscated.

6th. Charkhi, a tax paid on water-wheels in garden and grain lands. It varied in almost every district, and was proportioned to the dimensions of the Charkha.[23]

7th. Hakkabah, a partial water rate taken from certain Zemindars, but not by any means general throughout the province under its native rulers.

8th. Ijareh Kolabha. The Kolab, or tracts of inundated land, and the lakes, such as Manchar, Manyar and others, were farmed out to government servants, who paid from one-third to one-half the profit derived from reeds cut for matting, wild fowl, and water lilies,[24] together with the different edible roots there produced.

9th. Ijareh Pattan. Ferries were farmed out to Ijarehdars, who demanded a sum varying between two Pies and one Pice from each person who crossed the stream.

10th. Shikar i Mahi. Besides the poll tax taken from the Mohana or fisherman tribe, government claimed one-third or even one-half of their gains, especially from those who made a regular livelihood by netting and spearing the Pullah or sable fish.

11th. Sardarakhti and Zirdarakhti. Besides the land and garden tax, certain fruits, as mangos, dates and others, paid a small sum under the above names. The Kardar sent a person to look at the tree before its produce was gathered, and charged about one Anna for each, under the title of Sardarakhti. Zirdarakhti was the portion of the fruit claimed at the time of gathering it; the government share varied from one-third to one-half.

12th. Tarazu, or toll charged on grain, fruit, and other articles of food, when exposed for sale in the bazaar. This was paid in ready money, at an average rate of one Pice per five Seers.[25] In some parts of Sindh, they claimed Mahsul (or custom) at the gate for milk when brought to the towns for sale. And in many places, no man was allowed to milk his own cattle without paying "Ijareh Jughrat" for permission to do so.

13th. Salamati Kishti. Whenever a ship or boat with goods or passengers arrived at a Bunder (harbour), the Ijarehdar claimed four Annas as a fee for its safe arrival. When the anchor was cast, he received a further sum of six Annas, under the title of Nath (nosering).[26] Horses, when imported, paid eight Annas a head for Salamati or "safety."

14th. Mawesi. Such, in the government Khasra,[27] was the head under which was entered the sale of a horse, mule, ass, camel, or cow. The rulers fee was one Anna per Rupee.

15th. Rejki (properly Rezagi). This tax on retail dealers was generally farmed out. All purchasers paid one Anna per Rupee to government; and in cases where the value exceeded one hundred Rupees, five per cent. Sahukars (merchants) and wealthy traders were charged only four per cent.

16th. Pannacheri, the rate charged for cattle grazing in government lands. Camels paid eight, buffaloes four, cows two, sheep and goats one Anna per mensem. This tax was generally farmed out to Ijarehdars.

17th. Gutto, or Ijareh Sharab, the sum paid annually by each distiller out of the profits of his trade. The amount was intentionally undefined.

18th. Amini. When a dispute arose between two Zemindars, an Ameen was sent by government to settle the quarrel, the rank of the person deputed being proportioned to that of the disputants. As the Sindhis are very litigious about their land, affairs of this kind were of frequent occurrence under the native rulers. In some cases, serious quarrels and loss of life took place, and the Zemindars seldom hesitated to take up arms in defence of what they considered their rights. The Ameen, besides fees, bribes, and perquisites, always contrived to obtain Mihmani (guest money) from, and to live with his suite for nothing at the expense of, the litigants. When the dispute was settled, a fixed sum was paid by both parties, together with gifts of grain and cattle, nominally for the prince, in reality for his officer. The people being naturally fond of bribery and corruption, were never satisfied with unbought justice; and had the Ameen been honest enough to refuse the proffered gift, the offerer would merely have concluded that his opponent had been more liberal in his inducements. The umpire always had it in his power to settle the question any way he pleased; if his award appeared violently opposed to justice, he had but to desire the party cast in the suit to enter a blazing fire,[38] undergo immersion till he was half drowned, or to offer some other such convincing proof of innocence. The best Ameens were those who could plunder the most for their masters and themselves.

19th. Jarimanah or Dand. Fining for different offences was a favourite system with the native rulers, who found it more profitable, and doubtless more efficacious, to mulct than to put to death. Almost all punishments, whether fixed by the Koran, or established by the practice of Islam, were commuted into fines. Even in cases of adultery, the Sindhi, after being flogged by the Kardar, was made to pay a sum of money to government; theft, violence, and even murder were to be settled in the same way. The prince, however, profited but little by this branch of revenue, as the greatest part of it was embezzled by Kardars and other officers of justice.

This short account of the native taxation, may suffice to prove that the husbandman and the merchant were by no means lightly assessed in Sindh. Under our rule the system has been assimilated to that of our Indian possessions. The change hitherto has not met with the approval of the people, who erroneously refer the cause of their ever-increasing poverty to our way of raising the revenue.

CHAPTER III.

A LIST OF SINDHI LEGENDS.—THE LANGUAGES SPOKEN IN THE PROVINCE.—A SHORT ACCOUNT OF EACH DIALECT.

THE most popular productions in the Sindhi dialect consist chiefly of stories and traditions of the Kafir (infidel) kings who defended, and the Moslem heroes who conquered, the province. The number of these written tales is considerable; but far greater is the mass of legendary lore collected by the Langha, or professional bards, and diffused by them among the lower orders of the population. As might be expected from a wild and semi-pastoral people, the memory of each ruined fort or town is preserved by the clans who are settled near the spot; every hill and dale is dignified by some occurrence worthy of remembrance; and each little graveyard contains its own illustrious dead.

The following is a short list of the most celebrated Sindhi legends:—

1. Sassui and Punhu; a tale of two lovers, who are supposed to have lived nearly 900 years ago, or about the time when Islam was first introduced into Sindh. The story is remarkable, as being known throughout

the extensive tract of country lying between Mekran and Affghanistan, Jesulmere and Eastern Persia. It exists in the Persian, Jataki and Belochi languages, and is probably the one alluded to by Mr. Crow when he observes that, "Meer Futteh Alee Khan directed the loves of a Beloch pair, as related in some of the country tales, to be translated into Persian verse, upon the model of Jami's Eusuph and Zulaykha, that the diffusion of these poems may establish the fame of Scinde as well in letters as in arms." The pair are now considered as saints or holy characters, and are supposed to be still in existence under ground. Their tombs are visited by many pilgrims, and stories are recorded of the preternatural appearance of the lady to those whose faith or credulity have induced them to visit her last abode.[1] The Hindoos possess the story in the Panjabi, as well as in the other dialects, and generally write it in the Gurumukhi (or Sikh) character. Among them, Sassui is familiarly known by the name of Rul Mui, or "She that died wandering," to distinguish her from another celebrated beauty, Sohni, who happened to perish in the Indus, and is therefore called Bud Mui, "She that died by drowning." The beautiful verses of Shah Abdel Latif upon the subject of this tale have made it a favourite one among the higher order of Sindhis, and there are not many of them who cannot cite passages from this work of their great countryman. Very few of the wild tribes of Sindh and Belochistan are ignorant of the legend: the camel man on his journey, the herdsman tending his cattle, and the peasant toiling at his solitary labours, all while away the time by chaunting in rude and homely verse the romantic adventures of Sassui and Punhu.

2. The tale of Rano and Mumal; two Rajput lovers.
3. The loves of Hir and Ranjho.
4. The story of Marui and the Sumra prince.
5. The battles and death of Mall Mahmud.
6. The conquests of Dulha Darya Khan.
7. The loves of Sohni and the Mehar (buffalo-keeper).
8. The wars of Dodo and Chanesar.
9. The prophecies of the Samoi or Haft tan.
10. The story of Lilan Chanesar.
11. The legend of the Nang or dragon.
12. The tale of the Ghatu or fishermen.
13. The battles of Abdullah the Brahui.
14. The feuds of Subah Chandiya.
15. The quarrels of Jam Hala and Jam Kehar.[2]

The Arabic language is known to the learned Mussulmans; Sanscrit to the Hindoos. Neither of these tongues are commonly spoken. The few Affghan Zemindars settled in the north of the province still use the Pushtu of their forefathers; but the dialect is not sufficiently diffused among the people to be included in the languages of Sindh. The same is the case with pure Panjabi; it is confined to the small number of Sikhs who are settled in the different cities and towns. The generally known tongues are,—

1. The Belochi; 2. The Jataki; 3. The Persian; 4. The Sindhi.

The Belochi is a rude, mountain dialect, spoken throughout the country called Belochistan, and by those hill tribes who have migrated to the plains of

Sindh. It belongs to the Indo-Persian[3] class of languages, and though uncultivated, is said to be very ancient. It is remarkable for its similarity to modern Persian: one half of the words appear mere corruptions, or possibly similar forms, of the polished tongue. Like its sister dialects, Brahuiki and Pushtu, the vocabulary contains a few Sanscrit and Arabic roots, together with a considerable proportion of barbarous words. The latter, however, appear not to be the remains of an aboriginal tongue, otherwise they would be those expressing primary ideas: they are probably a new element, introduced by isolated position and the want of a standard of language. As must happen among a people divided into clans, and separated from each other, the dialect abounds in diversities of words and idiom, and being naturally poor, it borrows many vocables from the neighbouring countries. Its literature is confined to a few tales, legends, war songs, and the productions of the Bhats or Beloch bards. Few Europeans[4] have hitherto been tempted to learn Belochi, easy as it would be to any one acquainted with Persian and Sindhi; and this is the more to be regretted, as a critical knowledge of it might be valuable to students of the old and obscure Iranian languages, such as the Zend, Pahlawi, Dari, the dialects of the Dasatir, and others known only by name. It has been said of the Parsee sacred volumes, that in them "there is scarcely a single radical of any importance, which may not be traced to a corresponding term in some living dialect of Persian." And doubtless, the hill tongues of the Belochis, Brahuis and Affghans would explain several roots otherwise unintelligible.[5]

In Sindh, the following great clans preserve the use of the hill language :—

Domki, Magasi, Burphat, Kalpher; and many other smaller families.

These tribes speak either Jataki or the hill tongue, and their selection depends upon the district they inhabit :—

Rind, Talpur, Mari (Murree), Chandiya, Jemali, and Laghari.

The Jataki,[a] also called Siraiki, from Siro, or Upper Sindh, where it is commonly spoken by the people, and Belochki, on account of its being used by several of the Beloch clans settled in the low country,—is a corrupted form of the Multani, itself a corruption of the Panjabi tongue. It is extensively used throughout the province, and is spoken by probably one-fourth of the inhabitants. As usual, it abounds in varieties of dialect, and contains little or no original literature, except a few poetical pieces, and short tracts on religious subjects. The Langha or Sindhi bards seem to prefer it to their own language, and many well-educated natives, especially Belochis, have studied it critically, and composed works in it. The following is a short list of the most celebrated romances and legends which are to be found in the Jataki language :—

1. Sassui and Punhu, the Sindhi tale.
2. Hir Ranjha.
3. Yusuf Zulaykha (Joseph and Potiphar's wife; a fertile theme for composition among Moslem people). There are three or four different poems called by this name in Jataki.
4. Saif el Muluk and the fairy Badi el Jemal; a

poor translation, or rather imitation, of the celebrated Arabian or Egyptian story.

5. Laili Majnun, a metrical version of the tale of those well-known Arab lovers.

6. Mirza Sahiban, a translation of the Hindostani story.

7. The loves of Shaykh Ali (a Fakir), and Jelali, the fair daughter of a blacksmith. The scene is laid in Jhang Siyal, a tract of country near Multan, celebrated for its Fukara (religious mendicants), and lovers.

The above-mentioned are the most popular tales and romances: they are all in verse, as prose would be very little read. The Moslems have also a few works on religious subjects. Some of these, as for instance the Ahkam El-Salat, a short treatise on the Akaid (tenets) and Ahkam (practice) of Islam, are committed to memory by women, children, and the "seri studiorum," who find leisure to apply themselves to reading. Moreover, each trade, as smiths, carpenters and others, has its own Kasabnameh, or collection of doggrel rhymes, explaining the origin of the craft, the invention of its tools, the patron saints, and other choice bits of useful knowledge, without which no workman would be respected by his fellows. The celebrated Arabic hymn, generally known by the name of Dua Suryani, the Syriac or Syrian prayer, from which language it was borrowed by Ali, or, as is more generally believed, by Ibn Abbas, has been translated into Jataki, and is learned by heart as a talisman against accidents and misfortunes. The only vocabulary in common use is a short work called

Khalik-Bari, from its first line, "Khalik, Bari, Sarjanhar," the Creator.

The songs, odes and other miscellaneous poetry may be classed under the following heads:—

1. The Rekhtah, as in Hindostani.

2. The Ghazal; an excellent specimen of this style of composition is the translation of the Diwan i Hafiz into Jataki verse.

3. Dohra, or couplets, usually set to music.

4. Tappa, short compositions of three, four or five verses, generally amatory, and much in vogue among the Mirasi or minstrels.

5. Bait, an indefinite number of couplets, in which, very frequently, each line commences with the letters of the alphabet in regular succession. This trick of composition is much admired, probably the more so, as it is usually introduced into themes which, to say the least of them, are vigorously erotic.

The Jataki dialect is usually written in the Nastalik, and sometimes in the Naskhi, character. In the former, the system of denoting the cerebral and other letters which do not belong to the Arabic alphabet, is the same as in Urdu. The only exception is, that the letter *R*, which in Hindostani never commences a word, is often found initial in Jataki; as for instance in the verb ṛiṛana, to roll on the ground, to weep. The Naskhi hand, particularly when written by Sindhis, is often punctuated in the most confused and careless manner: as, however, the Jataki possesses only the same number of letters as the Urdu alphabet, and rarely uses the five sounds peculiar to the Sindhi, the learner soon acquires a knowledge of the character.

Hindoos, generally speaking, use the Gurumukhi, a beautifully simple modification of the Devanagari alphabet, venerated by the followers of Nanak Shah, as the chosen writing of their spiritual guides. The trading classes have a great variety of characters: towards the Punjab they use the Lande, a kind of running hand derived from the Gurumukhi. This again about Multan changes its form and name, and is called the Ochaki[7] alphabet. From the above two, proceed the rude and barbarous systems in use among the Hindoos of Sindh and Cutch.

The facility with which the Sindhi obtains a conversational knowledge of Hindostani, is probably owing to the diffusion of the Jataki dialect throughout the province. Among the Belochis, it is spoken by the great clans of Nizamani and Lashari. To the European, it is particularly easy of acquirement; and the late events in Multan and the Punjab will render a knowledge of it valuable in future years.

The Persian is, in Sindh, the language of literature, ceremony, office and epistolary correspondence. It is seldom used in conversation by the natives among themselves, except on public occasions, or in displays of erudition. In pronunciation, idiom and selection of words, it differs as widely from the dialect of Shiraz and Isfahan, as the patois of Northern Italy deviates from the standard of language in Rome and Tuscany. It is corrupted chiefly by the ignorant admixture of Sindhi, and has become thoroughly and systematically debased.

A short dissertation on the subject may not be uninteresting to the reader, especially as the people of

India, who speak different dialects derived from the Sanscrit, have introduced into their Persian many corruptions similar to those of Sindh.

The errors of the Sindhi[8] may be classed under the four different heads of vicious pronunciation, faulty selection of words, mistakes in grammar, and solecisms. Thus, he has converted the soft, varied, copious and expressive Persian into a barbarous Lingua Franca, difficult to acquire, imperfect when acquired, and all but unintelligible to an educated native of Central Asia.

The Sindhi pronounces Persian as he does his mother tongue. In the short vowels, he invariably articulates Fath so as to resemble "u" in our word "but;" whereas in Shiraz and Isfahan, that letter has a variety of intonations,[9] depending principally upon the class of consonant which follows it: its usual pronunciation being a mixture of the sounds of the "u" in "but," and the "a" in "bat." So, too, the Zamm is here always pronounced like our "ŭ" in the word "bull:" the Persian, however, has two distinct shades of articulation, one resembling that "u," another merging into the sound of our "o" in "obey." The Kasr in Sindh is invariably a short "ĭ," like that in bit:" in Persian, it varies with the letter placed after it, and not unfrequently has the sound of the French "e" in "relation," or "relais." It is not easy to explain this portion of the subject, as the shades of articulation are sometimes all but imperceptible: the practised ear, however, immediately detects the different way in which a Persian and a Sindhi pronounce the short vowels.

The same faults are committed in the long vowels. The Persian pronounces Alif like our "a" in "ball," "gall," and in certain cases it becomes very similar to the "oo" in our word "ooze," (úmadan for ámadan, Írún for Irán.) The Sindhi rejects altogether the latter sound, and pronounces the former like the sharp long Alif in Arabic, the Sanscrit (á), and the "a" in our "father." In the Ya and Vav, he has borrowed from the Indians the distinctions of Majhul and Maaruf, both the terms and sounds of which are unknown in Persian. For instance, he persists in pronouncing Ya as the è in the French père, and invariably says mèrawam, where a native of Shiraz would sound míravam.

In the consonants, the chief error is that of pronouncing the nine peculiarly Arabic letters exactly like the Persian sounds which approach nearest to them; *e. g.* Ain like Alif, *Ta*, like Ta, &c. Whereas the Shirazi, without adopting the harsh articulation of the Arabs, always makes these letters approach slightly to their original guttural pronunciation. The Sindhi, Hindoo or Moslem, is unable to articulate the Persian Zha, although a sufficiently simple sound, exactly similar to the French "j" in "jour;" he corrupts it into "y," as Yúlídah for Zhúlídeh, "dishevelled" (hair). He always retains the harsher sound, the twenty-sixth letter of the Arabic alphabet, and pronounces it as our "w" in "want," whereas the Shirazi, in many cases, softens it down to the "v" in "vent," as, for instance, in the name of the symbol, "Váv" is said, not Wáw.

The above may serve as a specimen of the most tangible forms of the Sindhi's vicious pronunciation. It is impossible to describe the effect produced upon the ear by his coarse and corrupted utterance, after hearing Persian articulated in all its beauty by the delicate organs of a native of Fars.

In selecting words, the Sindhi, who always learns the language from his brethren, introduces a heterogeneous mass of old and obsolete, learned and technical, low and vulgar, foreign and barbarous vocables. Thus, he will call a beetle, "Khabzduk," a cloud, "Saháb," and a kitchen, "Báwarchí khánah." When at a loss for a word, as frequently happens, he borrows one from his vernacular dialect, and inserts it either into his conversation or his writings. The curious effect of such words as Gil-bhanjú (clay), Mardum Khámriyah (labourers), and others originally Sindhi, but changed into Persian by merely altering the termination, is more easily conceived than expressed. In the case of compound words, such as "áb-kaláni," for "inundation," the violence done to the language is as great as in the simple ones. Finally, the Sindhi, as he learns principally from books, and teachers who have acquired their knowledge of the language by reading, is utterly ignorant of the difference between the spoken and the written Persian. And it may be remarked, that there are few modern dialects which abound so much in purely colloquial words and idioms, or which are better deserving of the honours of a Dictionnaire Neologique. That part of language which is usually called "Slang," is, in Persian, most copious, varied and energetic, and would rival our own in affording matter for a "Canting Academy," or a "Classical Dictionary of the Vulgar Tongue."

The grammatical errors of the Sindhi are of the most offensive description. He invariably neglects the peculiar rules of the Izafeh or sign of the genitive; and often omits it *in toto*, to the great confusion of the auditor. In the pronouns, he will use the plural when speaking of himself, as "Ma," and address, probably, an equal in the second person singular. This vulgarism is not uncommon among the Affghans, Brahuis, Belochis, and other hill people: in Persia, however, it is unknown. Of mood and tense, person and number, the Sindhi is equally ignorant; and he will often form the aorist of an irregular verb analogically after the manner of the regular formations, as Yafad, for Yabad, from Yaftan, "to find." Upon the same principle as in his own tongue, two, or even three, causals may be derived from a neuter root; he has introduced into Persian such solecisms as Goyánídan, "to cause to speak," Kunánídan, and Karánídan,[10] "to cause to do," and other such refinements, which no polite speaker can hear without astonishment.

To all foreigners, even those who study Persian under the most favourable auspices, the idiom always must be difficult. This arises partly from the copiousness and peculiarity of the phraseology, but is chiefly caused by the Persian system of borrowing from the Arabic. An indefinite number of expressions may be formed by adding an Arabic noun to a Persian verb, and the difficulty is to know the proper verb. The native of Sindh usually translates the phrase literally from his own language into Persian; he therefore abounds in such idioms as Hukm dadan (for Kardan), "to order," Sual pursidan, "to ask a question," and innumerable other blunders. The effect of this is not unfrequently to produce some offensive *double entendre*, or to express exactly the contrary of what was intended.

Such are a few of the most glaring colloquial errors of the Sindhi. His style of writing, formed upon the model of the Buhar i Danish,[11] garnished with a few phrases from Saadi and Nizami, with occasional imitations of the manner and idiom of Hafiz, is as ludicrous a cento as can possibly be imagined. Add to this, the usual pedantry of the half learned, poverty of idea, with the awkwardness of composing in a foreign dialect, and some conception may be formed of a Sindho-Persian book. Fortunately, however, they are neither commonly written nor read; and few literati, except the Sufis, who generally have had the advantage of foreign travel, would undertake so serious a work as that of composition.

The Sindhi generally uses his knowledge of Persian for "Insha," or epistolatory and official correspondence. After modelling his style from the "Forms of Harkaran,"[12] he is prepared for transacting business; many, indeed, learn to write by rote in the different Daftars (offices), without reading any work whatever. The consequence of this want of study is, that the style is involved and obscure, that wrong epithets are always applied, and that every rule of ceremony and politeness is violated. The Mirza (secretary) in Persia, on the contrary, begins, early in life, the systematic study of style and "etiquette;" and it is only after many years of application and constant practice, that he is considered to possess the multifarious qualifications required in one of his profession. The Sindhi again never learns to write the character properly, and his crabbed Shikasteh (running hand), with innumerable errors of spelling,[13] added to the difficulty of his jargon, combine to form an imposing mass of obstacles to the peruser. It is seldom, therefore, that a man is fully prepared for transacting business before his beard is grey, and certainly not less than five or six years' constant application would enable a Persian or Affghan Munshi to read, without hesitation, the Sanads (grants of land) and other unintelligible scrawls which abound in Sindh.

The origin of the Sindhi dialect appears to be lost in the obscurity of antiquity; but there are ample reasons for believing it is as old[14] as any of the vulgar tongues of modern India. It belongs to the Indian class of languages, and is directly derived from the Sanscrit; yet it is a perfectly distinct dialect, and not, as has been asserted, a mere corruption of Hindostani.[15] It is spoken with many varieties from the northern boundary of Katiwar as far as Bahawalpur, and extends from the Brahui Mountains to the desert which separates Sindh from the old western frontier of our Indian empire; and these limits well agree with the Moslem accounts of the extent of empire belonging to the Rahis or Hindoo rulers of Sindh. The classical or literary language is that of Lar, or Southern Sindh; the other principal dialects are,—

1st. The Siraiki, or language of Siro, Upper Sindh; admitting a mixture of Jataki and Belochi words.

2nd. The Kachi, spoken in Cutch, and made to approach the Guzerattee.

3rd. The Thareli or Jesalmeri, the language of the people about Omerkot, the Tharr, and Jesulmere; also used by the Shikaris, Dedhs, and the other outcast tribes of Sindh. It borrows largely from the Marwari, and has its own written character[16] and religious compositions.

4th. The Takkarana jíbolí, or dialect of the hill people to the west of Sindh, corrupted by a mixture of Brahui and Belochi terms, as well as possessing many names of things and idioms unintelligible to the people of the plains.

It may be observed, that a good knowledge of Sindhi introduces us to a variety of cognate languages, as the Panjabi, Jataki, Pushtu, Belochi, Brahui, and others spoken in the countries west of the Indus. In a vocabulary composed by a native, I observed that out of four hundred nouns, two hundred Pushtu and one hundred and fifty Belochi words were exactly or very nearly similar to the Sindhi. This may be accounted for in two ways; first, that these languages are all derived from some ancient and now unknown tongue, which was supplanted by or blended with Sanscrit; or that, secondly, they are all varieties of the rude and obsolete form of Sanscrit, which gave birth to the dialects of Central Asia, and extended its course westward as far as the Pelasgi carried it. The latter supposition enables us to account for the fact, that in Sindhi as well as in the cognate dialects of India, the most common words, and those in hourly use, as Put, a son; Dhi, a daughter; Gae, a cow, and Ghoro, a horse, are of Sanscrit derivation. But had the latter language been grafted upon an aboriginal stock, the vulgar names of things, and words denoting primary ideas, would, of course, have remained in the more ancient dialect.

The peculiarities of the Sindhi language are, the proportion of Sanscrit and Arabic words which it admits, and the heterogeneous structure of the grammar. Pure as well as corrupted Sanscrit vocables, for the most part unintelligible to unlearned natives of the western portion of the Indian Peninsula, perpetually occur. Of this class may be instanced,—

Achan, to come (S. root *Acha*).
Akás, the sky.
Achho, white (S. *Achha*).
Akhan, to speak (S. *Akhya*).
Apár, endless.
Dátár, the Deity.
Jas, victory (S. *Yas*—fame).
Joe, a wife (S. *Jáyá*).
Kukkur, a cock.
Sabbar, strong (fr. *Sa* with, and *bal* force).
Sáin, sir (S. *Swámí*).

The Arabic, contrary to the usual rule in the Indian languages, is sometimes used in Sindhi for the common, not the learned names of things. The following is a short specimen of this peculiarity:—

Abbo, a father.
Basar, an onion.
Dars, a saint.
Jabal, a hill.
Kadaho, a cup.
Káso, a pot (Ar. *Ka'as*).
Khás, good.
Kull, all.
Khutab, a school (in India and Persia, "*Maktab*" is generally used).
Mahkam, strong, firm.
Musáf, the Koran.
Mámúr, cultivated.

Khímo, a tent.
Mukám, burial ground.
Parch, a mat (Ar. *Farsh*).
Rikábí, a saucer.
Sát, an hour.
Shayy, a thing.
Mayyit, a corpse.
Tám, food.
Thum, garlic (Ar. Fúm).
Tohar, circumcision (Ar. purity).

This peculiar use of Arabic vocables may be accounted for by the fact, that during the Age of Ignorance, or the time that elapsed between the rise of Christianity and Islam, there was emigration on an extensive scale from Arabia to Sindh. In this point, the traditions of the province agree with those of Persia, Khurdistan, and Affghanistan, all asserting that they were either overrun or conquered by the wandering descendants of the Wild Man. Historians relate, that during the first ages of Mohammedanism, the armies that overran Balkh and Bokhara, there found Arabic inscriptions in obsolete characters, commemorative of former inroads; and it is reasonable to suppose that long before the mighty torrent of barbarians whom the early caliphs poured forth over the then civilized world, local causes, such as war, famine, or the ambition of a leader, may have occasioned similar eruptions. Thus, too, we may account for a circumstance which some English scholars have turned into an argument against the authenticity of the Parsee Scriptures,—that they contain many Arabic vocables. Ancient as well as modern Persian resembles the Pushtu and Sindhi in this peculiarity, that many of the words remarkably resemble in sound and spelling, Semitic roots of similar signification.

The Sindhi grammar is much more complicated than those of the modern dialects of Western India. The alphabet, to begin with, contains five sounds unknown to the cognate tongues, viz. :—

B, a peculiar labial, formed by forcibly pressing the lips together.

G, resembles our *g*, but it is articulated deep in the throat.

J, a mixture of dental and palatal sounds, somewhat resembling the rapid articulation of *d* and *y*, "dyă."

Dr, a cerebral *d* run into the liquid which follows it.

Tr, a compound cerebral and liquid, of the same formation as *Dr*.

In addition to which, the cerebral *R*, as in Jataki, is initial as well as medial and final.

The anomalous structure of the grammar is remarkable. The terminations of nouns, substantive and adjective; the formation of cases by means of insignificant affixes; the pronouns and pronominal adjectives; and in the verb, the inflexion of the infinitive and the forms of the future tense and the past conjunctive participle, all belong to the Indian tongues. The points in which it resembles the Persian, are the affixed pronouns of the three persons, and the verb which from the second person of the imperative forms an aorist, which is converted into a present by the addition of unmeaning particles. In the following particulars Sindhi is superior to both :—

1. The nouns substantive and adjective, together with the roots and infinitives of verbs, all end either in a long or a short vowel.[17] They form cases by

changing this vowel in the oblique state of the word; whereas in Hindostani and the dialects of Western India, the final consonant of a noun continues quiescent throughout the declension.[18] For instance:—

In Sindhi.

	Singular.	Plural.
Nom.	*Murs*^{u}, a husband.	*Murs*^{a}, husbands.
Gen.	*Murs*^{a} *jo*, &c., of a husband.	*Mursan*^{i} *jo*, &c., of husbands.

In Hindostani.

	Singular.	Plural.
Nom.	*Mard*, a husband.	*Mard*, husbands.
Gen.	*Mard ka*, &c., of a husband.	*Mardon ka*, &c., of husbands.

2. Many of the pronouns in Sindhi change their terminations to form cases, numbers, and the distinction between the masculine and feminine gender. So in the relative pronoun *Jo*, "he who,"—

Singular.

Nom. *Jo*, in the feminine *Ja*.
Gen. *Jenh jo*, of both genders.

Plural.

Nom. *Je*, } of both genders.
Gen. *Jinan*^{i} *jo*, }

3. The insignificant particles affixed to the aorist, and forming a present tense, are not always the same, as in Persian, but vary with number and gender. The verb, moreover, is much more artful than in Hindostani. From the root of the active a passive

form is procured, by adding *jan*; e.g., *Mári*, beat thou; *Márjan*, to be beaten: and this new verb has many of the tenses formed as regularly as that from which it is derived. The system of analogical causal verbs is more complete and complicated than that of the Urdu.

4. The Sindhi is superior to most of the dialects of Western India in various minor points of refinement and cultivation; as, for instance, in the authorized change of terminations in poetical words, the reduplication of final or penultimate letters to assist the rhyme, and many similar signs of elaboration.

The Sindhi language, again, is remarkable for a copiousness and variety of words, which not unfrequently degenerates into a useless luxuriance, and a mere plurality of synonymes. There is not a single article of any kind in the province for which the vernacular dialect, unlike the barbarous Sindho-Persian, has not a name. In the case of words denoting external objects, and those most familiar to the people, as, for instance, the camel, there are often a dozen different names, some synonymous, others distinct in their several shades of meaning. Abstract words are borrowed from the more cultivated tongues, Arabic Sanscrit, and Persian, almost *ad libitum*, and the result is a very extensive vocabulary.*

As regards the literature of the Sindhi tongue, it may safely be asserted that no vernacular dialect in India, at the time of our taking the country, possessed more, and few so much, original composition.

* In Appendix No. I. will be found a specimen of Sindhi copiousness.

Its principal wealth, however, consists in translations, chiefly from the Arabic, and in works of religion. It is of course difficult to make any calculation of the number of books procurable, but certainly not less than between two and three hundred MSS. could be collected.

In prose we find translations of annals, and almost all the religious sciences of the Moslems, with tales, sometimes profane, but generally borrowed from sacred history.[19] There are vocabularies[20] for teaching children the Arabic and Persian languages, books of Insha, or forms of epistolatory correspondence, and a few professional works on medical and other subjects.[21]

The styles of composition are two in number; first, the learned, which imitates the measured periods and rhetorical luxuriance of the modern Arabic and Persian. The adoption of a style so contrary to the genius of the Indian dialects, is probably owing to the practice of translating from the foreign languages; and we may observe that, not contented with imitating the manner, the Sindhi borrows also the matter of the original, by adopting and appropriating any number of words he pleases. To such an extent is this carried, that in some books it is only the skeleton of speech,—the auxiliary verbs, adverbs, prepositions, casal affixes and conjunctions, together with an occasional verb,—that is taken from the vernacular; all the rest being a mass of Arabic and Persian. The second style is the vulgar, which imitates the spoken dialect of the people, and is either written in pure Sindhi, or with a sparing admixture of foreign vocables. As might be expected, the former is the more usual as well as admired method:—Knowledge has not yet condescended to quit her sanctum in the closets of the learned and polite.

The poetical literature of Sindh is much more various and valuable than the prose, and yields not in importance either to the Mahratti, or the original compositions in the Hindi and Braj dialect. The elaborate rules of Arabic and Persian prosody are unknown in Sindhi, except when poetry is composed in imitation and in the measure of the classical languages. But Sindhi possesses an original description of verse,[22] when all its neighbours, even the Pushtu, are obliged to content themselves with borrowed metres. Its poetry is not without its charm. To a great variety of expression, it unites terseness of idiom, with much freshness, and some originality of idea and language. The numerous dialects which it possesses allow the higher class of authors to enrich their style, and give *vraisemblance* to their descriptions, by borrowing local words and idioms from the district assumed to be the scene of the tale. The favourite figure is alliteration,[23] and this, combined with omission of the casal affixes, and of other such prosaic appendages, gives a very distinct and peculiar rhythm. The effect produced upon the Sindhi by the poetry of his native land, is a proof that it has power and expression; even learned Sufis do not disdain to introduce an occasional couplet into their Arabic and Persian compositions.

The following are the principal kinds of poetry which have been cultivated by the Sindhis:—

1. Madah, a composition much admired by the Moslems. As its name imports, the subjects gene-

rally selected are "praises" of God, the Prophet, saints, and other religious themes.

2. Munajat, resembling the above, but common to all religions. It corresponds with our hymn, and is much read by the unlearned in the vernacular, whereas the Olema prefer those in the Arabic language.

3. Marsiyah, or elegies, generally upon the martyrdom of Hasan and Husain, are very common among the Mussulmans, Sunnis as well as Shiahs. Learned Sonnites object to them on religious grounds, and therefore avoid, as well as dissuade, others from observing the semi-heretical practice of annually lamenting the mournful fates of the Hasanain.

4. Kowar or Laanat, satirical compositions resembling the Hajw of Arabic and Persian literature. Like the latter, Sindhi has two kinds; Malih, or polite satire, and Kabih, gross personal abuse. If we judge of the merit by the effect of these effusions, we must pronounce it to be great; but the chief cause of its operating so powerfully, is doubtless the selection of subject. As usual among Orientals, the principal themes of satire are cowardice and want of generosity in man, unchastity and deficiency of beauty in woman; and most vigorously are these subjects handled. The poet who indulges his dangerous taste rarely lives to a good old age, but he has the satisfaction to know that the object of his satire is, and probably will be for life, the laughing-stock of society.

The four kinds above enumerated are derived from the classical languages, and are common to all the Moslem world; the next four are more original:—

1. Fath-namo, or songs of battle,[24] composed by the Langha (bards) to commemorate victory or disguise defeat. In style and subject they bear no slight resemblance to the vigorous productions of the old Arab poets.

2. Kafi or Wai, a song generally amatory, and containing from eight to a dozen verses. In Jataki, this style of composition is called Tappa or Khiyal. It is generally set to music, and is very much admired by the people.[25] Some beautiful specimens may be found in the Risalo of Abd el Latif.

3. Baita, or "couplets,"[26] which are sometimes in sets of two, but more generally of three verses. The first line rhymes with the second, and with the third at the cæsura of the latter, the terminating portion of the third line being rhymeless. This metre appears peculiar to Sindh, and is a great favourite with all classes. The Baita are set to music, and generally sung to the Tambur, a kind of guitar. The "Dohro" is the same kind of verse under another name, belonging to a different Sur, or musical mode, and accompanied by the Duhul (kettle-drum).

4. Sanyaro, the literal meaning of which is "a message," and thence it comes to signify an amorous poem, a mental missive as it were from lover to beloved. These compositions are set to a peculiar mode, and accompanied by the Nai or pipe; among the wilder clans no music is more admired than this.

In addition to these several kinds of composition, the people abound in *jeux d'esprit* called Gujartha and Pirholi, which resemble the Lughz, Muamma, and Chistan of Arabia and Persia, and the riddles, puzzles and enigmas of our own country. These are by no means without their merit, and possess a more than common share of terseness and sprightliness. As might be expected, too, from a semi-barbarous race, there is much poetry scattered throughout the country, which has not been, and probably never will be, collected. Much of this would, doubtless, be worthy the attention of Sindhi scholars, and a portion of it interesting to Orientalists in general. In this province, as was the case throughout India generally, the poetical literature of the vernacular is, at present, fresh, idiomatic, and sufficiently original, copious, and varied in words and expression, at the same time simple and natural. Under our system of education, the style of the authors seems to suffer from constant labour and attempts to imitate and borrow from the learned tongues. This may succeed in prose; it certainly fails in producing poetry. As a proof of my assertion, I may instance the old religious poems in the Mahratti dialect, compared with the productions of the last twenty years.

CHAPTER IV.

BIOGRAPHY OF THE THREE MOST CELEBRATED SINDHI AUTHORS.—SPECIMENS OF SATIRE.—THE PROPHECIES OF THE SAMOI.—EXTRACTS FROM THE TALES OF SASSUI AND PUNHU, MARUI AND UMAR THE SUMRAH.

Before submitting any specimens of Sindhi composition to the reader, it may be useful to offer a short account of the three most celebrated authors in the language, Makhdum Hashem, Makhdum Abdallah, and Sayyid Abd el Latif.

The former of these worthies was a Sindhi of the Ponhwar clan, and was born and died at Tattah. He flourished during the reign of the Kalora princes, and his descendants, who are still a wealthy and well-known family, are now living at Alima jo Kot. He travelled in India and Arabia, and studied with great success the Arabic and Persian languages, and theology. It is said that during his travels, he had several disputations with Christian missionaries, and wrote several tracts against their religion. On his return to his native land, he was appointed Kazi of Tattah, and treated by the rulers with the respect due to his learning and virtue. He is now considered a Wali or saint, and his mausoleum on the Mekli hills is a place of pilgrimage to his fellow-countrymen. His principal works in Arabic were,—

1. Ishbah; 2. Fakihat el Bustan; and 3. Bayaz Hashemi.

His fame rests principally upon the following compositions which he wrote in Arabic for the use of the learned, and himself translated into Sindhi, to render them intelligible to the vulgar:—

1. Akaid; 2. Faraiz; 3. Zibh i Shikar; 4. Aghsini; 5. Zikr i Khulafai Rashidin; 6. Zikr i Kiyamat; 7. Badr el munir; and 8. Maulud.

He wrote also some literal versions of parts of the Koran in an unlearned Sindhi style; and his translation of the last Juz (the thirtieth section) of the Moslem Holy Writ is invariably given to children when first sent to school. It is easy, simple, well calculated to illustrate the meaning of the original, and in sound learning not inferior to many well-known Tafsir (commentaries) in the classical tongues. His other works are read chiefly by the Hanafi Moslems, to which sect he belonged.

Next to Hashem, the most celebrated prose author in the Sindhi tongue is Makhdum Abdallah Nariyawaro. He was born at Nariya, near Bhooj, in Cutch, but belonged to the Sindhi tribe of Mandhro. He died at Suthari about thirty years ago. The Hindoo Rao, or prince, was his Murid (disciple), and allowed him an annual stipend. The following is a list of his best known works, and it is said that he wrote nothing in Arabic or Persian.

1. Kanz el Ibrat; 2. Kisas el Anbiya; 3. Khizanat

el Abrar; 4. Khizanat el Aazem; 5. Khizanat el Riwayat; and 6. Tambih el Ghafilin.

The Miar i Salikan i Tarikat, a biographical work in the Persian tongue, treating of the holy men of Islam, contains the following notice of Sayyid Abd el Latif i Tarik:[1]—

"This saint was the son of Sayyid Habib Shah, and was born in the beginning of the twelfth century of the Hijrah Æra (about A. D. 1680). He was celebrated for Riyazat (penance, mortification, &c.); became a Majzub i Ashik (a certain degree in Tasawwuf, or Sufi-ism), and finally rose to the rank of Mashaikh (teacher). Though he never studied,[2] he was master of the whole circle of the arts and sciences. His Murids[3] were numerous, many of them so much attached to him, that at his death, they died of grief; and the number that became celebrated as holy men is very great. He departed this life in A.H. 1161; and was succeeded by Sayyid Jemal Shah. His tomb is at Bhit,[4] and it is a very sacred spot."

So far his biographer. The people have, as usual, a long list of miracles performed by this saint, and tell wonderful tales of his travels and penances. The tomb is still visited by many, and there is an annual Melo (or fair) there in the month of Zulhijjah. His descendants are honoured as holy men, and possess considerable wealth.[5]

The poetical fame of Sayyid Abd el Latif rests principally upon his celebrated composition, "The Shaha jo Risalo."[6] His fellow-countrymen consider him the Hafiz of Sindh, and there are few of them, learned or unlearned, who have not read or heard his pathetic verses. In their admiration of his strains, they frequently quote the poet's own saying :—

"Bait^{a} ma bháenjá, Márhuá! hí áyat^{un} áhín
Piryán sande pára de, neo, lau laín."

"Think not, O man, that these are mere couplets, they are signs (from God to man):
They bear thee to thy True Friend, and have inspired thee with true love."

The following is a short specimen of satirical composition, the production of a Manganhan (minstrel), by name Mihru, and sung by bard and musician throughout the length and breadth of Sindh. It expresses the popular indignation against those traitors to their country, Mohammed Khan Thora, Kauro Narejo, and others :—

"Kal^{a} na peí mír^{a} khe kaid^{a} je, dádho Rabb^{u} sattár^{u}!
Likhiá Khatt^{a} khireb^{a} já saryal^{a} Sobdár^{a}
Kandh^{i} bhaggo Kaurejo pei Munshí Khe Mar^{a}
Khoinbria-wáro kharáb^{u} thío jenhkhe laânat^{a} jí laghár^{a}
Lakh laânat^{a} Thore khe jenh lái hambháriya báh^{i}
Thoro bhaggio tháh^{a} se, Sun gándú^{a} já pár^{a}
Lakh laânat^{a} Thore khe jenh lái dárú^{a} khe báh^{i}
Kalkatte-khán kotháyá en achí cháchá pagh^{a} badhá.
Kunjiy^{un} watho koth^{a} jún wehí Sindh^{u} halá!
Mihrú Manganhár^{u} chawe,
Saghon wijh^{i} tun Shera men awánge wália wágh^{a} waráe."

The bard laments the folly of the Ameer (Nasir Khan) in trusting to the English, and curses Mir Sobdar, who was said to have written to Sir Charles Napier for the turban, and to have stopped the armed hill clansmen when they were coming down to attack the invader. He pays a well-merited compliment to, as he passes by, Kauro Narejo, the civil officer, and Awat Rao, the Munshi, who betrayed Sobdar's forces in the field. The Sardar, Ghulam Mohammed,[7] is next mentioned, as he richly deserves, and then Mohammed Khan Thora is attacked with fierce invective. The latter individual, the Sindhis declare, agreed with the British to blow up Sher Mohammed's powder magazines at the battle of Dubba,[8] and did so accordingly. The author next ridicules the prodigious folly of the Ameers, who sent for strangers to settle their family disputes; and finally, speaking in his own name, invokes a blessing on the head of Sher Mohammed, the "Lion," and prays that he may soon return to enjoy his own. The following is as nearly a literal translation, as the difference of idiom, and the poetical licenses of the original, permit:—

1. "Little knew the Mir (Nasir Khán) what a prison was, O great God, that veilest our folly and sins!
2. And that burned (scil. in hell fire) Sobdar, with his foul treacherous letters!
3. May Kauro's neck be broken; may the Munshi be pounded with blows!
4. And an evil end come to the Khoinbri chief, with a heap of direct maledictions.
5. A hundred thousand curses on the Thora who ruined the country (literally, set fire to the heap).
6. Grandly and nobly fled the Thora (from the fight). See what a scoundrel[9] he was!
7. A hundred thousand curses on the Thora who set fire to his own gunpowder.
8. (Fools ye were) to send for men (*viz.* the British) from Calcutta, saying, 'Come, brothers, and bind on our turbans—
9. 'Take ye the keys of our forts, sit ye down and govern Sindh.'

10. Mihru the minstrel's last words are these:—
11. '(O Lord,) Strengthen thou the Lion (Sher Mohammed), and may the reins of his steed soon be turned towards Sindh.'"

The style of this fragment is rough and coarse. But even the European reader will confess that the sentiments are not deficient in patriotism or power, and do honour to the heart of Mihru the minstrel.

The tradition connected with the following bardic prophecies is this. On one occasion, Makhdum Baha el din,[10] the great saint of Multan, generally called Bahaulhakk, was visiting his Murids, or disciples, at Tattah. They plotted his destruction, in order to secure the blessings of his perpetual presence.[11] Shaykh Jiw, a follower of the saint, discovered the plot to him, proposed to take his Murshid's place, and was, by permission, martyred in his bed that night. The recreant Murids took the body, with the intention of cooking and eating part of it;[12] but when it was prepared, they repented their resolve, put the remains in a pot, and securing the lid, cast it into the Indus. By the decrees of fate, it was found by seven men of the Mohana (fishermen) caste, who incontinently devoured the contents, in ignorance of their nature. They at once became Siddhas (saints), or Walis, and are celebrated to the present day as the Samoi, Mamoi, or the Haft-tan.[13] Directed by heaven, they forthwith repaired to the court of Jam Tamachi,[14] at Tatta, and informed him, that under his capital was the head of a snake, whose tail reached to Delhi;[15] moreover, that as long as the animal in question retained its position, Sindh had nothing to fear from the lords of India. At the Jam's request, they secured the serpent's head by thrusting a spit into the ground. But the people of Tatta were incredulous. They derided the prince and his holy advisers, and insisted upon drawing out the spit, and seeing if any blood was upon it. In an evil hour Jam Tamachi consented, and heedless of the Samoi's warnings, directed the iron to be pulled up. Seeing its point dropping with gore, all were struck with horror, and confounded into belief; their apprehensions did not diminish when the holy men informed them that the snake had moved, and Sindh had for ever lost her protecting spell.

Jam Tamachi, in wrath, ordered the decapitation of the Samoi, when, to his dismay, each headless trunk arose, and holding its head, began walking towards the east. They did not cease to journey till they arrived at Amri, on the banks of the Puran river. There they fell to the ground, deprived of life and motion, and the crowd which had collected to witness their peculiar powers of locomotion, buried them in the sepulchres, which are still to be seen at Makan Amri.

The prophecies are seven sets of verses, as each saint, when he arose and took up his head, addressed a short speech to the Jam concerning the future destinies of Sindh. The curious fact of their all referring to modern events, which had nothing to do with Tamachi, or his times, must be regarded with the indulgence usually conceded to vaticination. The lines are undoubtedly ancient, for they are generally known throughout the country.[16] Like

"The prophecies of Rymer, Bede and Merlin,"

they are implicitly believed by the people. In vagueness, ambiguity, and other tricks of ariolation, they very much resemble the productions ascribed to the bard of Ercildoune, and our other seers in the olden time. They are probably mutilated remains of a considerable number of such rhymes; the major part of which have been consigned to well-merited oblivion.

To proceed: the first corpse raising his head, uttered these celebrated lines,—

1. "Hák^{i} wahando Hákro, bhajandí band^{a} Aror^{a}"
2. "Bih^{a} machhí en lorh^{a} wendí Samme sukrí."

1. "The Hakro shall become a perennial stream, and the dyke of Aror shall burst."
2 "And thus shall productions of lakes and streams be carried to the Sammah clan as presents." [17]

This prediction is yet unfulfilled. The dyke of Aror [18] has not burst; and the Hakro, a large bed of a river near Omerkot, has no water in it. The second line is a corroboration of the first, and literally means, that the rhizome of the Nelumbrum Speciosum (bih^{a}), fish, and certain little chesnut-like roots (lorh^{a}), which grow in Manchar and the other lakes, shall thus be conveyed to the inland regions about Jesulmere and Cutch, now occupied by people of the Sammah tribe. This prophecy may remind us of the Rhymer's lines,

> "At Eildon tree, if you shall be,
> A brigg ower Tweed you there may see."

And it is as easy to predict that a fertile country will, at some time or other, have bridges and canals, as it is to foresee that the sandy wastes of Arabia will not. [19]

The second corpse pursued :—

1. " Wasí wasí ár^{u} jadhen wanjí phittando,
2. Tadhen Bárocháno bár^{u} panje draman^{i} vikabo."

1. " Long and long shall the Ar remain full of water; but when at last it shall dry up;
2. In those days, the children of the Beloch shall be cheap and valueless in the land."

This prophecy, say the Sindhis, is now gradually being fulfilled: the Ar and Awar are other names for the Baghar creek, which is becoming more shallow every year; and the Belochis, who formerly were the lords of the soil, are regarded by the British with no more favour or respect than the Sindhis, Jats, or any other inferior clan. This is plainly indicated in the words of the prophecy, that the " Offspring of the Beloch shall be sold for five dirhems," or about half-a-crown,[20] a decidedly low price.

The third head declared that,

1. " Káre Kábáre, jhero lagandho cheh pahar,
2. Mirmichí máre, sukh^{i} wasandí Sindhrí."

1. " At (the town of) Karo Kabaro, a battle shall rage for many hours;
2. The Mirmichi shall be beaten, and our little Sindh shall become a happy abode for man."

The people explain this prediction, as referring to the battles and defeat of Sher Mohammed by Sir Charles Napier. The minor facts, that none of these fights lasted anything like " six watches," and that no affair took place at Karo Kabaro, are of course disregarded by the true believer. The word Mirmichi, in this ancient rhyme, has never been properly explained till now. When the Talpurs became lords of Sindh, the expression, it was supposed, alluded to the conquered Kaloras. Probably it was in anticipation of the confusion which would be created by so unintelligible a vocable, that the fourth carcase immediately enquired and replied,

1. "Mirmichí máre; Mirmichí kehrá pár$^{\underline{e}}$?
2. Hethín káriy$^{\underline{un}}$ potiy$^{\underline{un}}$ mathín kárá wár$^{\underline{e}}$."

1. "The Mirmichi shall be beaten; what are the signs of the Mirmichi?
2. Below (the waist) they have dark clothes, and dark hair on their heads."

This, though more distinct, is still ambiguous. The Belochis wear dark blue (karo) cloths round the loins, and are a dark-haired people, but so are many other clans. Sometimes the second line is recited with *variæ lectiones*, e.g.,—

2. "Zálin$^{\underline{i}}$ mathe ba chotá, mursan$^{\underline{i}}$ mathe wár$^{\underline{e}}$."
2. "On their women's heads are two braids of hair, and the men wear long locks."

The fifth body proceeded to describe the signs of the times to come in the following words:—

1. "Lagandí Lárán; sonko thindo Sire men;
2. Jadhen tadhen Sindhrí úgúnán venáh$^{\underline{u}}$."

1. "The war shall begin from Lar, (or, as the words may be taken, 'the battle shall be fought in Lar,' Lower Sindh); but from Upper Sindh (Siro), the rumour of an army's approach shall come down.
2. When this occurs, then indeed trouble cometh to our little Sindh from the south-east direction."

This is the celebrated prediction which, after agitating the whole of Sindh from 1839 to 1843, was at last curiously accomplished.[21] Lar, or Lower Sindh, was the scene of the battles of Meeanee and Dubba; the British force, however, was not sent up from the south, as might have been expected, but marched down from Sukkur to coerce the Ameers. The south-east direction points to the position of the Bombay Presidency.

The sixth corpse was at once specific and ambiguous :—

1. " Nírá ghorá dubará uttara khaun índá,
2. Ghagheriyun gassan[i] te wiráhe wendá,
3. Tihán poi thíndo tabal[u] Tájániyan[i] jo.

1. Their thin grey steeds shall come down from the north,
2. The petticoated females shall go about the streets divided (among the people),
3. After which the rule of the Tajyani begins."

The two first lines are curious. The natives always remark our fondness for grey horses, and the British cavalry had not grown fat at Sukkur in 1843. The second verse alludes, the Sindhis say, to the Beloch women, who when of rank wear a " Gagho" or petticoat, covering their persons from the waist to the ancles. It is a mark of respectability, and therefore is never seen among the lower orders, who content themselves with trousers, tight at the ancle. Peculiarly happy is the allusion to the way in which those ladies behaved when we first took the country; the ebullitions of society forming a striking contrast with its normal state under the Ameers, who made an intrigue with a Beloch woman an affair of imminent danger— in the expressive idiom of the country, "tied the sword to the strings of their petticoats."

The seventh body terminated the scene with these remarkable words :—

1. "Achí wehjá, Márhúá, Nangara je ádhár!
2. Puráná parár! nawa ma add! já nijhrá."

1. "Come and sit, O ye people, under the protection of the Nagar,
2. And beyond the Puran river build no new abodes !"

The Nagar, or "city," is a familiar name for Tattah, it being, by excellence, *the* city in Sindh during the prosperity of the province. This prophecy is, it is believed, fulfilled by our abandoning Hyderabad, the capital of the Talpurs, and selecting Kurrachee for the head-quarters of government.

To conclude this part of the subject, the philosophical reader will not be surprised to hear that these wretched rhymes have had a mighty effect upon the destinies of the province.[22] Like the people of Bhurtpore, when attacked by Lord Combermere,[23] the mass of Sindhians saw in the English a foe who was fated to conquer and rule over them.

The following are short translations[24] and specimens of the tales and songs most admired by the common people. The first is the well-known story of Sassui and Punhu. As the poet plunges "*in medias res*" after the most approved of injunctions, but at the same time neglects to introduce an episode explanatory of the beginning, a few prœlegomena will be necessary.

In the days when Islam had but partially spread over Sindh and the adjoining countries, a Brahman of Bhambuna had a daughter, of whom it was predicted that she would become a Moslem and disgrace her family. The father was dissuaded from killing his offspring, and, at his wife's request, putting the child into a box, he let it float down the Indus. Some days afterwards it was found by Mahmud, a washerman at Bambhora,[25] who, being childless, adopted the infant. When she grew up, her beauty and accomplishments, according to the Sindhis, became such as to cause the most disastrous consequences. But the poet now speaks for himself.

Babiho, a Hindoo trader, visited Bambhora with camels and merchandise belonging to Ari, the Jam or prince of Kech in Mekran. One day as he was passing by the Atan or Gynœceum, where Sassui and her female companions were sitting, the ladies called him and asked what merchandise he had with him. The man answers,—

> "Chúá, Chandana, Kewrá, múnsán wakkhar[a] jíyun wihun,
> Mul[a] mahange aun diyán bio khate bínún."

> "Choo, sandal wood and Kewra[26] I have by me, and of goods many scores,
> Dearly do I sell all these at double the price (that others demand)."

The ladies enjoin him to be more gallant,—

> "Sitting in our Atan, thou must not require (such) profit;
> Produce thy musk, rise and rub it upon those present."

To which the Banyan, Hindoo-like replies,

> "I am a foreigner and a wayfarer, why should I produce it?
> Ladies! behave not so tyrannically in this city of Bambhora."[27]

Sassui now displays the goodness of her heart—

"Banyan, approach and fear not; freely produce thy stores;
I will pay thee with ready money, the One Lord knows."

While the Hindoo is producing his wares, the lady turns to her companions and remarks,

"Wandering about this trading Banyan has reached our abode;
See his beauty, O my friends,—how handsome he is!"

The Hindoo modestly declines the compliment in favour of Punhú, the son of his employer,—

"Aun kujáro áhiyán disso mun pi dhanyom$^{\underline{i}}$,[28]
Tehín je sunh$^{\underline{a}}$ jo mun khe cháliho wantom$^{\underline{i}}$."

"What am I? you must see my own lord,
Of his beauty I have but a fortieth part."

Sassui and the ladies roused by this assertion, eagerly enquire—

"Banyan, by what name did thy parents call thee?
And who is the youth whose beauty thou describest?"

The Hindoo replies,

"My parents called me *Bábihal*[29] by name,
And the youth whose beauty I describe is Punhal Khan, the Beloch."

The lady, with a vivacity more striking than commendable, makes the following request:—

"My little Babiho, only bring that Beloch for me to see,
And I will pay the taxes and duties for all thy caravan."

Babiho objects at first to act as Mercury, and begins to raise all kinds of difficulties.

"He cannot get leave from his mother even to the chase,
How then can I bring to thee that well-guarded Beloch?"

This the lady treats very lightly,—

"Hundreds of Cafilas, lacs of people come and go,
What then is the difficulty for the Beloch to come?"

Babiho, seeing that the fair one is not easily disconcerted, puts in what he manifestly considers a *coup de grace*;

"Punhú parít^{i} sohnún wádho jenh já wár^{a},
Ba kuwáriyún tenh jún kowal^{a} jiharí kár^{i}."

"The beautiful Punhu, with the long flowing locks,
Has taken to wife two maids, whose voices are sweet as those
of the Kokila."*

Sassui, nothing daunted, pursues,—

"I, too, am a maiden, the pride of Bhambora,
And my accents are not less dulcet than the Kokila's song."

Under these circumstances, could man hold out any longer? Babiho presently relents, and says,—

"Aun pun halius Kech^{a} de, Bái, Alláhí tohár^{a}
Kiaram^{i} bol^{u} Baroch^{a} jo lagh^{i} Dhani^{a} ádhár^{a}."

"I now start for Kech. Lady! Allah be thy preserver;
I have promised (to bring) the Beloch to thee for the love of
the Lord."

Sassui, highly delighted, replies,

"My little Babiho, give my best salam to the Beloch,
(And say), Jam, I have sent thee an offering of rich clothes."

The first part of the story is now concluded; the Hindoo returns to his master, and gives him an account of his commercial doings. At the first opportunity he takes aside Punhu, the Benjamin of the family, and with much luxuriance of language and imagery, informs him of what has happened, and gives him the lady's message, with the offering of rich clothing. Fired with sympathetic ardour by the recital, Punhu[31] prepares to visit Bambhora, and expresses to Babiho his anxiety and affection in the following moving terms,—

> "Dos$^{\underline{a}}$! damámá dáirá mo khe wihan$^{\underline{u}}$ wih$^{\underline{a}}$ thiá,
> Tone bábo mokal$^{\underline{a}}$ na de, aun pí halandus to sán$^{\underline{i}}$."

> "My friend! kettledrums,[32] cymbals, and assemblies are all poison to me,—
> Even if my father permit me not, still will I journey with thee."

Babiho requests him to moderate his anxiety, and promises him success without having recourse to any such extreme measures. Accordingly when the old Jam proposes another mercantile trip, his factotum boldly declares that no one would go without Punhu being permitted to accompany them. The senior responds,—

> "Hoto, Noto, Jakharo, neo Babbur$^{\underline{a}}$ banhu$^{\underline{a}}$ sán$^{\underline{i}}$.

> "There are (my sons) Hoto, Noto, Jakharo, take them, with the slave Babbur, if you like."

Babiho remarks,—

> "Hoto, Noto, Jakharo, and Babbur the slave, are not wanted here;
> Give us Punhu that he may have intercourse with the great."

Ari positively refuses, but finding that his camelmen are more obstinate than himself, relents, and permits his son to go, on condition that the youth should obtain his mother's consent, saying,

> "Ta pí$^{\underline{a}}$ partoe Rabba khe ján mokal$^{\underline{a}}$ deí má$^{\underline{a}}$."

> "Thy father hath committed thee to God's care, if thy mother give thee leave to go."

The effect of which upon the caravan is described as great,—

> "The Cafila men betray their joy, and smile as if milk poured from their lips."

The old Jam now sends a Dadhi (minstrel) round his capital to give notice of his son's departure, and to call for the attendance of the latter's youthful comrades. At length, when all are prepared, Punhu, mounted on his favourite camel, and armed to the teeth, is going to start, when the old lady, his mother, exclaims,—

> "O youths! guard my little Punhu with anxious care."

Hearing these words, the truant's younger wife, Ayisa, comes forward, seizes the camel's nose-string, and says,—

> "Husband, leave me not thus, for the sake of the Lord!
> Either pass this night with me, or send me home to my father's house."

The elder wife, being more practised in such matters, requests the junior to desist, as some one had charmed away their husband's affections.

Punhu departs in great glee, and delights the Cafila men by the spirit and sweetness of his conversation. The only speech recorded is one of a prognosticating description[33] :—

> "Dao tittir$^{\underline{u}}$ je láe sago sirá$^{\underline{u}}$,
> Hik khátáo Sath$^{\underline{a}}$ jo bío piriann$^{\underline{i}}$ merá$^{\underline{u}}$.

> "If the partridge cry from the left or right, or in front,
> One advantage portended is profit to the Cafila; another is the meeting with our friends."

On the road they passed through a town where dwelt a lady more celebrated for beauty than correctness of morals. This fair dame, whose name was Sehjan, was struck with Punhu's beauty as she saw him ride by, and determined to meet him. Accordingly, she assumed the disguise of a man, and came up with the Cafila at a place called Loe, where the camel-men were dozing under the palm trees, and Punhu was playing at chess with his friend and confidant Babiho. The former immediately saw through the deception, and charmed with the frail one's beauty, not only accepted her invitation to a feast, but also delayed the caravan three whole days in order to enjoy her society.

In the meantime, Sassui became impatient to see her lover, and resolving to do her best, went to the house of Akhund Lal, the scribe. She requested him to write[34] a moving epistle to the fickle youth, to which the man of letters, who had long been a silent admirer of the lady, and was blind withal, responded "Akhyani Sán,"[35] and instantly recovered the sight which he had lost by weeping over his hopeless affection. Sassui immediately dispatched a Cossid or courier with the note, and her messenger, on reaching Loe, delivered it to Punhu. That amiable youth's charms had made such an impression upon the too-sensitive Sehjan, that he was unable to get leave to depart, and was finally reduced to the expedient of dropping opium into the lady's cups. Babiho was left behind to take leave of the outwitted Circe, when she might recover from her intoxication. As soon as the confidant disclosed the fact, the fair one was so much affected, that she would have murdered him, had he not invented a story of a Cossid's having brought to Punhu the news of his mother's death. Sehjan, with tears and sighs, thus addresses those around her :—

"Halo, halo, jedíyún halí paso lál^{i} Loe,
Uták^{a} Punhal^{a} je halí chashman^{i} sán^{i} chumo.

"Come, come my companions, come visit bright Loe,
And kiss with your eyes the place where my beloved Punhu abode."

Babiho was dismissed by the lady with presents, and soon joined his lord.

When the Cafila approached its destination, the crafty Babiho opened the camels' mouths, put a bit of musk[36] into each, and closed them up till they reached Bambhora. Crowds of people assembled to see them enter, and to admire the size and trappings of their animals. The camp was pitched in Sassui's garden, but for some reason or other the lady's modesty would not allow her to meet her lover after sending for him from his home. Punhu, after failing in many attempts, at length hit upon an expedient. Taking with him his bow and arrows, he observed a pet pigeon sitting on a mango tree, and shot it so skilfully that it fell into the lap of its mistress, Sassui's aunt. The old lady in wrath thus addresses him ;—

"Khúni bache khachro to khúniy^{a} khún^{u} kiyo,
Pakhí máre asan^{i} jo to jo kehro káj^{u} sariyo.

"Thou murderous boy, thou mule, thou hast done a murderous deed,
And what hast thou gained by slaying our bird ?"

Punhu replies,—

> "I am a murderer, and a mule, and have done a murderous deed;
> But I thought to slay her bird who brought me here from Kech, my home."

Sassui, overhearing the dialogue, takes up the arrow and hands it to Punhu. The latter, although without any excuse to remain, still lingers about the door, and receives another sharp rebuke from the testy old lady:—

> "Tillen werhan$^{\underline{a}}$ wich$^{\underline{a}}$ men tún kenhjo mor$^{\underline{u}}$?
> Ki tun káth^{a} hanandar$^{\underline{u}}$ ki tun kappar$^{\underline{a}}$ chor$^{\underline{u}}$?"

> "Thou struttest about the courts: whose peacock art thou?
> Art thou a digger of walls, or a cloth-thief?"[37]

Punhu denies these charges categorically;—

> "I strut about the courts, the peacock of my friends,
> But I am neither a wall-digger nor a cloth-thief."

At length Sassui took pity upon the young man, consented to meet him, and, in order to test his affection for her, told him that if he would win her hand, he must become a washerman under her father. Punhu did so, and his ignorance of the craft, together with sundry love-passages between him and his mistress, and certain semi-miraculous events which favoured his disguise, gave rise to many somewhat lengthy scenes. The adventure terminated, however, in a quarrel with Bábiho, and a marriage with Sassui.

Their happiness was not of long duration. The wife begged as a favour of her fickle husband, that he would never pass through one of the gates of

Bambhora, and he, husband-like, at once promised to avoid the place, and immediately sought it. There he happened to see one Bhagula, the fair and frail spouse of a Sonar,[38] or goldsmith. The lady admired the Beloch's handsome person, and to let him know her feelings, audibly exclaimed, "May God cause us to meet!" Punhu went home, and pretending that the scabbard of his sword was broken, repaired to the Sonar's house to have it mended. Sassui understood the deceit, and said to her female friends,—

"Ta Punhal$^{\underline{u}}$ halyum tevre bhanji tek$^{\underline{a}}$ miyán$^{\underline{u}}$,
Jekus$^{\underline{i}}$ Sonárí^{a} sehtio en Bhagul^{a} hayus$^{\underline{i}}$ bán$^{\underline{u}}$."

"My beloved Punhu is gone to the armourer's, having broken the scabbard of his sword;
Probably the Sonar's wife has conquered him—Bhagula has pierced his heart with the arrow (of love)."

Now, Bhagula was so wicked, that not contented with seducing Punhu's affections from his wife, she tried to persuade him that the latter was unfaithful to him. When Sassui went to recal the truant, she was addressed by her rival in these very rude terms:—

"Hit$^{\underline{i}}$ mathoi sabh$^{\underline{i}}$ waniyán ádáne korí
Ko na chadde ko bio hoe je Tharan$^{\underline{i}}$ men Thorí."

"Every Banyan has been thy favoured lover, the very weavers who sit at their looms;[39]
No one has missed thee; no, not even the Thori of the wild."

Sassui, indignant at such accusations, proposed to her rival to decide their quarrel by the trial of fire. When the affair became public, crowds gathered from all directions to witness the event, and a pile of three or four maunds of cotton, steeped in oil and clarified butter, was prepared for the ladies' reception. The unhappy Bhagula turned pale at the sight, and would have fled, but Sassui seized her ears and compelled her to enter. Virtue of course triumphed, and the Sonar's dame was burnt to ashes; her ears, which were in the pure hands of her rival, being the only portion which escaped. Punhu[40] acknowledged his wife's chastity, and returned with her to her father's house.

This little episode being duly concluded, the author passes on to the catastrophe of the tale. Babiho, the Banyan, had left Bambhora in high dudgeon, and, going to Ari, told him what had occurred. The senior, much scandalized by the event, sent his six stalwart sons to bring the fugitive *nolens volens* home. Their adventures are somewhat lengthily detailed, but conclude, as usual, with their administering an intoxicating potion to Punhu and his spouse, and carrying off the former at midnight, tied on the back of a camel. The author becomes very pathetic in describing Sassui's conduct when she awakes to the consciousness of her misfortune :—

"Sághari niháre Sassúi ta muhibbu na moháre,
Ditháin derani já utha na otáre,
Nayo niháre thí sajjara pera Punhua já.
Royo ratta phurá kara thí chappara chátáre,
Shíshá lála gulála já hai hai kiyo háre,
Sá gháilí kiyen ghára jenh jo jánibu Jata wathí wiyá."

"At dawn Sassui looks round, but her lover is not on the couch beside her;
She searches, yet finds not the camels of her brothers-in-law at the place where they alighted;
Stooping to the ground, she gazes, and recognises the fresh footsteps of her Punhu.

Then she weeps tears of blood, as if sprinkling the hills (over which her husband was travelling);
Crying, 'Alas! alas!' she scatters the red gulal[41] over her head.
How shall her wounded heart survive the loss of him, whom the Belochis have torn away from her?"

Then come the consolations of the friends. Sassui's mother reminds her of her household duties, the love of her female friends, and the impropriety of giving way to grief.

The lady replies :—

"My spinning-wheel gives me no pleasure, now that my husband is gone,
Nor feel I joy from the conversation of my companions;
My soul is among the hills, where the Belochis urge their camels."

At length, when the common places of consolation are thoroughly exhausted, Sassui declares to her friends a determination to follow her husband's footsteps. All dissuade her in these words, which graphically depict the dangers of the way :—

"Sunyí wanj^{u} ma Sassúí thá nai men nang^{a} sujann^{i}
Giddar^{a} bhaggar^{a} bholará thá richh^{a} rihániyun kann^{i}
Kárá nang^{a} nayyan^{i} mon agyán wák^{a} kiyo warann^{i}
Dádhá dembú dúngaren koráriyun karkann^{i}
Wijho war^{u} wanan^{i} men loháriyun ludann^{i}
Tenh khán poi sujann^{i} pakhá Punhu^{a} jám^{a} já."

"Go not forth to the wild, O Sassui, where snakes lurk in the beds of the mountain streams,
Where jackals, wolves, baboons and bears sit in parties (watching for the traveller);
Where black vipers, in the fiumaras,[42] oppose your way with their hissings;
Fierce hornets haunt the hills, Korars[43] utter their cry,

And Luhars, winding round the trees, swing and sway (in the wind).
After which dangers, appear the sheds,—Jam Punhu's village-home."

Still Sassui adheres to her determination, but dissuades her friends from accompanying her in the following words:—

"Waré thiyun waro, aun na warandí war[a] re
Matán unya maro munhje Punhú[a] khe páráto do,"

"O married females, return home, I will not return without my husband;
(I fear) lest, when you die of thirst, you curse my Punhu."[44]

Sassui starts upon her journey, and thus apostrophises the hills,—

"O ye high hills, why point ye not out the direction of my lover?
It was but yesterday that the string of camels passed over you;
Was not my lover, my friend, in that cafila?"

The author now enters upon a wide field of description,—the dangers of the road, the heat, the feelings of the lady in her novel position, and her praiseworthy perseverance in spite of sun, simoom, fatigue and bruised feet. At last, she meets a goatherd, and addresses him in the following words,—

"O my brother, the goatherd, God give thee many goats,
And may thy name be celebrated (for the beauty of thy flock) at every ford (where the animals are driven to water).
For the Lord's sake, goatherd! point out to me the path taken by my brothers-in-law."

Now it so happened that this wretch, who is described as a perfect Demon of the Waste in ugliness and wildness, had been told by the old witch, his dam, that on that day he should meet in the jungle a beautiful bride, decked in her jewels and rich attire. Seeing Sassui, he concluded that she was the person intended for him, and forthwith began to display a grotesque and unceremonious gallantry, which was rapidly verging towards extremes. The lady, to gain time, complained of thirst, and begged her horrible admirer to milk one of his goats. He replied, that he had no pot. Upon which, the fair one drew out a brass lota (pipkin), and, as he went to fetch the animal, knocked a hole in the bottom of it with a stone. The villain's eyes were so much occupied, and his senses so charmed, by the beauty of his prize, that he did not remark the unusual length of time it required to draw a draught of milk.

And now Sassui, driven to despair, offered up earnest prayers to Heaven to preserve her honour; begging to be admitted into the bowels of the earth, if no other means of escape existed. Heaven heard her supplications, and suddenly she sank into the yawning ground. The wretched goatherd then perceived his mistake, but unable to cancel the past, occupied himself in raising a Lorh and Manah[45] in honour of the departed fair one.

As usually happens in such cases, a few hours afterwards, Punhu, who had escaped from his brothers, together with one Lallu, a slave, and was travelling in hot haste towards Bambhora, passed by the spot. Attracted by the appearance of the Lorh, he went up to it and would have sat down there to rest, had he not heard the voice of his bride calling him from the tomb,

> " Enter boldly, my Punhu! nor think to find a narrow bed,[46]
> Here gardens bloom, and shed sweet savour around,
> Here are fruits, and shades, and cooling streams,
> And the Prophet's light pours through our abode,
> Banishing from its limits death and decay."

Punhu, called up Lallu, the slave, gave him the reins of his camel, and directed him to carry the tidings of his fate to his father and friends. He then prayed to Heaven to allow him to join his Sassui; which Heaven did by opening and swallowing up the lover. The tale concludes with the verse in which Lallu informs the old Jam of his son's last act,—

> " Wiyo wichoro, pirin gadyá pán^{a} men
> Ashikan^{i} ruh^{a} rattá, gul^{u} wiyo gulzár^{a} men.

> " Separation is now removed, and the friends have met to part no more,
> The souls of those true lovers are steeped (in bliss), and the rose is at last restored to the rose bed."

It is no less true than discreditable to human nature that these miraculous events are rejected by certain sceptical Sindhis, who declare that the recreant Lallu, when caught by Punhu in an intrigue with his bride, slew his master to prevent exposure. Moreover, it is asserted, that after this abominable action, the ruffian spent a week in the company of the beautiful Sassui, murdered her to keep the affair quiet, and concluded by inventing a pretty story to impose upon the credulity of the old Jam and his family. We must rank these unbelievers with those doubters who have not scrupled to treat as myths such veritable stories as the Siege of Troy, and the wanderings of Æneas.

The next tale in my little volume is that of Umar, the Sumrah prince, and Marui, the Sangiani.[47] It commences with a short account of one Palino, who ran away with a certain Mihrada, the mother of Marui, from the house of Phula Lako, her husband; and attributes that event to the will of fate.

> "By the Lord's will Mihrada became the butt of jibing tongues,
> Yet she was no born or purchased slave;
> She fell in love with a Maru, and eloped with Palino,
> But her being driven to the Tharr was the work of the Omnipotent."

The lady's condition prevented the celebration of her nuptials with Palino till the birth of Marui. The bard describes that event, and in the person of the Munajjim, or Astrologer, predicts the most remarkable occurrence in her life.

> "On the sixth day, and the sixth night, after the child's birth[48]
> He predicted in these words, 'Your daughter's fate shall be such
> That to you, O parents! Umar shall apply with joy.'"

To which speech the mother replies—

> "Let him do so, and he shall have Phul's daughter,
> The granddaughter of Sahir, the child of Mihrada,
> The protected by Palino—the dweller in the Tharr."

The chronicle proceeds to relate that the young woman, whose destinies had thus been settled for her, grew up, became very beautiful, and excited several *belles passions*. Her first victim was one Phog, a shepherd in the service of Palino, who, becoming desperate with love, went to his master and told him that he could serve him no longer. Palino, unwilling to lose a good servant, and at once understanding the cause of his disgust, promised him the hand of his step-daughter. Phog was highly delighted, and returned to his daily occupations with much zest. The bard says,

" Man^{a} men matáro thio senan^{i} je suhag^{a}
Hath^{i} dheri banh^{a} verhi tho katte unn^{a} ajagh^{a}
Chare manjhan chágh^{a} tho pahun pán^{a} muhariyun."

" His mind was joyful at the prospect of his (future) connexion,
With the clod in his hand, and the twist round his forearm, he spins a quantity of wool,
And in the gladness of his heart allows the cattle to graze where they please."[49]

After some time, seeing no prospect of success, the shepherd goes to his master and threatens to complain of his perfidy to the ruler of the land. The deceitful Palino replies,

" Umar the just King lives far off,
And he will not interfere with trade or marriages,
You will injure yourself by this conduct, O Phog!"

Phog, however, in his wrath travels from the Tharr to Omerkot, a long journey, and appears before the monarch, exclaiming,

" Pahuch^{u} tun Pohwaran^{i} khe E badshah^{a} Dodane dass^{i}
Wihan dei wadandaro munkhe char^{a} chakhaya^{un} chass^{i}
Mun tan Márúi bass^{i} ser^{a} tokhe Súmrá."

" O King, brave as Dodo,[50] aid thou the helpless hind!
After promising me a wife, they deceitfully change their minds.
Enough for me of Marui, now, she is a present to thee, O Sumra!"[51]

Umar remarked that this was a peculiar way to punish a breach of promise, and in order to test Phog's ideas of beauty, he introduced him into his harem, after ordering the ladies to put in requisition all the arts of the toilette. The shepherd, however, declared, with abundant tears, that not one of the high-born beauties was to be compared to the maid of the desert. At last becoming poetical he exclaims,

> " O Umar Sumra, even the charms of thy sister,
> Though faintly resembling, are not to be compared to those of Marui;
> Her nilufar-like nose,[52] her cheek, rich as the light falling on ambergris,
> The dark locks on her forehead, the braids which fall below her waist
> Must be seen to be appreciated, believe me, O Umar Sumra."

Umar then resolved to accompany the shepherd, and the bard thus describes their progress,

> " When the Sumro, that mighty prince, started on his journey,
> Phog following him on foot, Umar riding upon his camel,
> Both reached their destination at last, and beheld the outskirts of the beautiful Malir."[53]

The first objects they saw were two women standing at a well; they are poetically introduced as follows :—

> " Jiyen, Konwr$^{\underline{a}}$ men kungú tiyen Mihráde sen Márui."

> " As Kungu[54] in its casket, so was Marui by the side of Mihrada."

Seeing the stranger, Mihrada exclaims—

> " Ammán Umar$^{\underline{a}}$ ayo Sumre jo Sawar$^{\underline{u}}$
> Kádir$^{\underline{a}}$ lahe karár$^{\underline{u}}$ par^{e} Sindhí ḅhayán Súmro."

> " My love,[55] one of Umar the Sumra's horsemen approaches,
> God only knows, but I really believe it is the Sindhi Sumra himself."

The stranger stopped his camel, and pretending thirst as a pretext for commencing the conversation, asked Mihrada to draw some water for him. The fair one, with little respect for his incognito, remarks—

"O, wayfarer, thou callest for water, tell the truth,
Art thou one of a bridal procession,[56] or art thou Umar himself?"

Umar replied, that he was neither the one nor the other, but was most undeniably thirsty. Upon which, says the bard,

"Tadhen Márúi mágihin kadhio ábu achho kara khiru
Angrianni wechho kario lahio wijhe Niru
Manjhán hubba Hamiru tho ghorún wijhe ghotio."

"Then Marui immediately drew water as clear as milk,
And shrinking backwards poured out the stream;
The Hamir in delight offers up prayers for her happiness."[57]

After a protracted scene, Umar leaped from his camel, seized the young lady and carried her off to Omerkot, in spite of tears and struggles. There the beauty began to display her spirit by refusing to touch food or to speak a word either in address or reply. But, as the bard says, the former symptoms rapidly disappeared, and Umar determined to cure the silence of his refractory charmer. Every day she was chained and fettered, and, when night came, was carried to the couch on which Umar slept, a gold katar, or dagger, separating the pair. This lasted for some time, till at last the lady exclaims,

"This is not the way, O Sumra, in which men contract nuptial alliances;
Thou chainest those whom thou lovest—this is a strange manner of showing affection.

Alas! alas! I am dying for one sight of the Tharr;
Ye holy Pirs of Panwar,[58] O grant me to see my friends once more."

Umar consoles her with these words :—

" Mándí thí ma márúí, hanjún hadd^{i} ma hár^{i}
Dukhan^{i} puthiy^{a} sukhará sighá thín^{a} sukár^{a}
Bhanjí zeriyún bár^{i} to tán band^{u} bidá thió."[59]

" Be not afflicted, my Marui, pour not forth these tears;
After grief comes joy, and after famine, quickly reappears plenty.
Break and burn thy fetters, thy bondage is now done."

Having thus gained a minor point, Umar released his prisoner, and allowed her to live among the ladies of the palace. She waited for an opportunity, and sent a message to her cousin Maru, begging him to aid her in escaping from her prison. Maru accordingly mounted his camel, travelled to Omerkot by night, and alighted at the Khanakah, or hermitage, of some Pir there. Leaving his beast with the holy man, he scaled the palace walls, and entered the chamber where Umar and Marui were sleeping. The latter awoke, and persuaded her relative not to murder the prince, but to content himself with substituting a silver for the gold dagger on the couch. Maru was loathe to spare the sleeper, but after some conversation with his cousin, and settling their plans, he retired to the hermitage in the disguise of a Mujawir.[60] In the morning, Umar saw the dagger, and asked the lady what had happened; but she considered it advisable to be ignorant of the night's occurrences.

Five or six days afterwards, Marui obtained permission to perform a pilgrimage to the Khanakah, in consequence of a vow made to visit the holy man. She promised also, that if this boon were granted, she would comply with all the prince's wishes. The Hamir, highly pleased, sent his own sister and female attendants to accompany the lady, and to see that her object was devotion. After visiting the tomb, and performing the usual religious rites, Marui pointed to her cousin, and asked the women, "Which of you will wander about with my brother the Fakir?"[61]

Umar's sister replies, in jest,—

"Márú chadde Malíra men bio mun bháu hiti kiyo,
Ihrí niwarí tun wanju halí bie sen."

"Having left (thy cousin) Maru at Malir, thou sayest, 'I have acquired a new brother here;'
Free, indeed, art thou; go thou with this, thy other brother."[62]

Marui hailed her words as an omen of good, and presently finding some pretext for escaping from her companions, mounted Maru's camel, and in company with him, hastened to revisit her beloved Malir.

Apprised of the event, and persuaded by his friends and kinsmen, Umar at last gave up the idea of making Marui his wife. In order to inform her of his determination, he instantly rode over to the Malir, told her that she was his sister, and returned to Omerkot. Still the violence of his affection did not abate, and even though the lady came occasionally to see her "brother" during his sickness, the disease threatened to be a mortal one. The beginning of the end was, that Marui accidently heard a false report of the Hamir's death as she was preparing to visit him; and such was her grief, that her soul incontinently quitted its tenement of clay.[63]

Umar on his part, as in duty bound, no sooner heard of the fair one's decease, than with equal facility of exit, he also departed this transitory life.

The relator concludes this Tale of the Tharr with the appropriate but somewhat hackneyed quotation,

> "Verily we are God's, and unto Him (we are) returning."

CHAPTER V.

THE SAME SUBJECT CONTINUED.—THE TALES OF RANO AND MUMAL; OF SOHNI AND THE MEHAR; OF DODO AND CHANESAR; OF HIR AND RANJHA; OF DULHA DARYA KHAN, AND OF MALL MAHMUD.

The short specimens of composition given in the preceding chapter, orientally considered, speak well for the moral tone of Sindhi literature. The tale of Rano and Mumal is not quite so unobjectionable; the hero being an individual of questionable character, and the lady nothing but a fair Kanyari, or Hetæra, in plain English, a courtesan. The European reader must not, however, confound the idea of this class with that of the unhappy beings in his own country, whom necessity or inclination have urged to break through all restraints human and divine.[1]

The story opens with stating that the Hamir Sumra, the Sindhi prince who reigned at the time, called together his friends and boon companions, Don Bhutani, Sinharo Rajani, with his brother-in-law, Rano Mendhro, and proposed a trip to the banks of the Kak river, near Omerkot, to call upon the Lais of the age, Mumal the Rathorni.[2] The party started, and on the way met a man habited in Fakir's garb. The bard thus describes the adventure:—

"Bábú gadio barr[e] men ján pahar[u] sijj[e] khán poe,
Kissá kario Kák[i] já en ratt[a] warnun roe,
Kák[e] na wanjé koí matán mán jiyen thiye."

"A Babu[3] met them in the wilderness, one watch after sunrise,
When speaking of the Kak,[4] he wept tears of blood, (and cried)
'Let no one go to Kak, lest he become what I am.'"

The friends address him in the following words,—

"O, Babu, of the wild, what hast thou to complain of Kak?"

The Fakir rejoins,—

"Men (if you go there), the very trees will lament your fate,
The stones will cry aloud, and the waters shed tears for you;
Magic veils, like the lightning's blaze, will obscure your sight.
Mir[5] affirms that no one can gaze at Mumal,
Without bearing in his face wounds that never heal."

This somewhat startles the party, and the bard graphically depicts their proceedings:—

"Tadhen Hamír[u] niháre Ráne dánh[a] Ráno danh[e] Hamír[a]."

"Then the Hamir stood gazing at Rano, and Rano at the Hamir."

Rano addresses the mendicant in polite and flattering strains,—

"Babu of the wild, welcome art thou to day,
Sami! on thy neck the gold beads[6] brightly shine;
With what colour are they dyed, that they appear so beautifully red?
The Bhonwr pays tribute to the blossom on thy turban,
Wise Jogi! declare to us the tidings of Kak."

Upon this, as the bard says,—

" Tadhen duske en dass^{a} de tho roe ratto áb^{u}
Ta' ayus^{u} Ludráne khaun ákila ! sán^{i} asbáb^{a}
Aun nango hos^{i} nawwáb^{u} para Kak^{i} máre kiyus^{i} kápari !"

" Then sobbing, and pointing out the way, he weeps tears of blood,
(Saying) ' O, wise one ! I came with my suite from Ludrano ;
I, the naked pauper, was then a noble, but Kak has ruined and beggared me.' "[7]

Rano thus resumes :—

"Art thou a beggar from Kashmir,[8] or Kahu, the son of Jarrar ?"

The Fakir answers,—

" Mendhra ! my suite was composed of five thousand warriors ;
Sodha ! each man was lord of his own village ;
Each rode his steed with shield, dagger and sword :
That witch dispersed them by the might of her magic glance ;
She ruined all, my friend ! I now go forth alone, O Mendhra ;
Shun thou the road of Kak, and avoid the pit into which I fell."[9]

The advice was, of course, disregarded by the friends, who instantly started, and journeyed on till they reached the waters of Kak. Seeing a crowd of female slaves gathered round a well, they went up to them, and, as a preliminary step, enquired the name of the stream, the town, and other such particulars. The head of the party, a handmaid of Mumal's, by name Natir, feels somewhat indignant at seeing such ignorance displayed by the wayfarers, and thus replies to their queries :—

" Kak is crowded with the tents and pavilions of visitors ;
Who are ye that are ignorant of Kak and its deeds,
And the fame of the Rathor women who inhabit it ?
Here dwell Mumal and Sumal, Sehjan and Muradi.[10]

They deck the assembly with secret purpose;
On their heads are pink veils, and on their bosoms saffron coloured bodices,
Their dresses are bright as lightning; they delight in swinging from the lofty trees,
And in laving their fair limbs with rose-water from rich vases,
And pour Atr (ottar) over the heads of their visitors.
O, Mir Mendhra! such are the delights of Kak."

The friends repaired to an Otak,[11] and soon received a message from Mumal, who had been apprised of their arrival. The bearer approached with a low Salam, placed some toasted Chana (grain) and raw silk at each travellers feet, and retired. The latter, with the exception of Rano, all inadvertently ate the grain, and sent back the silk cleaned and spun. The hero of the tale, however, sent for Natir, twisted the silk into a rope for his horse, threw the Chana to him, and told the handmaid to let her mistress know what he had done.[12] Before she departed, the friends opened a little flirtation with the fair slave, the Hamir saying,—

"Tun ghumen já rang^{i} mehall^{a} men Ráni k^{i} Báni
Máre Mashukan^{i} khe je khanio naina nihárien."

"Thou who pacest the inner rooms of the palace, art thou queen or slave?
Thou murderest a lover each time thy glances are raised towards him."

Natir replies, with becoming coquetry,—

"Aun báni; Ràniyun biyun mun nainen ma bhull^{u}
Sandi Kák^{i} kandhí ahiyán kám$_{a}$ hall^{i}."

"I am a slave, very different are my queens, be not enchanted by my glances,
On the banks of Kak I rove on foot."[13]

When Mumal heard what had happened, she sent back Natir with a present of Halwa (sweetmeats) and bread to Rano. The swain administered a little gentle chastisement to the bearer, and asked her how she and her mistress dared to send him a woman's dinner.

Presently, the friends received an invitation to sup with Mumal, but to come singly, beginning with the bravest. The Hamir was permitted to start first, but on the road, he was startled by so many horrible forms of snakes and dragons, lions and ghools, that he returned home supperless. The courtiers followed, but with no better effect. Rano, when at last it came to his turn, took the natural precaution of securing a guide, and, for that purpose, chose the fair Natir. On the road she strove to escape, but the Sodha drew his dagger, and looked so fierce, that she desisted from any further attempt of the kind. Undaunted by the figures on the road, which he saw were put there merely to frighten him, the successful adventurer reached Mumal's abode, and was desired by her slaves to sit upon the Khatolo or couch.[14] Rano suspected some trick, and striking the seat with the horn of his bow, burst through the unspun cotton which covered the frame, and saw a well under the place selected for him. Being then ushered into another apartment, his eyes were dazzled by the beauty and dress of the line of damsels that stood up to receive him. Puzzled by the similarity of their appearance, he nearly failed to discover Mumal, when a Bhonwr, or large black bee, opportunely buzzed round her head.[15]

Rano's superior intellect thus provided him with a supper and a fair companion; but his happiness did not last long. The jealous Sumra waited for a few days, and when his brother-in-law left Mumal to return home, requested to be allowed to see the lady's face for an hour. Rano consented, upon the condition that the prince should disguise himself, and behave as a common servant. The Hamir assented, but, when desired by Mumal to milk a buffalo, obeyed in a manner that betrayed his real rank. The mistress of the house immediately guessed what had occurred, and said to her lover,—

> "Ráná na jántoí wadde wen^{i} wirsen,
> Sat^{a} bhatíro Súmro kojho kare ándoen."

> "Rano thou hast erred, and sadly erred,
> In bringing the handsome[16] Sumra here in such unseemly plight."

The prince feels the indignity most acutely, and resolving to punish Rano for his conduct, sends the following message to him :—

> "Art thou coming, O Mendhra! thy friends all sigh for thee;
> Or hast thou any message for the lords of Dhat?"[17]

To which Rano replies,

> "A hundred salams to fair Dhat, twenty salams to my neighbours;
> In Mumal's love, my lord! we care for nothing else."

Mumal, in an evil hour, persuaded Rano to go and take leave of his companions before they left Kak, wishing him to remain on good terms with them. He did so, and was instantly seized, bound on a camel, and carried off to Omerkot, where the Hamir confined him in a deep dungeon: nor did he release his successful rival, till the latter swore never to return to Kak.

But Jove is supposed, in Sindh as well as elsewhere, to laugh at lovers' perjuries, and Rano no sooner found himself at liberty than he revisited the lady of his heart. One morning his wife observing that the water in which her husband washed his head was of a suspicious colour, called her mother-in-law, and said to her,—

> "Petí putoí para-ghar^{a} handhaniyún kare shail^{a} shikár^{a},
> Kani wairíyen waddhio kaní dinnias^{i} már^{a},
> Kiyen jiyen manjh^{i} kapár^{i} rat^{u} relá kiyo nikare."

> "Thy greedy profligate son is ever wandering about in pursuit of strange women;
> Some foe has been wounding, some enemy beating him;
> See how the blood has poured in streams from his forehead."

The old lady, in alarm, carried the vessel to the prince, who immediately recognising the red tinge of the waters of Kak, again imprisoned Rano, and drove iron spikes between the toes of his best camel. At length the Hamir's wife interceded with him and procured the liberation of her brother, who resolved to revisit Mumal with all possible expedition. Summoning the head herdsman, he enquired after his favourite dromedary, and heard that it was dead; the man, however, told him that it had left a colt, which used to start alone at night and to return in the morning with its mouth red, lean and gaunt with excessive fatigue. Thinking this to be disease, the herdsman said to Rano,—

> "There is a camel,[18] the foal of thy camel, an animal of pure breed,
> He has long been sick, that colt, and besides he has lost his mother,
> And pines for her, and is now dried up and wasted away."

Rano replies,—

> "Show me the camel dried up and wasted away,
> I will physic it and cure its bodily ailments."

When Rano saw the colt, he perceived that it had been drinking the waters of Kak, and admired the beauty of the animal. Taking it home with him, he decked it out with bells and fringed trappings, mounted it, in the joy of his heart exclaiming,—

> "Hall^{u} miyán karahall^{a} ta passán máríyún Múmal^{a} jún,
> To khe chandan^{a} cháriyán tarah^{a} mocháriy^{a} tarahall^{i},
> Asín máníyún Múmall^{a} tún nayyo nágelun chare."

> "On, on with thee, master camel-colt, let me see Mumal's
> abode!
> I will feed thee with sandal leaves, and in the richest spots;
> While I break bread with Mumal, thou bending (thy long
> neck) shalt browse the flowery nangel."[19]

Fate, however, willed it otherwise. The fair Mumal, in order to beguile her grief, had hit upon the curious expedient of dressing her sister Sumal in Rano's old clothes, and of causing her to sleep on the same couch. As it was night when the lover arrived, he merely saw that the bed contained more than one occupant, and in the fury of his jealousy, drew his sword to kill the pair. After a few minutes' reflection, however, he put up the weapon, and planting a stick by the side of the couch, left the house in silence. When Mumal awoke and saw the sign, she guessed the full extent of her misfortune :—

"Thou hast ridden to Kak, and yet thou believest thy love faithless;
O Jat! hath thy intellect fled for ever?
With grief as thine only companion hast thou departed, O Mendhra!"

The bard now indulges in rather a prolix account of the sorrow and mourning of Mumal and her sisters. The ivory spinning-wheels lie neglected under the shade of the Kewra trees, and the silken swings hang idle from the boughs of the spreading Pippil; in fact every pleasure now ceases to please. At length, driven to despair, Mumal disguises herself as a merchant, goes to Dhat and throws herself in Rano's way. Attracted by some undefined feeling, the Sodha is not slow in forming a friendship with the new comer, and frequently invites him to his house. One day, when they had been playing at chess, Rano cannot help remarking aloud that the merchant was very like the "light of love," Mumal. She seizes the opportunity of throwing off her disguise, and, drawing forth a ring which the lover had given her in happier times, casts it into his lap. He understands the meaning of the action, but turns away in anger and loathing. The fair one then exclaims,—

"Human beings, O Mendhra! are liable to error,
But the good do good, and injure others as little as possible;
They carry on friendship to the last, and never (lightly) break its chains."

Rano replies,—

"Chhinní já hekárª kehí jorí tenh walª jí?
Ṇa jánán bihárª mero mue ki jiyare!

"How shall the creeper when once broken reunite?
I know not when again we meet (as friends) in life or in death!"

Mumal then seizes the hem of his garment, and says,

"My love! I come to thy abode as a suppliant, and cast thy skirt round my neck."[20]

Still Rano remains inexorable; and the unhappy Mumal leaves the house. Feeling sick of life, she collects a pyre of firewood, and exclaiming,

"If we meet not now, I go where our souls will reunite, O Mendhra,"

sets fire to the mass, and is burned to ashes.

When the obdurate youth hears of that melancholy occurrence, he repairs to the spot, and, with pouring tears, thus addresses the manes of his Mumal:—

"Our separation now ends, my beloved, our sorrows are over,
Fired with desire of thee, I quit the world which contains thee not.
Tell my friends (ye bystanders!) that Rano is gone to seek Mumal."

He then makes the servants throw up a heap of wood, lights it, and precipitates himself into the flames. In recounting this tragical end, the bard remarks,—

"True lovers are they who ever behave truly to each other,
And whose hearts are crimsoned with the dye of affection.
The fires of such love as this open the way to the realms of futurity."

The reader may possibly think otherwise. He cannot, however, but confess that the Sindhi author has very delicately handled rather a difficult subject in the tale above related, and that he deserves our gratitude for the pains he has taken to condense his subject: in Europe a similar thin web of adventure would be spun out, with threadbare common-places, to the long length of three volumes. All the three legends conclude tragically. The insecurity of existence and property in the East, and the every-day dangers of an Oriental life are too real for the mind to take any interest in the fine-drawn distress and the puny horrors which are found sufficiently exciting by the European novel reader. It is scarcely necessary to remark that in these tales we may discern the rude germs of that kind of literature to which, among us, Boccaccio's genius gave its present polished form.

The following stories are too well known and popular in Sindh to be passed over in silence. One of the most pleasing is that of Sohni, the Dub-mui, or "Drowned Beauty;" and it is one which the bards most delight to sing. The heroine was, according to some, a Hindoo woman; others say she was the daughter of a Jat of Sangar, a village on the banks of the Sangra river, in the province of Jhang Siyal. Her father gave her in marriage to one Dam, an individual of the same clan. As the nuptial procession went to a neighbouring stream, to perform certain rites and consult the omens, she was sent by her husband to fetch some milk from the jungle; there she saw a buffalo keeper,[21] and instantaneously fell in love with him. Reversing the well-known practice of Hero and Leander, at night she used to pass over the Indus upon one of the Ghara, or large earthern pots, with which the fishermen support themselves in swimming, spend the hours of darkness in listening to the sound of her lover's Bansli (shepherd's reed), and return home before dawn.

The "Mother-in-law" in Sindh, as well as elsewhere, is always a personage of baneful influence. The dame, who stood in that relation to Sohni, persuaded her lover, Kodu, a potter by trade, to make a jar of unbaked material, exactly similar to that used by Sohni in her nocturnal natations. One night, the heroine happened to be sitting in the moonlight with her Mehar, and remarked to him that there was a Phola, or pellicle, in his eye. He replied that she must have seen it there, without remarking it, for many months, and concluded with warning her that some misfortune would happen to them both.[22] The next time she attempted to swim the stream, the jar, which her treacherous mother-in-law had substituted for the usual Ghara, burst, and the fair one then and there met with a watery grave.

Her praises are generally sung in "Baita" like these—

> "Sohni was fair,[23] both in body and mind;
> Nor had she one defect you could remark;
> She left husband and home in search of happiness
> And in quest of love, but found a grave."

The story of Dodo and Chanesar is of a heroic cast; and the former of these worthies is very popular among the Langha, or bards of the province. They were brothers; the former the younger, the latter the elder son of Bhungar, a prince of the Sumra clan. When their father died, Dodo, who was the favourite of the soldiery, dispossessed Chanesar of his rights, and ascended the throne. On the day of inauguration, the latter's mother, hearing the shouts of the people, enquired what the reason was, and when informed of it by her son, exclaimed, "Would to God a daughter had been born to me instead of thee!"

His parent's taunt was the climax of misfortune, and the unhappy Chanesar, finding all other means of no avail, started off to Delhi to procure assistance from the Mogul. At that vast capital he passed some time in fruitless endeavours to make himself known to the monarch and his court. At last, when positively refused admission, he waited for an opportunity and slew the emperor's favourite elephant, Makua, with one blow of a miraculous rod which he had procured from a shepherd during his travels. For this offence he was dragged before Ala el din Padshah, and interrogated by Madan el Mulk, the Wazir. He stated his object in doing the deed, and moreover proved his power by killing a tiger single handed. The emperor was delighted with his valour, and prepared in person to restore him to his kingdom.

When the Mogul's host reached Jesulmere, Chanesar persuaded the monarch to write to Dodo, and to claim as a sign of homage, two or three Sumra women. The Sindhi assembled the clan, who were of opinion that the demand could not honourably be complied with, but agreed to refer the point to an old Manganhar, or minstrel, a prime authority in all such matters. The senior was accordingly carried into the presence in a basket lined with cotton, and unhesitatingly declared that for sixteen generations no such disgrace had ever been incurred by the Sumra tribe. Dodo, however, feeling desirous to avoid bloodshed, forwarded a hundred horses and an elephant as a Nazaranah, or tribute-offering, to the emperor. The latter was at first disposed to be satisfied with this tacit admission of inferiority, but Chanesar told him that the usurper, by sending the animals, and not coming in person with his present, had, under the semblance of submission, treated his majesty as a lord does his slave. Ala el din now advanced in furious mood. Dodo made all due preparation for receiving him. The "Sharm"[24] was sent first to Odar Kapurani, but afterwards was placed under the protection of the gallant Abro Abrani, the Samma ruler of Cutch. After a few days desultory fighting, a general action came on. The Sindhis performed prodigies of valour, according to their own account; Dodo went so far as to attack the emperor's body-guard single handed. After cutting his way through the crowd, he thrust his dagger into the thigh of the elephant which carried Alaeldin's steel howdah, and used it as a ladder; but pierced with a hundred wounds, he fell before he could reach the emperor.

The Sindhi host then fled, and the Moguls, after defeating Odar, went to attack the Samma. The latter mounted his favourite mare, fastened himself to the saddle, and sallied forth from his stronghold to meet the foe. His handful of followers were cut up in a few minutes, and when he was killed, the mare bore his corpse from the field of battle. His wife saw from her watch-tower what had occurred; she took the body of her husband and placed it upright at the window, in order to persuade the enemy that Abro was still alive; the fort, however, was invested, and the ladies, unable to defend themselves, drank poison and died like veritable heroines.

The traitor Chanesar, feeling that the honour of the family had been tarnished by his hand, now resolved to ruin Ala el din, as he had destroyed his brother and kinsmen. He went over to Dungar Ra, the only surviving son of Jam Abro, and with him concocted plans and projects. The result was a general rising, a "*levée en masse*" of the patriot population of Sindh and Cutch: the only recreant was the Hajjam or barber, who, to this day, is looked upon as one of the vilest of men. Repeated skirmishes, night attacks and battles soon reduced the mighty host of the Moguls, and at last the monarch, followed by only seven horsemen, fled to Mathela. There he heard that disturbances had taken place at Delhi, and in despair swallowed poison, and died. The poor remains of his mighty army shaved their beards, and became Fakirs.[25] How gallantly the Sindhis fight —in books!

The next tale in our list is the celebrated Panjabi legend, usually known as "Hir Ranjha,"[26] the names of the lady and her lover. The latter was one of the eight sons of Jam Mohammed, alias Fauju Zemindar, a chief of Jhang Siyal, according to some, or, as others say, of Takht Hazari. The father determined to provide his son with a wife, and with that intention, collected together all the celebrated beauties in the country. He then told Ranjha to select his bride. The youth accidently chose a dame who had no right to be in such an assembly, as she was already a married woman. Judging from the omen, we are not told how, all the spinsters there present declared that Ranjha was destined to love the fair Hir, of Jhang Siyal. The hero accordingly disguised himself in the garb of a Fakir, and, after a few unimportant acts of knight-errantry, managed to get an interview with the "polar star of his destiny." Having proved the intensity, if not the purity of his flame, by drinking a cup of poison without injury, the lady told him that she was his, and the happy pair immediately set out upon their wanderings. Both lived and died Fakirs.

This story is a very favourite one with the minstrels and lower orders of musicians. Some of them, in their enthusiasm, visit the tomb of the beautiful Hir, and join in the pilgrimage which takes place to that sanctified spot. The adventures of the lovers enter into a thousand songs, of which the following are short specimens. The lady speaks :—

"God grant that Ranjha may never be parted from me,
Aid us, O Lord! and let Vedan love none but me.
Where the holes of snakes and scorpions are,
There Ranjha fearlessly places his foot,[27]
Since the dark night when I visited him, dressed in crimson clothes.[28]
May Khora[29] die, may all this trouble cease,
And Ranjha ever be present at Jhang Siyal."

Another specimen :—

"When a hundred thousand physicians would fall back in despair,
Let my loved Ranjha appear, and I rise from my bed.
Where Ranjha lets down his long flowing locks,
There I will collect the clay.[30]
And I love to wander through the tamarisks,
Where Ranjha feeds his buffaloes."

The story of Dulha Darya Khan is another quasi-historical tale of Sindhi prowess and conquest. It is related that Jam Nanda, the chief of Kinjur, on the lake of that name,[31] had been for many years childless, and at last determined to adopt an heir. One day, when out hunting, he saw a shepherd boy lying under a tree, and observed that during many hours, the shade remained stationary over the sleeper's form. Convinced by this sign from heaven that the choice would be a good one, he adopted the child, and called him Dulha Darya Khan. The Khan soon becoming a great chieftain, and a doughty warrior, conquered many of the regions round about Sindh, and at last resolved to attack Candahar. He succeeded, and informed his foster-father of the glad tidings by means of a line of beacons which he had erected along the road. Sindh rejoiced with exceeding joy.

When Dulha returned, he determined to marry into the Sulangi clan; but they declined the honour, offering, as an excuse, the impossibility of finding a maiden fit for him. In mighty wrath, the Khan resolved upon a terrible revenge. He treacherously invited the greybeards and chiefs of the tribe to a Borgia entertainment, and blew up the house in which they were feasting. The head of the clan was a lady of a certain age, whose sex saved her from the general ruin of her family. Swearing to follow up the blood-feud to the last, she started for Delhi, to beg aid and assistance from the Mogul, who seems, at that time, to have been the general refuge for destitute Sindhis. By his favour, she was provided with a large army, returned to her country, and defeated the recreant Khan in a pitched battle. Dulha, aware of what he had to expect, fled in the disguise of a Fakir, but the lady's emissaries pursued, detected and bore him before his female foe.

Then ensued a scene which notably illustrated

"Furens quid fœmina possit."

The enraged Amazon directed the executioner to cut the luckless Khan's throat, and tear his head from his shoulders, in presence of the whole army. She concluded, the bard says, by drinking wine out of the bleeding head.

The legend of Mall Mahmud, or Mahmud the Brave, commemorates the gallantry, in both senses of the word, displayed by the proselytizing champions of Islam in the olden time. The "Brave," one of the Ashab, or companions, of Ali, in true knight-errant style wandered from Mecca with the intention of slaughtering all the fighting men who might decline to believe in Allah and Mohammed.

The fort of Hyderabad in those days was held by a Kafir, or infidel, Nerun by name. The daughter of this abomination, Bibi Nigar, when enjoying the pleasures of the chase, saw a fire in the jungle and went up to it. There she observed an individual broiling some game to satisfy the cravings of hunger; perceiving by his dress that he was a stranger and a soldier, the lady, being of masculine habits and disposition, and, as it would appear, fond of gymnastic exercises withal, challenged him to a trial of strength. He not knowing that his antagonist was a woman, prepared to gratify her by dealing a goodly buffet; but feeling an unaccountable weakness in the region of the arm, after three futile attempts, told his opponent that he could not strike. The lady smiled, exposed her face, and thus explained the phenomenon.

Of course both parties fell in love with each other instantly, and, of course, both being Orientals, settled the preliminaries of matrimony with a celerity unknown to the people of more frigid climes. The lady presently left her lover, informing him of her name and residence, and giving him a gold ring as a pledge of future fidelity. The swain also swore eternal constancy, but insisted upon a change of faith, and asked permission to travel to Mecca for the purpose of inviting Ali, his lord, to the nuptials.

The lady's attendants, however, no sooner reached the castle, than they informed her progenitor of his daughter's little love passage with a Moslem. The father resolved to get over the difficulty by marrying the lady to a kinsman, and gave orders for the nuptial feast, the attendance of musicians, and other preparations suitable to the occasion. Bibi Nigar, in despair, mounted a camel-man upon her swiftest camel, and giving him a message to Mall Mahmud, told him to ride for his life towards Mecca. The champion was soon found, and as he and the messenger were returning together, to the vast delight of the former they were joined by the holy and valiant Ali, mounted on his venerated steed, Zu'l Jenah. Arriving at Hyderabad, Mall Mahmud left his lord in a garden, and started in disguise for the palace, to view the locality before adopting any definite plan of proceeding. There he was soon discovered by the art of a female slave, and confined in a well[32] below the fort.

Ali waited some time for his follower, but seeing that he did not return, went to seek him, and was guided by Divine wisdom to Bibi Nigar's Hujleh, or nuptial chamber. He concealed himself till the newly married pair retired to rest; when, as soon as the bridegroom gave him an opportunity, he came forth from his hiding-place and slew him. The next step was to liberate the imprisoned "brave," which being happily effected, the lovers and their venerable protector mounted their horses and left the place with all possible celerity. The Kafir father was not slow to follow them. At the hour of morning prayer, a host of foes was close upon their track. The fugitives dismounted to perform their orisons, which gave the infidels time to come up with them. Bibi Nigar, having first concluded her genuflexions, rode at the pursuers, and fell after performing many deeds of valour. Her lover could not but follow her example, and Ali was in duty bound to revenge his friends by slaughtering immense numbers of the assailants. This done, he returned to Mecca.

Sindh, therefore, like almost all the other Moslem countries, has its peculiar tradition about the fourth Caliph; and, as will presently be shown, rejoiced in the presence of his two sons.

The above are the most important and the best known of the popular legends of our province.

CHAPTER VI.

MOSLEM EDUCATION AT SCHOOLS AND COLLEGES, UNDER THE NATIVE RULERS AND OUR GOVERNMENT.—THE STUDY OF MEDICINE, SURGERY, ETC.—HINDOO EDUCATION.—HOW TO INSTRUCT THE PEOPLE.—THE NASKHI ALPHABET ADVOCATED.

As might be expected from a semi-barbarous race, the native rulers of Sindh encouraged no branch of study, except that peculiarly belonging to their own faith.

The course of education among the Moslems is as follows:—The boy[1] is sent to a day-school,[2] from the hours of six A.M. to six P.M. to learn reading and writing.[3] The Akhund, or pedagogue, begins by teaching him to pick out the letters of Alhamdu lillahi rabbi 'l Alamin. This is a custom religiously observed. The pupil then proceeds slowly through the last Siparo or section of his Holy Writ, and generally masters this preliminary to his studies in about six months. A little present of money and articles of dress[4] is then claimed by the preceptor as one of his perquisites.[5] The boy next begins to commit select passages of the Koran to memory,[6] and at the same time commences writing. The Akhund, with a large reed, traces thick letters on an undried Takhti,[7] and the pupil exercises his hand in tracing over the marks left on the surface of the board. At the same time, Tahajji, or spelling, is taught; and six months are considered sufficient for the task.

After the first year at school, when the boy begins to read and write by himself, he is made to peruse the Koran, without, however, understanding it. The rate of his progress is slow, and he probably is nine years old before he proceeds to the next step—the systematic study of his mother tongue, the Sindhi. The course is as follows:—

1st. The Nur-namo, a short and easy religious treatise upon the history of things in general, *before* the creation of man. The work was composed by one Abd el Rahman, and appears to be borrowed from the different Ahadis, or traditional sayings of the Prophet. A mass of greater absurdities could not be put into the hands of youth. It gravely states[8] that the total number of hairs on Mohammed's person were 104,472.; of which three were white.

2nd. The works of Makhdum Hashem,[9] beginning with the Tafsir.

3rd. Tales in verse and prose, such as the adventures of Saiful, Laili-Majano, &c. The most popular works are the Hikayat-el-Salihin,[10] a translation from the Arabic by a Sindhi Mulla, Abd el Hakim; the subjects are the lives, adventures, and remarkable sayings of the most celebrated saints, male and female, of the golden age of Islam. The Ladano is an account of the Prophet's death, borrowed from the Habib-el-Siyar, by Miyan Abdullah. The Miraj-

Namo is an account of Mohammed's night excursion to heaven; as a satire upon miracles and things supernatural it would be inimitable. The Sau-Masala, or Hundred Problems, is a short work by one Ismail, showing how Abd-el-Halim, a Fakir, married the daughter of the Sultan of Rum, after answering the hundred queries with which this accomplished lady used to perplex her numerous lovers.[11]

The youth finds an immense number of such works as these to supply him with ideas, and to strengthen his imagination; he usually studies their profitable pages for two or three years.

About the age of twelve or thirteen, the scholar is introduced to the regular study of Persian, beginning with—

1st. Vocabularies, as the Duwayo, Triwayo, and Chashm-Chiragh. The first is a string of Sindhi words translated into Persian, whence its name. The second adds the Arabic vocable. The third is intended to teach the tenses of the Persian verb.

2nd. Easy and popular pieces of poetry; such as the verses attributed to Saadi, and called Karima and Nagahan, from their first words. These occupy in Sindh the literary position of the "Deserted Village" and Gray's "Elegy" in England.

3rd. History, epistolary correspondence, and the works of the chief poets, as the Gulistan, Bustan, Hafiz, Jami, Nizami, &c. The three latter are never properly understood without commentaries and note books;[12] and these aids are not always procurable. The really difficult works, such as the Masnavi of Jelalodin, the poems of Khakani, and others of the same class, are far beyond the powers of either pupil or instructor. Firdansi is seldom read.

If the scholar was determined to become one of the Olema, he proceeded to one of the Madrassa, or colleges, at the age of fifteen or sixteen. Sindh, in the time of the Talpurs, contained, it is said,[13] six of these establishments.

1. At Sehwan; 2. Trippat, near Sehwan; 3. Khohra, north of Sehwan; 4. Matalawi, generally called Matari; 5. Mohar, or Walhari, near Omerkot; 6. Chotiyari, on the Narrah River.

The college was supported by Wakf, or presents and bequests made by the wealthy and religious. The system is one of the redeeming points and meritorious institutions of Islam, which encouraged its followers to support seminaries and schools, instead of monasteries and convents. In purely Moslem countries, Affghanistan for instance, many men pass their lives as Tulaba, or students, supported by the Wakf, or foundation of a college or mosque. This is an advantage in some ways to the poor scholars, who are sure to find some person capable of teaching them well, and who probably has devoted all his time and energy to the study of one branch of science, as logic, philosophy, or even grammar. Moreover, the Wakf is a good and economical arrangement for supporting the dreamy student,[14] who is constitutionally unfitted for an active life, as it turns his indolence to some account, and yet offers few inducements to the idle and depraved to imitate his example. The Talpurs used to contribute a monthly sum, proportioned to the expenses of the several establishments. Each college had one or two Makhdum, or heads of houses, that lectured to the more advanced scholars;[15] they received liberal salaries, and were treated with the greatest respect. This office was therefore much coveted, and the highest Sayyid in the country would not have been ashamed of filling it. The other instructors were three, four, or five Maulavis, who received monthly sums, varying from thirty to sixty Rupees, and occasional honorary presents. There was no fixed number of Khutabi, or scholars; it was regulated by the accommodations which the Rubat, or college building, afforded.[16] The pupils received a daily allowance of food, and, in some cases, money; they were also clothed at the public expense. They studied all day, except on Tuesdays and Fridays; the other vacations were the two Eeds, and the Ashurah in the Moharram. After every second year, the scholar, if considered worthy of the indulgence, was permitted to go home for a few weeks. Absence without leave, and disobedience, were punished with expulsion; immorality, especially when the fair sex was concerned, with a solemn application of the Daro,[17] or scourge. They were allowed to carry swords and daggers, or rather claimed the right of doing so; but they seldom abused the permission, as the Affghan students are wont to do.

The following is the usual course of study; and the reader will not fail to remark (comparing Sindhi with our vernacular tongue, Persian with Latin, and Arabic with Greek,) the similarity of the "pabulum" afforded to the youthful mind in the universities of the Christian, and the Madrassa of the Moslem world:—

1. Sarf and Nahu, grammar and syntax;—2. Mantik, logic;—3. Fikh; 4. Tafsir; 5. Hadis; different branches of divinity;—6. Maani-bayan, rhetoric (more rarely studied.)

A short account of the text-books may be found not uninteresting. The pupil had probably been taught at his school the simple parts of Sarf, or the forms of Arabic conjugations. The first work[18] read was the little treatise called Mizan i Sarf, the work of the celebrated saint and scholar Lal Shah-Baz, upon the subject of the regular verb Faala. It is usually committed to memory, as is also the work called Ajnas or Munshaib, a set of simple rules for the formation of the increased derivatives. The "Kism i doyyum" treats of irregular verbs, and teaches the Sarf-i-Saghir,[19] or the Paradigma. These two books were written in Persian by the same saintly pen, Lal Shah-Baz. The third treatise usually read is one called Akd, also the work of that author, but composed in Persian and Arabic mixed. It treats upon the almost endless subject of the permutation of letters, applying the rules to the several descriptions of irregular verbs. The fourth volume is called Zubdat; it further illustrates the same branch of language; some pupils learn the prose by heart, others commit to memory a poetical version, rhymed for mnemonic purposes. The pupil now commences the study of Nahw, or the declension of the noun, pronoun, &c., and first reads the well-known Miat Amil, or the Hundred Governing Powers, with its Sharh.[20] After the repeated perusal of these works, he returns to the subject of Sarf, reading either the work of Mir Sayyid Ali Sherif,[21] or more commonly, the Sarf i Zarradi, composed in Persian and Arabic by the poet Jami. He now either terminates this course of reading, or if anxious to attain high proficiency, studies the Shafiyah, a most valuable book written by the "marvellous boy," Ibn Hajib.[22] This, however, is, generally speaking, beyond the powers of either professor or pupil, especially as very few of them have the valuable commentaries of Jahrehburdi, or El Razi. Returning to Nahw, the scholar studies the Nahw i Zariri, an Arabic treatise by Abu'l Hasan Ali El-Zariri El-Kohanduzi (Kunduzi?); and begins to learn Mantik or logic. In Arabic grammar, the line of demarcation between the latter study and syntax is very faintly drawn, and no student can, with any degree of facility, progress in one without the aid of the other. To conclude, however, the subject of Nahw, the highest books read are, the treatise of Sejawandi, a work more valued than it deserves; the Hidayat El-Nahw, and lastly, the Kafiyah.[23] The latter is committed to memory, and the celebrated commentary called the Sharh Mulla (Jami), together with the Hashiyah (marginal notes) of Abd-El-Hakim, and Abd El Ghafur.

In Mantik, the first treatise perused is the Isaghuji (Isagoge of Porphyry), translated into Arabic by Asir El-Din Abhari. This is always the first step; the next, is the study of the Kalakuli,[24] a commentary on the above. Some students next read Shammah and its two Sharh: the text-book being committed to memory. The few pages called Nim-Ruzi, and Yek-Ruzi,[25] from the length of time it took to compose them, are next studied. After these, the student proceeds to the serious study of the Shamsiyah, a highly prized work on dialectics by the poet Hafiz. A somewhat bulky commentary on the above, called Kutbi, concludes the course, though some have been known to learn Zubdah, Tahzib, and Sullam. The tenebrious works of the Mirzas and the ancient logicians are never read. The science has a bad name in Islam, especially among the half-learned, who object to it on religious grounds.[26] All, however, are agreed upon one point, that it sharpens the intellect, although some assign the *modus operandi* to certain devilish influences.

The curb chain of theological and religious study is applied to the young student's imagination, as soon as he enters upon the intricacies of high syntax, and is exposed to the seductions of dialectics. The first step in that study is to read and learn by heart the common works upon the Hanafi branch of divinity, as the Hidayat, Wikayat, and other books too well known to require any mention here. For the benefit of very young readers and the fair sex, there are numerous vernacular treatises of the simple points of faith and practice in prose and verse; these the boy would usually read at his school, and therefore be in some degree prepared for the more systematic study of the Madrassa. The next step, is to peruse some Tafsir (commentary on the Koran), as the Jalalain, Madarik, Baizawi, Ismai, Kashshaf, Jawahir, Hosayni, and others. At the same time, the Ilm i Hadis is taught; superficially, however, as it is of little use to those who do not intend devoting their lives to the exclusive cultivation of the religious sciences. Very few youths advance so far in syntax and logic as to attempt the study of Maani-bayan (rhetoric); and those that do so, seldom proceed beyond the text-book called Talkhis, with its commentaries, the Mukhtasar and Mutawwal, as they are commonly termed.

The other studies are,—

1. Kiraat.
2. Munazarah.
3. Uruz.
4. Tibb.
5. The occult sciences as Raml (geomancy), Nujum (Astrology), and Jafr (a peculiar method of divining by numbers, &c.)
6. Tawarikh; or history, very seldom read.
7. Hikmat, or philosophy. I have heard of individuals in Sindh, who are said to have studied the works of Avicenna, Chelepi, and the other standard books, but I never met with one.
8. Ilm i Khat (caligraphy).

Kiraat, or Tajwid, (the art of pronunciation, reading and chaunting, as applied to the Koran) is little cultivated in our province. Of the seven Kari, or authors that systematized the study, Hafs, as in India,[27] is the only one generally known. The short tract of El-Jazari, abridged from the large work called Tayyibat El-Nashr, is the usual text-book, but there are many other treatises in Arabic, Persian and Sindhi, composed in rhyme as well as prose. The people of Sindh pronounce Arabic in a most extraordinary manner; except in some rare instances, when a pilgrim returns to his native country after a long residence at the holy cities, no amount of study can master their cacophony. At the same time the country swarms with Huffaz, or drones who have learned the Koran by heart, and live by repeating it at mosques and over tombs. They generally begin early in life, and commit the whole to memory in five or seven years.[28] All learned men, however, are expected to be able to recite the following portions of their scripture:

1st. The Fatihah, or first chapter.

2nd. The last Juz, or section: the short chapters being used in prayer.

3rd. The thirty-sixth chapter, which is peculiarly efficacious at the hour of death.

4th. The forty-fourth, seventy-first, and seventy-third chapters, which act as talismans against danger, difficulty, poverty, &c., &c.

5th. Generally, those portions of the volume which contain Ahkam, or commands, *e. g.*, the few lines explanatory of Wuzu and Ghusl (ablution) in the second chapter.

The Ilm i Munazarah, or art of wrangling is fortunately very little known. It is a branch of logic and divided as among the Greeks into ερωτησις, or interrogatory disputation, and εριστικη disputation in general. The only work of the kind I met with was a little volume containing seven separate treatises illustrating the most approved methods of confuting the adversary when he is in the right, and establishing the correctness of one's own opinion when wrong.

The Ilm i Uruz, or prosody, is not included in the Arabic system of grammar, and therefore seldom studied in a regular manner. The Nisab El-Sibyan, and several commentaries, are the only works generally used.

The student of Tibb, or medicine, begins by reading the few pages called the Tibb i Yusufi,[29] composed in verse and prose, committing the rhymes to memory. He afterwards studies the Persian works called Mizan and Tohfat El-Mominin upon the subjects of Materia Medica, and the practice of Physic. At the same time he frequents the Gandhi's (druggist's) shop, and there learns that part of his profession. He then selects the line he intends to pursue. Medical practitioners in Sindh are of three descriptions: the lowest, unable to read or write; the middle, capable of perusing a work in the vernacular tongue, or in easy Persian; the highest class, men of rank and education,[30] well versed in the classical languages. The student must become the Shagird (scholar) of a well known physician, and under him learn the simple treatment usually adopted. The use of the lancet is acquired by diligently thrusting it into the leaves of the Ak (Asclepias) or Pippar (Ficus Religiosa); the contents of the Karura (urinal) are carefully scrutinised; the peculiarities of the pulse are learned, and the operation of the Dambh, or actual cautery, is illustrated by the professor. The student is now sufficiently advanced to be entrusted with pauper cases, and upon their persons he studies the dressing of wounds, opening tumours, and removing cataract. He concludes his course of instruction with acquiring a most superficial knowledge of anatomy and surgery, and a fair stock of dietetic rules, prescriptions and simples.[31]

The young physician now begins "manslaying on his own account," to use the native phrase, and in order to acquire knowledge and a name for skill, distributes drugs and advice gratis to those who are willing to receive them. This way of winning fame is not so dangerous as it appears, because the chances are that out of the dozens that flock to the aspirant, demanding his advice and remedies, no one will do more than carry off, and promise to take, the drug he prescribes.

After, perhaps, a few poisonings and other mishaps, the physician begins to take fees. The bargain is made before the treatment commences, and the patient is usually obliged to pay previous to the cure being effected. The doctor well knows that in case of death the family will certainly refuse to remunerate him, and should it so happen that the patient recovers before paying, there is little chance of his ever doing so. The sums are regulated by the rank or wealth of the sick man: when he is a person high in authority, the fee is left to his generosity. Professional honour is utterly unknown. The Hakim (doctor) is seldom allowed to see female patients, otherwise an intrigue would follow every visit. He must be treated with all kinds of ceremony, such as sending a horse for him, offering a high seat in the room, and other such observances, otherwise a mistake in the prescription would certainly occur, to teach the patient better manners.[32] The visit is managed as follows: The physician sits down, observes the sick man, asks his symptoms, feels the pulse, or calls for a Karura, drops some strange words, generally in Arabic for the sake of unintelligibility, and, declaring that a cure is the simplest thing in the world, takes his leave. He retires for the benefit of consulting his books, and what is called Tashkhis i

Maraz (diagnosis): he then writes out a long prescription[33] in Persian, usually beginning with venesection, proceeding with a cathartic dose, and concluding with dietetic directions. The latter are very rigorous, and if the patient can resist the two preliminaries, he may recover. When this event happens, the relations meet, and the Hakim, with due solemnity, informs them that the sick man may now perform the Ghusl i Sihhat, or ablution of recovery; those present all cast some pieces of money upon their relation's head, and the amount, when collected, becomes one of the medical attendant's perquisites. When, on the other hand, the case turns out badly, the physician consoles himself, and the friends of the deceased, by attributing the event to the will of God, the decree of destiny, or to the untimely intervention of a Jinn (demon).

The great deficiency of the profession in Sindh is in point of surgery. The Ilm i Tashrih, or anatomy, is never properly studied; and the books which contain the plates and descriptions of the body, are copied and recopied by ignorant scribes, till the drawings are more like anything than what they are intended to represent. Religious prejudices forbid the use of the scalpel, and consequently the teacher is as ignorant as his pupil. In Sindh, and indeed throughout the East generally, the people have the greatest confidence in the skill of European surgeons. Not so when medicine is required: we study the constitution, diet and habits of the natives so little, that, with all our advantages, we are by no means respected as physicians. Our ignorance of aphrodisiacs is considered the most remarkable phenomenon: there being scarcely a single oriental work on physic that does not devote the greater part of its pages to the consideration of a question which the medical man in the East will hear a dozen times a day.

As, in almost all cases, a respectable person would let his spouse die in childbed rather than call in a medical man, the Dai, or midwife, is the only practitioner of the obstetric art. The consequence is, that any but a common presentation usually kills the woman. Under these circumstances, the approved treatment is to give alms to the poor, recite certain orisons, or tie a Tawiz (charm) to the patient's thigh. When she dies, the Jinn[34] is abused accordingly.

The people of Sindh were at one time celebrated for their skill in caligraphy; at present, however, they have only three hands;—

1st. Naskhi, generally called "Arabi Akhara," (Arabic letters).

2nd. Nastalik, or "Chitta Akhara," (the plain handwriting).

3rd. Shikastah, or "Bhagel Akhara," (the broken or running hand).

I have seen some excellent specimens of the Naskhi, and, generally speaking, this character is well written in Sindh. The Shikastah is detestably bad. The Cufic alphabet is quite forgotten, although the walls of tombs and mosques prove that at one time it must have been common. All the ornamental characters, as the Shulsi, Rayhan and others, are unknown. The Talpur Ameers were great patrons of caligraphists, and used occasionally to send to Persia for a well-known penman.

To conclude the subject of Moslem education in Sindh, the first thing that strikes the European observer, is the deficiency of mathematical study. The system of loading the memory with the intricacies of Arabic grammar, and of learning text-books by heart, deserves very little praise. It is, however, facilitated by mnemonic methods, although they are equally ignorant of Simonides' local system, or the fanciful *aide-memoires* invented by modern Europeans. The representation of numbers by means of the formula called Abjad, is not only useful in the *jeux d'esprit* called chronograms, but also of solid service in enabling the students to remember dates by means of significant sentences.[35] Artificial words, expressing different formulæ of cyphers, calculations in astrology, geomancy and other studies, are much used, and generally thrown into a metrical form. Technical verses are commonly committed to memory, and by means of them the minute points of syntax, logic, and prosody are easily learned and readily retained.[36] These devices, however, though sufficiently useful, are poor succedanea for the strong and permanent effect that the study of the exact sciences has upon the human mind.

I am little acquainted with the Brahminical education in Sindh, and am therefore obliged to rely upon information gathered from conversations with individuals of that caste. They agreed in one point, that the only studies are those of Sanscrit grammar in general, Jotishya,[37] or judicial astrology, and the common Dharma Shastras (religious works). Some learn the Bhagawat Purana, or the Mantra Shastras (magical formulæ); a few study the Sanhita of the Yajur Ved, and still fewer peruse the whole book. The Hindoo Amil, or civil officer, who is almost always of the Vaishya, or third caste, seldom studies Sanscrit. At an early age he goes to some Brahman, who, after a few religious preliminaries, makes the pupil read through, for good omen, the Devanagari alphabet. After this, the work of education seriously commences; the boy is sent to an Akhund, generally a Moslem, to learn the reading and writing of the Persian language. When sufficiently advanced to understand the Gulistan, the Insha of Harkaran, and the elements of arithmetic,[38] he is taken to some Daftar, or government office, by a relation, and is there thoroughly initiated in the mysteries of Arzi (petitions), and of making the simple calculations required in the routine of business; he is also imbued with a thorough knowledge of the intrigue, chicanery, and intricate rascality that belong to his trade. His Persian is of the vilest description. He is ignorant of the simplest grammatical rules, and would be unable to comprehend the distinction between noun and verb. He is fond of reading, or rather pretending to read, Jami, Nizami, Khakani, and other difficult authors, though, at the same time, he is unable to gather sense from the simplest page of Hafiz. His style of writing is formed from the solecistic productions of the authors of Insha, his pronunciation from that of the ignorant Akhund, and his handwriting from the abominable models in the different Daftars. If attached to the tenets of Nanah Shah, the Hindoo Amil often learns to read and recite certain portions of the Granth, but seldom, unless of ambitious character, attempts to master the difficulties of understanding what he is reading, and of learning the Gurumukhi character. The usual plan is to procure a copy of the prayers deemed requisite in the Nastalik hand, and to peruse the same with devotional fervour and faith in the efficacy of utterance. As regards Arabic, I have heard of only one Hindoo who had the courage to attempt the dangerous study.[39]

Under our rule at, present, the Moslem has fewer opportunities of study than the Hindoo. Instead of six establishments for the promotion of education, all that we have done hitherto is to authorize the foundation of a school at Hyderabad, and to support an "Indo-British" one at Kurrachee, in addition to a place of instruction maintained, I believe, by private contributions, and superintended by a converted Hindoo. The Mussulman, therefore, is reduced to the limited means of acquiring knowledge, offered by the petty day-schools which abound throughout the country. Not so the Hindoo.[40] His greater pliability of conscience and tenets allows him to take any step towards improving his position, except the last and irrevocable one,—that of becoming a Christian. He will apply for, receive, and read the religious tracts and translations of the gospels, which our countrymen are fond of distributing, especially if the injudicious[41] donor possess the means of temporal advancement. The Hindoo will even study the Bible for the purpose of getting up some phrases to quote before his patron, will punctually attend his school, and even engage in its devotional exercises. When the object is permanently secured or lost, like the "rice Christians" of early Goa, our supple Polytheist not only throws off the appearance of amendment, but also infuses a little additional bigotry into his heathenism, in order to regain that position in his own caste which worldliness has tempted him to peril. The Moslem, on the contrary, stands aloof, scrutinizing these signs of the times with a jealous eye, and quoting the traditional apothegm of his faith, "An-Naso ala' din i Mulukihim,"—"people are religionized by their princes."

Of late, there has been an abundance of very unprofitable discussion amongst the rulers of the province as to the language which should be selected for literary and official purposes. The linguists prefer Sindhi, seeing that it is sufficient for the objects required, and is, moreover, generally understood.

The other party supports Persian, or advocates Hindostani, opining that the "language of Scinde is in a very crude state," has "no standard dialect, no universally prevalent character, and no literature;"—that "its literature is depressed without extinguishing the language."[42] The linguists, it is presumed, will succeed eventually in spite of ignorance and apathy, as they are in the right. The point to be considered, is the best means of improving the dialect (practically speaking) by diffusing a knowledge of it, and bending it to our purposes. And with such object, the establishment of places of instruction is manifestly indispensable.

At the five large towns of Kurrachee, Tatta, Hyderabad, Sehwan and Sukkur, Sindhi vernacular schools might be founded. The course would be, Sindhi reading and writing, a little grammar, and epistolary correspondence. The number of scholars might be limited to forty or fifty. The term of instruction would be from three to four years, as in such a country, length of preparatory study would be considered time wasted.

After doing this much for the vernacular dialect, it would be as politic as profitable, to encourage the study of our own. If we would give the natives of Sindh opportunities of acquiring knowledge, and connect them with ourselves by proving to them our superiority, they should be taught the English language. Schools might be established at the three chief towns, Kurrachee, Hyderabad and Shikarpore (or Sukkur). The course would be, English reading and writing, grammar and composition, arithmetic, account keeping, and a superficial knowledge of history and geography. The probable duration of the course would be about five years. Pupils of the English schools should be taken directly from the vernacular establishments, and, unless the prospect of government employ be clearly held out, students would be scarce.

That such measures will eventually be carried out under our enlightened rule, there is no doubt.

The characters in which the Sindhi tongue is written are very numerous. Besides the Moslem varieties of the Semitic alphabet, there are no less than eight different alphabets used principally by the Hindoos, viz.,

1. The Khudawadi, or Wanikhakhar.

2. The Tathai, of which there are two varieties, viz.:—1st. The Lohana; and 2nd. The Bhatiha hand.

3. The Sarai, used in Upper Sindh.

4. That used by the Khwajah tribe.
5. The Meman handwriting.
6. The Ochki form of Panjabi.
7. The Landi form of Panjabi.
8. The Gurumukhi, or Panjabi.

The average number of letters is forty, ten being vowels, and thirty consonants.

The origin of these characters may fairly be traced through the Landi[43] and Gurumukhi, to the Devanagari character. As the immigration of Hindoos into Sindh has always been from the north, it is most probable that these alphabets were brought down from the Punjaub, in the form used by Nanak Shah. This was gradually altered into running hand: and underwent almost as many changes as there are castes or tribes.[44] The learned Mr. James Prinsep was completely at fault when he supposed that Marwari had been corrupted into Sindhi, or that the latter is a mixture of Guzerattee, Tamul and Malayalim.

But however numerous these alphabets may be, they are all, in their present state, equally useless. This arises from one cause, the want of a sufficient number of vowel signs.[45] The consequence is, that the trader is scarcely able to read his own accounts, unless assisted by a tenacious memory.

The selection of a character which will be practically useful, is necessary, if we would establish schools: the choice, however, is not without its difficulties. Four systems have been advocated, viz.:—1. Devanagari; 2. Khudawadi; 3. Gurumukhi; 4. Naskhi.

The Devanagari is certainly the most scholar-like and analogous system, and therefore, perhaps, the best for dictionaries, grammars and other works, intended solely for the purpose of teaching the language to Europeans. At the same time, it has many imperfections. No less than twenty letters[46] would require diacritical marks to render them intelligible. Moreover, this character, however well adapted for books, is tedious and cumbersome for official papers.[47] Finally, it would not easily be learned by the people, and is at present utterly unknown to them. The last objection appears to be the strongest of all, for surely no undertaking could be more troublesome or useless than an attempt to supplant a well-known alphabet by one unknown to the people.

The adoption of the Khudawadi[48] character has been advocated, on account of its being already extensively used by the people. It is, however, confined to a particular, though influential, caste of Hindoos, and even amongst them is only known to the traders, and generally neglected by the Moonshees and Amils. The main objection to it is that, in its present state, it is all but illegible. And to dress it up in Guzerattee, " vowel points,"[49] as has been proposed, in fact to remodel it, might be an easy work, but at the same time it would be an improvement very unlikely to be generally adopted by the Sindhis.

The Gurumukhi is an admirably simple form of Devanagari, and perfectly fitted for Panjabi, imperfectly for Sindhi. The disadvantages attendant on its introduction would be the same as belong to its Sanscrit progenitor, viz., it is very little known to the people, would require extensive alteration, and, though useful for books, would be slow and clumsy to write.

The Naskhi form of the Arabic alphabet appears to be the most favoured by circumstances in Sindh. The intrinsic merit of the character must be acknowledged, when we reflect that it has spread from Arabia, its origin, to Algiers and the Ganges, to Bokhara and Ceylon. For centuries it has been tried, and found capable of adaptation to a multitude of dialects: by a few simple additions and modifications, it has been trained to denote the cerebrals of India, and the liquid tones of the Persian and Malay tongues, as well as the gutturals of Arabia. It may be termed, *par excellence*, the alphabet of Asia: nor is it likely to be supplanted by any innovating Romanized systems, or to decline as civilization progresses. In elegance of appearance, and brevity without obscurity, it yields to no other written character, and it is no small proof of its superiority to many, that it offers a symbol for every sound existing in the language for which it was invented.

But, as might be expected, the further it deviates from Arabic the more imperfect it becomes. At present it has been rudely and carelessly adapted to the language of Sindh, and by the confusion of points and the multitude of different sounds expressed by one letter appears difficult and discouraging. Still its intrinsic value remains, and we may safely hope that as education advances, much will be done for it. As a case in point, we can instance the many little changes and improvements which have been lately introduced by the natives of India into their system of writing the Nastalik hand.

My reasons for advocating the adoption of the Naskhi character are as follows:—

1st. That all the literature of the country has been for ages written in this hand.

2nd. All educated Moslems are able to read it and most of them to write it.

3rd. Although the Hindoo Amils throughout Sindh are at present unable to read it, their knowledge of the Nastalik or Persian hand would render the difficulty of learning it nugatory. It must be recollected that religious bigotry formerly forbade any infidel to open a book written in the same character as the Koran.[50]

4. It converts itself with great facility into a running hand sufficiently rapid for all practical purposes. The epistolary correspondence of the Arabs is a sufficient proof of this.

Such are the reasons for preferring the Naskhi character. On the other hand, it may be argued that the Nastalik has the one great advantage of being known to every writer in the province, that it has been successfully adapted to Hindostani and Panjabi,[51] and therefore might be made equally useful in Sindhi. The chief objection to it is that however practicable for Parwanahs, Arzis, Hukms and other official papers, it partakes too much of the character of stenography to suit the language we are considering. The dialect of Sindh is so complicated in sound, construction and number of vocables, that, as is proved by the practice of the people, a more complete alphabet is required for it. Any Sindhi scholar may observe that the best educated native will find considerable difficulty in reading out the vernacular hemistichs and tetrastichs written in

Nastalik, which are frequently introduced by authors into religious or metaphysical works composed in Persian. Whether habit and education would or would not do away with a considerable portion of this difficulty, is a consideration which I leave to the profound practical linguist.

CHAPTER VII.

PRESENT STATE OF SOCIETY IN SINDH.—EXTRACT FROM A NATIVE WORK UPON THE SUBJECT OF MATRIMONY.—CEREMONY OF VISITING.—PREVALENCE OF INTOXICATION, AND THE DIFFERENT PREPARATIONS IN USE.—PECULIARITY OF THE NATIONAL FAITH.—THE OCCULT SCIENCES, DEMONOLOGY, MAGIC AND ALCHEMY.—OSTEOMANCY, THE BOOK OF FATE.—ONEIROMANCY.—PALMISTRY.—OMENS.—CRIMES AND THEIR PUNISHMENTS.

It is almost impossible, by mere description, to convey to the mind of the civilized reader, a full and just idea of the state of society in a semi-barbarous country. Probably the best plan is to illustrate it by an account of the manners and practices, habits and customs of the inhabitants, and by selections from the different books which are written with the view of producing an effect upon the great body of the people.

The work from which the following extracts are taken, is a summary of advice upon the subject of matrimony, composed by one Sayyid Hasan Ali in the Sindhi dialect, and called the Lizzat El Nisa Sharai,[1] or the "Lawful Enjoyment of Women." It contains two chapters written in a very unadorned style. The

European reader will readily compare its matter with that of the Romance of the Rose, and other compositions which belong to the age when the West was nearly in the same state in which the East now is.

The author begins by quoting the traditional saying of the Prophet, " Marriage is my practice, and he that turneth from my practice, then he is not of mine." Matrimony, it is stated is a Wajib, or religious duty, when the man can afford it: it is a Sunnat, or practical duty,[2] when he has the means of obtaining a livelihood. A life of celibacy is only allowed when the individual has not the wherewithal to support a wife, and is not of an amorous complexion. If the former deficiency exist with the latter condition, debt, which is so rigorously forbidden by Moslem faith, is not only permitted but encouraged with the promise that God will become security for its being discharged. In case of celibacy, much fasting and prayer are enjoined.

After these preliminary assertions, the Sayyid proceeds to offer advice, moral and physical, about the selection of a spouse. The Cœlebs is directed to consider the two grand points, viz., Nasab, or respectability of birth and parentage, and Hasab, or individual eligibility. Widows are to be avoided, and four qualities to be sought for in the marriageable virgin. In the first place, her stature should be shorter than her intended's. Secondly, she should be younger; thirdly, possess less property, and fourthly, be his inferior in rank and station. The best complexion is dark with black hair, as it denotes modesty, and virtue: red and white, as well as pallid skins, are always to be avoided as indicative of choleric and sensual temperaments. The Sayyid cautions his readers against eight descriptions of females: those of low caste as Langhi (musician), Mohani (fishwives), &c.; the very beautiful, the wealthy, the tall and thin (as it is difficult to love such women); the talkative, the too amorous, and finally any woman with whom Cœlebs may previously have intrigued. At the same time the reader is warned that there is no religious objection to matrimony with the latter.

As regards the marriage ceremony, it is considered preferable to perform it in the mosque, and not at home. To be present at a nuptial feast is equal in merit to fasting, and a tradition states that the "day of wedlock is better than the worship of a thousand years." No less than five ounces of food from the banquets of Paradise are miraculously mixed up with the dishes placed before the wedding party. The first kiss which the bridegroom gives is equal to one hundred and eighty years of worship.[3] It also enables him to escape the torments of the tomb, causes a light to be shed over his grave, and procures the ministering of eighty angels. Before consummating the marriage, the happy man is directed to wash the bride's feet, and to throw the water into the four corners of the Hujleh, or nuptial chamber, as this act is productive of good fortune. After which the bridegroom holds his wife's "front hair," and repeats the following prayer: "O Lord, bless me and my wife! O Lord, give to me and mine thy daily bread! O Lord, cause the fruit of this woman's womb to be an honest man, a good Moslem, and not a companion of devils!"

The Sayyid next enters upon the long and difficult subject of a woman's peculiar duties, religious and domestic. These he enumerates as follows:—

1st. She is to pray five times a day, and fast: also to exhort her husband to devotion: always bearing in mind that on the day of resurrection the first question put to a woman will be concerning her prayers; the second, how she performed her duty to her husband.

2nd. To meditate on the sanctity of a wife's duty to her spouse, to obey him in all things,[4] except when the order is contrary to a higher command.

3rd. Never to break, by thought, word, or deed, the laws of modesty, recollecting the tradition, "A woman without shame is as food without salt."

4th. Not to apply for divorce without the best of reasons; also not to fall in love with handsome young men, and lavish upon them the contents of the husband's purse.

5th. To stay at home, except when the husband permits her to go abroad; not to visit even her parents without leave of absence, though those parents might be dying or being carried to their graves. Any woman who quits the house against orders, exposes herself to the curse of Heaven, and to sixty stripes religiously administered; she also loses all right to Nafakeh, or maintenance money.

6th. To devote herself to household affairs, such as cooking (for her mate, not herself), sewing, darning old clothes, spinning, washing, milking cattle, lighting the house, and attending to the furniture and stores. It is very sinful to eat before the husband has fed, and to refuse coarse victuals, because others live more luxuriously. To comb the spouse's hair, to wash his clothes and spread his couch, are, in a religious sense, equal to Haj and Umrah (the different kinds of pilgrimage).

7th. When at home, to dress as well, and when going out, as plainly as possible.[5] In the house, to apply oil, antimony, henna, and other cosmetics, to keep the person very clean, and by no means to neglect the teeth. At the same time, the virtuous wife must not be extravagant in dress, or torment her husband for Tattah silks, Multani muslins, embroidered slippers, and similar articles of luxury.

8th. If wealthy, never to boast of supporting the husband; and if poor, never to be discontented with humble living.

9th. Always to receive the husband, especially when he returns from abroad, with glad and smiling looks.

10th. Never to speak loudly and fiercely to, or even before, the husband; the words Laanat and Phit (curse!) are particularly to be avoided. Never to taunt her spouse with such words as these; "thy teeth are long and thy nose short;" or "thy head is large and the calves of thy legs small;"[6] or "thy face is a black creation of God's!" or "thou art old, weak, and scarcely a man!" or "thou art a real beauty, with those grins and exposed teeth!" or "lo! what a fine turban and charming gait!"

The Sayyid concludes this enumeration of female duties with a pathetic lament that the Ran (wenches) of Sindh are in the habit of utterly neglecting them. Probably, like the great Milton, he was a better author than husband, and generalises from his individual case. Another charge might be brought against him, as the second chapter of his work is quite unfit for the perusal of the fair sex.

Another key to the manners and customs of the people, is their peculiar style of ceremony. The Sindhi is inferior to the Arab in dignified deportment and manliness of address; he also wants the soft and exquisitely polished manners of the Indians. Among the Ameers and the highest orders of society, the Persian style of ceremony was very much cultivated; and as usual with such imitations, failed in the point of courtliness, dignity, and habit of society. The lower classes of Sindhis are remarkably rough in their manners and speech. No Moslem, however humble, ever enters the room without at once sitting down upon the floor and joining in the conversation. Under the elder Ameers, the court, if it could be called so, was remarkably watchful and jealous of any appearance of familiarity; their successors, however, failed in keeping up their dignity, as the following description of a Salam i Am, or levee, may prove. When the prince thought proper to receive his subjects, a chair was placed for him under the verandah of the palace, and conveniently close to the door. At the cry of "Salami" (audience!) the mob rushed in, and found their ruler surrounded by a body of the tallest and most muscular Farrashes[7] belonging to his establishment. The first attempt was to break through the line by sheer force; the servants, on the other hand, opposed the people with as little ceremony; the mob, when defeated in its endeavours to reach the prince, began to pelt him with petitions and addresses, vociferating prayers and curses with all their might.[8] When the ruler could endure the scene no longer, he quietly opened the door and slipped through it into his own apartment. By this time the people would probably have broken through the line of fatigued Farrashes, and finding themselves again foiled, would amuse themselves by trying to break open the door. Such scenes took place periodically in the palaces of all the younger Ameers, not excepting even Sher Mahommed, though the latter was, generally speaking, feared and respected. On one occasion, when very much pressed by a petitioner, he availed himself of his religious reputation, and stood up to say his prayers. As it is forbidden to the Sunni to look around him at such times, it might be expected that the petitioners would have waited for the close of his devotions; the more eager applicants, however, thrust their petitions close under his eyes, and pertinaciously held them there till dragged away by the servants. How different the formality of Runjeet Singh's Durbar, or the apparatus of Fath Ali Shah's Salam!

The higher orders of Sindhis are fond of being uncivil to strangers, particularly if the latter permit it; but like true Orientals, they seldom venture upon rudeness when they expect a rebuff. The easiest way of treating such individuals, is by a display of anger proportioned to the offence, or by some fiercely satirical reply. To be "not at home" is considered insulting, and the visitor, if not received with due respect, never enters the house again. The ceremony of a visit is as follows :—A servant is despatched to announce one's approach, and the master of the house comes out to meet his guest, proportioning the distance he advances to the dignity of the latter. If the visitor be of superior rank, all in the room rise from their seats as he enters; his degree regulates how much they are expected to move. The compliments are long and tiresome, generally expressed in Persian, sometimes in the vernacūlar tongue. The host then leads his guest to the seat appointed for him; the place of honour is a large cot covered with Ghali or Toshah (silk coverlets). The gradations are as follows ;—1st. A smaller cot, with or without the coverlet; 2nd. a carpet or rug spread on the ground; 3rd. a mat, also on the ground; 4th. the bare floor; 5th. a place in the verandah outside the room. Sherbet, cardamoms, betel-nuts, and hookahs are introduced after the ceremony of sitting down is settled; of late years, wine, Bhang, and opium are often offered. It is, however, by no means safe for a stranger to encourage the latter practice, as the more civilized Oriental seldom touches an intoxicating preparation in the house of another, and few of them are pleasant companions when in the jovial state. Contrary to the Persian customs, no solid food but fruit is placed before a visitor. The length of the call is proportioned to the rank of the visited; a short visit is allowed only when calling upon inferiors. The guest leaves the house with the same formality as when he enters it; and if very much superior to his host, is accompanied home by the latter.

It is needless to enlarge upon the necessity of studying such apparently trifling matters in a semi-barbarous country. A knowledge of language and manners is all powerful in the East, and the civilized Englishman is called Jangli[9] in many parts of India, on account of his neglect of or contempt for the only way to impress his fellow subjects with a feeling of respect. The petty princes of Sindh had each his separate title; for instance, Mir Nasir Khan was addressed as Sarkar i-faiz-asar—the beneficent majesty; in conversation, they were called Mir Sahib or Mir Sain.[10] When speaking of their wives, the term used was Dereyeh kalan,[11] the concubines being Dereyeh khurd. All such forms were considered *de rigueur*, and ignorance or unobservance of them could be looked upon in no other light but that of direct and aggravated insult.

A bad feature in the present state of native society in Sindh, is the peculiar prevalence of intoxication.[12] From the highest to the lowest orders of the people, the fair sex included, only the really religious can withstand the attraction of a glass of cognac. The form in which it is usually taken is with water in equal parts. A Sindhi of high rank, if addicted to drinking, begins before dinner. When sufficiently intoxicated, he eats, and finishes the meal with a cup full of milk to aid digestion, previous to the siesta, as we take coffee. They have little objection to drinking in each other's houses, or to being seen by strangers, a great proof of degradation in the East. When determined to indulge in deep carousal, they begin with drinking Bhang, and then proceed to wine or spirits, strictly observing this order of things, as the sensation is supposed to be more pleasant. The Persian poet says,

> "First drink Bhang, and then wine,
> Beautifully flows the stream over the verdure."[13]

There are many natives of the highest rank in Sindh who do not object to any of the intoxicating preparations known. The poor people are compelled to drink the Pichak or dregs of the different alcohols and wines: the draught, as may be imagined, is very cheap and very nauseous.

The alcoholic drinks principally used are two in number, viz., 1. Gura jo darun, made from molasses with Babul bark, and other ingredients. Though fiery, and disagreeable in flavour, the Hindoos of Sindh are remarkably fond of it, and some will finish as much as a bottle a day; they drink it out of small cups, containing about a tea-spoonful, and repeat the dose every quarter of an hour. 2. Kattala jo darun, a spirit extracted from dates, and very generally drunk by the lower orders. It is hot and nauseous.

The principal wines, if they can be so called, are,—

1. Anguri, made of the Sindh grape at Hyderabad, Sehwan, and Shikarpur. It is generally qualified with the spirit of Gur. When wine is made of dried grapes, it is called Kishmishi.

2. Sonfi; extracted from aniseed with Gur brandy; it is considered a superior kind of drink.

3. Mushki, perfumed with musk and other perfumes.

4. Turanji, extracted from citron peel.

5. Misri, made with sugar-candy, and perfumed. It is one of the most expensive preparations.

6. Gulabi, perfumed with rose water.
7. Kaysari, coloured with saffron.

The lower orders of the Moslems are extraordinarily addicted to the use of Indian hemp, and take it to such an extent, that, like the Guzerattee opium eaters, they find it necessary to existence. Under the Ameers, a Seer (2 lbs.) of Bhang was always procurable for an Anna; now, under our contract system, it costs from five to six times that price. The general use of this deleterious preparation has doubtlessly done much towards causing physical and mental degeneracy in the Sindhi: it produces madness, catalepsy and a multitude of other disorders. The principal varieties used are,—

1. Bhang, Sawai, or Sukho. The small leaves, husks and seeds of the hemp plant, ground, and drunk with water or milk. The "Bhanga jo Ghiyu," or hemp butter, is prepared in two ways. The best prescription is to boil the hemp in milk, skim off the cream, and turn it into Ghee or clarified butter. The common way of making it is to toast a Seer of Bhang in a brass pot, into which a Seer of Ghee must be poured; the vessel is then covered up, and the mass allowed to remain on the fire, with occasional stirring, till reduced to about one-half. When the colour turns dark, the pot is removed, and the hemp butter poured off, drop by drop, into another vessel. It is used by surgeons as an anæsthetic agent during operations.

2. Ganjo: The top of the hemp plant. It is smoked, not drunk like the Bhang. There are no less than three different ways of preparing it for the pipe. When the smoker desires to cause as much intoxication as possible, he throws the whole top into water, and sepa-

rates the seeds from the leaves; the latter are then taken out and rubbed in the palms of the hands, till all the moisture is expressed, and the mass becomes solid. It is placed at the bottom of the Chillum or pipe head, a certain portion of wetted tobacco is put above it, and at the top of all a lighted bit of Nori.[14] A less intoxicating preparation is procured by rubbing the seeds and leaves to powder, and washing them three times in water. The third way, is to toast on an iron plate all that remains of the top after the little leaves have been removed. When it becomes hot and brittle, it is rubbed in the hands till the whole of it, including the seeds, is reduced to a rough powder; water is then added, till the Ganjo becomes of the consistence of wax, in which state it is mixed up with, not placed beneath, tobacco, as is done in the two other varieties. Ganjo is not very much smoked in Sindh. One pipe is sufficient for a novice; the habitué requires from four to five at short intervals. The antidote applied to its frequently violent effects upon the nerves is, generally speaking, lime juice, sometimes pickled Mango.

3. Charas, or the gum of the hemp. In Sindh it is never eaten raw, either for intoxication or medicinally, as has been tried amongst us: in fact, it is considered poisonous in this state. It is either smoked with tobacco, or eaten when made up into Maajun. The best quality comes from Affghanistan[15] and Central Asia.

The above are the principal ways of using hemp. As regards the quality of intoxication, the Bhang is believed to cause fearfulness, and great vivacity of imagination; it produces unnatural hunger, followed by painful indigestion. Ganjo is celebrated for exciting the perceptive faculties, animating the conversation, and at the same time keeping the talker on his guard against any attempts to draw from him the "Tacenda." Charas resembles Ganjo in its effects upon the perceptives.

The other intoxicating preparations common throughout Sindh, are the following:—

1. Maajun; any intoxicating confiture made of Hemp-butter, Charas, or Dhatura seed, mixed up with sugars and sweetmeats. The Maajun is used by natives, generally of the higher classes, for the three purposes of Kaif (intoxication), Kuwwat (aphrodisiac tonic), and Imsak.[16] The two latter objects are considered so desirable, that even rigid Moslems will break the order against their touching intoxicating substances, for the purpose of securing them.

2. Khash-khash, or poppy seeds, used chiefly in preparing.

3. Tadhal, a refreshing beverage, drunk during the hot weather, made of water sweetened with sugar-candy, and flavoured with cummin, aniseed, and sometimes spices. A little Bhang is occasionally introduced to produce a refrigerating effect.

4. Dhature jo bijj, the seeds of the Datura Stramonium. This most dangerous article is used by the Halwai (or confectioners) in preparing the different Maajuns which are sold in the bazaars. It is sometimes used by those veteran debauchees who are too unexcitable to rest satisfied with milder preparations.

5. Kohi (or Jabali) Bhang; a kind of henbane, smoked and drunk, after being prepared, like Bhang.

It is usually taken by Fakirs and religious mendicants, as it is supposed to produce aberration of intellect. Novices find the contraction of the nerves of the throat caused by it peculiarly painful.

6. Afim, or Ammal (opium); formerly much eaten (never smoked) in Sindh; now less common on account of its increased price, It is supposed to produce a disregard for life, and contempt of danger; the consequence of which is, that chiefs and soldiers who are preparing to distinguish themselves by single combat, generally go into battle under its influence. The Belochis are celebrated for this practice; hence their ferocity and recklessness when once engaged.

The usual ways of taking opium are, either to swallow it in the form of pills, with a little sugar or sweetmeat afterwards, or to dissolve it in water; and if impure, to strain it through a cloth previous to drinking it. It is sometimes mixed up with saffron, and used in a variety of manners, which, however, are not so well known in this country as in India.

Sindh is sufficiently civilized to possess fixed places, where these intoxicating preparations are consumed. A little outside all the large towns there are several Daira,[17] as they are called, walled gardens, planted with Bhang and the Nazbu (a kind of Ocymum, supposed to excite mirth), and containing an Otak, or hall, for the convenience of the company. There, at about five or six o'clock, P.M., the Bhangi, or hemp-drinkers, congregate. At first, there is a scene of washing, pressing and rubbing the plant; and the prospect of their favourite enjoyment renders it an animated one. The potion is drunk in solemn silence, after which some smoke, and others eat sweetmeats, or dried and parched grain. Presently, one begins to sing, another calls for music, a third amuses himself and his friends by talking in the most ridiculous way, and a fourth will fall asleep. At about eight, P.M., they disperse.

Women are never allowed within the walls of the Dairo, so that it is a far more respectable place than the abominable dens called Akhara, in Western India. It is not, however, frequented by men of good reputation, although Sayyids and Munshis may sometimes be observed to enter. The Jelali Fakirs are constantly present at these drinking bouts.

Another thing which acts strongly upon the general state of society in Sindh, is the peculiarity of the national faith.

In most countries, civilized or uncivilized, the traveller and ethnologist may remark that when a new religion has raised itself upon the ruins of an old and cultivated form of worship, the intruder is compelled to borrow much from its predecessor. Indeed it may be doubted, to judge from general experience, if the spirit of the latter ever departs. In the case of Christianity, how much does Protestantism owe to the stern and rugged animus of Druidism, and the different faiths peculiar to the nations of the North? Along the shores of the Mediterranean, again, it palpably partakes of the Pantheistic character of the old religion which peopled earth, air and sea with forms of ideal beauty, and gave rise to the arts and sciences which humanized that portion of mankind.

So it is with Islam. Conceived and born in the deserts of the Arab, it went forth conquering and to conquer. But when the excitement of battling and plundering had passed away, and the converts had the time and opportunity to insert a few of their old tenets and traditions into the system of Monotheism, violently thrust upon them, Islam began to feel and show the effects. In Persia, the wailings for the death of Siyawush, the martyr of Guebrism, were *mutato nomine*, transferred to the pathetic tales of Hasan and Hosayn; and Islam there put forth the great branch of Tashayyu, or the religion of the Shiite. In India, the superstitions of the Hindoos have been adopted as points of practical faith, in such numbers, that the Arab of the present day exclaims, "O thou returner from Hind, renew thy Islam!" Sindh displays the working of the same principle. The dancing of the Nantch girls at the tombs of the holy men, the adoption of sacred places from the heathen, and the respect shown by the Moslems to certain Hindoo saints and devotees, are abominations in the eyes of the old stock of the faithful; at the same time they are acceptable acts of religion here. To quote a notable instance of ancient Paganism peeping through the veil of their adopted faith: In the hills to the northward of Kurrachee, a great Haji,[18] (pilgrim) turned a flower into an alligator, whose descendants still wallow in the mire of a marshy pool. The largest of these beasts is, *ex officio*, the Pagaro (*i. e.*, turban-wearer) or head of the house; when speaking of the hideous reptile, the natives invariably term him Mor Sahib, or Mister Peacock,[19] a Euphuistic style of expression. Whenever the Sindhi has any desire, which he thinks Heaven may be induced to grant, he repairs to the pool, kills a goat, and offers a bit of the flesh to the intercessor. If the latter deign to accept it, the votary feels assured of success, and *vice versâ*.

In the month of Ramazan, there is a large Melo, or fair, held at this place; and the courtesans, who here as well as in India, are, generally speaking, the most strict in their devotions, flock to it in numbers. My companion, an Arab, after looking at the scene, declared that Satan was clearly at the bottom of all that was going on, and opined that Katl Am, or a general massacre, was the only way to purge the land of such abominations. Certainly, nothing can be more clearly an excrescence upon the body of Islam, which forbids even the graving of an animal's image, lest the simple and unwise should be induced to respect it too much.[30]

Superstition is rife throughout Sindh; scepticism, rare. Among the learned, one may occasionally meet with a Dahri, or materialist; and some few of the Sufi persuasion have so curiously mingled Atheism with Pantheism, its contrary, that the European mind can hardly conceive or follow out the combination. These cases, however, are rare, and confined to those who have read themselves out of their depth in logic, or who have attempted the science of Hikmat (philosophy).

It is not my intention to trouble the reader with a detailed account of the demonology, magic and other branches of the occult sciences studied and practised in Sindh. Perhaps, however, a few words upon the subject of their peculiar superstitious practices may not be uninteresting.

The list of supernatural and preternatural apparitions

is a formidable one. Khwajah Khizr[21] is of course known: he often appears to travellers in different guises, but generally as an old man. They believe in the Rijal el Ghaib;[22] in the Jinns or Genii: in Bhul, ghosts or disembodied spirits; in Ghool, or demons of the wilderness: in Peri, fairies,[23] and in Dew, Rakas, and Pap, powerful fiends, corresponding with the Arab "Marid." The Dakan or Den, is the same as our witch, usually an old woman, decrèpid, poor, of humble family, and angry disposition. She has the power of turning men into beasts, killing cattle, flying to any distance on a tree by reciting a Mand (magical formula) and mounting a hyæna. Unlike the Arabian witch, she is, however, unable to ride a besom. With such powers, ugly old women generally are feared and hated by the common people; they take advantage of the reputation by acting as the Mercurys of illicit love, and not unfrequently lose their lives in consequence of carrying one or the other of their occupations too far. This Lynch law, however, was not recognised by the native government or religion, and unlike our own country, Sindh has never considered witchcraft a punishable crime. Some understand by the Dakan a kind of female fiend that assumes many shapes, and is to be driven away by stripping oneself stark naked.

The Banbh and Mamm are frightful beings, half female, half hellish. They live in the hills and jungles where they frequently appear to travellers, are covered with hair like bears, have large pendant lips, and live on fruits and herbs.

The Shir is a creature that partakes of the Satanic nature. He, generally speaking, appears as a low-caste man, very dark, tall, and frightful: sometimes as a headless body. He lives in the Mukam, or burial ground, where he lights fires, and amuses himself by throwing the brands about, frightening folk by vociferating their proper names, or pursuing them in the form of some beast. Hence the universal fear of approaching a burial ground by night.

The Shaitan (Satan) curious to say, is only seen by learned and religious men, to them he appears as a young man of white complexion and handsome form which he can change *à discretion.*

This mania for demonology and tales of wonder is very prevalent among the Hill people, and the nomadic tribes of Sindhis. The bear, for instance, as in Persia, is supposed to display at times a degree of intelligence for which we do not give him credit. Many travellers have seen him riding on a wild ass, with a turban of twisted grass round his head: his object being to delude the wayfarer into the belief that he is a man, and thereby the more easily to secure his prey. This credulity is authorised by the Koranic assertion of men having been metamorphosed into beasts, as a punishment for their sins. It is interesting to observe that here, as nearly all the world over, popular superstition has created Marhun Machhi (mermen and mermaids), either by mistaking some kind of fish for a human being, or, more likely, by reasoning on false analogy, that as the earth was made for man, so millions of spiritual and ethereal beings inhabit the air, consequently the sea must be equally well populated. The Sindh mermaids, like Leyden's, have warm hearts under cold skins, and occasionally make splendid offers to those who consent to live with them, and become their lovers. Even the inanimate creation is dignified by a connection with human nature. There are probably a hundred large trees in the province, called after the celebrated saint Abd el Kadir Jilani. Each has its pole and flag hung upon it to fulfil some vow made in sickness or adversity. Sweetmeats are distributed to the poor in honour of it, and the fruit and leaves are not allowed to be touched even by cattle. As in Arabia,[24] India, and Persia, strips of cloth are suspended from shrubs and trees. The reasons given for this custom are various. Sometimes the trees are thus decked as a mark of respect to some holy man who may have visited the place, at others as a votive offering; but the more general idea, I believe, is, that any one suffering under a malady, may, by hanging up a rag, transfer his complaint to the vegetable.

The practice of magic[25] in Sindh, as in the east generally, consists of talismans and different ceremonies for inspiring love, causing hatred, destroying enemies, raising oneself in the world, escaping mysterious dangers (such as the evil eye, or the praise of a foe), averting and curing pain, disease, barrenness and abortion, securing wishes, and detecting thieves. The writing of these Taawiz,[26] or Tilism (talismans), is a profitable employment; they are generally composed in a jargon of Hindostani and Panjabi, mixed with Sindhi; and their Hindoo origin[27] is evident from the names of the pagan gods which occasionally occur in them. Moslems here, as elsewhere, divide all magic into two branches, lawful and unlawful. The former is studied by prayer, the Chillo (or forty days' fast), invocations of angels, a knowledge of the Names of the Supreme Being, and a right comprehension of the peculiar properties of certains parts of His Word. The latter is, of course, diabolical, and often of an abominable nature,[28] especially when philters are concocted.

The following are short specimens of some of the most peculiar talismans :—

When a man desires to excite love in a woman, he selects seven large cloves on the seventeenth day of the month, and recites the following prayer seven times over each of them :—

> "Laungá laung saláhí
> Laungana badhí rahí na káí,
> Jis kun laung parhí diyán háth,
> Uh kirandí paundí aundí mere sáth."

> "O cloves! O cloves! ye are truly good;
> She that is bound by the cloves can never remain away from me!
> To whomsoever, after this recitation, I give the clove,
> She, falling and rising (*i. e.* eagerly), will come to me."

The amorist then contrives that the woman may eat the cloves, and feels assured of success.

Salt is pressed into the service of Cupid in the following manner. On the first Sunday of the month the lover recites these lines seven times over a handful salt :—

> "Lúna tú, lúnáru tú, satten samudren páru tu!
> Lúna merá khá tu, fuláni, pera chúmandí ao tú."

> "O salt! O thou salt one! thou essence of the seven seas!
> O certain person—(naming the woman)—eat my salt, and kiss my feet."

The reciter then dissolves the salt in water and drinks it; the consequence of which is that the other party falls violently in love with him.

Should the lady resist these measures, the disappointed lover becomes desperate, and proceeds to extremes. From the harmless specimen subjoined, it will be evident that passion frequently gets the better of delicacy. Agathu̱ chinnanu̱, or "breaking the trowser string," is done by reciting a charm over seven or nine threads of raw cotton, spun by a girl not yet betrothed. The bits are then rolled up and knotted seven times; after which the lady is duly warned of the punishment of disdain. Should she persevere in cruelty, one of the knots is opened, and by a curious coincidence, the string which confines the fair one's trowsers, breaks of itself and leaves that garment unsupported. This operation is repeated till she yields; an event which, says the book that details the plan, may soon be expected.

The system of philters and amatory talismans is probably borrowed by the Moslems from the Hindoos, to whom it has long been known by the name of Washikaran. It is to the advantage of all parties to support the idea. The magician gains money by teaching his craft, the fair sex have a valid excuse when detected in a grave delinquency, and the husbands are consoled by the reflection that the chastity of their spouses could yield to none but preternatural influence. Belief in it is almost universal; as a proof of which, no woman would allow a lock of hair to be taken even by her husband, for fear of the power it might give him. The art has a bad name, and it is probably with reason the people assert that adepts in it generally meet with accidents. It is not, however, used for illicit love only; there are many semi-religious charms, containing texts of the Koran, to be recited by those who desire to marry, or who wish to retain the affections of a wife.

The contrivances for destroying a foe are numerous and various, generally resembling those incantations of the ancient Romans which have been handed down to us. The worst feature, perhaps, of the case is, that religion is almost always used for this unholy purpose; and certain chapters and verses of the Koran are supposed to possess mysterious powers of ruin or destruction. A common practice is to make an earthen image, supposed to represent the enemy, dressed in saffron-coloured clothes. An incantation is then recited over a needle, with which the joints of the figure are subsequently pricked. A Kafan, or shroud, is then thrown over it; a small Charpai (couch) is prepared, and prayers for the dead are duly recited. Finally, the figure is buried in the graveyard, and consequently the foe dies of disease. The efficacy of this procedure is so devoutly believed, that doubtlessly success must often have resulted from it.

The most curious and complicated charms are those used in the recovery of stolen property, and the detection of thieves. Strange to say, the Egyptian practice of seeing figures shifting over the ink poured into a boy's hand is, with certain small differences, known in Sindh. The Vinyane-waro,[29] or finder of lost goods, rubs some dark substance upon the thumb-nail of a youth not arrived at the age of puberty, or directs him to look at a black spot painted on the bottom of a bright brass pot. The soothsayer, during this period, recites the Azimât (charm) three different times, after which the seeing commences. The boy first sees a Bhangi, or sweeper, appear in the ink and clean the floor; after which Farrashes (tent pitchers) approach and prepare a pavilion. They are followed by a train of servants, who spread carpets and erect a kind of throne for the king of the Jinn, who presently advances in state, accompanied by his suite. Before him the loser of the article presently appears as a complainant, and the monarch sends his Chobdars (mace-bearers) for the thief. The latter being violently dragged into the presence, is bastinadoed till he shows the spot where the goods are concealed, and then dismissed. When the charm is concluded, the boy accurately describes the person of the guilty man, and the place where he deposited his plunder.

The natives of Sindh aver that this incantation is not a diabolical one, as it is only to be mastered by the forty days' fast, and the other ceremonies usually gone through during the study of Taskhir (or acquisition of power over angels and demons). Consequently few apply to it, and the knowledge is confined to certain families. I never saw the operation, but have heard of it sufficiently often to be assured that my informants were not deceiving me as regards the practice of it; moreover, traces of it are to be found in Southern Persia, and other parts of the eastern world. It probably originated in India, that poisonous source of three parts of the superstitions which have inundated

Europe and Asia; thence it might have travelled westward to Egypt and the Maghrib. As a support to my conjecture, it may be mentioned, that in Sindh it is practised by Hindoos as well as Moslems.

The charm which is called Koran-gardan (the turning of the Koran) in Persia, is known to few here. The way in which it is done is as follows:—A key is so placed among the leaves of the holy book, that the handle and part of the shaft may protrude; and it is secured by a bit of cord fastened tightly round the volume. Two persons then put their fore-fingers under the handle, and so support the book, which hangs down lightly between the hands. A certain verse is repeated once for every suspected person, and at the name of the thief the volume turns round of itself, so that the handle slips off the forefingers of the two persons that hold it. This superstition was formerly common in Europe, the Bible being the *locum tenens* of the Koran; it is now obsolete, except in a few remote localities. The Portuguese of Goa, being a people of strong faith, will use a hymn or mass-book as well as the holy volume, and recite an Ave Maria, sometimes with, sometimes without, a Pater Noster in the Lingoa Baxa.

Some methods of detecting thieves are not without a certain amount of pucrile ingenuity. For instance, a Mulla, Fakir, or any other religious character, is sometimes summoned to read a prayer over a bit of paste, composed of wheaten flour kneaded with water. The household is then assembled, and a small portion is distributed to each person, with the information that the thief cannot easily swallow it; and that moreover, if he succeed, he is likely to lose his life. Of course it frequently occurs that the felon's powers of deglutition are considerably impaired by the action of his imagination and that the tell-tale morsel in his mouth leads to detection. In India this is done with rice, and the quantity of saliva in the grain when masticated, enables the master of the house to determine who the delinquent is.

Some of the charms are such palpable impostures, that it only excites our admiration to see how human nature can allow itself to be so cozened. An empty Tasri, or metal basin, performs the duty of a detective force in the following way:—A Nakhsh, or figure, is drawn on the bottom of the pot, and the Azimat is recited over it a thousand times. A person is then selected, told to perform Ghusl, or the greater ablution, to dress in clean clothes, and then to grasp the Tasri with all his might. The pot, duly adjured, commences its journey towards the spot where the stolen article is concealed, and draws its holder with such force, that were two or even three men to pull against it, it would infallibly draw them along with it. Yet withal, strange to say, when the same Tasri is not in the man's hands, it lies upon the ground bereft of motion.

Of these contrivances there is an immense number. They are, however, confined to private houses, and are never admitted into a court of law; as Islam, contrary to the Hindoo and Guebre faiths, and the practice of Christianity in the dark ages, rejects the trial by ordeal. However, the confidence of all classes in these incantations remains unshaken, and this fact will account for the occasional success which attends experiments. The failures, as may be imagined, are not much talked of.

The faith of the Sindhis in alchemy, and the way in which it is studied and practised, affords a fair specimen of the workings of native society. In the infancy of natural science among the Arabs, Kimiya (alchemy) at once took its rank as the Ajall el ulum tabiiyeh (the most luminous part of philosophical learning). They borrowed it from the Hindoos, to whom the permutation of metals had been known from remote antiquity by the name of Rasayan. The Hajar el hakim (philosopher's stone) of the Arabs is clearly a direct importation from India, where the Sparsha Mani (touch-jewel) was first dreamed of. The Hindoos, it may be conjectured, derived their ideas of Rasayan from considering the changes which take place in the three kingdoms of nature. They remarked that the seed became a tree when planted in the ground; and when swallowed by a bird, the same atoms of matter might become living flesh and blood. It was assumed that the seven metals were of the same essence, but dissimilar in accident, each being in a different state of progression towards the highest grade.[30] The conclusion—a simple but erroneous one—was, that metallurgy would enable the student to permute the baser into the more precious ores.

The Arabs seized the idea with their accustomed avidity in adopting all strange learning which combines the attractions of science and wonder. They divided their Kimiya into two sections, Ilm, or theory, and Amal, practice. In course of time, the study became an arduous one. Many alphabets were invented, signs introduced, and hundreds of volumes were composed in a style so scientific and sibylline, that it became the labour of years to comprehend a simple recipe.

The moderns have considerably simplified the study, and, probably, there is not a native of Sindh who could understand ten lines of an ancient work on alchemy. They content themselves with oral instruction and imperfectly working out Persian prescriptions. Professional alchemists are, usually speaking, cheats, surrounded by dupes, whom they fleece in the most barefaced manner. A remarkable case in point came to my knowledge. A rich Banyan, known to have spent many years and rupees in the pursuit of permutation, met with a religious mendicant who gradually let out the secret[31] that he was able to make gold. The Banyan took the bait, treated the impostor with the greatest distinction, and paid him liberally with money and promises. At last the alchemist, yielding to importunity, directed the dupe to procure from a certain shop, in a distant place, a peculiar kind of earth essential to their success. The gold seeker did so, and was overjoyed to find that he could produce no less than an ounce of the precious metal with the assistance of the mendicant and his earth. The end of the tale can easily be guessed. The cheat disappeared, after making his pupil pay several thousand rupees, a large sum for a lesson in the shallow artifice of filing down a gold mohur and mixing it with dust. But wiser nations and more civilized people than the Sindhis are not above illustrating the truth of the Arab saying, "greed of gain hoodwinks the eyes of the wise."

The would-be alchemist usually begins his studies as follows:—After due enquiry he finds out a proper instructor, generally a religious mendicant of any faith whatever. The reason of which is, that holy men who despise the world and things worldly, are either more likely to become possessed of invaluable secrets, or owe their disregard for mundane events to the possession of those very secrets. The holy men, on the other hand, being generally very poor, are glad to be able to gain a few rupees out of the expense of experiments, and encourage the experimenter to believe that although they could change his house into gold, their voluntary penury disables them from buying an ounce of copper. The student passes all his spare time in the company of his instructor, waiting upon him with the utmost deference, and eagerly listening to every scrap of knowledge which falls from his lips. At the same time search is made for manuscripts and note books which may be useful, and choice extracts are diligently copied. The instructor, if fairly feęd, will begin by initiating his pupil into the art of preparing oxides[32] of the different metals, a kind of stepping stone to the heights of Alchemy. Here instruction ends. If the pupil be a rich fool, he is deluded till he becomes a wiser man: if a useful knave, he may rise to become an assistant to the arch impostor. The legitimate offspring of alchemy in this part of the east is coining. In semi-barbarous and poorly populated countries, forgery and counterfeiting the coin of the realm are not considered such crimes as in more civilized lands: and the natives of the former hear with wonder that men have been put to death in the latter for such peccadillos. Under our rule, the Orientals, who can scarcely hope to copy the Company's rupee without detection, apply themselves to imitate the rude and artless native coinage before it totally disappears. My curiosity to see the tools which were used was disappointed, although I superintended many alchemical experiments; but there is no doubt that the people possess them, and the ability to use them.

The first business of an alchemist in Sindh is to prepare his Buto or crucible. For this purpose, he mixes with water, and exposes to the night air, a sufficient quantity of powdered Kheri (chalk), into which a few shreds of San[38] and Moong rope are thrown. It is then moulded with the hands into a pot of the rudest construction, dried in the sun and finally warmed over a fire till the colour assume a reddish tinge. The cover is made of copper, and the crucible before being placed in the furnace is rolled up in wet rags, and luted with clay, mixed with chaff or chopped straw.

The following prescription for making silver, may serve for a specimen of the present state of alchemy in Sindh. Take of Sankhiyo Pilo (yellow orpiment), one ounce; and procure twenty-two green and juicy branches of the Thuhar, or Euphorbia plant: each stick of which should be about a yard long. Make an incision in the centre of one of these sticks, insert the orpiment, close the hole and lute it with cotton cloth and wet clay. Toast it over a slow fire, in such a way that both extremities may be burned to cinders, while the centre remains scarcely charred. Repeat this operation twenty two times, till the orpiment changes to a bright red colour. It is now ready for making silver. Melt an ounce of copper in a crucible, and add to it, when in a state of liquefaction, about one-twelfth the quantity of yellow orpiment. The *silver* produced will, as may be imagined, be very light, yellow, and smell strongly enough. Before it can be used for coining, it must be subjected to the operation called Rijaran, or polishing. Take of alum, borax, sal ammoniac, and white salt, one pice weight each, pound together, and mix in the water till the mass becomes of the consistency of paste. Then rub it well on the metal, and heat the latter in it three times over a slow fire. The consequence will be that the silver, for a few days, shows a dull white colour, and loses a portion of its strong coppery odour.

As may be imagined in the case of a pursuit so interesting as alchemy, it often draws its votaries into real dangers. The wonderful and the horrible are so closely connected that the former appears to lead directly to the latter. A Hindoo shudders at the thought of mutilating the corpse of a fellow creature, even for the purposes of science; as an alchemist he will become a "resurrectionist," with the idea that copper and quicksilver, inserted into the cranium and mixed with the brains, will, when exposed to the action of a cowdung fire, produce a certain quantity of gold. And the friends of the deceased, who might have been appeased had their relative's cranium been permuted to gold, are apt to proceed to extreme measures when they find only animal charcoal.

The science of Osteomancy is the Ilm el Aktaf (knowledge of the shoulder-blades) of the pagan Arabs and some Bedouin tribes of the present day: the Ilm i Shaneh of the Persians and Affghans, and is known to the shepherd clans of Sindhis and Belochis by the name of Phannia jo fannu.[34]

The instrument of divination is the scapula of a sheep divested of its muscles and integuments. The dorsum is considered: six of the "houses" are disposed in regular order running from the neck of the bone down to the fossa which, in the human subject, would serve for the attachment of the supra-spinatus muscle, to the superior angle of the bone. The other six are contained in the space on the other side of the spine, and correspond with the former.

The total number of the houses, therefore, is twelve, and each is connected with one of the signs of the Zodiac,[35] in the following order:—

Houses.	Signs of the Zodiac.	Houses.	Signs of the Zodiac.
1.	Aries.	7.	Libra.
2.	Taurus.	8.	Scorpio.
3.	Gemini.	9.	Sagittarius.
4.	Cancer.	10.	Capricornus.
5.	Leo.	11.	Aquarius.
6.	Virgo.	12.	Pisces.

The points to be observed are, the colour of the

bone; the veins and streaks, the foramina which may appear upon its surface and what is called its "Jauhar" (texture and waving lines).

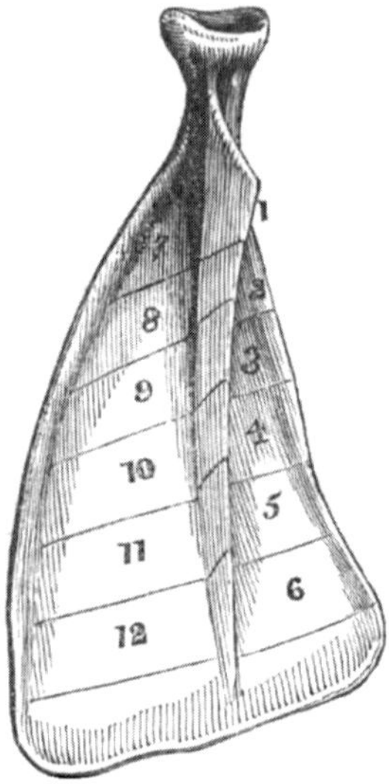

When divination is to be practised, they select a ram or he goat, without blemish; observing also that the skin be not torn or hurt in any place. The animal is slaughtered according to the Moslem form, in the name of the Almighty, and the flesh is devoted to charitable purposes. The right shoulder-blade is consulted during the dark half of the month, and *vice versâ*. The several houses are then inspected, and the following are the general rules for ascertaining the propitious or unpropitious appearances.

The first house gives answers to enquirers. If the bone be smooth, clear and without holes, the consultor is known to be a good man, and the omen is propitious. The contrary presignifies wickedness, sickness and violent death.

The second relates to the herds: if the bone be clear and clean, they will thrive and grass will be abundant. Should layers of white and red streaks appear upon the surface, robbers are to be expected.

The third announces facts concerning the flocks, and in every point corresponds with the second. When there is any unevenness in the bone, or if the side be rough, as if chipped, the shepherd knows that his animals are likely to suffer from a disease called Takanu̱.

The fourth belongs peculiarly to hills and mountains. When of a deep dark colour, it is a sign of abundance of grass: if white and clear, it threatens famine among the cattle.

The fifth house, if white and clear, announces abundant rains, and is a sign that ice and hail may be expected.

The sixth is that remarked when the consultor is suffering from any disease or complaint. If its surface be of a pure clear colour, there is no fear: when of a dull, cloudy white, three months of unhappiness must ensue. When foramina appear, the omen is very unpropitious.

The seventh answers enquiries respecting nuptials. When it is tinged with dark, extending to, and not beyond the boundaries of the house, good fortune is predicted. If the colour be pure white, danger is to be expected, and when there is redness, much unhappiness, disease or even death to the bride.

The eighth forewarns the questioner against the depredations of robbers. If the colour be clear and white, no danger is to be apprehended: black spots predict contests, the result of which will be auspicious. Holes denote danger, and waving lines foreshow the arrival of locusts.

The ninth decides the fate of cities and towns. Whiteness is a sign of good fortune, waving lines of plenty and successful trade. A black tinge is a sign of disease: holes, of violent epidemics. When red is the prevailing tint, marriages will be numerous.

The tenth is the house which respects armies and hosts. As usual, clear white is auspicious, black, a sign of violence and bloodshed, red denotes war and plunder: wavy lines predict defeat, and holes, much suffering and great toil.

The eleventh respects plains and leas. A dark colour is a sure foreteller of plenty, and, *vice versâ*, white, of want.

The twelfth decides the arrival of Kafilas. A clouded white tinge is a good and safe sign, and blackness shows that many caravans may be expected. Pure whiteness predicts drought; redness, ill-luck to the travellers.

The cavity which in the human subject receives the head of the humerus (marked 13 in the figure) proves when white and clear that the person who slaughtered the animal is a virtuous and pious man. As Moslems depend much upon the efficacy of supererogatory holiness, it is by no means an unimportant point that the soothsayer should be carefully selected.

The system as here described appears to me to be borrowed from a celebrated work on the different branches of ariolation, called the Kashf el-Rumuz.

The Sindhis are also well provided with cheap and

efficacious means of diving into futurity by means of Sortilege. The following specimen may remind the curious reader of the trifles somewhat extensively spread abroad[35] among ourselves, such as Napoleon's Book of Fate, and similar ineptiæ. It is said to have been invented by the Hindoos, who attribute it to four Rakshasas, or demons, that fought against Ramachandra at Lanka.

The Oraculum is consulted by means of a Kurah, or oblong die, with the first four letters of the Abjad inscribed upon the long surfaces. The consulter offers up a short prayer, with firm faith rolls the instrument up and down his extended palm, and throws it three times. Then remarking the combination of the letters which appear, he refers to the table and the number directs him to the answer.

The science of Oneiromancy[36] is not much studied. The only Sindhi treatise on that subject is a short translation from the Persian by one Mohammed Mukim. The rules appear to be borrowed from the celebrated work of Ibn Sirin.

The hill people, and some of the wilder clans of Sindhis, have a peculiar kind of divination by means of knotted strings. Seven pieces of equal length are twisted round the thumb and tied together, *secundum artem:* when the line is drawn out, the different combinations of knots that appear upon its length, enable consulters to judge of what is likely to happen. The art is called Mansing, and though not much practised by the higher orders of soothsayers, it has been reduced to a system, and gravely described in divers most unintelligible treatises.

The Ilm i Kaf, or Palmistry, is common among Moslems and Hindoos; but better known in Cutch than in Sindh. The "canons of true and catholic chiromancy" are much the same in Asia as in Europe, and the pages of Torreblanca, or the notable volume which boasts Aristotle's name, prove that the art is of purely Oriental origin.

The Sona[37] jo ilm, or knowledge of Omens, taken from the flight of birds, the appearance of beasts, and other similar phenomena, closely resembles the art of the Indian Thugs. The Belochis are considered great adepts in this branch of the occult sciences, and the Sindhis have a short treatise upon the subject called Sugun-namo.

There is no better clue to the peculiar disposition of any race of men, than that obtained by observation of the popular crimes, and the way in which they are punished. Judged by this test, the Sindhis are by no means a bad people, as atrocity is rare amongst them, and consequently justice is not severe. A murderer is condemned by all classes high and low: the word "Katil" (manslayer) being used as a term of reproach. The crime was punished in two ways: death or fine. The former was adjudged in certain cases, settled by Moslem law, and the manner of execution was this:—The servants of the Kazi (judge) pinioned the murderer's arms, and gave him up to his victim's relations, who either cut his throat with a knife, or struck off his head with a sword. In cases of death by guns, sticks, stones, poison, throwing into a well, and other means duly settled by the custom of Islam, the relatives of the slain received from the slayer a certain sum of money, called Diyat.[38] The practice called Badli, in India, where a murderer paid a substitute to take upon himself the blame and consequences of the offence was very uncommon and now does not exist in Sindh. Suicide was universally reprobated among the Moslems: Hindoos, as usual, with metempsychosists, regarded and regard it as justifiable or not according to circumstances. In cases of *felo de se* among the Sindhis, the corpse was not bathed or shrouded, but buried as it was found in an unconsecrated place. Kisas, or lex talionis, was the punishment of mutilation; and the blame of so barbarous a law belongs to the faith, not to the people. It was, however, rigorously observed. If, in a quarrel, a man blinded his neighbour, the Kazi directed the executioner to destroy his vision by means of a mirror held up to the sun. In the same way if a tooth was lost; the Lohar, or blacksmith, with a huge pair of pincers, extracted a corresponding portion of the dental process. The punishment of cutting and wounding, was the infliction of a similar injury.

Larceny, petty and on a grand scale, was the prevailing offence, though considered disgraceful by the people,[39] unless when done with arms in their hands. The penalties were numerous and various; but the Koranic order of mutilation was an exception, not the rule. In lesser cases, theft was visited with imprisonment, fine, and compulsory fasting. The lower orders were disgraced by shaving the beard, hair and eyebrows, by blackening their faces, and mounting them on asses. Sometimes the thief was compelled to wander about the town with slippers hung round his neck, and so beg his bread. When greater shame was intended, there were a variety of punishments similar to the mullet-penalty for adultery at Athens.

In the times of the Ameers of Sindh, prisoners were kept in the Chabutaro, or Kotwal's office. These dungeons were well provided with Niyyara (chains) Hathoriyun (handcuffs), Katha (stocks), Gatta (heavy iron collars for the neck), and other similar instruments. The higher classes of criminals were sent to the forts intended for their reception, or confined in a Chaukidar's house.

Justice, under the native princes, was administered in the large towns by the Kotwal; in the villages, by the Kardar of each province. In all cases which were to be decided by the Koran, the Kazi used to act, and appeal from one of these officers to another was generally permitted. The principal Ameers had power of life and death, each in his own territory: the Beloch Sardars (chiefs), and the Pirs, or religious teachers, could not claim, but often exercised, the right. Hindoos were allowed to settle any affairs which occurred amongst themselves by means of the Panchayat, or committee of the caste: but in cases of murder, they came under the jurisdiction of the Kotwal.

Forgery, coining, and using counterfeit seals, were considered political offences, and were punished with fines, imprisonment or flogging. Perjury was and is common amongst all classes. An oath taken upon the Koran was considered decisive, as it is supposed that the offended Deity would certainly punish the perjurer. The result was that the educated classes acted upon the principle—

"—— Certe lenta ira Deorum est,"

and foreswore themselves accordingly. The poorer order of Moslems have a terror of the offence, which only Rupees will do away with. The Hindoos of Sindh are not inferior to their Indian brethren in utter contempt of an oath. The result of experience in this province leads an observer to believe, that when a native makes an assertion, he is to be doubted: when he asseverates, to be disbelieved; and when he swears, to be suspected of a black and exaggerated lie. Falsehood and prevarication are considered minor forms of perjury, and anything but criminal. Where truth is unsafe this must be expected from human nature. To so general a rule there will be some exceptions: the latter, however, appear very rarely.[40]

Intoxication, fornication and prostitution were not punished according to Koranic law, which, like some other faiths, is not acted up to by those who believe in it.

CHAPTER VIII.

TASAWWUF, OR SUFYISM, IN SINDH.—THE SUFI POETS.—THE PIRS, OR RELIGIOUS TEACHERS.—TWO GREAT DIVISIONS OF TASAWWUF, VIZ., JELALI AND JEMALI.—DESCRIPTION OF THE JELALI.—ACCOUNT OF LAL SHAH-BAZ.—THE JEMALI SUFIS, AND THEIR PECULIARITIES OF IMITATION, TENETS AND PRACTICES.—THE MOST CELEBRATED SAINTS IN SINDH.

THERE is nothing more remarkable in Sindh than the number of holy men which it has produced, and the extent to which that modification of Pantheism, called Tasawwuf throughout the world of Islam, is spread among the body of the people.

The tenets of Tasawwuf, or Sufyism, have been eloquently given in summary by Sir W. Jones;[1] and in these days the literati of Europe are probably as learned in them as most of the Maulavies. But if De Bode's "Bokhara" be taken as a specimen,[2] much ignorance as to the practices of the sect still remains.

It will be necessary to preface with a few words upon the origin of Tasawwuf. It is still doubtful whether the source of it may be traced to Persia or to India: the date assigned to the establishment of the community called Essenis, who may be supposed to have borrowed their mysticism from the Zoroastrians,[3] shows that Central Asia held such tenets at a very early period; and the philosophical works of the Hindoos prove that the ancient Indians had made great progress in them. Orthodox Moslems generally trace Tasawwuf back to Hindustan. They assert that when the Mohammedans entered that country as conquerors, their fame reached as far as Kamru Dwipa, where dwelt a sage Hindoo, deeply skilled in philosophy and metaphysics. The wise man, they say, attracted by the reputation of the new comers, left his country to meet them at Lakhnauti, was converted to the true faith by Kazi Rukn el Din, and from a Hindoo work, the Anirat Kandha, composed a treatise in Arabic and named it Hauz el Hayat. This garbled account,[4] at any rate, shows the popular belief. The Shiah heresy attributes the introduction of mysticism to the caliphs of the house of Abbas, who were determined to oppose some new and enticing doctrine, borrowed from a polytheistic people, to the sanctity and orthodox tenets of their Imams. There is certainly a wonderful resemblance between Tasawwuf and the Vedantic system;[5] and the modern Indian's opinions concerning the efficacy of Jog (penance and abstinence), exactly contain the Sufi's ideas of Riyazat. Both believe that, by certain superstitious practices, the *divinæ particula auræ* in man so emancipates itself from the tyranny of impure matter, that it acquires supernatural powers of metamorphosing the body, transferring the mind to men and beasts, forcibly producing love, causing the death of foes, knowing what is concealed from humanity, seeing spirits, fairies, devils and angels, flying in the air, counteracting magical arts, prevention of pain, curing the venom or wounds of animals, alchemy, healing the sick, subjugating the planets, visiting the heavens, and obtaining by prayer all that one desires. But human nature always presents a general resemblance; and among similar races, in similar climates, and under similar circumstances, the same developments may be expected and are found to be exhibited. The prudent archæologist will probably be inclined to believe that the tenets of Tasawwuf or Vedantism are so consistent with man's reason, so useful to his interests, and so agreeable to his passions and desires, that their origin must belong to the dark beginnings of human society.

A system of belief adopted by such minds as Jami, Hafiz, Saadi, Jelal el Din, Abd el Kadir, Ibn Fariz and others, must be supposed to possess some intrinsic value. And the merit of Tasawwuf, is its *beau ideal* of goodness as connected with beauty, and universal charity and love as flowing from the source of all goodness. The Persians, with their wonderful powers of ideality and comparison,[6] applied themselves to the perilous task of blending Polytheism,[7] the poetry, with Monotheism, the prose of religion. By this means they not only secured to themselves the means of indulging their fondness for revelling in the regions of imagination, but also authorised such flights by making mind, to a certain extent, paramount to revelation. The Koranic idea of the human soul or spirit, for instance, is similar to our own; but the Sufi, deducing the doctrine of the soul's immortality from its immateriality, assigns to it Azaliyat, immortality without beginning, as well as Abadiyat, immortality without end. And convinced by reason that nothing can be at once self-existent, immaterial, and unbounded by time except the Deity, he concludes that the spirit of man is nothing but the breath,[8] the particle of the Divine soul lent to mankind, the noblest of God's works. In the same way, his appreciation of the beautiful and the good is explained as the unconscious tribute of the human heart to the spiritual perfection of the Author of its being. Consequently he abandons himself to the sentiment, and not unfrequently becomes either an utter ascetic by contemplation of spiritual, or a debauchee by yielding to the seductions of the material loveliness. Oriental nations show very little practical admiration of the golden mean. They are almost always in extremes, and their conceptions of virtue, heroism, devotion, love, and friendship, are of the most enthusiastic and impossible description. It is curious for the European to observe the method by which they justify their exaggeration of themselves.

Tasawwuf then may be defined to be the religion of beauty, whose leading principle is that of earthly, the imperfect type of heavenly, love.[9] Its high priests are Anacreontic poets, its rites wine, music, and dancing, spiritually considered, and its places of worship meadows and gardens, where the perfume of the rose and the song of the nightingale, by charming the heart, are supposed to improve the mind of the listener. This is thorough Epicurism in the midst of one of the most gloomy of faiths: the contrast is striking, but its existence is easily explained. It depends for support entirely upon the favour which the poet finds with all classes of men. The Sufi bard is, generally speaking, a profound student of the different branches of language and metaphysics; he is gifted with a musical ear, and fearlessly indulges in luxuriant imagery and description, which contain a simple sense agreeable to all—a *double entendre* seldom understood by any but the few learned. The most striking specimens of the class appear to me to be Ibn Fariz among the Arabs, Hafiz in Persia, Shah Bhetai[10] in Sindh, and Abd el Rahman among the Affghans. The nationality of each of these individuals is remarkable. For instance, Ibn Fariz composes in a rich and mechanical language, addressed to the eye as well as the mind; and his ideas are borrowed from the wild hills and desert sands of his native country. As might be expected, his poetry displays all the manliness, fervency, and contempt for life, combined with the eloquence, the modulation, and the choice of words required to attract and charm the ears and souls of his countrymen. In Hafiz, who uses a very inferior language, we find learning, and love of pleasure, wonderful powers of imagination, and a fulness of meaning, which none but Persians can appreciate. Nothing is more remarkable than the ardour for devotion to which he abandons himself,[11] and the spirit of tenderness and love for all things (including even inanimate objects), which breathes from his poetry. The effect is, that even his most rigid readers are delighted with his attractive Pantheism, and persuade themselves that every word he utters is to be understood in a mystic sense. Shah Bhetai, the Sindhi, had the disadvantage of contending against a barbarous dialect, and composing for an unimaginative people. His ornaments of verse are chiefly alliteration, puns, and jingling of words. He displays his learning by allusions to the literature of Arabia and Persia, and not unfrequently indulges in quotation. His compositions are all upon subjects familiar to the people, strained to convey a strange idea. As might be expected, he is more homely and common-place than Ibn Fariz or Hafiz; at the same time, he is more practical, and some portions of his writings[12] display an appreciation of domestic happiness scarcely to be expected from one of his order. Hence his poetry is the delight of all that can understand it. The learned praise it for its beauty, and are fond of hearing it recited to the sound of the guitar. Even the unlearned generally know select portions by heart, and take the trouble to become acquainted with their meaning. Abd el Rahman, or Rahman as he is familiarly termed, is a perfect specimen of the rugged race which preserved the independence of the Affghan hills. The Pushtu, a dialect more barbarous than that of Sindh, becomes in his hands a very tolerable vehicle for poetry stern and gloomy as his. He abounds in fierce invective against the world, its falseness and treachery, its passing good and permanent evil: his contempt of life is scarcely tempered by devotion, and he seems to indulge in an occasional pleasant thought with regret. I have never heard an Affghan read one of his odes without a sigh.

Tasawwuf, under the native governments, was as

formidable a political engine as most of the secret confraternities recorded in history. Hasan Sabah, the celebrated "Old Man of the Mountain," to mention no others, showed what use could be made of it by a talented and unscrupulous villain. Even among the mild Sindhis, a noted Pir (religious superior) formerly might safely order one of his Murids, or disciples, to murder an enemy. Yet the native princes encouraged it, partly from superstition, and partly because the price of every Pir was well known to them. Unlike the Assassins, the order in this province had no Grand Master, nor was the material that composed it equal to that of the Fidawis.

To the Pirs, great advantages accrued. Of these individuals there are between fifty and sixty in Sindh,[13] most of whom can trace their genealogies up to the Prophet, and the principal saints that succeeded him. Under our government they have of course lost the right of flogging and beheading their followers, so that their power now depends principally upon the ignorance and superstition of the populace. As they are usually the vile descendants[14] of some ancestor celebrated for virtue or learning, they think it necessary to keep up appearances; yet their garb of goodness is a very flimsy one. The Pir who calls himself a Fakir, or beggar, will probably maintain an establishment of a hundred servants, and as many horses; it is sufficient for him occasionally to show a camel-hair vest under his garments, and his followers will excuse his ostentation. The vanity of the disciples induces them to believe in, and to vaunt the supernatural powers of their superior; his being able to work miracles and to visit heaven[15] gives *them* additional importance. Timidity of disposition on the part of the followers, favours the imposture in no small degree. The manly Wahabi of Eastern Arabia derides the idea that even his prophet, much more a mere mortal like Abd el Kadir, can intercede for him, or interfere between him and his God. The pusillanimous Sindhi and Hindoo, like the nations of southern Europe, cling to the idea that the supererogatory works of their saints and holy men, will be, as it were a wall between them and the gulf of eternal perdition.[16] The power of ideality in the Persians, and the strange fanaticism of the Affghans, operate in them as cowardice does in the Sindhi. Like the mysteries of the Druses, Tasawwuf, in our province, admits female as well as male initiated; many of the former rise to distinction in the order. This is another advantage to the Pir, as even the most religious woman would consider it an honour to intrigue with his holiness; the less scrupulous could not refuse any member of the holy family, and the looser kind would admit all the Pir's followers to the same privileges. Seduction, if it can be called so, is carried on in two ways. The religious superior, if determined on secrecy, manages the affair himself, either by visiting the husband or summoning the wife; and he has little to fear from marital vengeance, as the dishonour would in most cases be considered an honour. The other plan is to employ a confidential servant, who, as a reward, receives the promise of eternal beatitude, or what he values as much, a present of a few Rupees. In a pecuniary point of view, the position of the Pir is an enviable one. He levies a tax of from one-eighth to one-half upon the income and produce of his followers, who are too timid to defraud the saint,[17] and not unfrequently make him expensive presents when any unexpected stroke of good fortune, attributed to his intercession, enables them to do so. It is not too much to say, that some few of the chief Pirs could, by good management, command an annual income of 30,000*l*. Besides emolument, these holy men enjoyed and enjoy the power of committing any villany, upon the principle that from the pure nothing but what is pure can proceed. Their excuses are ingenious. To vindicate luxury and polygamy, they quote the cases of Solomon and David among prophets, Abd el Kadir and Baha el Din among saints. Celibacy, continence, penance, and religious discipline are dispensed with after they arrive at a certain pitch of holiness. When a public scandal occurs, they tell a tale of the great Shaykh Bayezed Bustami, who, to punish himself for pride, told a courtezan to bring him his turban and staff and claim money from him, at a time when a select body of revering disciples was collected round their instructor. Or they may instance the not less celebrated Shams el Din Tabrizi, who, on one occasion, asked a Murid to lend him his wife, for the purpose of trying the disciple's faith. Pride and vaunting are justified, by quoting the verse of the celebrated Sufi Junayd, "how high and how great is my degree (in creation)!"—although Mohammed expressly said, "we know Thee not as Thou oughtest to be known."[18]

So tenacious of respect are most of the chief Pirs,

that they would never rise to any of the Ameers, or condescend to treat them with civility; the prince, on his side, was glad to make an easy show of religious humility, and stoop to conquer when forcible victory would have been valueless. Sometimes these saints will openly transgress the orders of their faith. The Koran, for instance, limits the number of wives to four, whereas the family of Pir Ali Gauhar, a noted religious character in the north of Sindh, allows each male to marry from twenty to thirty women. They explain away their disobedience by supporting the dogma, that wives were limited to the number four because that sufficed for ordinary Moslems; and as it would be sinful to marry one woman and make her unhappy, so it is lawful and right to take thirty to oneself, provided the measure be equally agreeable to all parties. Such reasoning is of course conclusive.

The practical results of the Pirs' imposition are, that the Murids, in their delusion, look upon him as the under door-keeper of Paradise, and respect him accordingly. Even the cowardly Sindhi would assault a man that ventured to curse his Pir; the Affghans and Persians would consider the instant murder of such an individual a highly meritorious action.

The effects of Tasawwuf upon the people in general can easily be conceived. The disciples sink capital in a speculation that can never pay in this world; and besides their monetary loss, they throw away all chance of moral improvement. It would be impossible for a government of strangers to check the system by active measures, as their efforts would only increase its evils. The safest plan is to do away, as much as possible, with the political importance of the Pirs, and to oppose such superstitions by the diffusion of knowledge.

Tasawwuf in Sindh has two great divisions, viz., 1st. Jelali;[19] 2nd. Jemali.

The Jelali is supposed to occupy himself in contemplating the terrible qualities of the Supreme Being. The idea is clearly derived from Hindustan, as may be proved by the practice of the Indian Arpanthi of the present day, who systematically endeavours, by committing every species of crime, to anger the Deity into granting him absorption by annihilation. The Jelali, as a Moslem, at least apparently so, dares not own to such tenets, but adheres rigidly to the practice. He eats forbidden meats, and drinks to intoxication, excusing himself by quoting the divine saying, "Eat ye and drink ye." His immorality and debauchery are known to all: in vindication of himself he quotes the Hadis—"The heart and intention of the believer are of more importance than his words and deeds." The whole of this vile class profess the greatest respect for Ali, and in Sindh are generally the disciples of the celebrated Kalandar,[20] Lal Shah-Baz, to whose tomb at Sehwan they perform frequent pilgrimages. In India, much study and knowledge of a peculiar kind are required from the Jelali Fakir. For instance, one of these individuals might ask another what are the Adab-i-Kachkol (*i. e.*, what is the mystic lesson conveyed by the bowl in which they carry about grain, &c., given as alms?) The answer should be, "Before it his daily bread, behind it death, to the right Heaven, on the left Hell; below it is the animal that supports the earth (viz., the bull), and above it the firmament." This reply is the only proper one; any other would secure to the replier a blow with the interrogator's staff.

The initiation of the Jelali is a long and ceremonious one, beginning with Ghusl (the greater ablution) and prayer. The candidate is then invested with the cap, the coat, and the other appurtenances of his order; each gift has its own appropriate lesson, and nothing is omitted to impress the "brother" with an idea of his important duties. When all is duly concluded, the newly-made Fakir is sent out into the world, a sturdy, irretrievable beggar, unfit for any useful occupation in life, sure of Heaven, and, meanwhile, permitted to make earth as pleasant a place as he can, by the liberal use of hemp or spirits, and the pursuit of the most degrading sensuality.

The following are the articles of dress used by the Jelali and other Fakirs :—

1. The Taj, a felt hat in the shape of our fools' cap; the Jemali prefers white cotton for the material.

2. Kafni (Khafni), or Alfi, a coat made of black wool, with white threads, in shape somewhat like a shroud, without sleeves, and reaching down to about mid-calf.

3. Godri, a blanket of the same material, used during the cold weather, and when sleeping.

Some Jelalis religiously confine themselves to the above three articles of dress; others condescend to adopt short drawers, or to wrap a cloth round the thighs. The professional implements carried about by these beggars are :—

1. Tasbih, a rosary made of some red stone, generally cornelian, with large beads, the rattling of which may warn people that the holy man is engaged inh is devotions. Like most Orientals, the Fakir, by perpetually manipulating his rosary, gets into the habit of doing so mechanically.

2. Asa, a staff, generally of ebony or black wood, with sometimes a ferule and an ivory top. The Jelalis often carry huge and formidable clubs; the most debauched of the class walk about with pestles to bruise the intoxicating hemp.

3. Beragan, a black wood stick about a foot and a half long, with a fork on the top, intended to support the Fakir's forehead during meditation or sleep, as it is considered vulgar to lie down.

4. Dhaga, cords made of black wool twisted, and about as thick as a man's little finger; they are used as a girdle wound round the waist.

5. Gano, threads of black wool, with a little red silk in them, worn as a necklace.

6. Gabri, a wallet, generally speaking of red cloth, to contain food and the necessaries of life.

7. Tumbi, a cup made from a gourd, used to drink from and receive alms of grain or money.

8. Sing, a horn of the wild goat, formed into a most unmusical instrument, and performed upon at dawn, in the evening, and before the doors of almsgivers. Much importance is attached to this exercise, and the origin of it is said to be as follows:—Ali, the only hero of Islam that did not fly at the battle

of Ohod, was toiling to rally his fugitive soldiery, when a voice from Heaven directed him to call a wild sheep, which came and gave up its horn into his hands. The hero blew through it the dread blast[21] of "Kutb! Kutb!" and the desired effect was of course produced.

The Jelali Fakirs in Sindh, are, generally speaking, poor, and live from hand to mouth. Their Pirs are said to receive about one-third of their gains.

Some account of Lall Shah-Baz,[22] the great superior of this order in Sindh, may be acceptable to the reader. His real name was Usman i Merwandi; he was a great grammarian, philologist, traveller and saint: and died at Sehwan in A.H. 673 (A.D. 1274). As a Kalandar, he was a rigid celibatarian, and left no children: his modern disciples are initiated by his Khalifeh (successors) and Mujawir, or those that attend the holy sepulchre. His place of burial is much respected. Every year a girl of the Khonbati (Safflower dyer) caste is married to the tomb, with music, dancing and all due solemnities. The worst part of the affair is, that she is never permitted to contract any more substantial matrimonial alliance. The rite of initiating candidates is made as humiliating as possible, in order to prepare the Fakir for the kind of life which he is to adopt. All the hair on his person (including even that of the eyebrows) is shaved off, as a preparatory measure. The Mujawirs approach and blacken his face: they then hang a bit of cord round his neck, show him a looking-glass, and ask him how he likes his own appearance. He replies, very much. His shoulder is then seared with a hot iron, his body is stripped and smeared with the ashes of cowdung, and, lastly, he is told to go forth into the world and beg his bread professionally.

Sometimes, but rarely, respectable people submit to this initiation, and continue for a short time to act as mendicants, either in performance of a vow, or in order to obtain some wish. The tomb is perpetually surrounded by a multitude of devotees, who believe that by perseverance or obstinacy they can succeed by tiring out the saint. The wealthier classes bribe him. One half of the gifts belong to the Khalifeh; the other to the Mujawirs, who are two great families of Sayyids, viz., of Lakhyari, and Mathari.

The Jemali Sufis in Sindh, as in the Oriental world generally, are a much more respectable class than their Jelali brethren. The latter openly dispense with the formalities of religious worship: the former do not, except in the rare instances when inward sanctity is felt, known and acknowledged to be superior to outward forms. In addition to prayer and fasting, the Jemali Sufi is recommended penance and seclusion; silence; meditation in dark and gloomy spots; perpetual devotion; abstinence from food, sleep and carnal enjoyments; perfect love and obedience to his Shaykh, or religious superior; abnegation of self and all worldly ties, and, finally, the strictest attention to the rules and regulations of his order. In the cases of the wealthy and dignified, vicarious penance and presents of money are taken as substitutes: but rank in the brotherhood is only to be acquired by strict devotion or inheritance.

The four principal divisions of the Jemali Sufis in

Sindh are—1. Kadiri;[23] 2. Nakshbandi; 3. Sohrehwardi; 4. Chisti.

The Chisti order follows the path of their founder, Kh'ajeh Muin el Din Mohammed i Chishti (so called from Chisht, a village in Khorasan), who was born at Sejistan, educated in Khorasan, died and was buried at Ajmir, on the 6th Rajab, A.H. 633 (A.D. 1235.) Their Silsileh,[24] begins with Mohammed, like those of the other three divisions. In many points their practices are similar to those of the Maulawis of Turkey, but they object to allow infidels to witness their meetings. Music is considered a religious duty. When intending to produce ecstacy, they repeat the following lines in honour of Allah and the Prophet.

> " Hasbí Rabbi jall 'Alláh!
> Má fi kalbí ghair 'Alláh!
> Núr Muhammad sall 'Alláh!
> Lá iláha ill 'Alláh!"

When the fit is induced, the rest of the company look with great respect at the patient till it is over. Formerly, as a trial of faith, a pot of water was thrown upon the devotee's back, and if not absorbed by his person before any could reach the ground, his sincerity was called into question. Of late years the practice has been abandoned.

The tenets of the Nakshbandi order are too well known to require description: the following account of the formalities they have adopted in Sindh may, in some points be new to the Orientalist.

When a candidate of rank or education is to be initiated, the Pir prepares himself with prayer, and afterwards takes his seat upon a clean Musalla,[25] turning towards Mecca. He then causes the candidate to sit upon the same carpet, in the position called Duzanu, and to perform the Fikr i Surat, *i. e.*, to meditate with closed eyes upon the appearance of his religious instructor. The latter, at the same time, employs himself, if sufficiently high of degree, in Fanah fi 'llah, or "merging the creature into the Creator." After about five minutes the Pir raises his hands, as in prayer, and repeats the Fatihah, or first chapter of the Koran, directing his disciple to pronounce the words after him. Lastly, the instructor, placing his hand upon the candidate's breast, mutters a few words,[26] and finally, blows once in the direction of his disciple's heart, who is to be occupied in meditating upon the Shafakat i Murshid (the kindness of his Pir). The initiation is then ended.

Before undertaking the system of religious exercises, the newly made Sufi is directed to improve his local memory by reflecting upon the Pir's appearance for four or five days. He sits in the position of Murakabah,[27] and begins this preparatory rite about an hour after sunrise.

The young Nakshbandi in Sindh usually commences with the three Shughl or Practices of the Kadiri order. After the morning ablution and prayer, he commences the Zikr,[28] "La iláha ill' Allah," repeating it one thousand times. He then repeats "Ill 'alláh;" next "Allah," and lastly "Hu." The total number of repetitions is thus four thousand: after each hundred of which the words "Mohammedu Rasulu 'llah," are pronounced. Whenever strange thoughts intrude, the Deity's name, "Ya Faal," effectually removes temptation to wander.

After this Zikr comes the Tasawwur, or Meditation. The pupil is directed to think of the Pir's form, to retain his breath,[29] and to suppose his heart to express the word "Allah." During the operation, the mind is fixed upon a spot[30] supposed most unanatomically to correspond with the position of the heart. This ends the first Shughl, which is to be performed morning and evening, for forty days in succession, and ever afterwards as often as possible.

The nature of the second Shughl is as follows: after prayers the young Sufi is directed to repeat slowly the words "Ya Allah," causing them to pass, as it were, from the heart to the right shoulder. After a hundred repetitions he is to utter Ya Hu, carrying it downwards from the shoulder to the heart the same number of times. The duration of this Shughl is also forty days.

The third Shughl is called "Pas i anfas ala'd dawam," or the "Continuous observance of inspiration and expiration." The candidate is directed to master all his senses, external and internal, and thinking of the Shaykh, to breathe through the nose "Allah," when inspiring, and "Hu," when expiring. This exercise is repeated five hundred times after the morning, and one thousand times after the evening, prayer.

These three exercises belong both to the Kadiri and the Nakshbandi orders. The three following are confined to the latter, who commence them when directed to do so by the religious instructor.

The first Nakshbandi Shughl is called Lataif Sitteh,

(the Six Mysteries), and is performed thus :—The body is divided into six Darajat (steps or degrees), viz. :—

1. Nafsi, about two fingers below the navel.

2. Kalbi, about two fingers below the nipple of the left breast.

3. Ruhi, about two fingers below the nipple of the right breast.

4. Sirri, about the middle of the breast.

5. Khafy, in the forehead.

6. Akhfai, in the poll of the head.

The above is the order adopted by the Banuriyeh Sufis, who follow the path of Sayyid Adam i Banuri. The latter saint seems to have modified the system of his master, Kh'ajeh Ahmed i Faruki i Sirhindi i Nakshbandi, surnamed "Mujaddad i Alf i Sani (the reviver of the second thousand years of the Hijrah era). Kh'ajeh Ahmed reckoned only five steps, and made some difference in their positions.[31]

The young Nakshbandi is directed to perform this exercise twice a day before sleeping. He begins by retaining his breathing, and mentally repeating "Allah" in the first or Nafsi position. When fatigued, he applies the forefinger of the right hand to the right nostril and puffs out his breath. He then removes the forefinger, breathes freely till refreshed, and resumes the exercise. This operation is performed from three to five, and so on to twenty-one times in each step (Nafsi, Kalbi, &c.,) in regular order. At the last Darajeh—the Akhfai—the word "Allah" is repeated mentally twice, not once as in the others. The more experienced are able to perform the operation as many as twenty-one times in each step, during the period of one retention of the breath. The moral effects of this exercise are said to be exaltation and attraction towards the Deity; purification of the heart, even as a room is swept by the broom; intense love for, and "*desiderium*" when separated from, the Supreme Friend; and, finally, a total abnegation of self and the world. The duration is at least forty days, and the Murid,[32] when directed by his Murshid, passes on to the next practice, without, however, totally abandoning the first.

The second Nakshbandi Shughl is called by a royal title, the "Sultan i Zikr," on account of its peculiar efficacy. The Salik, as he may now be termed, after inspiration retains his breath, and mentally conducts the word "Allah" from the first step below the navel, in a straight line, through the fourth and fifth, up to the sixth or brain; thus neglecting the cross formed by the second and third. The Holy Name is then cast out, as it were, from the brain through the nostrils, which are not closed by the forefinger, and should be "dashed like water from a bucket over the whole person." The body of the devotee must be taught to expect it; when in a promising mental state, every limb should be mesmerized by its influence, and when in progress towards perfection every created thing, animate or inanimate, around the Salik, should appear to join in his emotion. The number of times appointed for this Shughl is determined by the Murshid. There is no fixed duration to the exercise, and it may be practised at any or at all hours in the day.

The third and last Shughl is called "Nafy wa Isbat," Negation and Affirmation. It is done thus: the Salik obtains complete mastery over his senses, retains his breathing and fixes his thoughts in the Nafsi position below the navel. He then inhales breath, and conducts the word "La" from below the navel to the brain: the word "Ilaha" from the brain to the right shoulder: the word "Illa" from the right shoulder to the Ruhi position, below the right breast, and the word "Allah" from the right nipple to the middle of the breast. Finally, he fixes the terminal letter of "Allah" in the Kalb, or heart.[33] This formula must be repeated from one to two hundred and ten times [34] in succession, and when fatigued, any odd number of breathings may be inhaled. The effects of this Zikr are an increased intensity of affection for the Supreme Being, and a more complete relinquishment of self.

The Salik has now terminated his religious exercises and becomes, if duly approved of, a master in the mystic craft under the name of Sahib Irshad, or one capable of directing others. At the same time he never omits occasionally to practise the several Shughl, conceiving that each has a beneficial effect upon his mind. Some Saliks are termed "Salik i Majzub"[35] and continue to observe all the external forms and ordinances of their faith. Others are called in contradistinction "Majzub i Salik," as being so much affected by their mystical affection for the Deity and Gnosticism that they are dead to excitement, hope and fear. This class is of course rare, and requires a peculiar conformation of mind. The pretenders to it are common in proportion as the pretence is easy and its advantages great. A Majzub is usually a professed debauchee, and a successful beggar. He is a staunch free thinker, explains away the necessity of all such rites as ablution, prayer, fasting, and fighting for the faith. He believes not in the miracles of the Prophet, the resurrection of the dead, or the doctrine of a future state. When a man of education arrives at this point he resembles the Hukama, or metaphysicians, who think nothing so unfashionable as belief in the Koran. The religious fanatics usually hold the tenet of Wahdat el Wujud,[36] or the unity of existence (in kind),—utter Pantheism, as the very phrase denotes that God is all things and all things God.

The Sahib Irshad, or Master Sufi, may now, if considered sufficiently advanced in mysticism, be appointed a Khalifeh,[37] or be invested with the prophetic mantle of his Pir. He has reached the second order, and become Kamil,[38] or perfect (comparatively, not absolutely). The other steps are to be gained by the assiduity of devotion necessary to secure the favour of the Supreme Being. In addition to the regular prayers and Shughl, or preparatory practices, the Sahib Irshad has now to commence a system of meditations called Huzur, as they must be " present " with him at all times and fill his thoughts the whole day. The book from which I have borrowed part of the contents of these pages, gives a list of twenty Huzurs, some of them sufficiently curious, the others trivial and uninteresting in the extreme. It will be unnecessary to offer any more than a specimen, as every Murshid may compile his own list of profitable meditations.

The first Huzur is called Fana fi'l af'al: the meditater must suppose his entity to be that of a stone or clod of earth, every action of which proceeds from the One Actor. By contemplating this Spirit within him, the devotee now becomes "Maslub el af'al,[39] and may act in a way by no means permissible to the vulgar herd.

The second Huzur, undertaken after a thorough intelligence of the preceding one, is called "Fana fi's sifat." The nature of man is supposed to have seven accidents, viz., life, volition, power, learning, hearing, sight and speech; all of which must be merged into the Sifat, or accidents (of life, &c.,) attributed to the Almighty. By this means the Gnostic hopes eventually to attain a knowledge of the Zat, or entity of the godhead. At any rate, the Murshid arrives at the comfortable position of requiring none of these Sifat, or accidents, for his own use; as life and learning, however necessary to the crowd, cannot be required from one who has parted with them to the Deity.

The fifth Huzur is called "Fana fi'sh shaykh," or merging one's existence into that of some holy man. This is called Kufr i Hakiki "true or faithful infidelity," a contradiction signifying that such disbelief is so far laudable, that in its adoration of the creature, it worships the Creator that animates the creature. Here lies the true danger of Tasawwuf. The Shayk or Murshid is by it invested with power over the property, life, and soul of his follower: the respect paid to him is of an extraordinary nature, and even when in his tomb, his dominion has not ceased.[40] It is easy to see the vile use to which a clever and designing man may apply such a belief. The benefit of this meditation to the deluded meditater is supposed to be the increase of his love to the Deity, and consequently a rapid advance towards a higher grade of sanctity.

The ninth Huzur is a meditation upon the excellence of the five great Prophets, Adam, Noah, Moses, Jesus and Mohammed. Each has its own peculiar position in the body: to Moses, for instance, belongs the Nafsi place, and to Mohammed, as most dignified of all, the Akhfai, or brains. It must be recollected that most Moslems place Abraham next to their own Prophet, and consider that the former surpassed all others in excellence of Sifat: the latter in Zat.

The twelfth Huzur is called "Fana fi'r rasul," or absorption into the Prophet. By intense endeavours to picture in his mental eye the appearance of Mohammed, and by reflecting upon his dignity in creation, the devotee loses himself in the superior nature and acts and thinks as if he were the Prophet himself. Very few of course ever reach this dizzy height of dignity, and fewer would be so fond of martyrdom as to dare to claim it.

The twentieth and last Huzur enables the Gnostic to arrive at "Fana fi'llah," or absorption into the Deity. His soul is now so thoroughly purged of the alloy of matter, that nothing impedes his free contemplation of the Godhead, or prevents his recognising the Eternal Origin of all things. The Sufi is now justified in exclaiming,—

> "How high and how great is my degree (in creation)!
> There is nothing within my coat but God."

With the celebrated fanatic Mansur, he may indulge himself in asserting Ana'l Hakk ("I am God"), especially if equally ambitious of the crown of glory. It would be difficult to believe that men who are pious according to their creed, could ever justify to themselves such daring blasphemy, did we not know the effects of philology and philosophy upon the eastern mind, and the prevalence of certain forms of insanity[41] throughout Oriental nations.

The above may serve for specimens of the nature of a Sufi's meditations. To show how many of this order in Sindh have risen to the highest grades of sanctity, the following passages from the Tohfat el Tahirin[42] may be quoted.

Mohammed Aazam enumerates between seventy and eighty saints of the first magnitude, whose sepulchres grace the Mekli[43] hills, near Tattah. The latter city, it is said, contains the bodies of about a hundred devotees of minor importance; and their names only are given. The holy tenantry of the hills is treated with more ceremony; their lives and miracles are described with great care. The chief are,—

1. Sayyid Mohammed Hosayn, popularly called "Pir Murad," as by his aid the petitioner invariably obtained from Heaven his "Murad," or whatever he desired. This saint was originally the pupil of Shaykh Isa Langoti,[44] a very holy man, whose peculiar toilette gave him a surname. Pir Murad, immediately after birth, positively refused to open his eyes till the Shaykh appeared, and the latter owned that he was fated to become the child's Murshid and Murid. After the age of forty, our saint began to make such progress in sanctity, that he was compelled to wear a veil over his face, because any person that saw the light of

that countenance instantly became a Wali, or saint. Of the latter class he created about five hundred, and the number of his own pupils that rosé to distinction was at least two thousand. Shaykh Sadr el Din, the son and heir of the celebrated Multan devotee, popularly termed Bahawal Hakh,[45] determined upon a trial of skill with Pir Murad. With this object, the former sent from Multan a cup of milk, and a message to inform Pir Murad that Sindh was as full of his (the Skaykh's) religious dignity as the cup was of milk: The Pir saw that he had no common person to deal with, as the milk had travelled all the way from Multan to Tattah without turning sour or losing a drop. After some meditation, he drew forth from beneath his prayer-carpet a handful of flowers, and dropped them into the cup, as a sign that there was still room for him in Sindh, and sent to remind Shaykh Sadi that the descendants of Abubekr were expected to wait upon those of the Prophet. The flowers never faded till the messenger reached Multan, and the Shaykh, seeing that he had failed in the first point, arose, girt his loins, and went down to Tattah, there to settle the dispute personally by a trial of skill. The meeting of two such distinguished men was, as may be imagined, spirit-stirring and edifying in the extreme. After some conversation, they agreed to repair to the mosque and pray. On the road, Shaykh Sadr saw a dead cat and restored it to life by saying, "Kum b'izni 'llah,"—"Arise with the permission of God."[46] Pir Murad paid no attention to this feat; but when they arrived at the place of worship and found no Imam to recite the prayers, he sent a servant into the streets, to summon the first person he might meet. This, curious to say, was an old Brahmin, a veteran idolator, who, however, no sooner heard the words than he hurried into the Pir's presence, tore off his priestly thread, prayed and preached in most eloquent Arabic, explained the words "Bis millah" in fourteen different ways, to the intense delight of the congregation, and, in fine, became a most luminous Moslem. Shaykh Sadr had the candour to own that he had met with a better man than himself; and, after paying a long and interesting visit, returned to his own land.

The Sindhis are fond of quoting one of Pir Murad's sayings, that "it is better to restore one dead heart to eternal life, than life to a thousand dead bodies."

2. Sayyid Ali Shirazi; a disciple of Makhdum Nuh, under whose tuition he reached the high degree of "Baka Billah,"—"eternal life in God." In early youth he went on a pilgrimage to Medineh, where the people declared that he was too black to be a Sayyid.[47] He immediately went to the doorway of the Prophet's sepulchre, and exclaimed, "O my grandsire!" A voice from the tomb replied, "Here I am, my son!" to the great confusion of the listeners. This Sayyid was so devout, that he would continue a whole week in a state of ecstacy, without eating, drinking, or sleeping. His miracles were very numerous, and some of them sufficiently curious. On one occasion, a Tattah grandee built a magnificent mosque on the Mekli Hills, but refused to pay the

workmen, as the Mihrab, or arch, which ought to front Mecca, was about one cubit out of the line of direction. The poor people applied to the Sayyid, who, fortunately for them, was at that time praying, together with his Pir, in a neighbouring place of worship. The holy men arose, walked up to the mosque, and moved it bodily into the required position, each holding one end of the building. After this wonder Dives paid his workmen; the affair of course became public, and the mosque, which remains to this day, is proof positive of the fact.

The Sayyid was as stern as he was holy. One day, an ancient pair, whose united ages amounted to two hundred and ten years, came to him and begged that he would procure for them the blessing of children. The reply made, after due deliberation, was a promise of three boys, who appeared in the course of three years. But when the Sayyid sent to demand one of the children as a Murid, the ungrateful parents refused. Their unkindness so irritated the holy man, that he instantly prayed that the blessing of issue might be withdrawn from them. The consequence was, that all the boys died that very night of an intense and mysterious pain in the stomach.

Another anecdote related about the Sayyid[48] is this:—One of his servants, an alchemist and magician, observing his master's parsimonious way of living, taught him to permute the baser metals into gold. As, however, the holy man continued to live as poorly as ever, the servant reproached him for avarice. The Sayyid rejoined by sending him to the most ignoble locality in the house, where, wonderful to relate, cartloads of gold and precious stones were found piled up in heaps. The master did not fail to make use of the opportunity for instilling a moral lesson into the mind of his man, by enlarging upon the insignificance of an article which the wise and religious consider to be fit only for certain places.

3. Two brothers, who bear the unpromising names of "Miyan Mitho" and "Miyan Ratho."[49] They are so holy, that on the day of resurrection they will not only go to Paradise themselves, but also carry with them the portion of the hill where they are buried. This circumstance, as may be supposed, gives no small value to the ground in the eyes of those that purpose to be inhumed there.[50]

4. Kazi Mir Sayyid Shukr Ullah; a very holy man, and, curious to say, also a Kazi, or judge. The following proof of his courage and equity is still remembered in Sindh. When Shah Hasan Arghun, the then lord of the land, was complained against by a poor man, whom he had refused to pay, the Kazi summoned the prince, and made him, as defendant, stand by the side of the plaintiff before his judge, and there plead as a Moslem should. The cause was decided against the ruler. The Kazi then arose, saluted the Shah according to court ceremony, and placing him on the seat of justice, apologised for the apparent uncourteousness of his behaviour. The prince drew a sword from beneath his robe, and, showing it to his judge, declared that with that weapon he would have slain him as a punishment for his hypocrisy, had he not manifested himself a dealer out of equity. But the Kazi was not far behind the Shah, as he imme-

diately produced another sword from under the carpet of justice, and explained to the prince that he had resolved to cut him down had he in any way acted against the rules of his faith.

It is needless to add that after this pleasantly ferocious scene the prince exclaimed " happy the subjects that have such a judge to judge them !" and that he promoted the righteous Kazi to the highest honours of the state. Who does not recollect the story of Mohammed II., the great conqueror of Constantinople, and his architect ? The event is likely to have occurred in almost every country that possessed a law and a religion : at the same time it is only fair to observe that probably such events become historical only because they are very rare.

The Kazi, in his old age, retired from the law and became a great Wali. He was buried by the side of sundry other devotees, and after his death, has appeared to thousands of votaries in visions and in the flesh. The prayers of many poor people have been miraculously granted by the intercession of this distinguished saint.

5. Miyan Maluk Shah, a devotee of such temperance, sobriety, and, it is to be presumed, chastity, that during a long life he never touched aught but water, and only consumed 112 lbs. of flour. His great delight was to listen to the creaking of the water-wheels, and in this amusement he used to indulge, reckless of time or place. On one occasion, he was sitting under a tree in a garden near Tattah ; night came on, and the gardener loosed his bullock from the wheel and left the place. The water-wheel, however,

continued its gyrations, and, when the gardener returned in the morning, he found the whole place overflowed with water. Suspecting the stranger, he forcibly ejected him, but great was his astonishment to see that not only the tree, but also the part of the garden where the holy man had been sitting, began to follow his steps. The poor gardener, now aware of his mistake, fell at the feet of the holy listener to water-wheels, and promised never again to interfere with his pleasures.

Miyan Maluk Shah at times could do a kind thing. He once saw a Hindoo carrying a pot of buttermilk on his head, and instantly directed him to throw it upon the ground. The infidel obeyed, when, suddenly a black snake, in a state of venomous putridity, fell from the broken pot. Of course the Hindoo was converted to Islam.

To this saint belongs the honour of discovering the spot which had been visited by the Hasanain [51] on the Mekli Hills. A shepherd came to Miyan Maluk, and asked him how it was that the flock always passed a certain spot with holy awe, refusing to tread on or even to graze near it. The saint's mind was instantly illuminated, and he understood the reason of their peculiar conduct. He was afterwards favoured with several visions of learned devotees whose testimony was unanimous and convincing. He therefore marked out the spot with stones, Nawwab Saifullah Khan enclosed it with walls, Khudadad Khan Abbasi built a grand dome over it, and crowds of people visit it to this day. How many holy places throughout the world have no better foundation for their honours!

The reader will by this time be tired of the subject of sainthood. It may, however, be interesting to give a short description of the kind of miracles attributed the holy men of Sindh.

1. Causing the birth of children, especially in cases of barrenness and advanced age.

2. Curing complaints and diseases, such as impotence, madness, deafness, dumbness, blindness, ophthalmia, issue of blood, epilepsy (especially), lameness, wounds, the bites of serpents, &c. The disease usually selected is one popularly considered incurable, and the *modus medendi* is either by giving the patient a drop of water to drink, or passing the hand over the part affected. This fact may be interesting to the mesmerist.

3. Causing prayers to be granted; saving distressed mariners or wandering travellers when invoked by them; appearing in person at a distance in order to protect a friend against some unseen danger; stilling storms, especially when far off; changing female into male children; converting sinners and infidels to the true faith; turning man's heart by a look, thought or word; compelling inanimate objects to act as if they possessed life and volition; benefiting friends; destroying foes; exercising dominion over birds, beasts and fishes; making youth's beards to grow, and *vice versâ* restoring juvenility to worn out old men: raising the dead; putting to flight the fiend, summoning angels and spirits; causing trees to produce clarified butter and honey; refining sensual to spiritual love; knowing men's thoughts and plans; breaking through chains, fetters, doors and walls; living without food, drink or

sleep; causing a pot of water to support a whole caravan for several days without palpably diminishing, commuting the death of one person by procuring a substitute, and giving learning to fools.

As might be expected from a semibarbarous people, collateral or contemporary evidence is never sought for, therefore an immense superstructure of falsehood is built upon a slender foundation of truth. None but those that have sojourned amongst them can understand the facility with which the most ridiculous invention gains credence. The miraculous lie is, generally speaking, useful to many who exert all their efforts to adorn and promulgate it: those who know the truth are either sensible enough to keep silence, cunning enough to pretend to believe it, or weak enough to lose reputation and to be considered liars by opposing it. And so, after a generation or two, the miracle finds its way into a Persian book or becomes universally known to the people in the shape of a legend or tradition.

To the credit of the Sindhis it must be said that they do not refuse to admit the religious merits of the the softer sex. One of the holy personages buried on the Mekli Hills is a certain Bibi Fatimah, surnamed Hajiani, from her having performed the pilgrimage. She was a Hafizeh (*i. e.*, knew the Koran by heart), and when at the Holy Sepulchre, used to recite the whole of it once a day, giving the religious merit of the action to the soul of the Prophet. Her miracles were very numerous; the most celebrated one was stilling a storm which threatened destruction to the pilgrim ship in which she was returning home.

Many women in Sindh become Fakirani (religious

mendicants) Murids and Sufis. A few of them occasionally rise to the high rank of a Murshid. There is at present a lady named Nur Bai, the relict of one Rahimano Fakir, of the Jahejah clan, living on the banks of the Goonee river. Her progress in the Nakshbandi path has been such that she is termed a Mashaikh (teacher), and instructs a number of pupils of both sexes. She lives in great pomp, with no small show of respectability: there are, however, certain well authenticated scandalous reports concerning her morals and private habits. Every celebrated Murshid has about him a number of Fakirani, married and unmarried, Hindoos as well as Moslems. These women, especially the widows, wear green clothes, carry a large rosary, and are, generally speaking, remarkable for their disregard of decency and morality.

CHAPTER IX.

ACCOUNT OF THE DIFFERENT STRANGER TRIBES SETTLED IN SINDH: —THE SAYYIDS AND RELIGIOUS FAMILIES.—AFFGHANS OR PATHANS.—BELOCHIS.—JATS.—MEMANS.—KHWAJEHS.—MOHANA, OR FISHERMEN.—AFRICAN SLAVES.—SPECIMEN OF THE LANGUAGE SPOKEN BY THE LATTER.

Before commencing a regular account of the Sindhi, properly so called, and the Hindoos who have inhabited the province from time immemorial, it may be as well briefly to describe the several stranger tribes settled in the country. These are,—1. Sayyid; 2. Affghan; 3. Belochi; 4. Jat; 5. Meman; 6. Khwajeh; 7. Mohana; and 8. African slaves.

The two great families of Sayyids, viz., Hasani and Hosayni, are both numerous in Sindh. Individuals belonging to the latter class have the title of Pir,[1] as Pir Bhawan Shah. The Hosayni race is termed Sayyid, as Sayyid Jendal Shah. As is usual in our province, these two large bodies are subdivided into clans, called after their original place of residence, as Bokhari, Mathari, Shirazi, Lakhirai, Sakrulai, &c. Most of them are of the Shieh or Rafizi persuasion, and therefore they suffered severely during the various Affghan invasions. Many of these Sayyids are learned men, much respected by the commonalty, in spite of the discrepancy of belief. Under the Kalhora dynasty they became possessed of large landed estates, granted as Inam (or free gift) *in perpetuum*. When the Talpurs came into power the priesthood declined, as these rulers prided themselves chiefly upon their literary acquirements, and laid little or no claim to holy descent.[2]

In Sindh, a Sayyid seldom will allow his daughter to marry a Moslem who is not of the same lineage. Formerly no man, however rich or respectable, would have dared to address a maiden of the sacred stock; cases are quoted to show that individuals have been forced to leave the country for proposing to a Sayyid's widow, who was a common Muslimah. The consequence was, that many of the women were left unmarried, and old maids are not common in the East. The custom is now disappearing. Another peculiarity in Sindh is, that if either of the parents be a Sayyid, all the children must be called Sayyids.[3] It is, therefore, not uncommon to see African features among them, and thus their great number is easily accounted for.

The other religious families in Sindh are,—

1. Kurayshi, or Siddiki, descended from Abubekr. They are sufficiently numerous, and have the title of Makhdum, or master, as Makhdum Nuh Siddiki. Under the head Kurayshi (descended from the Koreish tribe), are included the Faruki family, that claims descent from Umar. Their name usually begins with Miyun ("master"), as Miyun Ibrahim Faruki.

2. Alawi, the posterity of Ali by any of his numerous wives, except Fatimah. They are all Shiehs, are not often met with, and bear the title of Khwajo, "Sir," *e. g.*, Khwajo Murad Ali.

3. Abbasi, the descendants of Abbas, very numerous in Sindh. They are called Mullo ("priest"), or Buzurg[4] (the "great"), *e. g.*, Buzurg Maaruf Abbasi.

The other families, such as the Hamzawi, Musawi, Razawi, Mahdawi, &c., &c., so common in different parts of the Moslem world, are here either unknown, too inconsiderable to merit any notice, or included under the above three heads.

The Affghans, or Pathans, are generally found about Hyderabad, and in the north of Sindh. Many of them have been settled in the country for some generations, and become possessed of considerable landed property. Some of the men are talented, and sufficiently educated to read, write, and speak four or five languages. In appearance they are a large and uncommonly handsome race of people, perfectly distinct from the common Sindhis, whom they regard as quite an inferior breed. The women are not inferior to the men in personal appearance, and display all the fondness for, and boldness in, carrying on intrigue that characterize them in their native land.

It is probable that many Affghans settled in Sindh after the celebrated invasion of this country by Sardar Madad Khan Nurzye, who was sent in A.D. 1781, by Taymur Shah to restore the Kalhoras after they were dethroned by the Talpurs. Madad, as he is commonly and disrespectfully termed by the Sindhis, behaved very cruelly; he laid waste the fertile tract about the Goonee river, by cutting down the trees and destroying the towns. Moreover, he either carried off the people into captivity, or tortured them in order to make them discover their treasures. For these acts he is cursed by bard and annalist as a robber and no soldier.

When the Kalhora rule first began, about A.D. 1740, the aristocracy of Sindh, which, as in most Oriental lands, was purely one of rank conferred by office, consisted either of Sindhis or of Jats. But Miyan Mir Mohammed, the first prince of that dynasty, made the fatal mistake of sending to the Belochi country, and inducing, by offers and promises of feofs and favour, two of his mountaineer Murids, Mirs Aludo and Masudo,[5] to emigrate from their barren hills, and settle in the low country. The entrance of the barbarians is thus described by the native annalists:—When the Belochis arrived within fifteen miles of Khudabad, the prince sent out several of his ministers and nobles, with presents of clothes and horses with gold saddles, to receive and escort his distinguished guests to the capital. As the procession advanced, it met a troop of beggarly shepherds, followed by their flocks, and women mounted on asses. The ministers enquired for Mir Aludo, and were much astonished when told that the ragged wayfarer with the Dheri in his hand and the Kambo[6] on his shoulders, was the personage whom they were sent to conduct with such ceremony. However, like true Orientals, they saluted him with due courtesy, took the Dheri and Kambo from him, mounted him upon the best horse, and accompanied him on his way to the capital.

After this first step, the Belochis began to flock into Sindh under their different chiefs and heads of clans, who receiving grants of land, settled and built towns on the Narrah River and other fertile parts of the country. About thirty-five years after the first entrance of the mountaineers, Miyan Sarfaraz Khan, the Kalhora prince caused the murder of Mir Bahram and his son Sobdar, the Talpur chiefs. The cause of the assassination was the ruler's fear of the valour and increasing power of his military vassals; but the deed was looked upon as an atrocious one, because it was done in public Darbar, in presence of the prince, who was also the Murshid of the murdered man.[7] Mir Bijjar, the son of Mir Bahram, on his return from pilgrimage, consulted a certain Fakir, Abd el Rahim, a Sindhi of the Mangariyo clan, and was greeted with a promise of success, provided he would never restore the Kalhora race to power. After a short campaign, Mir Bijjar succeeded in dethroning the tyrant, but unhappily for himself, he broke the condition of success. The popular story is, that when he went to visit Abd el Rahim, he found his spiritual adviser seated in the company of another Fakir, who immediately exclaimed,—

" Bijjara asá^{n} pári, to na pári :
Háne weyí to je ghará^{n} Sardári ! "

" O Bijjar we have—thou hast not—kept the promise ;
Now, indeed, hath the power departed from thy house ! "

The other Fakir, Abd el Rahim, also remarked, in supplement to this poetical address—

"Addá kí^{n} ma chúensi;
Indá Kúkaní petu phárí wendasí."

"Brother, say nothing to him,
The Kukami will come and rip open his stomach."

Mir Bijjar was shortly afterwards murdered by three men of the Kukani tribe, who had been sent by the Rajah of Joudpoor at the instigation of the Kalhora Prince. By his death the chieftainship came into the hands of his nephew, Mir Fath Ali Khan Talpur.

The Belochis thus rose to be lords paramount of Sindh, and so continued until the conquest of the country by the British. The native annalist, from whose pages the above extracts are made, appropriately enough remarks, "See the wonderful changes of that revolving heaven, which makes beggars of princes and princes of beggars!"

The Ethnology of Belochistan has been too accurately described by modern travellers to require much further elucidation. One point, however, deserves to be noticed. Pottinger and Postans seem determined to derive this people from the Jews: the former depends upon the similarity of customs, forgetting how much the Koran owed to the Law and the Prophets: the latter relies upon the unsatisfactory testimony of dress. The Belochis themselves claim descent from the Arabs, and assert that their original home was Haleb (Aleppo.[8]) The Burhan i Kati explains the words Kuch and Baluch to mean barbarous tribes, inhabiting the mountainous borders of Mekran, and originally descended from the Arabs of Hejaz. The author of the Tohfat el Kiram, probably in order to flatter the clan, traced its origin up to Mohammed bin Harun, a descendant from Mir Hamzah by a fairy. A popular tale derives the word Baloch from Bachh, "a son," and Luch, the name of a slave girl who became pregnant by Mohammed bin Harun. Native testimony, therefore, seems in favour of the Arabian descent of the Belochis, although observation detects one great objection, viz., that they have forgotten every word of their original language, and speak an ancient and apparently indigenous dialect of the Iranian class. The question is not of sufficient importance to deserve any further consideration.

When the Talpur succeeded the Kalhora dynasty, as before mentioned, they encouraged a multitude of their fellow countrymen to settle in the country by gifts of land, feofs and other privileges. The tenure of their Jagirs seems to have been a rude form of the feudal system. Every chief was expected to attend his prince in all his campaigns. No fixed number of retainers was laid down, but each head of a family considered it a point of honour to lead as many vassals as he could to the field. Thus the Belochi chiefs became under the Talpurs a military aristocracy, similar to that of the Normans after the conquest of England. The mutual jealousies of the Talpur Ameers tended to aggrandize the Belochi power, as each prince was compelled to attach as many brave adherents as possible to himself by a ruinous display of generosity.

But phases of society in Oriental lands are often wonderfully ephemeral. Sir Charles Napier, in less than six months, so altered the position of the Beloch clans, that, as their own prophecy warned them, their importance became nugatory. The measures which proved so eminently successful were the following:—

First. Disarming the population, or rather, forbidding men to go about armed. This order had two results: the first was to strike the minds of the natives with astonishment, as for generation after generation few ever dared to leave their houses without matchlock, sword and shield. The second and more important effect was that large armed bodies of men could not meet unobserved.

Second. The prompt notice and sudden punishment of all acts of violence, such as murder, highway robbery, and cutting down their wives. The abstract justice of hanging a Belochi for the latter offence may be questioned; its policy and advisability cannot.

Third. Weakening, diminishing, and eventually destroying the importance of the Sardars, Jagirdars and other feudal superiors by taking from them all power over their vassals. Thus the latter were taught to look up to Government as their ruler, and the former felt that his dominion had ceased.

The Belochi is far superior to the common Sindhi in appearance and morals. He is of fairer complexion, more robust frame and hardier constitution. He has his own ideas of honour, despises cowardice as much as any belted knight in the dark ages[9] and has no small portion of national pride and aristocratic feeling. At the same time he is violent, treacherous and revengeful, addicted to every description of debauchery,[10] dirty in person, rough and rude in manners. His amusements are chiefly drinking and field sports; he considers reclaiming a hawk or breaking a horse, a far nobler occupation than reading and writing: and would rather be able to cut a fat sheep in two with his sword than master all the science of Bagdad and Bokhara. The consequence is that there is scarcely a single learned Belochi in the country. Even the princes contented themselves with an imperfect knowledge of Persian, with writing books of poems composed for them, and sending westward[11] for works never to be perused. One of the chiefs of the Talpur family told me, in the true spirit of the middle ages, that he himself could not write, but that he never went about the country without a Moonshee or clerk who could.

The Belochi is not a bad soldier, as he is trained from his youth upwards to the use of weapons and to brave danger. He is a bold and strong, but by no means a skilful, swordsman, utterly ignorant of the thrust, relying upon the shield to parry the cut, and decidedly inferior to the Hindoo in sword playing. His only merit is that, like the Arabs, he has learned by practice to cut with considerable force, and to do the utmost damage with his heavy, well-tempered and trusty blade.[12] Under the native princes, the most armed were, of course, the most respectable part of the army. The offensive weapons were matchlocks, with long and very tolerable barrels made in the country, pistols (rare), swords, spears, javelins, daggers and straight poinards, of peculiar shape, called Katari. The bow was seldom used, as the Beloch wants that power of arm which made it so formidable in the hands of the Saxon, and enables it still to keep its place among the Affghans.[18] The heavy defensive armour invented in Europe during the chivalrous ages was never known to the Belochi chief, who fought with face, throat, arms and thighs quite unprotected. The head was defended by a Kangor, or steel cap lined with silk: over this a silk turban was twisted, and sometimes a Torho, or chain of small steel rings, was worn outside the turban. For the body they had the Zirah (coat of mail) tightly fitting, and extending down to the thighs. The best came from Khorasan and Persia, they are made of silver or steel annulets sometimes gilt and coloured; so that the appearance is brilliant in the extreme. Some of the Ameers used to wear instead of, or under the Zirah, a silk coat, called Chiltaho, made of foreign material, with numerous folds strongly fastened together. It was impenetrable to a sword cut, but was heavy and uncomfortable. To protect the hands they had Dastana, or short gauntlets, made of the same material as the Zirah; this was the more necessary, as the hilt of the sword offered no defence to the fingers. The shields were of different sizes and shapes according to the owner's taste, and were generally made of leather or rhinoceros hide.

The Ameers of Sindh, like most native sovereigns, had no regular army, nor were their forces regularly disciplined. What is much worse, of late years they were half drilled after the European fashion. Yet the Belochis generally, and especially the Murrees and wild tribes living towards the north, prefer their own plan of rushing on, in furious charge, probably more than half intoxicated, against the enemy, to the systematic advance of a regiment of Sepoys. Their plan has its merits, as has been proved in Arabia and Affghanistan, though of course it would fail when tried by and against large bodies of men.

The pay of the soldiery under the native rule is variously estimated by different authorities. The smallest sum paid to footmen was about three and a half Rupees per Mensem: some of the horsemen received the respectable salary of one Rupee a day. The Sardars, or officers, had fixed allowances proportioned to their rank; besides what they made by plundering in an enemy's, and forgetting to pay in their own, country. Military license was all but unchecked, and even between the different grades in the same army the want of discipline did away with respectfulness of behaviour though not with affection or devotion.

Connexions between the sexes are formed in three ways. The Belochi is allowed the usual number of wives (Zal or Joe); he can contract a kind of left-handed marriage with as many as four Sureth, or lawful concubines, and may have children by any number of female slaves (Bani or Goli). The latter must have been duly paid for, inherited or taken in warfare, provided that in this case they refuse to become Moslems. Polygamy is not common, except among the highest classes.[14] The wife is usually equal in rank to her husband, and claims the greatest respect: in fact, as much as would be found among any nation of Europeans. As with the ancient Greeks, the ἑταίρη, or, in her stead, the concubine and female slave are expected to divert their lords; the wife is generally speaking treated with ceremony and deference, rather than with affection or familiarity. The Belochi females, especially those of high rank, are believed to be fond of spirituous liquors.

Adultery and fornication were rare under the native rule; among the wealthy the greatest precautions were taken to secure the women, and the free use of the sabre kept the lower orders of females in the right path. When we conquered the country, and forbade the husband to take the law into his own hands, the women felt, to translate a native phrase, that "the sword was no longer tied to their trowser strings." The result was, that they freely indulged in all kinds of depravity. This first burst ceased, as might be expected, after a short period, and society gradually subsided into its normal state; the lock and bolt taking the place of the knife and sabre. Belochi women are rarely sufficiently well educated to be able to read any thing but a little Persian and Sindhi. Very few of them can write; and their time is chiefly taken up in spinning, making clothes, dressing, and other such occupations. They are fond of intrigue, but will not risk so much for it as the Persians and Affghans; at the same time they display more boldness than the Sindhi or Hindoo women. Females of the upper classes are rather formal and serious than otherwise; contrasted with the laughing and jest-loving dames of India, they appear very grave. The use of poison is all but unknown to them, and suicide is extremely rare. Many of the widows refuse to marry again; some from bad motives, others with the idea that it would be indecent to pass into the arms of a second husband. I heard of one man who offered his sister the choice of another spouse, or to live at home in perpetual Rozo (fast[15]); she chose the latter alternative. Some women, aspiring to the rank of Zahid (devotees), refuse to marry, and condemn themselves to a life of celibacy. Such instances, however, are rare. The Belochi females are good mothers, and particularly attentive to their religious duties; even the difficulties and dangers of a pilgrimage to Mecca do not deter them from attempting it.

The Belochis are in the habit of putting to death their female children[16] by concubines and unmarried girls, either by means of opium or drowning in milk.[17] Abortives were sometimes given, but, as usual, with very doubtful success. These practices, however, chiefly prevailed among the highest classes, who imitated their rulers, and considered the murder a point of honour: at the same time they were aware of the enormity of the action in a religious point of view. Under our rule female infanticide has diminished, but by no means ceased. The Beloch seldom feels towards his daughter as he would towards a son: in most Oriental countries female children are considered nothing but incumbrances and the unsettled state of society renders their position precarious. What is commonly called "natural affection," appears to be the growth of habit, strengthened by duty, gratitude and inclination. The philoprogenitiveness of philosophical Europe is a strange idea, as well as term, to the Nair[18] of Malabar, who learns with his earliest mind that his uncle is a nearer relation to him than his father, and consequently loves his nephew much more than his son.

The passion of the Belochis for war and hunting made them attach great value to their horses, camels, and hawks. As in Arabia, the mare is preferred to the stallion; she becomes an inmate of the family among the poorer classes, and most men would rather go without a meal themselves, than let the favourite animal want it. The chief breeds are those belonging to the Gehrai Sayyids, and the Khosa, Karmati, Mari (Murree), and Nizamani clans.[19] The price of a good mare in the hills was formerly about 400 Rupees; at present, half, or even a quarter of that sum, would be sufficient. After forty days, the foal is taken from its mother and fed with camel's, goat's, or cow's milk; the former being preferred, as it is supposed to produce greater powers of endurance. Buffalo's milk is avoided, from the idea that it causes the horse to lie down when passing through water. Training is commenced before the first year, and in six months the colt is taught to walk, amble, canter and gallop. The Belochis are fond of ringing their horses, teaching them to turn quickly, stop suddenly, prance when required, to fall down on the ground, and other arts of the Oriental *manége*. Drugs are seldom given, and the simples required for horses and hawks are rather those that are learned by experience, custom, or tradition, than culled from the pages of the Faras-Nameh and Baz-Nameh.[20] As in forays a man's life often depends upon the speed and bottom of his mare, great care is taken to prepare her for the expedition. For many days before the start she is fed with grain, boiled sheep's head and other flesh, clarified butter, and raw sugar; as little water and green meat as possible are allowed.

The exercise taken is rather long than violent, and the sweatings frequent but not excessive. Their system of training is a very successful one, and the animals are brought into an excellent condition of flesh and wind.

The clannish feeling among the Belochis was as strong as might be expected from a semi-barbarous nation of mountaineers, imbued with feudal prejudices. Except the Talpurs, no family refused to marry a daughter to an eligible suitor, because he belonged to another clan; all, however, preferred not doing so. The clansmen paid Sar Shumari (head money) to the chief annually, besides making presents on certain occasions, such as a birth, marriage, or death in the family.

In the Appendix will be found a list of the principal clans of hill people settled in the plains.

The Jat,[21] or, as others write the word, Jath, Juth, or Jutt, was, in the time of the Kalhoras, one of the ruling classes in Sindh. It was probably for this reason that the author of the Tohfat el Kiram made them of kindred origin with the Belochis, who now repudiate such an idea with disdain. The Jat's account of his own descent, gives to Ukail, the companion of the Prophet, the honour of being his progenitor. But what class of Moslem people, however vile, do not claim some equally high origin? As Jatki, the dialect peculiar to the people, proves, they must have come from the Panjab,[22] and the other districts, as Ubho (or Baladasht), Jangh Siyal, Multan, &c., dependent upon the great Country of the Five Rivers. Driven by war or famine from their own lands, they migrated southwards to Sebee and the hills around it. They are supposed to have entered Sindh a little before the accession of the Kalhora princes, and shortly afterwards to have risen to distinction by their superior courage and personal strength. At present they have lost all that distinguished them, and of their multitude of Jagirdars, Zemindars, and Sardars, now not a single descendant possesses anything like wealth or rank. Their principal settlements are in the provinces of Kakralo, Jati, Chediyo, Maniyar, Phulajee, and Johi. They are generally agriculturists or breeders of camels, and appear to be a quiet inoffensive race of people. In the eastern parts of Central Asia, the name Jat[23] is synonymous with thief and scoundrel.

The Sindhi Jats have many different Kaums or clans; the principal of which are the following:—Babbur, Bhati, Jiskani, Joya, Kalaru, Magasi, Mir-jat, Parhiyar, Sanjarani, Siyal, and Solangi.

The term Meman, a corruption of the Arabic word "Mumin" (a true believer), was probably given to the people that go by the name now, when they were converted from Hinduism to Islam. The word, in its fullest signification, is applied to two distinct races of people; in the first place, to the Khwajeh tribe, of whom an account is given below; secondly, the Meman Sayyat (*i. e.*, "green," from the Sindhi Sawo), or Achhra (white),[24] who are followers of Abu Hanifeh.

Many Memans are found settled in Sindh, especially about Hyderabad, Sehwan and Kurrachee. Cutch is probably their original country, as large numbers of them are still found there. In our province they are employed chiefly in agriculture and breeding camels. Their dress is that of the common Sindhi, except that they frequently shave the head, especially when old, and wear the turban; sometimes, though rarely, they adopt the peculiar Sindh hat. They have produced many very learned men, and have done much to introduce the religious sciences into this country.[25] The tribe merits some notice, as it has either abandoned or never adopted the practice common among their brethren in Bombay, viz., that of depriving the females of their pecuniary rights in wills and inheritances. Among the Memans, the widow and daughter are provided for according to the Koranic law. Their Pirs, or holy men, are the family called Rashid Shahi (descended from one Mohammed Rashid Shah), or the Rohri-wara Sayyids; remarkable for nothing but excessive polygamy. Rashid, the founder of the house, took unto himself thirty-two wives (instead of four), and justified the practice by the usual sophistical arguments of the Sufi order to which he belonged. The Sindhi divines pronounced his tenets to be heretical, and his conduct damnable. The Memans, however, did not object to it, and still reverence his descendants.

Altogether the Memans must be considered a respectable race; though, like the Jews, they have acquired a bad name by their rapacity in dealing with strangers, and "Wadho Meman" (a great Meman), in Sindhi means a miserly usurer.

The Khwajeh[26] (or, as the word is generally pronounced, Khwajo and Khojo), is a small tribe of strangers settled in Sindh, principally at Kurrachee, where there may be about three hundred families. Their own account of their origin is, that they emigrated from Persia.[27] Probably they fled the country when the Ismailiyeh heresy (to which they still cleave) was so severely treated by Holaku Khan. They differ from the Ismailites in one essential point, viz., whereas that race believes in only seven Imams, the Khwajehs continue the line down to the present day. They are, therefore, heterodox Shiehs, as they reject Abubakr, Umar and Usman, and reverence Ali, Hasan, Hosayn, Zain-el-Abiden, Mohammed-i-Bakir and Imam-Giafar-i-Sadik. In Sindh they have no mosques, but worship in a Kano, or house prepared for the purpose. For marriages and funerals they go to the Sunni Kazis; but their Mukhi, or head priest at Kurrachee, settles all their religious and civil disputes. Under the Mukhi, who is changed periodically, are several officers called Waris, and under these again are others termed Khamriya. Their present Imam (chief), Agha Khan, for years a pensioner of the British Government in India, has done much to injure the tribe by his rapacity and ill-judged extortion. The Mukhis are ordered to keep a most rigid account of each individual's profits every month, and to deduct one-eighth as the regular income tax. Without reckoning the numerous fees which the reverend rebel[28] claims on every possible occasion, he probably receives no less than one lac of Rupees from the unfortunate Khwajehs of Sindh. His success amongst the same tribe in Bombay[29] and other parts of India, was by no means great, as the people observed his too great predilection for drinking and intriguing with their females.

The Sindhi Khwajeh is rarely a well-educated man. In this point he is, generally speaking, inferior to his brethren settled in India and Muscat. In our province they have progressed just sufficiently to invent a character for themselves, and to write out the Koran in it. They are fond of the Marsiya, or elegiac poetry on the subject of Hasan and Hosayn's martyrdom; such compositions are common among them, and the nature of the theme interests their feelings strongly. Their prayers are similar to those of the Shiehs. They also use the Tikhi, or bit of Karbala clay, during their devotions, and make rosaries of the same material.

The Khwajeh wears either the Sindhi hat, or a turban; he always shaves his head, leaving a Zulf, or side lock, on each temple. Both sexes wear red or white clothes, avoiding dark blue, the common colour of the country. The rest of the dress resembles that of the Sindhis in general. All allow the beard to grow long, and young men do not trim the mustachios according to the Sunnat.

The Khwajehs are termed Tundo[30] by the Sunni caste; the name is considered to be an insulting allusion to their bad habits of abusing the memories of the Caliphs. The former refuse to eat food with the latter, and the Sunni, if a religious man, would always suspect that a dish offered to him by one of these heretics contained some impurity. It is certain that the Khwajehs have occasionally gone so far as to defile the Sunni mosques and places of worship; they cannot, therefore, complain of the bad reputation given to them, even though some exaggeration may enter into it. For instance, the many tales of debauchery told about the meetings of the Khwajehs at the annual fair of their patron saint in Sindh, Taj Din Turel, are probably founded on fact, but few would credit the scandalous scenes said to take place there, as such practices would be at least as repugnant to the principle of the Shiehs as to those of the Sunnis. Yet so it is with most faiths in dealing with those of different opinions. And the more minute the heretical differences are, the more violent is the display of hate and malice.

The Mohana, or fisherman caste, appear to be a tribe of converted Hindoos: their own account of their origin, however, is as follows:—When Sulayman, the son of David, was amusing himself by ballooning[31] over Cashmir, he saw a horrible looking woman, and, although the wisest of human beings, was puzzled to conceive what manner of man it could be that would marry her. Some time afterwards, the Prophet King lost his magic ring by the wiles of Sakhar the demon, who ascended his throne, seized the palace and drove out its lawful owner. Sulayman, impelled by destiny, wandered to Cashmir, and there became tho husband of that "grimme ladye." Her dowry was every second fish caught by her father, who happened to be a fisherman. As usual in such tales, the demon soon lost the ring, and it was found in the stomach of one of the fishes. Thus Sulayman recovered his kingdom. His wife, who remained behind in a state of pregnancy, had a son, who became the sire of the Mohana.

The Mohana do not look like Sindhis. Their features are peculiar and the complexion very dark: some of the women are handsome when young, but hardship, exposure to the air, and other causes, soon deprive them of their charms. They are to be found chiefly about the lakes of Manchar, Maniyar and Kinjur. At the latter of these places are some ruins of a palace built by Jam Tamachi, one of the rulers of Sindh, who married Nuren, the beautiful daughter of a fisherman. The event is celebrated in the legends of the country, and Shah Bhetai, the poet, has given it a Sindhi immortality in one of his Sufi effusions. The Mohana are by no means a moral people. Their language is gross in the extreme, and chastity seems to be unknown to them. The men are hardy and industrious, but incurably addicted to bhang, opium, and all kinds of intoxication. Probably, their comfortless[32] and precarious life, half of which is spent in or on the water, drives them to debauchery. They are admirable swimmers, as might be expected: the children begin that exercise almost as soon as they can walk. The Mohana, though depraved, are by no means irreligious. They keep up regular mosques and places of worship, with Pirs, Mullas, and all the appurtenances of devotion. The river Indus is adored by them under the name of Khwajeh Khizr, and is periodically propitiated by a cast offering of rice, in earthen pots covered with red cloth.

There are many different clans among the Mohana race. Their caste disputes are settled by the head men, who are called "Changa Mursa," and invested with full powers to administer justice to those who consult them.

The African slaves in Sindh were of two kinds; the Ghara-jao, or serf born in the house, and those imported from Muscat, and other harbours on the eastern coast of Arabia.[33] The former were treated as inmates of the family; prædial, or rustic labour was not compulsory in Sindh, as in India, where great numbers were attached to the soil, so as to be sold or inherited with it. Hence it was, that when emancipation came, the boon was to them a real evil.[34] Under the Ameers from six to seven hundred Zangibari, Bambasi, Habshi (Abyssinian), and other blacks were annually imported from Africa: of late years the traffic has all but entirely ceased. Their value was from forty to one hundred and fifty rupees; girls were more valuable than boys, and were imported in greater numbers. Abyssinians, especially the females, sometimes fetched as much as £40 or £50. According to their own account they were generally sold when children to merchants for grain, cloth, and other necessaries: kidnapping was common, and not a few had been made captives and disposed of by the Sawahili to the traders that frequented their coast. The greatest number came from a district called Kitomondo, adjoining the Sawahil country: the chief towns they mention are Lamo, Baramaji and Kinkwhere. They describe the country as peopled by Moslems,[35] and a few idolators, and talk largely of their forts, chiefs and armies. The following is a list of the principal tribes of Sidi (as the African black is generally called in this part of the world) found in Sindh:—

Dengereko.	Murima.
Dondere.	Murima-phani.
Gindo.	Muwhere.
Kamang.	Myas.
Makonde.	Myasenda.
Makua.	Mzigra.
Matumbi.	Nizizimiza.
Mkami.	Nyamuezi.
Msagar.	Temaluye.
Mudoe.	Zalama.
Mukodongo.	Zinzigari.

The African slaves were, generally speaking, employed as horse-keepers, grass cutters, day labourers, and apprentices to the different trades, as carpenters, blacksmiths, and others. They received an allowance of food and clothes, but were seldom allowed to eat with their masters. In some cases they rose to distinction, and, as confidential servants of the princes, exercised no small authority over their inferiors. Of this class was the Sidi Hosh Mohammed, the favourite attendant of the Ameer Sher Mohammed: a celebrated historian has suspected, though I could never discover any relationship between him and Marshal Hoche. The African blacks usually married females of their own race: in large families they were not permitted to connect themselves with the property of another master. Their children were of course slaves, and manumission appears to have been rare, except from religious motives. Many Sindhi Moslems used to marry Sidiyani or female Africans: the off-spring of such unions is admired by natives in general, but to European eyes possesses few attractions. The half-caste is called by the Sindhis "Gaddo," and the quadroon "Kambrani."

The Africans now in Sindh are ignorant and illiterate to the last degree. In disposition they are at once cheerful and surly, merry and passionate: the natives declare that they are as revengeful as camels, and subject to fits of sulkiness so intense, that nothing but the most violent corporeal punishment will cure them. Their pugnacity is such that under the native rulers few Fridays passed without the sword being used by the slaves of one trade against those of another, and their great strength of body and endurance of punishment rendered them the terror of the peaceful inhabitants. Brave and remorseless, they are also the most daring and treacherous of villains: nothing, in fact, except the certainty of death can deter them from robbery and bloodshed.

This character well agrees with that given to them throughout central Asia, where, as inmates of families, their dispositions are well known. At the same time they are capable of affection and gratitude, and when in good humour appear to great advantage. Their fondness for sensual pleasures is remarkable, and so susceptible of the tender passion are they, that deliberate suicide is by no means uncommon among them. Their great delights are eating, drinking, music and dancing. The two latter exercises are usually combined, and present a most grotesque appearance. The males and females are either mixed together, or placed in two bodies opposite each other. The dance is a monotonous one at first, the ladies merely advance and retire, performing occasional pirouettes: the males look on and admire till it becomes their turn to amuse the assembly with jumping and distortions of the limbs. At last, excited by the furious music of the kettle-drums, with the singing and the peculiar cry[36] uttered by the females, the slaves, who are seldom found in a state of complete sobriety, become almost demented. On several occasions I have seen them dance so long and so violently that more than one performer has been carried off quite insensible. At a well known place of pilgrimage near Kurrachee, called Magar-Pir, their dances are more ceremonious and systematic: they are performed under a tamarind or other tree, to which a preliminary offering of incense is made. It is impossible to say too little for the charms of the female slaves: among several thousands it would be difficult to select a tolerable face. Notwithstanding this, many of them did, and some still do, make their living by prostitution.

Most of the African slaves in Sindh are ignorant of their native languages; many of them having been born in the country have picked up only a few words of them from their parents, and those that were imported when young have had time to forget their mother tongue. Besides, the dialects found among them are seldom if ever written,[37] consequently there is no standard of language. Generally however they can discourse with each other in a tongue unintelligible to the other natives of the country, by using their own names of things and supplying Sindhi words for those which they have forgotten.[38] Some of their peculiar expressions, "Kuttumba," for instance, are common enough to be known to all the people around them.

CHAPTER XI.

CEREMONIES OBSERVED BY SINDHIS AT THE BIRTH OF INFANTS. —AKIKO, OR SHAVING THE BOY'S HEAD.—CIRCUMCISION.—BETROTHAL AND OTHER CEREMONIES PRELIMINARY TO MARRIAGE. —THE NUPTIAL RITES.—DEATH AND BURIAL.—TOMBS AND GRAVEYARDS.

WHENEVER a child is born, whether it be a boy or a girl, rejoicings take place in the family proportionably to its means. On the night after the birth, the mother's female relations assemble together, and, carrying a certain quantity of milk with them, pay her a visit. These calls are repeated for a succession of six days; the usual extent of refreshment offered to the guests, being milk, sweetmeats and tobacco. A Mulla, or priest, is then summoned, and, after much ceremony and some trifling presents, a name for the child is taken either from religious works, or decided upon according to the rules of judicial astrology. The wilder Sindhis of the hills are in the habit of calling their children by the names of plants and fruits, as Kando (thorn) and Ambu (Mango).[1] Among the higher classes the date of each child's birth is registered in a book kept for the purpose. None of them, however, practice the celebrating of birthdays as is done in Europe.

The ceremony of Akiko,[2] or shaving the hair (of male children only), takes place when the boy is between three months and one year old. The principal part of the festivity is the sacrifice of a sheep without blemish, which must be slain according to the usual rules. They then remove the flesh from the bones, carefully observing that none of the latter are broken, and with the former prepare a feast for the Olema, relations and mendicants, When the child's hair has been shaved by a barber, it is placed, together with the sheep's bones, in the animal's skin, and buried either in a Mukam (burial ground) or at the threshold of the door. The popular idea is, that on the day of resurrection the contents of the skin will arise in the shape of a horse, and triumphantly carry the child over the bridge of El Sirat into Paradise.

At the age of four years and four months the boy is sent for the first time to school. On this occasion presents are given to the pedagogue, but no great rejoicings take place.

The ceremony of Sathri, or Toharu (circumcision) is generally performed when the boy is in his eighth year. A feast of rice, flesh, and other dainties is prepared for the company; musicians are summoned, and fireworks are kept in readiness. The patient, dressed in saffron-coloured clothes, and adorned with Sihra (a kind of paper or flower garland), is mounted on horseback, and led round the town to the sound of instruments, singing and firing of guns. When he returns home the barber performs the operation in the same way as it is done in India: but not nearly so skilfully. Clarified butter, wax and the leaves of the Neem tree, are used as a dressing to the wound, which is expected to heal in eight or ten days: sometimes however the case is a very tedious one.[3] Immediately after the operation, clothes and money are waved round the boy's head and given to the barber and the minstrels who are present. When the patient recovers, his feet are washed in public, and a small present of money is made to the operator, food is distributed to beggars, and other acts of liberality are customary. The poor, who are unable to afford such expenses, merely pay a few pice to the barber for performing the rite. Female circumcision is not practised in Sindh.

The ceremony of betrothal generally takes place when the recognised signs of puberty appear, that is to say, in the fifteenth year of males, and the twelfth of females. Early matches are fashionable among the wealthy and proud: want of means, secret attachments, and family objections often compel respectable people of the middle classes to wait till the age of twenty or thirty before performing the rite which their religion renders obligatory. It is a general rule to marry a girl as soon as possible: the reason of the custom is palpable. Betrothal is only a preparatory measure to marriage: and some time ought to elapse between the two ceremonies. The former has become by Rasm,[4] or practice, not by faith, a necessary preliminary to the latter: none who can afford it would endeavour to dispense with it, even though the expenditure entailed thereby would compel them to wait for years before they could collect the means to conclude the affair. The popular idea is that to marry at an expense below one's station in life is a sign of a miserly and low disposition: the consequence is, that even rigid Moslems will not object to contract a debt for so laudable a purpose as good repute. It may be observed that such extravagance is only permitted in the first nuptials: less ceremony is observed in marrying a second time, or when the female is a widow. Some authors [5] condemn this custom as a waste of money: it appears, however, to have been established with the object of impressing upon the public mind the religious importance of the first marriage, and to throw some obstacles in the way of polygamy. After betrothal, the prudent parents do all they can to prevent the parties meeting: both, however, are permitted to visit one another's relations of the same sex. Among the upper classes any *prægustatio matrimonii* is considered disgraceful: it is not however difficult, here as elsewhere, to persuade the betrothed female to grant favours which, under any other circumstances, she would refuse: consequently accidents are not of rare occurrence. It is the same in Affghanistan, and other parts of Central Asia, where the mother of the betrothed not unfrequently connives at what is called Namzad-bazi, or visiting the future bride, unknown to the father. The word, however, does not imply any scandalous occurrence, and of course where the use of the sabre is so unrestrained the danger is diminished. In Sindh the lower classes, such as the Mohana and others, think they have a right to intrigue with their future brides: some of them will go so far as to consider the mother-in-law a substitute for her daughter until the latter is of an age to be married.[6]

The ceremony of betrothal, called Namzadagi, in the Persian, and Manganun or Pothi in the Sindhi language is performed as follows. A lucky day is selected for the purpose: the best being any Monday, Wednesday, Thursday or Friday in the months of Ramazan, Rabi el Akhar, Rajab and Shaaban. A Wakil, male or female "go-between," duly selected for the purpose, is sent to the girl's relations. After some preliminaries he pays a visit to the family, and with much cajolery and a hundred promises, all worth their weight of wind, discloses what his object is. Fashion compels the young lady's friends to refuse him at the first time of asking, as it would be "vulgar" in the extreme to accept at once. Thus the first visit terminates abruptly. About a month afterwards the same Mercury is again dispatched, and he goes through the same forms. This time the relations, if they dislike the match, return a direct and explicit refusal: in the other case their answer would be an ambiguous one. A favourite formula is "If God pleases, we cannot escape our destiny; we have, however, no present intention of giving away our daughter." When any such signs of encouragement are visible, the parents and friends of the boy begin a course of visits to those of the girl: the same are duly returned, and this is considered the proper time to observe the habits, manners, and education of the young people, as well as to ascertain the wealth and respectability of the families. The individuals most concerned are not, however, allowed to see each other, although aware of what is going on. This peculiarity is remedied by the extreme minuteness of the descriptions, the caution of the parents and probably the total unconcern of the future couple. For some weeks the same kind of proceeding is kept up: all manner of politeness is forced upon the seniors: the juniors are beaten, if necessary, into their best behaviour: the neighbours are bribed by the hope of a marriage festival to be eloquent in their praises of both parties; and a vast quantity of little cunning is expended in divers ways. At last, if there should have been no reason to retreat (which is still permitted), the boy's relatives, with much ceremony, propose an auspicious day for the betrothal. If accepted, at the appointed time they repair in force to the lady's house with a present of clothes, generally speaking a Rida (veil), Cholo (boddice), and Suthan (pantaloons), a little henna, five or six rupees worth of sweetmeats, and a few ornaments, such as Har (necklace), a Var and a Khirol (different kinds of rings).[7] They find the house duly prepared, and divide into the two parties: the males sit chatting with the men, and the females, accompanied by a Hajaman (barber's wife), carrying the presents, repair to the inner apartments. The future bride is then dressed in the clothes and ornaments, henna is placed upon her hands, and she is seated in a conspicuous part of the room, whilst her mother sends back the barber's wife to the mens' assembly with a large pot of milk directed to the father of the bridegroom. This the Hajaman presents to the males, and compels them to drink with many compliments and congratulations: they then discuss a portion of the sweetmeats provided for the occasion; and send what is left into the womens' apartments. All the males then raise their hands and recite the Fatihah: after this the girl's father is asked to appoint some time for the marriage. He does so, naming the month and day, upon which all parties rise up and leave the house. When arrived at this part of the proceeding, it is considered improper to break off the match: an opinion founded on custom, not on religious reasons. The father of the boy may retire under certain circumstances; the other parent never, unless he would have every minstrel sing of him—

> "Ahíráno akul muráin wiyo,
> Mangáe hekro paranáe biyo!"

> "The low fellow's intellects are quite offuscated,
> He betrothes (his daughter) to one man, and marries her to another!"

An anecdote is related by the Sindhis, which illustrates the extent to which this point of honour is carried. A woman of the Abra clan was nursing her daughter, and singing the following lullaby to her:—

> "Monjí dhija kanna lammá,
> Tenh khe sonꟹ wijhandá Sammá."

> "My girl hath long ears,[8]
> The Samma (clan) will put gold into them!"

When the child arrived at the age of puberty, the mother exhorted the father to marry her as usual to one of her own race. The Abra, however, refused to do so, and reminding his wife of the words of her song, gave his daughter to a Samma, lest the promise of the parent should be broken.

The above is a short account of the betrothal, as usually performed by the middle classes. The exact programme of the ceremonies depends of course upon the means of the parties; the very rich do all they can to squander money by keeping open house with feasting, dancing, singing and largesse to the poor for a period of from seven to fourteen days. The lower classes are compelled to rejoice as cheaply as possible, by substituting dates for sweetmeats, silver for gold ornaments, and cotton for silk clothes.

Between the periods of betrothal and marriage, the bridegroom's parents and relatives on all great occasions, take or send as a present to the bride, a little money and sweetmeats, together with a dress or two. About a month before the marriage day, the ceremony called Wana Wihanu is performed. The family of the Ghot (bridegroom) repairs to the house of the Kunwar (bride) with some sweetmeats, clarified butter, perfumed oil, henna, and an Akhiyo, or small circular piece of embroidered cloth used as a veil;—no one, not even a female, being permitted to see the girl's face at this particular period. The unfortunate bride is invested with the Akhiyo, and committed to prison, as it were, for the whole time that elapses between the Wana Wihanu and the actual nuptials. Her person is now prepared for the important event; she is fed with a kind of bread called Churo, made up with the sweetmeats and the clarified butter sent by the bridegroom; its effect is supposed to be an increased delicacy of skin and complexion. The barber's wife attends every day to bathe and wash her with Pithi (a succedaneum for soap, composed of sweet oil and flour of wheat or Mash, the *Phaseolus radiatus*), and the hair of the body is removed by depilatories[9] and vellication. All the different arts of the toilette, such as staining the hands, feet, and hair with henna, dyeing the lips with Musag (walnut bark), the cheeks with Surkhi (a preparation of lac, corresponding with our rouge), and the eyes with Kajjal, or lamp-black,[10] are now tried as experiments. The locks, parted in front, and allowed to hang down behind in one or two plaits, are perfumed with oils,[11] and carefully braided to see that the back hair is all of the same length; the front part is trained to lie flat upon the forehead by applications of gum and water,[12] and the Namak, or brilliancy of the complexion, is heightened by powdered silver-leaf or talc, applied with a pledget of cotton to the cheeks and the parts about the eyes. At times sandal-wood and rose-water are rubbed upon the head and body, after the former has been thoroughly combed and washed with the clay called Metu and lime juice. The young beginner is instructed in the science of handling a bit of musk enclosed in embroidered cloth, and Tira, or moles, are drawn upon her face and lips with needles dipped in antimony and other colouring matters. The Missi, or copper powder, so much used in India with the idea that it strengthens the teeth and relieves their whiteness, is seldom applied in Sindh by modest women. These experiments and preparations continue for many days;[13] and, during the whole period, visitors flock to the house and are feasted by the father of the bride.

The bridegroom has not so much to go through; three days are considered sufficient to clean him with Pithi, dress him in rich clothes with garlands and flowers, and show him to the public at Maulud (commemorations of the Prophet's nativity), Nautches, and feasts given to the relations and friends of the family. Properly speaking, the Wana Wihanu is part of the nuptial ceremony, for on the third day of the bridegroom's preparation the marriage rite commences.

The Wihan, or Shadi (marriage ceremony), is usually performed at night. Early in the evening the barber repairs to the Ghot's house, strips, bathes and dresses him in a turban, shirt, waistband, shawl, trowsers, and a pair of slippers sent by the bride's relations. At the same time, the Kunwar is decked out by the barber's wife in a suit of clothes, together with various kinds of jewels,[14] procured for her by her future spouse's family. After the toilette, the expiatory ceremony called Ghora is performed, by waving or throwing money over the heads of both parties. The cast-off clothes are the perquisites of the Hajjam (barber) and his wife. As great attention is paid to the dressing, it is seldom concluded before midnight. About that hour the Kunwar's father sends to inform the Ghot that the bride is ready, and repairs to the house of his son-in-law, where he finds a large gathering of relations, a Mulla, and other persons necessary for the performance of the rite. The priest, seated between the bridegroom and the bride's father, selects two legal witnesses and sends them to the Kunwar's house that she may appoint a Wakil[15] or agent. This occasions much delay, as etiquette forbids the lady to show herself, and prescribes as much nonchalance and coquetry as possible, in token of modesty and propriety of demeanour. At length some near relation, generally the father, is named for the task, and the witnesses return and inform the assembly that one of them is duly nominated to act as Wakil. The Mulla then addresses the Wakil in this set form of words: "Dost thou, A. B., agree to give thy daughter, C. D., the granddaughter of E. F. to this man, G. H., the son of I. J., and grandson of K. L.?" The other replies in the affirmative, using the same expressions. This is done three times in succession. The priest then says to the bridegroom, "Art thou, G. H., willing to marry C. D., the granddaughter of E. F.?" After this question has thrice been asked and answered, the Ghot proceeds to the Mahr or settlements, which must be made according to the Moslem law. The sum of money to be paid is specified in the presence of legal witnesses; it is also decided whether the presents of jewellery[16] made before marriage are to be the property of the husband or the wife in case of separation or divorce. When such matters, which are numerous and minute, have been duly settled, the Mulla recites the common prayer called "Allahumma Inni," the whole assembly repeating the words after him; this is followed by a long address to Heaven, invoking its blessing upon the young couple, and quoting the names of such prophets as Adam and Hawwa (Eve), Ibrahim and

Sara, &c., &c., who rendered the state of matrimony so peculiarly respectable. Next comes another portion of the Khutbo (sermon or address), explaining the excellence of marriage, and its rank as a holy rite among the Faithful. All present then recite the Fatihah with raised hands. This concludes the religious portion of the ceremony. The priest now congratulates the bridegroom in set phrase, and each member of the assembly does the same in his turn; the bridegroom replying "Salamat." Presents are made to the Mulla, as a reward for his exertions, by the Ghot's father; their value of course depends upon the wealth of the family; the nobles bestow horses, camels, gold-hilted swords, and other such expensive articles; the middle classes offer a few Rupees and some handfuls of dates or sweetmeats, whilst the lower orders give merely a few Pice. The father of the bridegroom must now distribute presents of confitures or dress to each man present according to the guest's rank.

At about two A.M., the bridegroom, accompanied by his relations and friends, proceeds to perform the ceremony of Sargasu,[17] or the nocturnal procession. Riding a horse selected for the occasion, he parades through the streets, surrounded by the male members of the two families, with females singing and following behind, whilst gymnasts dance before him with naked swords, to the sound of drums, horns, and the firing of guns. They reach the bride's house in about an hour's time; one of her near relatives then takes the Ghot's arm, assists him to dismount, and leads him in. The women of the procession are allowed to enter, but the Jani (or male portion) return to the place where they met early in the evening, and, after sitting there for a short time, disperse homewards.

When the Ghot enters the bride's house he is conducted in by the women, who take the opportunity to perform a number of puerile ceremonies, which may have been instituted for some grave or moral object, but certainly serve for no such purpose now.

The usual formalities are as follows:—The bridegroom is seated on a Khata, or bedstead, with his face towards the west, in front of his bride; between the couple a large bolster is placed. A Sohagan[18] then performs the ceremony called "La$^{\underline{a}}$ diyan$^{\underline{u}}$," and compelling them to touch foreheads seven times in succession, recites these words:—

"Hekrí lá$^{\underline{a}}$ Chhandr$^{\underline{u}}$ ba Hure,
Asán babal^{a} dhiy$^{\underline{a}}$ ghúmande núre."

"This is the first time that the moon and the houri touched foreheads:
May our father's daughter always walk about with the anklets on."[19]

When this is over, they perform what is called "Phul$^{\underline{a}}$ Chundan$^{\underline{u}}$;" the Sohagan throws at the bride about a dozen cotton flowers dyed with saffron or turmeric; these the Ghot takes up and puts aside; a dry date is then placed in the Kunwar's right hand; she is told to hold it firmly, and the bridegroom desired to take it from her. As he must use only one hand, he is sure to fail and to excite a general laugh; a fine of about five Rupees, to be spent in sweetmeats, is the penalty if he joins in the merriment.

"Tir^{a} Maan^{u}" is done as follows:—A quantity of white and dry Tira (Sesamum) is brought in upon a large Thali, or metal platter, and placed before the bride. She joins her palms together, fills them with the grain, and pours it six or seven times into the Ghot's hands. The Sohagan, in the meantime, sings—

> "Jetrá Tir^{a} máindí,
> Otrá put^{a} janíndi."

> "As many grains of Sesamum as thou metest,
> So many sons mayest thou bear."

To this interesting ceremony succeeds that called "Chanwar^{a} Maan^{u}." The Sohagan places before the bridegroom a platter filled with salt and white rice in equal proportions. The Ghot now takes the initiative, and pours six or seven palmsful of the grain into his bride's hands, whilst the Sohagan is singing—

> "Lún^{a} sarb^{a} salún^{a},
> Je kinh Wanaro de, so sabh Wanarí jhale."

> "These are salt and nicely salted (things),
> Whatever the bridegroom giveth, that the bride receiveth."

The object of this proceeding is probably to inculcate obedience in the wifo.

Besides the common ones above mentioned, there are various minor ceremonies prevailing in different parts of the country. Sometimes an earthen Dhakkanu (pot-cover) is placed upon the ground, and the Ghot is desired to stamp upon it. If he succeeds in breaking it, all the ladies augur well of his manliness, and quote the verses,—

"Dhakkanu bhaggo,
Buddo lattho—
Asarajá E Alláh!"

"The cover is broken,
Our desires are granted—
Protect us Thou, O Lord!"

In other places they fix a Kandi (thorn branch) firmly in the ground, and placing a sword in the bridegroom's hand, desire him to cut through it with a single blow.

When the various formalities are duly concluded, the Sohagan causes the happy couple to rise up from the bedstead, and conducts them into the Pakho or Khudu (nuptial chamber). As the bridegroom is about to enter it, his bride's sister or a female cousin opposes him and demands a present of a few Rupees. The door is then closed.

The best time for entering the bridal chamber is considered to be between midnight and the dawn of day. The female relations of both parties pass the night together in singing, talking and eating. At sunrise the bride's mother enters the room to warn the sleepers that it is time to bathe and dress.

It is usual among the Sindhis for the Ghot to pass seven days and nights in the Sahorano Gharu (his father-in-law's house). After that time the couple may return to the Maetano Gharu (the bridegroom's home). Even when mere children are married they are made to sleep together, and to live under the same roof.

Until the birth of her first child the bride is permitted to call upon her parents once a week, generally on Fridays. After that event, she is permitted to visit them every Eed or Great Festival. Usually, however, much more indulgence is allowed: but all the terrors of religion are directed against ladies who insist upon leaving home without the permission of their spouses.

The other great ceremonious event relating to the Sindhi is that of his funeral obsequies. Owing to his natural timidity, increased probably by the peculiarities of his gloomy faith, he turns away from the idea of departing this life with a feeling of peculiar horror. Any allusion to it always excites his fear and disgust: I have often observed that individuals, even when in the best of health, could not describe or allude to the different ceremonies of burial without trembling and changing colour. It is likely that this remarkable cowardice may account for the many well-authenticated cases of "forewarnings" and foreseeing death, which are perpetually being quoted by the Sindhis. An individual for instance, after perhaps seeing a camel[20] in a dream, knowing that such vision is an omen of approaching dissolution, will be seized with a profound melancholy. After a few days his observing friends discover the cause of his grief, and are informed by him that the "bitterness of death is on his tongue." The forewarned prepares himself for the next world, by abjuring the pleasures of this, by leaving off his usual occupations, and by repeated prayers, weepings, fastings, and other penances, not neglecting to make all the requisite temporal arrangements. His family, never for a moment doubting the truth of their relation's warning, of course do not try to divert his mind from dwelling upon the approaching sad event: but rather, by their tears and manifestations of sorrow, give an appearance of reality to the fancied state of the case. Can we wonder that the forewarning often turns out to be exactly true? When by some chance the individual does not die, his salvation is accounted for by a direct interposition of the Almighty will, and the whole story is soon forgotten. On the other hand, should the threatened person die, a strong preternatural case is immediately made out, established by the fears and love of wonder common to vulgar minds, and confirmed by the interested voice of the priesthood. The mainspring of human action, Acquisitiveness, has induced the Mulla to prepare a multitude of events which must occur to every Moslem that enters the grave. Among Christians who have been informed of little that occurs between the periods of death and judgment, the simple idea of an incomprehensible eternity, contrasted with ephemeral mundane existence, is that usually offered to the imagination. In the East, where a microscopic minuteness of description is a *sine qua non* when a strong effect is to be produced, more details are judged necessary. The Kanz El Ibrat, a work translated from the Arabic, and much studied by the population of Sindh, gives the following account of the Azab el Kabr, the pains and punishments of the tomb. When the usual prayers have been read over the body and the mourners leave the grave, the angels Munkir and Nakir, "with grey eyes and black faces," enter and perform the Sual, or interrogatory.[21] Should the dead man have been a Kafir (infidel), a Munafik (hypocrite), or one of the wicked, he is then visited by a procession of ninety-nine snakes, endowed with such powers of biting and stinging, that the pain of the same endures till the day of resurrection. He is then indulged with a full view of that portion of the bottomless pit which he is to occupy, and for this purpose a hole opens in the side of the grave leading directly to Hell. The next torture is that which is called in Persian the Fishar i Kabr, or the "squeezing of the tomb." On both sides the earth closes upon the sentient corpse till its ribs are pressed against each other; and lest the discomfort should not be sufficient, snakes, scorpions and other vermin are thrown into the grave. Finally, the Ruh (life or soul) is taken from the body and cast into Sijjin,[22] the place appointed for reprobates.

These puerile ideas are well adapted to the comprehension of the people for whom they were invented or modified. Their wonderful capability of belief in the unknown, their intense apprehensions of the unseen, and appetite for the marvellous, all combine to produce the necessary effect. Such an account read out to an assembly of Sindhis would never fail to cause weeping and groaning. Of course the priest derives benefit. The more detailed and horrible the accounts of futurity are, the greater is the fear excited by them, there is more application to religious exercises, and, consequently, greater deference and more money paid to the class that can avert evils so tremendous. Well educated Turks and Persians feel disposed to question the probability of these anile tales. I heard of a man at Shiraz who filled the mouth of a corpse with flour, and proved to his friends that no verbal answers could have been returned to Munkir and Nakir during the interrogatory, as the mouth was found a few days afterwards as full as ever. The Mullas had their rejoinder, and confuted the reasoner,[23] by proving that the voice did not necessarily proceed from the throat. In Sindh, however, there is no such latitudinarianism. The fear of consequences would always deter a man from opening the grave of a newly buried corpse; thus all experiments are prevented. And it may be observed, that whenever an idea founded upon religion has been diffused through a people, confirmatory instances and events will also abound. Thus in Islam history does not disdain to chronicle cases in which Munkir and Nakir have by mistake or intentionally been seen by the living. The Hindoo Triad has at different times appeared to its worshippers. Guebres have been favoured with visions of Zoroaster. And in Southern Europe, saints, that probably never existed except on canvas, still condescend occasionally to visit the devotee.

When a Sindhi is seen to be in the state of Sakarat (the agonies of death), all present recite the Shahadat, or confession of the Mussulman faith. If water from the sacred well, Zamzam, be procurable, it is squeezed into the man's mouth,[24] and a traditional saying of the Prophet informs his followers that it is a meritorious deed: the holy fluid, however, is not common in Sindh. The corpse, after the eyes and mouth have been closed, is laid out with straightened limbs upon a Takhto, a framework of sticks. Under the latter they excavate a hole about knee deep, and six feet in length: a kind of sink, over which the body is washed. Ber (jujube) leaves are steeped in water, which is heated over a fire, made with the wood of the same tree, or, preferably, with the dead man's Miswak, the sticks used as tooth-brushes; also a pot of the clay called Metu, mixed up with water, is kept in readiness. A Ghassal (corpse bather) is then summoned. He begins by stripping the body, and covering the parts from the navel to the knees, with a clean white cloth, called a Satr-posh. He then draws a cotton bag, intended to act as a glove, over his hand, and with a clod of earth begins the cleaning process. This bag is thrown away, and a second taken in its stead. The Ghassal now performs Wuzu (the lesser ablution) for the corpse, purifying its nostrils and mouth with cotton. Bits of the same material[25] are used to stop up those orifices, and the whole of the face is washed. The hair and beard are then cleaned with the preparation of Metu. After this all the body is thrice bathed; the third time with camphorated water. The Ghassal wipes the corpse by throwing a clean white sheet over it, and rubbing it so that the remaining moisture may be dried up. The body is then placed upon another sheet which is spread over a Charpai or Khatolo (kinds of bedsteads). Next they put on the Kafan or shroud, a large piece of cotton torn so as to pass over the head: usage directs that it should not be sewn in any part, that it should reach down to the calves of the legs, and that religious sentences should be traced with clay from Mecca upon the portion that covers the dead man's breast. Various perfumes such as rosewater, attar of roses and the powder called Abir[26] are sprinkled over the body. It is then covered with a sheet, the skirts of which are tied together at both ends with that upon which the corpse is lying. Finally, a shawl, or some such covering, is thrown over the sheet, a Koran, belonging to the priest, is placed at the head of the bier, and the corpse is ready for interment.

The procession is now formed, and four of the friends or relations of the deceased raise up the Jenazo (bier). They are preceded by two or three men chaunting Maulud, and themselves reciting the Shahadat, they proceed at a rapid pace[27] towards the Mukam (burial ground). The grave, which is usually dug beforehand, is about four cubits square, with a hole called a Guja in the middle, as nearly as possible the size of the body. The Akhund, or priest, now takes the Koran from the bier, and gives it to the nearest male heir of the deceased, telling him to fix a price for it. When the sum has been formally settled, the Akhund thus addresses him:—"Dost thou give me this Koran in lieu of any prayer, fasting, or debt-payment which the dead man may have omitted?" When the heir has replied in the affirmative, the priest duly states that he accepts the offer, takes the Koran, descends into the Guja and reads aloud the whole chapter "Tabarak." He then places a little mould from the grave in the palm of each man present, and desires them all to repeat after him the "Kul huw'Allah." After this the earth is returned to the Akhund, who scatters it over the tomb. The corpse is then lowered into the Guja by three or four relations: the limbs must be straight, and the head so inclining towards the shoulder, that the face may turn towards the Kaabah.[28] They next loosen the skirts of the sheets, but not so as to uncover the head, and prepare to fill up the grave. Strong sticks are placed over the mouth of the Guja; if wood be not procurable a slab of stone is used: in both cases, however, contact with any part of the body is avoided. Over the framework matting is carefully disposed to support the mould, and prevent it from occasioning uneasiness to the corpse. They then recite the Ayat (verse of the Koran), "From her (the earth) We (God) created you, and into her We return you, and from her We will draw you forth another time." During the recitation the earth is filled in. The company now forms in a circle round the grave, each member touching his neighbours' forefingers, and in this position repeating the chapter, "Ya Ayyuha'l Muhammal." They then raise both hands in the posture of prayer, while the Akhund recites the final orison and dismisses them to their homes.

On the Treyo, or third day after the funeral, the principal Waris (heir) kills a cow or a goat, according to his circumstances, and gives the first funeral feast to the family, and all that were present at the interment. This, too, is the proper time for settling legacies,[29] and discharging the outstanding debts of the deceased. After the feast, the Akhund and his coadjutors perform a Khatm, or reciting the whole Koran by each repeating a single section; they receive in payment small presents of money, scented oils, betel nuts and other such articles. The Ghassal is rewarded with gifts; one of his perquisites being the clothes of the deceased. Prayers are then offered up, and the company separates.

Another feast is given by the Waris on the Daho,

or tenth day after the death. The ceremonies differ little from what take place on the Treyo.

The same may be said of the Chaliho, or feast on the fortieth day, which terminates the first portion of the mourning, if it can be so called. Up to this time the friends and relatives of the deceased visit his family, generally twice a day, morning and evening; and the women of the house are all clad in Sua[30] (dirty clothes).

The last feast given is on the Baraho, or anniversary of the death. It usually concludes the funeral rites, though some families are so affectionate as to keep up the practice of sending food to the Akhund, twice a day, on all great festivals.

The higher orders usually pay several Akhunds to read the Koran over a relation's tomb for forty days in succession; even the poorest do their best to secure the luxury for a week or fortnight. Among the more literary classes, it is not unusual for an individual occasionally to peruse the sacred volume in the presence of the dead many years after their decease. The idea of course is, that the religious merit of the act will belong to the person in whose favour it is done on the great day of reward and punishment.

When the grave is filled in, earth is heaped upon the top in different shapes. Sometimes it is raised in cylindrical form about one span high, sprinkled with water, and smeared with Kahgil; others merely make a heap of mould covered with pebbles,[31] or spread over with leaves of the tree called in Arabic "Arak," and in Sindhi "Jara." Over the remains of respectable men they erect tombstones of bricks and lime;

anciently sandstone slabs were common. The shape is usually long, though square tombs are to be met with; the top is of convex form, rarely flat. There is not, however, any distinction of shape between the graves of the Sunnis and Shiehs. Epitaphs are not much in fashion; they are limited to an Arabic quotation, a verse or two in the Persian, and sometimes the name, with the date of birth and death of the occupant inscribed upon a blue glazed tile at the head of the tombstone. A similar tile is placed at the foot, but it bears no inscription. Men of high rank, great wealth, or religious celebrity, are buried under domes of cut stone, some of them handsome and elaborately built, with arabesques and other ornaments. The tombstones of such worthies as Shah-Abdellatif, Lal-Shah-Baz, &c., &c., are always covered with richly-embroidered cloths, and their mausolea are closed by silver doors, sometimes with golden padlocks and keys.

Every traveller in Sindh must have remarked the immense tracts of graveyard which it contains. The reason of this disproportion between the cities of the dead and those of the living is, in the first place, that the people are fond of burying their kin in spots which are celebrated for sanctity, and secondly, they believe that by interring corpses close to the dust of their forefathers, the Ruha, or souls of the departed, will meet and commune together after death. Hence it is that when a Sindhi dies in a foreign place, his heirs or friends will generally agree[32] to remove the body to the family graveyard, at a certain period or within a stated time. The corpse is then exhumed, and carried in a box on horse or camel-back to its final destination. And it is believed that when such promise has been given, the two angels never visit the provisional tomb, but defer their questioning till the second interment takes place. The Ameers, though generally speaking Shiehs, did not direct their bodies to be sent to Karbala. The unhappy Mir Nasir Khan is said to have expressed a wish that his corpse might be inhumed there, in order to avoid the degradation of resting in a land belonging to the Infidel. He is, however, buried at Hyderabad, in the tomb of his uncle Mir Karam Ali. The rich Persians about the court of the native rulers usually would direct the transmission of their bodies to the "place of martyrdom" (Karbala). Other Shiehs, not being wealthy enough to afford themselves this luxury, were contented to occupy a corner of some graveyard in Sindh.

CHAPTER XI.

THE SINDHI PROPER DESCRIBED.—CUSTOMS OF THE MEN: THEIR DRESS, DIVERSIONS, GYMNASTIC EXERCISES AND GAMES.—THE CUSTOMS OF THE FEMALES: THEIR MORALS, HABITS, INTRIGUES AND DRESS.—THE DANCING GIRLS, PROSTITUTES AND MUSICIANS. —OUTCAST TRIBES IN SINDH.

THE Sindhi proper[1] is a taller, stronger, more robust and more muscular man than the native of Western India. His hands, feet and ancles have none of that delicacy of formation observable amongst the nations that inhabit the broad lands lying on the other side of the Indus. The Sindhi, in fact, appears to be a half breed between the Hindoo, one of the most imperfect, and the Persian, probably the most perfect specimen of the Caucasian type. His features are regular, and the general look of the head is good; the low forehead and lank hair of India are seldom met with in this province. The beard, especially among the upper classes, is handsome, though decidedly inferior to that of Persia or Affghanistan. At the same time, the dark complexion of the Sindhi points him out as an instance of arrested development.[2] In "*morale*" he is decidedly below his organisation; his debasement of character being probably caused by constant collision with the brave and hardy hill tribes who have always treated him as a serf, and by dependency upon Hindoo Shroffs and Banyans, who have robbed and impoverished him as much as possible. He is idle and apathetic, unclean in his person, and addicted to intoxication; notoriously cowardly in times of danger, and proportionably insolent when he has nothing to fear; he has no idea of truth or probity, and only wants more talent to be a model of treachery. The native historians praise him for his skill in tracking footsteps, a common art in the Eastern world, and relate more wonderful instances of such sagacity than were ever told of the American aborigines, or the Arabs of Tehamah. His chief occupations at present are cultivation, fishing, hunting, and breeding horses, camels and sheep.

The Sindhi does not in general dress so handsomely as the natives of India. Moslems in this province wear little gold about their persons, except a ring or seal. The old usually shave off the hair, according to the ancient practice of Islam;[3] the young take no small pride in their long locks, which are parted in the middle of the head, curled, and allowed to hang down to the shoulders, or tied up in a knot under the cap or turban. The grey beard is dyed with henna, to which a little alum is added in order to deepen the colour; young men sometimes stain the hands and feet with it. Perfumed oils, antimony, and the powder called Missi, are used; the latter, however, much more rarely than in India.[4] As Hammams are unknown in this country, depilatories are not in fashion; the hair of the body is generally removed by means of a razor.

The peculiar Sindhi cap, which has been compared, not inaptly, to a European hat inverted, was known in the time of the Kalhoras, but came into general use under the Talpurs. It is now worn by all but religious characters, who prefer the turban. The square hat, made of black cloth or Kimcob (cloth of gold), and called "Mogho topu," belongs to the higher and wealthier classes. There are three different kinds of turbans: 1. the Paga, a long cotton cloth, generally white, sometimes dyed; 2. Patako, resembling the former, but smaller; 3. Phentiyo, a fold of cotton stuff, loosely twisted round the head. The lower orders prefer clothes dyed with indigo to white dresses, as the latter show the dirt too much; some of them, especially the Fakirs, affect green colours. The articles of dress worn by the poor are, a Puthiyo (or Kiriyo, a cotton packet resembling the Mirzai of India), a pair of Kancha (drawers wide at the ancle), or Suthana (trowsers very loose about the waist and gathered in at the instep), a Gandhi (Chadar or Pothi, a piece of cloth thrown loosely over the shoulders), a Bochanu or Cummerband (sash), and a pair of slippers. To the articles above enumerated, the rich add a Pehranu, or shirt with sleeves, and a Kaba (a long coat made of white cotton, in shape resembling a European nightshirt). The Angarkha of India has lately been introduced, but the short waist which distinguishes that garment is here considerably lengthened. The Sadri (or Phatui, a waistcoat of rich or coloured stuffs) is another late introduction. During the cold season they wear a Kurti (long coat in the shape of a Kaba wadded with cotton), or a Nimtano (a jacket of the same description, with arms down to the elbows). The rich are fond of handsome furs; the poor content themselves with an Affghan Posteen, a Masho, or Chogho (cloaks made of felt, goat's and camel's hair). The slippers generally used are of two kinds: 1. Jutti, made of red or yellow leather, in shape not unlike those worn by the Egyptians; and 2. Ghetalo, of the same material embroidered with cloth or silk. Wealthy men when travelling, wear a kind of leathern top boot called "Mozo;" the best come from Affghanistan, but a cheaper and inferior article is manufactured in in Sindh. In the hills, a sole, made of the leaves of a kind of dwarf palm called Phisa, is used to protect the feet; in appearance it resembles the peculiar sandal of the Pyrenees.

The following are the amusements most popular in Sindh :—

Pattanga, or kites, are flown by all classes, high and low, but the diversion is not so favourite a one with grown up people as it is in India. There are five or six varieties of the toy; one kind, called Bharkani, or Guddi, was a great favourite with the native princes, who used to amuse themselves with flying them with a Nakkara (kettledrum) hanging to the tail. The bumping of one kite against the other decides the victory when a wager is laid.

Kabutar-bazi, or betting on pigeons, is an amusement peculiar to the higher classes. A Bazigar, or tumbler of the best breed, is selected and trained to tumble as quickly and as often as possible when thrown up by the hand. The wager is generally decided by upwards of seven tumbles; should the pigeon accomplish less, the bet is void. As heavy sums are laid upon the result of a trial between two noted pigeons, the price of a single one will sometimes be as high as a hundred Rupees. About twenty Rupees is the usual value of a good pair.

A small bird called Burbuli (a kind of shrike), is taught to fight here like the quail in Affghanistan. A male bird is chosen, and tamed by not being permitted to sleep. After that preliminary, he is starved at times for eight or ten hours together, in order that he may learn to follow a person when called. He is also taught to catch falling objects, by tossing up a cowrie with a bit of bread fastened to it. Whilst training, he is fed with a kind of cake called Churmo, or with chewed Bhugra.[5] When the fight is to take place, food is thrown between a pair of them, and they set to immediately; their backers excite their birds by pushing them with the finger. The Burbuli is by no means a game bird, and as he only can use his bill, a death rarely occurs. Wagers are seldom laid upon the fight; the victor merely wins the other bird. Boys are very fond of this amusement, and have invented a number of different terms to distinguish between the several kinds of birds, their peculiarities of pecking, &c., &c.

Kukkur-bazi, or cock-fighting, is a common, but not a fashionable, amusement in Sindh. The birds are generally fought by Moslems at the Daira, or drinking houses, on Fridays, as was anciently the practice with our swains on Sundays. Formerly, no

Hindoo dared to be present, as circumcision would probably have been the result; even in these days they are seldom seen at the cockpit. The game cock of Sindh is a very fine bird, distinguished by the bright yellow leg and a peculiar brilliancy and transparency of eye.[6] The feeding and training very much resemble the Indian way, and require the greatest attention, as the use of steel and silver is unknown. There is no peculiarity in the mode of lifting or fighting the birds.

The Sindhis are very fond of fighting Ghata (rams). The best breed is the large and strong black animal of the hills. He is trained, as early as possible, to butt against the hand when excited by a peculiar sound; when full grown he generally becomes so savage that he will attack any one that comes in his way. The usual food is grain, clarified butter and a little green meat: a very small quantity of water is allowed, and during training as much exercise as possible is given. Rams are fought in the cold season, as they are easily killed in the hot weather. The Dairo is the usual place, and Friday the day selected for the sport. A fight seldom lasts longer than half an hour, and the eyes of the fugitive are immediately bandaged, otherwise he would refuse to meet his conqueror another time. The young Ameers were very fond of this amusement, and it became a fashionable one, probably on account of the expense attending it. The price of a good ram is from fifteen Rupees upwards.

Horse racing, as practised in Persia and Arabia, is unknown here. In the former country the state of politics frequently renders it advisable to have in one's stable a horse that is equal to a twenty or thirty miles gallop: and this accounts for the great length of the distances marked out on the course. By the ancient as well as the modern Arabs, the importance attached to breeding the horse would lead to trials of speed and bottom: and Mohammed, who retained as many of the time-honoured customs of his country as he consistently could, allowed horse racing when he forbade other sports and games. In Sindh, during the two Eeds,[7] the people assemble about sunset in the plain of the Eedgah, and ride short heats of a quarter or half a mile, on untrained horses. This is considered a semi-religious exercise, and profitable to man and beast. As they never race for money, the acclamations of those around him are the only reward of the winner.

The Taalim-Khana (Gymnasia) of India, are unknown in this province. The Sindhis, however, are very fond of wrestling, but the Malla (wrestlers) are, generally speaking, African blacks. Those selected for this exercise are broad and powerful men, with prominent muscles and large bones, rather below the middle height, splay footed, bandy legged, and with curved shins. They are carefully trained on flesh, clarified butter and milk, and compelled to abstain from flatulent food, drinking and smoking. They are not fattened up with sweetmeats, as in India, and generally enter the ring in first-rate condition. An Ustad (trainer) teaches the different Ari (or Band,—tricks and feints). The dress worn during the contest is the Patko, wound round the head, a pair of drawers and a waist-band. It is not necessary to throw the adversary on his back, as in India; he is beaten if he comes down upon one knee, and the best of three falls usually decides the contest. As the people became violently excited at these encounters, frequent quarrels and some bloodshed used to result from them. The Sindhis are decidedly inferior in science to their neighbours the Persians and Hindoos, nor have they the numerous gymnastic exercises common to the other nations of Asia. They are ignorant of the use of the chain bow, the practice called Dand[8] (Shinau in Persian) and even the Mugdars. Wrestlers are exercised in running, jumping, hopping on one leg, raising the Mall (a large stone pierced with holes to admit the fingers), breaking Kathi, or rods, over the wrists or muscles of the arm, and struggling with each other to open the fist, twist the arm, grasp the wrist whilst the adversary tries to disengage it, and pull a stick away from each other. The other popular exercises are—1. Muthiyan jo Zor, placing the fists on the ground, and raising up a boy or a man who stands upon them. 2. Chambo Wathan, interlacing the fingers and trying to disengage them from the grasp of the adversary. 3. Pera te Uthan, squatting on the hams, lifting one leg off the ground, and then slowly rising up by means of the other—no easy task. 4. Kakk Khanan :—the gymnast, in the squatting position with both arms behind the back, picks up with the lips, a bit of straw placed on the ground before him. The above are the principal exercises ; there are also many different combinations and minor varieties.

Gambling being forbidden by the laws of Islam, the native rulers used occasionally to fine those that transgressed. This did not, however, prevent the lower classes of Moslems imitating the Hindoos,[9] so much as to believe that their religion permitted or rather enjoyed such recreation during the Eeds. The Sindhis are one of the most gambling of Oriental nations, all sexes and orders appear to have an equal passion for play, the result, probably, of early habit: as the women are very fond of games of chance, and are skilful players, the children, who are exceedingly quick in early youth, soon learn to imitate their mothers. A boy of seven years thus becomes well grounded in all the mysteries of gambling, and then begins to make money by play. By constant practice he learns all the popular games of cards, dice, cowries and pice, and devotes the whole of his time to them. The idea of a debt of honour being utterly unknown, a Sindhi is seldom ruined, as he never pays when he can avoid it. He is a very eager player, even when there is no betting; he is insolent when winning, and sulky if he loses; quarrelsome about disputed points, and perpetually cheating. A native when playing at any game, such as chess, or Baita-bazi (capping verses[10]), which is supposed to require talent, will never admit that he is fairly beaten. If he be a man of rank, his attendants and sycophants are expected to praise every move, and to be ready with some good excuse when his skill fails.

The games most played in Sindh are,—

1. Shatranj (chess); 2. Nard (backgammon); 3. Pachis; 4. Dhara (dice); 5. Ganjifa (cards); 6. Chanarpisi; 7. Tritran, and other similar games, as Nautran, Sorahtran, &c.

Chess is played in many different ways. That

called Faranji (Frankish) very much resembles ours, but the queen is always placed on the right of the king; pawns never move two squares, and when one reaches the end of the board, it is changed for the piece belonging to the particular square attained. A checkmate wins the game; but when the antagonist loses all his pieces (except the king of course), only half a game is reckoned. Finally, what we do in one move by castling, with them takes three; thus, (1) the rook must be moved next square to the king; (2) the king makes one move like a knight beyond the castle; and (3) the king takes the square next to the castle. The game called Rumi (Turkish) is puzzling to Europeans, owing to the peculiar use of the queen and bishop. It invariably begins with queen's pawn two squares, and queen one square; after which the latter piece can only move one square obliquely, and must take other pieces or give check in the same way. The bishop moves obliquely like the queen, but passes over one square, even when it is occupied by another piece. Some Sindhis play very tolerably at this game. Another modification known in the province, but originally derived from India, is called Band. Its chief peculiarity is, that when any piece is defended by a second, provided the latter be not the king, the former cannot be taken. This, of course protracts the game considerably, so that two or three days may elapse before the checkmate is given.

Nard[11] (Backgammon) is generally played by those Sindhis who have visited Persia or learned it from the natives of that country. The Persians, from perpetual practice, are the greatest adepts at this game that I ever saw.

Pachis[13] is derived from India, and no alteration in its form has been made in Sindh. It is a favourite game among all sexes and classes: the females being perhaps the more skilful at handling the cowries and cheating whenever an opportunity presents itself.

Dhara, or dice, are four sided pieces of ivory, about two inches long, and one third of an inch in diameter. The sides are marked with an ace (Paon̲), a deuce (Duo), a cinque (Panjo), and a sice (Chakko). A set of three dice is generally used, and, when not combined with any other game, playing with them is called Jua. No skill is required: when the bets are arranged, both parties throw the dice, and the highest number wins. Hindoos are particularly fond of this kind of play: good Moslems avoid it, as in their religion it is considered the worst species of gambling.

Ganjifa, or cards, are of two kinds. 1. Angrezi, the full English pack of fifty-two. 2. Mogholi. The former is the kind most commonly used; it has been adapted to a great variety of games and provided with as many technical words as the most complicated European language could afford. The Ganjifa Mogholi were, it is said in Sindh, invented by one Changa Rani, in order to prevent her husband perpetually pulling his beard: a portrait of the inventress is always painted on the lid of the box. The pack consists of ninety-six in all: these are divided into eight different sorts, each of which has twelve cards, viz., a Badshah (king), a Wazir (prime minister), and ten others, viz., from the ten to the ace included. It would be tiresome to describe, or even to enumerate, the many games played with this huge pack.

"Chanarpisi" resembles Pachis, but is more simple, and more easily learned. The board is divided into twenty-five squares, and each player has four pieces (Saryun or Gitiyun), with the same number of cowries. The latter are used like dice at backgammon to decide the number of squares to be moved over. The name of the game is derived from "Channar," the technical term, when all four Cowries fall to the ground with the slit upwards, and "Pissi," when only one is in this position. The game may be played by either two or four people, and he wins that first reaches the centre square. Whenever a piece is in one of the crossed Ghar (squares), it cannot be taken by the adversary.

The Tritran ("Three Corners") of the Sindhis is the same as that called Katar by the Persians and Affghans. The latter people are very fond of it, especially the lower orders in the country villages, where the greybeards assemble and play together for hours over a few lines marked with a stick on the ground. Even in Sindh it is rare to find such an article of refinement as a board or a cloth made for Tritran. The game is very simple: each player has three pieces (generally pebbles or cowries), which are put down in turn, and he wins that first can place all three in a straight line. Nautran (nine-corners), and Sorah-tran (sixteen-corners) are games resembling Tritran in all points, except that the lines and counters are more numerous.

Games peculiar to children in Sindh much resemble those of India, and the well-known European diversions of forfeits, touchwood, blindman's buff, prison bars and tipcat. Grown up people do not disdain to enter into the spirit of the thing, and in the ruder games many have been maimed and some killed. The Kheno (ball) made of cotton twisted round a betel nut and covered with leather, plays here, as elsewhere a conspicuous part in such sports. Even the ladies do not disdain to display their grace and agility when using the Kheno; the consequence is that it has merited frequent honorary mention in the amorous poetry of the country.

Throughout the Moslem world, the two great points of honour are bravery and chastity in woman. Judged by this test the Sindhis occupy a low place in the scale of Oriental nations. Under the native rule, however, several instances of honourable conduct (orientally speaking) are quoted in favour of the Sindhis. One of the reigning clan, Fatteh Khan Talpur, was slain by a Langho, or common musician, who detected him in an intrigue with his wife. A Shikari (sweeper) one of the vilest of classes in Sindh, ripped up with a sickle the belly of Ahmed Khan Numdani, one of the chief Sardars, for the same reason. There are two causes in the province why the punishment[13] for adultery was made so severe; in the first place the inadequacy of the Koranic law; secondly, the physical peculiarities of the people. As is often the case in warm and damp countries,[14] lying close to mountains, the amativeness of the female here appears to be stronger than that of the male. We find, accordingly, that in all the vernacular books the fair sex is represented as more worthless in Sindh than in any other part of the world. It is amusing to observe the virulence of abuse with which the ladies are assailed, especially when the reason is duly considered.

In point of personal appearance the Sindhi woman is of fairer complexion and finer features and form than those of Western India: the latter, however, are superior in grace and delicacy of make. Towards the north of our province there is a considerable portion of personal beauty, especially among the females of the higher classes. Their education is much neglected. Few can read, and still fewer can write, their own language: to peruse the Koran without understanding a word of it is considered a feat, and in a large town not more than four or five women would be able to spell through a Persian letter. Still there are female teachers who, when required, can educate a girl; their chief occupations, however, are reading the billet-doux of absent lovers, and inditing answers to the same. The usual Moslem prejudice against female education is strong in Sindh. All are agreed upon one point, viz., that their women are quite bad and cunning enough, without enlarging their ideas and putting such weapons as pens into ther hands. In manners the Sindhi female wants the mildness of the Indian and the vivacity of the Affghan and Persian. She is rather grave and sedate than otherwise in society, and is not so much at ease in it owing to the want of Hammams and frequent social intercourse. She is fond of play and can cheat with formidable dexterity. The chief games are Pachis, Cards and Cowries (thrown like dice) and the excitement caused by them is so great that violent quarrels frequently occur, even when no wagers are laid. Sindhi women are most indecent in their language, especially in abuse; they have very few expressions peculiar to their sex,[15] but deliberately select the worst words used by the men. They are fond of drinking liqueurs and the different preparations of hemp: intoxication is always the purpose of their potations. Many of them take snuff and almost all smoke Sukho (tobacco) in the Hookah. Their other amusements are dressmaking, the toilette, visits and intrigues. The preparations for the latter occupations throughout the country are rather extensive. For instance, in the small town of Kurrachee there are no less than seven Kutni (procuresses) three of them Hindoos and four Moslems. The custom is to go to the old woman's house and there sit down. She closes the door that no stranger may enter, offers water to drink, with a pipe of tobacco, and at the same time enquires the name and other particulars of her visitor. After much preparatory conversation, the man discloses his object, and requests the Kutni to procure him the means of meeting the fair dame. The old woman at first positively refuses, on account of many alleged difficulties: then she reluctantly agrees to undertake a trial, but insists upon the expense, and finally after receiving her Lawazimo (the technical name for the small present of a few Annas made on such occasions) and making a formal bargain for what she is to get in case of success, dismisses her employer with many promises. She afterwards, if properly paid, allows the parties to meet at her house, and manages their different interviews. The employment is a lucrative but not a safe one: the Kutni being perpetually exposed to the resentment of injured husbands, who sometimes use the stick without remorse. These old hags are accused of many actions of gross villany, such as administering narcotics, preventives and abortives, and practising unholy rites, in order to subjugate the wills of their victims. Probably their promises and flattering tongues are the natural magic which works such wonders. Women in Sindh are devotedly fond of flattery, and find no description of it too gross or ridiculous. Their chief inducements to intrigue besides passion and want of employment, are avarice[16] and pride. Curious to say (among Moslems) it is no small honour for a woman to boast of her intimacy with some great man, such as a Kardar or a Kazi. In intrigue the Sindhi woman is far more daring than her Indian sister, though much inferior, when there is real danger, to the Persian or Affghan. Some cases of considerable audacity are quoted. For instance, the wives of Mir Mohammed, one of the reigning family, had the boldness, it is said, to introduce into the palace by means of an old woman a young Beloch dressed in female clothes. The lover in his attempt to escape, when he found a longer stay impossible, fell from the roof, broke his leg, and was secretly put to death by the Darban (guards). The ladies escaped all the evil consequences which might be expected to result from so barefaced an affair.

Prostitutes in Sindh are of two kinds. The Rangeli, or Khobli,[17] is a low courtezan of the Jatki race, from the districts of Ubho and Jhangsiyal. They inhabit villages close to the main roads, and support themselves and the males by the contributions of travellers. The sum usually paid is from three to four

Pice, besides which the visitor is expected to make a present of hemp or tobacco. Some of these women have very fine features and forms, particularly in early youth. The debauched life they lead soon makes them look old. In spite of their depravity they are very attentive to the duties of their religion, and never object to devote a certain portion of their ill-gotten gains to the support of a mosque and its officiating Mulla.

Another and a more respectable class is the Kanyari, who, like the Nautch girl of India, generally unites the occupation of dancing with the more immoral part of her trade. An individual of this order has, generally speaking, her own house, is often married to a musician, who attends her at the different dances, and lives comfortably enough. Nautches frequently take place at sacred spots, and invariably on occasions of marriage and other feasts. At such times it is customary for the master of the house to give two or three rupees to the dancing girl when she comes round to collect money; all the visitors present are expected to do the same, under pain of being reputed miserly in the extreme. The sum thus raised in one night is often considerable. A first rate Nautch girl expects about one hundred rupees for an evening's performance; the inferior ones will take as little as ten or twelve. Some of these Kanyari strive to attract attention by fixing the price of their favours extremely high. They calculate upon and often succeed in finding amongst the natives, despite of their usual parsimony, fools who court the celebrity of wasting their money in this species of debauchery.

On one occasion, I heard of a respectable merchant giving as much as two hundred rupees for a single visit. As the Kanyari grows old, she is compelled, if she has been extravagant in youth, to depend upon the exertions of her daughters or her slave girls. When money is saved, it is invariably laid out in ornaments and jewels, which, as in India, are handed down from parent to child till urgent necessity compels the family to part with them. This practice, which occasionally collects several hundred pounds' worth of articles easily robbed, in a poor country is often dangerous; many murders have been caused by it. Under the native governments, the Kanyari used to pay a certain annual sum for permission to exercise her craft. They were, however, only tolerated, not encouraged as in India; no respectable woman was permitted to degrade herself by joining the class, and to the honour of the Sindhis it must be said, that like the Arabs, they considered visiting the houses of prostitutes a disgrace to the visitor—not the person visited. The Kanyari is, generally speaking, well dressed and clean in her person, she seldom drinks more than other women, and, like the lower orders of the frail sisterhood, is scrupulously obedient to the injunctions of her religious teachers.

Sindhi women are fond of rich and expensive clothes. The wealthier orders have a number of dresses made of brocades, gold and silver stuffs, fine velvets, painted silks, satins, and other such articles of luxury. Unmarried girls usually dress in red colours; old women and widows wear white. As a general rule, the more clothes worn on the person the greater is the respectability of the wearer. The different articles of dress are as follows:—Over the head a silk or cotton Chadar (veil or sheet) is thrown; of this kind of mantilla there are several varieties, as the Chunni and Pothi. The chief distinction between them is the size of the veil, as all colours are used indifferently, and there is no difference in shape. On the body they wear a Cholo[18] (shift opening in front, and sleeves reaching down to the elbows); the material is either silk, cotton, muslin, or other such stuff, the favourite colours white, blue and red. Under the shift a bit of cloth called Kanjari, Choli, or Gaj,[19] conceals the bosom; when it passes round the sides like a bodice and is fastened behind, its name is Puthi. This advisable article of dress is very often omitted in Sindh; a fact which may in some measure account for the pendent shape which the bosom assumes even in young women after a first or second child.[20] The Suthan, or trowsers, very much resemble in cut and material those worn by the men; the only difference is, that they are made to fit the ancle so tightly that there is often no small difficulty in putting them on. Among the rich the Agath (or Naro, the trowser string) is generally made of expensive materials embroidered with pearls and other precious stones. The Jutti, or slipper, is of leather, with Tonr or tassels of coloured silk on the upper part. It is a most inconvenient kind of shoe, consisting of a mere sole, scarcely covering the toes, and presenting peculiar difficulties to the walker. When women of good family leave the house, they hide the Suthan under a wide Paro (or Peshgir, petticoat), which conceals the person from the waist to the ancles. Over the upper part of the body they throw a Rawo (or Salur, large white veil). Among females of the Sayyid race, especially in the northern parts of Sindh, the Burka of Arabia and Persia is much used. It is intended to present an appearance of peculiar modesty, but fails to do so, if we may believe the native proverb, which declares that the wearer of the Burka is a little worse than her neighbours. Hindoo women wear the Paro larger and longer than the Muslimah; they usually prefer the Cholo without a Gaj, and throw a white veil over the head. They are also distinguished by some minutiæ of make in their ornaments and jewels, but these are unobservable except to practised eyes.

Sindhi women are fond of wearing a multitude of ornaments; they are not, however, so profuse in their decorations as the natives of India, who will rather wear bangles of glass and gum than leave the wrist bare. In Sindh these bangles are unknown to the people. Their chief peculiarity is the fondness for large rings of ivory covering the fore arm; these are worn by all sects and classes. A list of the jewels and ornaments in common use would present few attractions to the reader, especially as any description[21] of the same articles in India will serve equally well, with some few alterations of names, for those of our province.

The musicians in Sindh are of two kinds,—1. The Kalwat, or respectable singers; 2. the Langha, or Mirasi,[22] the bards of the country. The latter term is derived by the people, who are most fanciful etymologists, from some Mir, or great man, who, after acquiring the unenviable soubriquet of "Asi, the sinner," by condescending to eat with a Shikari (sweeper), became the father of the bards. The clan, as might be expected, gives itself a noble origin. Some connect themselves with the Samma tribe, which once reigned in Sindh; others mount up as high as Kaab el Ahbar, the renowned poetical contemporary of Mohammed.[28] The Langha are of Jat or Sindhi extraction. They are considered a low race, and certainly are one of the most vile and debauched classes to be found in the country. Every clan of any consequence, as, for instance, the Laghari, has its own minstrels, who attend the weddings, circumcisions, and other festive occasions, and expect to be well paid by the chief. In former times they used to accompany the head of the house to battle, armed with sword and shield, with the Surindo or Rebec in hand, praising the brave, and overwhelming cowards with satire and abuse. The people had, and still have, a great horror of their tongues. One of the Talpur family, who had not distinguished himself for bravery at the battle of Meeanee, was so much tormented by their ironical praises that he pays them liberally to keep out of his presence. Anciently the chief bards were in the service of the several Ameers; now they are obliged to live by begging, singing in the bazaars, and attending at the different houses where any ceremony is going on. At the same time they will spend every farthing they can gain in drinking and other debauchery; their idleness is even greater than their poverty, and their love of pleasure compels them to be most importunate in their demands for pay and largesse. In knowledge of music they are inferior to the Hindoos, but some of their popular airs approach nearer to the Persian style than the interminable recitative of India. They have no means of writing down a musical phrase, and therefore learn everything by oral instruction. Their voices are tolerable in the lower notes, but the use of the falsetto being unknown, and the higher the key the more admired the music, the upper tones are strained and disagreeable in the extreme. Some of them can be compared to nothing but the howl of a wild beast. No care whatever is taken of the organ, consequently in the rare cases where it is good, its powers soon decline. The words sung to music are, generally speaking, the kind of poetry called Baita, Wai and Dohra, in the Jatki and Sindhi languages. The Langha have some little knowledge of the simple and popular parts of Sufiism, and can explain their amorous and bacchanalian songs according to the usual system of double meaning. They, as well as the Kalwat, have a great and almost religious respect for the name of Tan Sen, the famous musician of Akbar's court.[24]

The Sindhis being all Moslems, no distinction of caste, properly so called, prevails among them. As in most Eastern countries, however, the Kori (weaver), and Chamar, or worker in leather, are considered low and vile. There are two outcast tribes in Sindh, the Bale Shahi and the Shikari: they must originally have been Mussulmans, and appear to be classes degraded by their occupations, and now all but banished from the society of their fellow-religionists.

The Bale Shahi are professionally called "Banghi,"

or "Chuhro," (sweeper), and politely "Halal-Khor," the Indian name. They delight, however, in the royal term, and derive it from the following legend, which may be quoted as a proof of the utter degradation of their minds. According to the sweepers, Balo Shah and Rabb Taala (or Khuda, the Almighty) were twin sons of one Mehtar Sanwri. They describe the former in their peculiar dialect to have been a Dhing-jawan (a strapping youth), whereas the latter was a Shisho-basho,[25] or frail and delicate person. On one occasion there was a dispute between them as to how their rights were to be settled; Bale-Shah being determined to reign in heaven. As Rabb Taala refused to be contented with the dominion of earth, the brothers quarrelled, and determined to settle the dispute by a wrestling match. In this trial they both proved perfectly equal. At length they were separated by Mullo Musro, who assigned to Rabb Taala the celestial, and to his brother the terrestrial, sovereignty. Thus Bale-Shah became the lord of the whole world, and the sweepers, who are his descendants, ought to occupy the same social position. This splendid account of the origin, compared with the actual occupation of the Bale-Shahi, affords no small merriment to the other classes of Sindhis. Yet not only do many of the sweepers relate the legend with perfect confidence in its veracity, but also display a pride of caste utterly at variance with our notions of common sense. In this point they resemble the outcasts of India,[26] where the twenty or thirty tribes of Banghis (sweepers) have their several dignities and precedence as distinctly defined as any subdivisions of the pontifical and regal races. It is possible that the ridiculous tale above related may be a mangled scrap of Sikh history. The prophet of the Panjab had two chief Chela (pupils), Balo and Mardano; the former used to prevent flies setting upon the august person of his superior; the latter had the office of playing to him on the rebec. In the stories of the Guru, there is frequent mention of sweepers; and many of them, after conversion, rose to high rank. The use of the Jatki language partly proves the Panjabi origin of the Bale-Shahi; the rest of the invention may easily be attributed to pride and ignorance.

The Bale-Shahi of Sindh is generally a large and tall man, with a dark complexion, and a degraded cast of countenance. They dress like the Belochis, marry in their own tribe, and live outside the towns and villages, subsisting by the chase and their peculiar occupation, for which they receive about an Anna a month from each family. These sweepers cannot now be considered pure Moslems.[37] They circumcise, repeat the Kalmah, pray, reverence the Pirs, pay Mullas to marry and inter them, and have no sectarian books. At the same time they are not allowed to enter a mosque; and as they are known to eat carrion, no Moslem will sit at meals or drink with them. The Hindoos consider them so impure, that in cases of contact, the body must be bathed and the clothes washed.

The Shikari (huntsmen), or Dapher, are, if possible an even more degraded race than the Bale-Shahi. Their second name is probably derived from the Dapho, or broad-headed javelin with a shaft six or seven feet long, their favourite weapon. The Sindhis deduce from the word etymological reasons for proving that they are descended from a plurality of fathers.[28] The Shikari are neither Moslems nor Hindoos. They are very numerous about Omerkot and the Thurr, where they subsist by manual labour, agriculture and hunting. In these regions there is something remarkably wild and savage in their appearance. The only garment worn is a cloth round the waist, except in winter, when a tattered blanket preserves them from the cold. Armed with his usual weapon, the Shikari generally seeks the wildest part of the country where he can find the greatest number of hogs, jackals, lynxes, and a kind of lizard called Giloi. At night he sleeps, and during the day he squats, under a cloth spread over some thorny shrub to defend him from the chilly dews and the burning rays of the sun. His food is the produce of the chase and whatever carrion he can pick up; his only drink the small quantity of water which he carries about in a leathern pouch. Yet he is not professionally a robber or an assassin, although the inducements to such crimes must sometimes prove too strong for him to resist. Thoroughly a wild man, the Shikari will seldom exchange his roving and comfortless life for any other; he knows no mental exercise, and is ignorant of the elements of education. Yet, although such a thing as a book has never been found among them, the Shikari have some idea of religion. The only part of worship they know is the Moslem Kalmah. They are married and buried either by the regular Mulla, or by certain religious characters of their own, called Bhopa, or

Gurara. The Dapher in the north of Sindh is generally circumcised; the wilder portion of the community inhabiting the Thurr neglect that rite altogether. Both, however, join in asserting their superiority to the Bale-Shahi, or sweepers, who retort by declaring the contrary to be the case. The Shikari is never allowed to enter the mosques of the Faithful. When any one of this caste wishes to become a good Moslem, he lights four fires and stands in the midst, till sufficiently purified by the heat. The Kazi causes him to bathe and put on pure clothes; he is then given over into the charge of some person who undertakes to teach him the elements of his religion, and becomes a member of the Machi clan of Sindhis.

The females of the Shikari class are generally of dark complexion; some of them, like the Bale-Shahi, have fine features and good figures, though by no means so remarkable as the Halal-Khors of Guzerat and the adjacent parts of western India. Their charms, however, have often proved sufficiently powerful to introduce them into higher society, and royalty itself in Sindh has not disdained to intrigue with them. This fact may probably account for the fair skins sometimes to be seen amongst this people.

CHAPTER XII.

THE HINDOOS OF SINDH.—THEIR CASTES, BRAHMAN, KSHATRIYA, THE FIVE DIVISIONS OF WAISHYA AND SHUDRAS.—THE SIKHS; RELIGIOUS MENDICANTS AND OUTCAST TRIBES.—PRESENT STATE OF HINDUISM.—SPECIMENS OF HYMNS AND PRAYERS.

THE Hindoo portion of the community occupies, in Sindh, the same social position that the Mussulmans do in India. As in Arabia, Affghanistan and other parts of Central Asia, the Hindoo here is either employed in trade, or in ministering to the religious wants of his caste-brethren. We, therefore, find among them none of the properly speaking outcast tribes (as Parwari, Mang, Chandala and others) so numerous in their own country. It is probable that few or none of the Hindoo families that flourished in Sindh at the time of the first Moslem inroad have survived the persecution to which they were then subjected: most likely they either emigrated or were converted to Islam. The present race is of Panjabi origin, as their features and manners, ceremonies and religious opinions, as well as their names, sufficiently prove. It may be observed that they show a general tendency towards the faith of Nanak Shah, and that many castes have so intermingled the religion of the Sikh with their original Hinduism, that we can scarcely discern the line of demarcation.

As usual among the Hindoo race, wherever it is settled, they have divided themselves into different tribes. The Satawarna, or seven castes of Indians, in Sindh, are as follows:—1. Brahman; 2. Lohano; 3. Bhatio; 4. Sahto; 5. Waishya (including a number of trades as Wahun, grain-toaster; Khatti, dyer, &c.); 6. Panjabi; and 7. Sonaro.

Five of these belong, properly speaking, to the Waishya (the third, or merchant) division of pure Indians. The seventh is a mixed caste, descended from a Brahman father and a Shudra mother. In Sindh he is usually considered as belonging to the servile tribe.

Of the first, or Brahminical class, we find two great bodies, which are divided and subdivided as usual. These are—1. Pokarno; 2. Sarsat or Sarsudh.

The Pokarna are the priests of the Bhatia Banyans. They belong to the Telinga-kul of the Panjadravida race, and worship Maharaj, an Avatar of Vishnu.[1] Tradition differs as to their original home: one account represents them to have derived their name from Pushkara-Kshetra, near Benares: another declares that they were called Pushpakarna because they offered up flowers to Lakshmi, and being cursed by Parwati for refusing to eat flesh, migrated from Jesulmeri to Sindh, Cutch, Multan, the Panjab, and other remote localities. Other castes affirm that the Pokarno is the illegitimate offspring of a Brahman Tapeshwar (devotee) and a Mohani (fisherwoman), who imprudently undertook to ferry the holy man across a stream. Moreover, the name is facetiously composed of the Sindhi words *Pohu* lage so *Kare* (" he does exactly what he pleases "). However this may be, it is clear that the Pokarno, although the purest Brahman in Sindh, is by no means of high family: he seldom refuses to trade, and sometimes will condescend to become a cook.

The Brahmans[2] take the words Das, Ram, Chand, Rae, Mal, Ji or Misr, before or after their names, as Misr-Sukh-Deoji: Taro Misr, &c. Many of them can read, if not understand, Sanscrit; they are celebrated for their knowledge of judicial astrology, and make a profession of drawing out the Janampatri (horoscope), deciding horary questions, writing out the Tripno (astrological almanack[3]), performing the ceremonies and superintending the religious education of their followers. Their knowledge of astrology is very limited, yet it is sufficient to secure them the respect of their inferiors, and even of stranger castes, such as those professing the Sikh faith. Moreover, they lead a tolerably strict life, Brahminically speaking: seldom learn Persian or enter into public business, eat no flesh, never drink spirits, and marry in their own caste. The Pokarno wears a turban (not the Sindhi cap) usually of red cloth, shaves the beard, and dresses like the Sahukar or trader. He is not distinguished by any peculiarity of Tilak, or sectarian mark, but draws on his forehead a horizontal or perpendicular line indifferently, whereas in India the latter distinguishes the worshippers of Vishnu from the Shaivya, who is known by the line across the brow.

The Sarsat or Sarsudh (properly Sariswatiya, as derived from the vicinity of the Saraswati River), belongs to the Panja-Gaur race. Of this tribe there are about forty pure families in Sindh; they abstain from all irregular practices, and call the rest of the caste Sindhur,[4] because they allege the others were originally Numryo Belochies made Brahmans by Rama Chandra, who when in want of a priest, applied a tilak of vermillion to the Mlenchha's forehead. The Sarsat are supposed to have emigrated to Sindh about two centuries ago. They worship Mahes (Mahadeva or Shiva) and Bhawani his Sakti. The latter deity is known to them by many names and under a plurality of forms, as Devi, Durga, Kali, Parwati and Singhawani (the "rider of the lion"). She presides over most of the Hindoo sacred spots as Hinglaj, the Mekli Hills near Tatta, Dhara Tirth near Sehwan, &c., &c. The Sarsat abstains from certain impure meats, as beef and fowls: he eats fish, wild birds, onions and the flesh of the deer, kid and sheep, because ordered to do so by the Mountain Goddess in a time of famine. The meat is always bought, as the higher castes of Hindoos here as elsewhere will not kill animals themselves. Most of the Sarsat tribe drink wine and marry widows, though only those of the same caste. They shave the beard and wear the dress of a common Sahukar, namely, a white turban, Angarkha (long cotton coat), Dhoti (cloth round the waist instead of trowsers), Bochan (kerchief or shawl thrown over the shoulders), and cloth slippers: in the hand a Mala or rosary of sandal wood, with twenty-seven beads is usually carried. Sometimes a Sarsat will assume the dress of an Amil (revenue officer) whereas the Pokarna rarely, if ever, do. There are considerable numbers of the Sarsat class, settled at Hyderabad and Sehwan. They seldom learn Persian, or enter into the service of Government: their principal occupations being the study of Sanscrit and the Gurumukhi writings. The Sarsat, having but a modicum of astrological learning, make up for their deficiency in that kind of imposture by rather a rude invention. Their peculiar mode of prediction is called "Nashkan Karanu:" it is done by fixing the mind upon any question proposed, at the same time inhalation is stopped, and the nostrils tightly pressed with the fingers. After due meditation, the issue of an event is pronounced upon *ex cathedrâ* and a fee duly claimed.

Properly speaking, there is no remnant of the Kshatriya in Sindh. Those who lay claim to the regal origin are generally Banyans, who have partly conformed to the practice of Nanah Shah's religion: they are therefore heterodox Sikhs. It may be observed that it is general throughout India for the fighting Shudras whose peculiar Dharma, or religious duty, it is to seek occupation in warfare and plunder, to call themselves Kshatriyas. So the Nair of Malabar, who is notoriously of servile caste, will describe himself as belonging to the military division, wears the string of the twice-born and conducts himself accordingly. The Kshatriyas in Sindh have in reality no rank among Hindoos. Their chief occupations are trade and government employment: their studies are confined to the writings of the Gurus, and sufficient

Persian to keep them in office. They wear no peculiar costume, and do not necessarily shave the beard: their food is the same as that of the Sarsat Brahmans, except that they eat only animals that have been killed, either by themselves or a fellow casteman, according to the Sikh rite termed Jhatko. Finally, they are either pure theists, or, as is more generally the case, they mix up deism with the old idolatry of the Hindoos.

Of the Waishya, Wani, or Banyan caste, we find, as has been said before, five great divisions in Sindh. The two chief are undoubtedly the Lohano and the Bhatio: of these the first is the more numerous and influential; a description of them, therefore, will be a general portrait of the Sindh Hindoos. The Lohano derives his origin and name from Lohanpur in Multan: the date of his emigration is lost in the obscurity of antiquity. That the event took place at a remote period, we have ample proofs in change of language and invention of several alphabets. Moreover, the Lohana are found dispersed throughout Belochistan, Affghanistan, and the eastern parts of Central Asia: they have traded for years on the neighbouring coast of Arabia, amongst a barbarous and hostile people, enduring all kinds of hardship and braving no little danger in pursuit of wealth. This race is an interesting one, as showing the way in which, during ancient times, the Hindoos colonised distant countries, and propagated the tenets of their now exclusive faith. A Lohano is not expelled his caste for visiting the lands of the Mlenchha: nay, scant enquiry is made as to whether he did or did not connect himself with them by marriage or cohabitation. His children would belong to the Hindoo race, and if they visited their father's native land, might rise in caste by becoming Vishanvohu. There is little doubt that even the descendants of strangers belonging to respectable tribes might, after the lapse of some time, become Hindoos in Sindh. If, for instance, a European were to entrust his child, before it had tasted impure meats, to the charge of a Brahman, and that the boy were educated according to the rules of that faith, he would certainly be able to marry a Shudra woman, and possibly a Banyan: he could always enter the Sikh religion, and thus lay claim to Kshatriya rank. As a proof of this, I may adduce the fact, that under our rule the Hindoos in Central Sindh proposed, if they did not carry out, the measure of admitting converts from Islam, in retaliation of the numerous forced conversions that had been put upon the worshippers of Brahma in the olden time.

Of the Lohana race there are at least fifty divisions and subdivisions, the chief of which are the Khudabadi and the Sehwani. There is little union amongst them, they only agree in abusing every family but their own. All of them wear the Janeo, or Brahminical thread. They are, properly speaking, Pujara (worshippers of the Indus-god): many of them are Shewak[5] of Vishnu and Shiva: a few have adopted the faith of Nanak Shah. They eat meat, are addicted to spirituous liquors, do not object to fish and onions, and will drink water from the hand of their inferiors as well as their superiors in caste. Their devotions are neither frequent nor regular, they content themselves with reciting a few verses in Panjabi or Sanscrit, and attend the different Mela, Jat and Darsan,[6] where much more licentiousness than piety is found. It is said that they possess a few devotional works written in the Sindhi tongue, in Khudabadi characters. These are read out and explained to the people by their religious instructors; they are carefully concealed from the eyes of foreigners.

The Lohana may be divided into two great classes, according to their occupations.

1. The Amil or Government servants. An account of them will be found in the next chapter.

2. The Sahukar (Merchants), Hathwara (Shopkeepers), Pokhwara (agriculturists), and all that live by traffic or manual labour.

These people generally avoid the costume of the Moslems and wear turbans or skull caps Angarkha (long cotton coats), with a Lung or Potiyo (a scanty cloth wrapped round the waist and thighs) sometimes a cummerbund, and a kerchief or shawl thrown over the shoulders. They shave the beard, the crown and back of the head, so as to leave merely a Choti (or lock on the poll) and Chuna, bunches of hair on both sides. The mustachio is not trimmed, and is never removed except when in mourning.[7]

For education the trader goes to a Wajho or Hindoo schoolmaster, who teaches him to read and write that Sindhi alphabet in which the Wahiyun[8] or account books of the family are kept, together with a little arithmetic. After a year the studies are laid aside for practice in business. In this the Lohana, like their Indian brethren, are uncommonly acute. Some of them make large fortunes in foreign lands. Their staple articles were cloth and Hoondees (bills to discount); the latter was their especial favourite, as they could charge upon it what interest and premium they pleased. Under the British government their system of remittances has been changed for a better one. Shikarpur used to send forth a multitude of these wanderers; the number now is considerably reduced. As it was not the custom for respectable individuals to travel about with their women, the latter were usually left under the charge of their parents and friends.[*] The consequence was, that too often when the husband returned after a long sojourn in distant countries, like the European crusader, he found his wife surrounded by a small family of her own. The offended party, however, seldom allowed this trivial incident to interfere with the domestic tie; and after inflicting corporal chastisement upon his faithless spouse, dismissed the subject from his thoughts, and treated the fatherless offspring with truly paternal kindness. In other parts of Sindh, the Banyans have been so much scandalized by the frequency of this occurrence among their Shikarpuri caste-brethren, that they have proposed to put them under the ban of the tribe, unless they can compel their females to behave more respectably.

There are few varieties of the Shudra or servile caste in Sindh. Those that exist have all adopted the Janeo; they apply the Tilak to their foreheads, and imitate the Banyans in all points. At the same time the Shudra marry in their own caste. The Wahun exercise the craft called in Persian Nukhudpazi, and subsist by preparing for sale the different kinds of toasted grains.[10] The Khatti, or dyers, are numerous, as coloured clothes are generally worn by both Hindoos and Moslems. They usually live at some distance from the large towns; the reason of which, as assigned by the natives, is that they thereby acquire a greater facility for overcharging the price of their labours. Many of them, however, are found in the different cities, and there is no religious prejudice against them. Most probably they are obliged to establish their manufactories near the wells that afford the sweetest water. The Sochi, or shoemaker, will not dress leather; he buys it from the Moslem Mochi (tanner), sews it, and embroiders it with silk if required. The Hajjam (barber and cupper) comes from the district about Jesulmere, but he is of Sindhi extraction, and wears the dress of his own country, with the exception of the turban, which is of foreign form.

The above are the principal Shudra castes in our province. They generally worship Mahadeva and Devi; their only priests are the Brahmans. Their names may be known by the use of the appellation of the trade after that of the individual, as Teju Wahun, Haru Katti, Khatta Sochi.

Besides these different classes of Hindoos, there are many of the nondescripts called Sikhs, resident at Hyderabad, Sehwan, and other parts of Central and Northern Sindh. They are easily recognised by the fairness of their complexions, and a peculiarity of look and general appearance. There are two chief orders of them:—1. The Akali Khalsa, or pure Sikh; 2. the Lohano Sikh. The former imitates the devotee of the Panjab in all things; he never allows a razor to touch the hair on any part of his person, eats several kinds of meats which the other deems impure, as, for instance, the domestic fowl; has the usual religious hatred to tobacco, anoints his locks with clarified butter instead of oil, and touches the flesh of those animals only which have been killed according to the form called Jhatka. He wears no Janeo, but is distinguished by the Chakkar (quoit), Kangani (iron ring worn on the wrist), and short drawers called Kachh. The Lohano Sikh is also called Nanak Shahi and Munnee Singh (a "shaver," because when in mourning he shaves the head and beard). He is allowed to smoke, wear the Janeo, and eat flesh that has been killed by Moslems; sometimes he carries the Kangani, but never the Chakkar. The marriages and funerals of this class very much resemble those of their kindred, the Lohana Banyans. Both sects are known by their rings made of Amritsir iron, which is supposed to have the property of causing sleep, and the Sumarno,[11] or rosary of the same material, used by them to number the recitations of the different Ism and Mantra (forms of words half magical, half religious), in which their faith abounds.

In Sindh the Sikhs will make converts from all classes, Moslems, Hindoos and Christians. When the rite is to take place, the individual is caused to perform Ishnan (bathing the whole body), after which he visits the Thikana or Dharmsala (the place of worship), and offers up a gift to Nanak Shah. If the neophyte intend to become a Khalsa, the Udasi (high priest) drops a little sweetened water thrice into the palms of his hands, making him each time repeat a certain formula called Khando. If he prefer becoming a Nanak Shahi, after the bathing he is told to offer his gift, recite a secret Mantra with his palm full of water, immediately drink the latter and repeat the following lines of the Satanam. They are in praise of the Almighty, and taken from the book called Jap, the first section of the Panja Granth[12]:—

> "Satanám Kartá Purukh
> Nirbhau, Nirwair, Akála-murat
> Ajúni Sambhau, Guru Prashád
> Jap 'Ada sach; Jugáda sach;
> Hai bhí sach: Nánaka[13] hosín bhí sach."

The neophyte of either order is then instructed in the duties of his religion. Every day in the morning he is to perform Ishnan, repeating the prayer called Bani. Before eating, reading the Granths, and certain other occasions, Panjasnani (washing the five parts, viz., face, hands and feet) is enjoined. In the morning, after bathing, the young Sikh is expected to visit one of the Thikana, and hear or bow to the Granth Sahib.[14] About sunset he must read or listen to the Sandar in a place of worship; at such times the swinging frame upon which Granth Sahib reposes is waved to and fro, but the book is not opened. If unable to attend the Thikana, Sikhs should repeat aloud the Bani, Jap, and Sandar at their own houses. In each Thikana there are, generally speaking, one Udasi, or Gadiwala, who lives upon the Bheta (offerings to God) and Ardas (presents made to Nanak Shah or his scriptures); five or six Chela (pupils or aspirants to the priesthood), and several Trahlia (servants and religious followers).

The principal religious mendicants among the Hindoos of Sindh are the Shanasi (Sunnyasee), Jogi, Gosain and Ogar. There are a few Jangams, but they are all natives of Hindostan. The Shanasi is a Brahman who has abandoned the world and its vanities; he has become a beggar for the sake of futurity, ought to subsist by alms and presents made to his young followers, to lead a life of abstinence, and never to marry. He is often a decent-looking man, who does not refuse to engage in such mundane matters as taking up government contracts under a Parsee, acting as physician, selling Mantra and Jantra (magical forms), practising alchemy, and counterfeiting the coin of the realm. Many of these Shanasi come from Cutch and other provinces adjacent to Sindh; they are usually depraved characters, who eat flesh and fish, and will even drink wine and spirits. The sect is known by ochre-coloured clothes, and a turban of the same hue. Shanasis, like other religious mendicants, seldom burn their dead. They sometimes commit suicide by what is called Ghuffah (or being buried alive by the Chela). When they die in the course of nature, they usually direct their bodies to be disposed of either by Dharti-dak (burial in the earth), or more rarely by Jala-dak (being thrown into the water). A Dillo (large earthen pot) full of sand, is fastened to each leg and arm of the corpse; it is then conveyed in a boat and cast into deep water with much ceremony.

The Jogi also has ochre-coloured clothes, but wears a cap instead of a turban. His dwelling-place is called an Astan. This class of mendicants is known by a large hole pierced in the lobe of the ear; hence they are called Kana-phar (ear splitters). When dying the Jogi is placed in a sitting posture, leaning forward upon a Beragan;[15] it being against rule to depart life in a recumbent position. For his tomb they dig a pit and half fill it with salt; upon this the body is placed, cross-legged, with a Pahori (mattock) in one hand, and the arms resting upon the Beragan. Salt is then thrown over the corpse, and earth heaped upon the grave. Some respected individuals of this order have tombs of bricks with lighted lamps and other decorations.

The Gosain is not often met with in Sindh. His value, however is sufficiently appreciated; and when he appears, he is generally surrounded by a multitude of followers. In appearance he resembles the Shanasi, lives by alms or presents, and often amasses a considerable sum of money. After death he is generally disposed of by Jala-dak.

The Ogar resembles the Jogi, as the Gosain does the Shanasi. He is known by a bit of hollow wood fastened to a thread and worn round the neck. Through this he blows, before undertaking any action whatever. Like the Gosain, the Ogar is seldom found in Sindh.

None of the four classes above described wear the Janeo. Their names are thus distinguished—Bao Natgur Shanasi; Surajgar Gosain; Goraknath Jogi; Sarsatinath Ogar, &c. They all worship Mahadeva, Goraknath (a son of Mahadeva, according to their accounts), and Bhabaknath, an Avatar of Goraknath, so called [16] because when a votary approaches the sanctum at Hinglaj the mud boils up of its own accord.

About the Thurr, or little desert, to the East of Sindh there are a few outcast tribes such as the Koli (Coolies), who occupy themselves in hunting and cultivation: the Bhils (Bheels), who in life, customs and occupations very much resemble the Dapher tribe, and the Dedh or Meghawar [17] (tanners, shoemakers and weavers). The latter are supposed to have come originally from Malwa, and the language and character in which their Pothi or sacred books are written, are said to belong to that province. They are now to be found in many parts of Sindh: in greatest numbers however about Ghara, Hyderabad, Mirpur and Omerkot. Near the latter place they are in a flourishing state, far superior in numbers to the Moslems, and sufficiently wealthy to support a Mehman-khano or caravanserai for the housing of travellers. The pride of caste, if it can be called so, manifested by these outcasts is sufficiently ridiculous. The following is one of their favourite assertions: "Asráf Sindh meṉ kaun hai? Yadhra ghar hamáro: ghar Sayidenro: adh ghar Fath Aliro: bi merei dándá-dundá." [18]—"What great families are there in Sindh? Ours is one: that of the Sayyids another: Fath Ali's was half a family, and all the rest are riff-raff." As regards religion, the Dedh are neither Hindoos nor Moslems. They have, however, numerous ceremonies directed by their priests (called Gurara), who are compared by them to Sayyids, and greatly respected as the expounders of their Pothi, or sacred works.

In burying the dead they cast the earth upon the corpse, instead of protecting the latter by a gravestone as the Moslems do: and bodies are generally buried in the direction of east and west. Their Pir (patron saint) is one Pithoro, the son of a Dedh called Mandan, who, when the great Sufi, Bahawal Hakk, honoured Sindh with a visit, called upon him and begged his intercession with Heaven for a son. Bahawal Hakk was pleased to do so and gave a little bit (Pitthu) of wet date to his visitor: no sooner had the wife of the latter tasted the blessed morsel than she conceived, and in due time bare a son, who was called Pithoro, from the piece of date. He is buried in a building at Gurahor, near Omerkot, and his memory is respected by the Moslems as well as the Dedh.

The Hindoo religion is not to be found in a state of purity in Sindh.[19] To this general statement the only exceptions are a few Brahmans, who study their Scriptures in Sanscrit, and possibly have visited India, the fountain-head of their superstitions. As has been before said, Hinduism here is mixed up with the heterogeneous elements of Islam, and the faith of Nanak Shah. A Hindoo will often become the Murid (follower) of a Mussulman, and in some cases the contrary takes place. When we consider that the religion of Brahma was at one time established throughout the province, that as late as the seventeenth century, the Hindoos were reckoned to be ten times as numerous as their conquerors, and, finally, that all the great Pirs revered by the Moslems have classical Hindoo names, we must conclude that the spots accounted holy by the pagans were seized upon by the followers of Mohammed. Some of them bear indubitable signs of their Polytheistic origin, in Yonis (natural or artificial holes in solid rock), Lingams carved in stone and placed upon the margins of tanks or pools, together with many other equally unmistakeable evidences. From the Sikhs, the Sindh Hindoo has learned to simplify his faith: to believe in one God, whom he calls Khuda, Thakur and Bhagwan, and to assent to the doctrine of a future state of rewards in Sarg [20] (Paradise), and punishments in Narg (Hell). The male and female Avatar, such as Vishnu and Shiva, Lakshmi and Devi, are considered by them as intercessors with the Deity, and hold the same position as the Paighambar or prophets of the Moslems. The Pirs and holy men are revered as sub-intercessors, whose superogatory piety enables them to aid their fellow creatures in a spiritual way. These saints never die, but even in their tombs can listen to and forward the prayers of their votaries. They are thus invoked:—The Suali, or person, that wishes to make a request, approaches the Turbat (sepulchre) of some well-known saint, as for instance Lal Shah-Baz, and addresses him in the following words, "O Kalandar! O thou with a great name, well known in both worlds. Thou listener to thy friends! only grant me my desire and I propose to distribute a Deg [21] to the poor in honour of thee!" The shrine is visited every morning and evening; if the devotee be a stranger and his business very urgent, he takes up his abode on the spot. Perseverance is of course the only means of success, and when the Pir has been so slow in his movements as to allow his visitor to die before the prayer has been granted, all believe that there will be a greater proportion of reward in heaven. Some votaries are so grateful as to continue their visits to the tomb, and presents to its guardians, even after success.

The names of the principal Pirs, who are reverenced by all classes of both faiths, are—

1. Lal Shah-Baz, called by the Hindoos, Bhartari Raja.
2. Patto Sultan (or Pir Alim Shah), designated Pir Patto.
3. Khwajah Khizr, termed Jenda Pir.
4. Pir Mangho, known as Lalu Jasraj.
5. Shaykh Tahir, also called Uddhero Lall.

There are many others of less celebrity in different parts of the province.

Of these worthies Jenda Pir is believed by the Hindoos to be the personification of the Darya or Indus. It is difficult even for an European, to view that noble stream without admiration, not unmixed with awe: the Oriental goes a step beyond, and from admiration directly proceeds to adoration. The Pujara (votaries of the river) are remarkable for the rigidness of their fasts, which generally last forty days together. During that period they avoid eating, drinking, smoking and other enjoyments, at all times from midnight till sunset. Every evening before breaking the fast, they recite the Sindhi verses called "Panjará Darya Shah$^{\underline{a}}$ já."[32] When the forty days are concluded they go to the Indus, or if the river be far off, to some well; repeat certain prayers and hymns; sip water three times from the palm of the hand, and after eating a bit of the kind of cake called Patasho, return home.

The following is a specimen of a Sindh Munajat or hymn often recited in honour of the Indus—

O thou beneficent stream!
O Khizr, thou king of kings!
O thou that flowest in thy power and might!
        Send thou joy to my heart!

I have sinned times innumerable;
Pardon my transgressions!
Thousands weep and pray at thy threshold.
        Send thou, &c.

I am wretched, I am ignorant,
I am a fool—the fool of fools;
O King, hear my prayer!
        Send thou, &c.

Intercession becomes thine exalted rank,
Bright art thou, and bright is thy look,
Above thee there is no (earthly) power.
        Send thou, &c.

O giver of daily bread, send it to me!
Give my heart purity and truth!
Difficulties surround me.
        Send thou, &c.

O Sultan! O verdant Lord![23]
Aid thou the weak one!
Thou knowest my case.
        Send thou, &c.

Make my foes my slaves!
Destroy my obstinate enemies!
Aid thou the aidless!
        Send thou, &c.

Thou art great in learning,
Powerful and lordly,
A worker of miracles, a brave benefactor.
Send thou, &c.

(Through thee) all the sorrowful are joyful,
All the hungry are fed,
All the weak are strengthened.
Send thou, &c.

Thou art our aid, our stream, our horseman,
Thou takest our boats to shore,
Thou art our defence in time of need.
Send thou, &c.

Be with me in all things,
Give me power before men,
Support me in difficulties.
Send thou, &c.

O friend! I bear thee in mind,
Thou corner-stone of the weak!
Hear the prayer of Eesar![24]
Send thou joy to my heart!"

In the specimen above quoted there is a little Oriental exaggeration in epithet, and an attribution of certain offices and power likely to offend the European mind. It is not, however, intended to ascribe to the river that omnipotence which we consider to belong peculiarly to the Almighty. A native of the East, especially a Hindoo, allows his power of veneration to lead him astray: his warmth of imagination and language never permits him to stop short of the highest possible grade of adulation. The following hymn[25] to the Deity may be contrasted with that addressed to the river-god.

"O All Powerful! do with me as thy wisdom directs.
Thou supportest the firmament without pillars, and causest the spheres to revolve.
Thou givest brilliancy to the sun, that it may enlighten the world:
Thou causest the moon to shine through the darkness of night.
If thou wishest to turn the beggar into a monarch, verily thou art able,
And thou canst change the monarch into a beggar who wants a loaf.
At thy threshold, a hundred thousand worshippers continually pray.
From a single blade of grass thou causest a hundred events to arise.
In the greatness of thy mercy thou hast given intellect to man,
And yet thou eludest the intellect and comprehension of mankind.
Thou cherishest the helpless, and pardonest their sins in this world:
From thy store of kindness thou canst grant the prayer of this thy worshipper.
Thou canst either reward the infidel, or cast him into hell:
Such powers are thine, whether thou actest in this or in that way."

The next in rank to Jenda Pir, the river-god, is his Wazir (prime minister) Uddhero Lall. The legend told about him by his Hindoo votaries runs thus:—In the days of Aurungzebe, there was a Moslem Kazi in Sindh, who resolved by moral and physical means forcibly to propagate his faith throughout the province; and such was his success that the worshippers of Brahma began to fear for the very existence of their religion. At length Heaven heard their prayers, as the time was come when the persecution grew intolerable.

At Nasrpur (about twenty miles from Hyderabad),

a town built on the Indus, which then flowed down the channel now called Phitto, dwelt an aged Banyan, whose name was Puggar Wani. Others call him Ratan; all, however, are agreed that he and his wife were not only childless, but also much too old to hope for the blessing of issue. He being the head of the caste called together a Pench, or meeting of the Banyans, requested them to join him in supplication, and for that purpose led them down to the river side, where for forty days they persevered in the exercises of praying, fasting and vigils. After that period when all began to despair of success, a human voice was heard to issue from the stream, conveying the gratifying intelligence that the committee of Banyans might be dissolved, as the Kazi's persecutions should shortly be changed to a favourable view of the religion against which he was so violent. The Banyans departed, but as after a short time no alteration appeared in the conduct of the Kazi, they returned to the stream, and requested that it would be more explicit. The kind-hearted River vouchsafed to inform them, that he proposed to manage the matter by means of a child who should be born to Puggar Wani and his wife. Again the Banyans returned home in a state of joyfulness. In due time a boy appeared, and received the propitious name of Mangal, the "auspicious one." No account of this wonderful youth's education and occupations is given, except that when he reached his fifth year his parents used to send him together with the other children of the neighbourhood to sell Kuhar (boiled grain or pulse) in the adjacent villages. Mangal was in the habit of leaving his home every day, and after getting rid of his companions by different means, of going to the river side alone and occupying himself with prayer to the stream. When it was time to return, he threw his basket of Kuhar into the waters, which requited him by upheaving the same vessel full of money, honey and other delicacies. At length the parents, judging by the sum they received from their son, suspected that all was not right: no adjurations, however, could force the secret from the boy. All he said was that he had gained the money honestly. One day Puggar Wani resolved to follow his son and watch his proceedings. When Mangal reached the river, he performed his orisons, sat down to meditate, and finally threw in his offering. Upon this two men issued from the stream and in presence of the father, drew the boy into the water. Puggar Wani shrieked in despair, but was presently comforted when he saw his son return from his visit with the usual basket upon his arm. At this time it so happened that in consequence of the Kazi's increased vehemence for converting the Banyans, all agreed once more to have recourse to the river. Again their prayers were responded to by a voice, which informed them that they might be of good cheer, as Mangal was now an efficient protector. The boy undertook that office with pleasure, and only requested that whenever a Hindoo was chosen out for persecution he might be informed of the event. A few days afterwards the Kazi came to Nasrpur, and being in a bigoted frame of mind, openly declared his resolution to circumcise the whole place; and as he had heard some curious tales about Mangal, that he would commence with making an example of him. After summoning the boy, the Kazi began by setting forth the advantages of Islam, and its superiority to all other faiths: his juvenile auditor, however declared himself not to be convinced by unsupported assertions, and demanded a polemical discussion, to which the Moslem agreed. As is commonly the result of such exercises, out of as well as in Sindh, neither party, at the termination of the argument, saw any reason to alter his own opinions. Mangal then proposed that it should be resumed at the river side, and stated his conviction that no spot could be better fitted than the banks of the Indus for discriminating truth from falsehood. When they arrived at the place appointed, the Hindoo remarked that on such occasions he was in the habit of casting his white cloth over the water and seating himself upon it as on a carpet. Moreover, he opined that if his opponent would only join him, the question would easily be settled, as the true religion would swim and the other sink. The Moslem was as strong in faith as the pagan, he instantly accepted the test, and only bargained that his own Chadar,[26] which was stained with indigo, should be used instead of the Hindoo's cloth. When the antagonists reached the middle of the stream the Kazi began to sink. After enduring two or three immersions, he lost courage and called to the boy for aid. Mangal, nothing loth, merely ordered his persecutor to place the tips of his fingers upon the corner of the Chadar, where five white spots instantly appeared. He obliged the Kazi to swear by that sign he would cease his persecutions, and then landed him in safety.

To the present day the Sindh Moslems, especially the Mohana, who have a superstitious regard for the river which supports them, wear blue coloured sheets with white spots on each of the corners. As might be expected the Moslems deny the truth of the whole story and declare that the marks are purely ornamental, adducing as a proof that many more than five (which ought to be the number) are found in each of the four places where they are disposed. A great fair, in honour of the river, takes place at a village called Jahejan jo Goth, about ten miles from Nasrpur, on the first day of the month, Chait. It is dignified with the name of a Jat, or pilgrimage, and is remarkable for the trafficking and debauchery that go on there. At such times the Hindoos are in the habit of taking their pregnant women to the spot, and seating them upon a Lingam dedicated to Uddhero Lall: with the idea that, by the power of that holy man, a female fœtus will miraculously be turned into a male one. In derision of their credulity the Moslems sing these satirical lines :—

> "Láll Uddherá druggajens,
> Dhi hoe, ta put[u] kijens.
> O Sancto Uddhera hanc subige mulierem,
> Ejusque filiam in filium converte."

However, Lall Uddhero, under the name of Shaykh Tahir, is much respected by the Mussulmans; who still show his Dairo and the place where he taught the Koran. Of course they treat with contempt all the inventions of the pagans, and their claims to the possession of so holy a fellow-religionist.

The Munajât, or hymns composed in honour of Uddhero Lall, resemble in most points the specimens quoted above. From a number in my possession, I select the following as a sample:—

"O Uddhero thou art ever near us;
For this reason, O Lál,[87] I clasp thy skirt.
Thou fulfillest the desire of the desirer
And listenest to the entreaties of men.
Great indeed are thy gifts,
O thou that shadest the heads of thy petitioners!
I have brought my prayer and offering to thy shrine.

O Uddhero, thou art ever near us;
For this reason, O Lal, I clasp thy skirt.
O lord, in thy hand is the key of daily bread,
Without the refuge of thy threshold I should be a wretched wanderer:
At thy door thousands of petitioners are standing,
Thou sendest away the sorrowful in joy,
And the barren conceive and bear children.

O Uddhero, thou art ever near us;
For this reason, O Lal, I clasp thy skirt.
Thou art a king of kings,
A hero, and a noble monarch.
Cause thou our fates to be happy,
Blacken the faces of our foes,
And let the prayer of the poor be heard!

O Uddhero, thou art ever near us;
For this reason, O Lal, I clasp thy skirt.
I am weak in mind and bad withal,
Abundant in sin and shame,
O Pir! thou canst pardon my sins,
O Brahman! receive my Ardas
And Vriddhi and Siddhi[88] shall fill my abode.

I will conclude this part of the subject with the translation of a short hymn in honour of the Kalandar, Lal Shah-Baz. The original is in Persian, and, consequently very much admired by the small literati of the Amil class.

> "O Kalandar! thou art indeed a king,
> Who in time of difficulty can remove our grief.
> Throughout the world thy pure name is known.
> By thee every wretched one has been cured of his wretchedness.
> Thy look falling upon brass acts as Alchemy,
> So is thy regard to every one that openly owns his sins.
> We entertain great hopes from thy (well-known) kindness,
> O true friend! give us our daily bread.
> Thou king of kings, Shahbaz! show us thy favour,
> For I, thy worshipper, am in trouble and confusion.
> Thou knowest my case, O lend me thine aid!
> Thou art the king of mighty kings, lend me thine aid!
> Make green the tree of my hopes,
> Open the gates of grace before my face!
> From thee I hope for kindness, disappoint me not!
> Draw me forth from the gulf of pain and despair.
> Thou art the Mir of Merwand,[*] the lion of the Lord,
> Pity the case of this thy hapless supplicant."

Most Hindoos of any education in Sindh have a Pothi, or prayer-book for private devotion. The character used is Shikastah of the worst description, written either by the devotee for his own benefit, or handed down from father to son. Such volumes are treated with the greatest respect, and covered with one or more cloths, lest profane hands should touch the binding: they are seldom shown to strangers. The following is a list of the usual contents of such books:—

A short poem in Persian called the Sri Kishan Namo, because after every fourth line come the words "Sri Kishan Gao, Sri Kishan Gao."

The Sri Ganes Namo, an address (poetical as usual) to Ganesha, praying for prosperity and the acquisition of wealth.

Sri Gopal Hari, a prayer to that well known Avatar.

Short extracts, in verse and prose, from the Bhagawat: these are generally in the Persian and sometimes in the Panjabi language.

The Sukhmani of Nanak Shah.

A number of Madah, Panjara and Munajat to the different Pirs, in Persian, Panjabi and Sindhi. Most Hindoos know several of these by heart and are in the habit of reciting them daily. They are believed to be peculiarly efficacious in a temporal, as well as a spiritual sense, if repeated at a time of need.

A few prayers and hymns addressed to the Creator in the Shastri (Sanscrit), Persian, Panjabi and Sindhi tongues. Those composed in the dead language are rare, and seldom, if ever, understood by the reciters. Compositions in the three latter dialects very much resemble those of the Moslems in style and ideas. As a general rule the Creator is not nearly so often addressed as his creatures.

Detached verses in praise of Krishna and the other Hindoo demigods, generally in Panjabi or Jatki, so composed that they may be sung to the different Rag and Ragini—musical modes. A few of these are in the form of a dialogue, as between Krishna and a worshipper; a mother and her son: suggesting the idea of rude beginnings of a drama.

The Pothi concludes with a variety of astrological tables, simple computations for determining lucky and unlucky days, a Fal-Namo[30] or two, prescriptions in medicine, and other such semi-religious compositions.

CHAPTER XIII.

THE AMIL CLASS: ITS ORIGIN, OFFICE, AND CHARACTER FOR FRAUDULENCY.—THE CEREMONIES, SUCH AS INVESTITURE WITH THE JANEO, MARRIAGE, AND FUNERAL OBSEQUIES.—CONVERSION OF THE HINDOO TO ISLAM, AND HIS RETURN TO HINDOOISM DESCRIBED.

THE typical class of Hindoos in Sindh is the Lohano Amil (or officer in government employ); a short description of the different rites and ceremonies, as performed by that caste, will therefore suffice to give the reader a general view of Hindooism as now existing in the province.

The Amil class was created by the exigencies of the native rulers, who could not collect or dispose of their revenues without the assistance of Hindoos. Throughout the east, the people least fitted for any business in which calculation is required, are the Moslems; and even the old Ameers, with all their hatred and contempt of Kafirs, were obliged to own the superiority of the Infidel over the Faithful in this one point. The princes that followed them lost a great portion of the ancient bigotry, and became very careless of caste; I have seen one of the chiefs of the present family embrace a Hindoo Diwan[1] with as little repugnance as he would have shown to a Sayyid of the purest blood. When the Hindoo found that he was necessary to his lords, he made the best use of his acuteness and readiness, and soon succeeded in improving his political standing in the country. Thus, most probably, arose the Kardar system, which, though of a totally different nature, is in Sindh what the Patell and his little republic are in India. After gaining a certain footing, the Amils began to abuse their powers. The native rulers had two great checks over their officers; capital punishment and torture. A Hindoo who went too far, was liable to be beaten to death with clubs and thorny sticks, or buried up to the neck in the ground; for minor offences a Tobra, or horse's grain-bag, full of red pepper well pounded was put over his head; he might be hung up to a tree by his legs, with pots of sand fastened to his arms; have a few scorpions introduced into his pantaloons, or undergo the discipline of the Billi (she-cat), a peculiar instrument furnished with hooks to tear the flesh. Such extreme measures however were seldom resorted to, and the subjects of native governments generally are not terrified by the prospect of the severest penalties, because they may fairly calculate the chance of evading them. So it was in Sindh. No Ameer could consider himself safe from the most impudent frauds.

By diligently studying the art of deceit, the Amils not only maintained but elevated their social position. They alternately served and sold, flattered and forsook the princes; bribed and bullied the middle ranks of Moslems who were dependent upon them; and they ruled with a rod of iron the common people whose debts and necessities enslaved them to Hindoo

Shroffs and Banyans. The Amils looked rigidly to their own advantage; and in pursuit of it they were held by no oath, feared no risk, and showed no pity. Though cowardly in action, they were brave in endurance, and the rulers have sometimes owned that they were fatigued with torturing them before the tortured seemed tired of the torture. The dexterity with which they forged documents, orders and seals, was acquired by long and diligent practice. Some were so skilful that they could copy the impression of a seal ring with pen and ink, and disguise the forgery by slightly rubbing it with the thumb. Another, but a less favourite way was, after procuring an old impression, to revive it, and then stamp it upon a bit of moist paper. This second impression was again touched up and stamped on the part of the deed where the seal is generally placed. The usual way of forging a seal was to take a little wet Met (clay), and, after cutting it into the requisite shape, to apply it to one of the best impressions that could be procured. A penknife (if much delicacy was required an instrument made on purpose) was then used to pick out the parts left white on the clay, and by this means they formed a seal which could safely be used ten or twelve times. Thus the finest and most complicated seals, cut in India and used by our politicals, were so successfully imitated that none but a professional graver could detect the fraud. Sometimes wax was substituted for the Met; but it never was so favourite a material on account of its being so liable to be spoiled. When all schemes failed, some Amils would go directly to the Wejhan-Waro (seal cutter) and bribe him to assist them.[3] This, however, was a hazardous experiment, as all seal gravers were known to the officials, and detection would have led to a severe punishment. The skill of the Amil in forging documents was not inferior to his other acquirements. In simple cases, after the deed was written out, it was sufficient to lick the paper, place it between the ground and a dusty carpet or rug, and stamp upon the latter till the ink lost the gloss.

In appearance the Amils are more robust and better looking men than the common Sindhis. Some of them are remarkably athletic in form, and their features are frequently regular and agreeable. They were compelled by the Moslems to adopt the costume of the Faithful, such as the Sindhi cap and drawers, to cultivate long beards, and shave only the crown of the head. They do not, however, trim the mustachios according to the Sunnat; moreover, they affix the Tilak or sectarian mark, and wear shirts with the opening down the left breast, to distinguish them from the Mussulmans. They delight in rich dress, and indeed are, generally speaking, fond of show and expenditure, offering in this point a contrast to the parsimonious Hindoo of India. Their religious opinions are the same as those of the Lohana who are engaged in trade, and they use similar food. In consequence, however, of superior education, and perpetually mixing with members of another faith, not a few of these Amils are Dahri, or materialists.

The education of the Amil has been treated of in a preceding chapter. On entering office, he used to repair to the Daftar (secretariat), and there copy from the Rakab,[3] or Dastur el Amal, the different particulars which he might require in the province to which he was appointed.

The chief ceremonies observed by the Hindoo Amils are those of investiture with the Janeo, marriage and funeral obsequies.

The rite of Janeo payanu̲ (putting on the thread of the twice-born), is thus performed. After five or six days preliminary feasting, with music and other signs of mirth, as at a marriage,[4] the parents of the boy who is to be invested summon a Sarsat and Pokarno Brahman, together with a Jajak, or player on the cymbals. One of the priests is then asked to name the articles necessary for performing the ceremony. The set form of his reply is "Chhebbi bhajaun,"— "let me break a basket," *i. e.*, fill it with a variety of things which he then specifies. Different kinds of dry fruits, grains and drugs, new clothes and ornaments, incense, twine, red paint for the Tilak, an axe, a ladle, a Sarai and Surmedani (needle for applying, and small vessel containing antimony), two wooden pestles, and some pieces of Mango wood, make up the list of requisites. All these things are prepared the day before the ceremony takes place. The rite called Dikh is a peculiar form of Puja (worship), performed by the Brahmans at night over the boy, who is previously bathed and dressed for the occasion in a new suit of clothes, with a golden Duri[5] round his neck. On the morning of investiture, the family prepare a quantity of Rot or Kuti (dish consisting of wheaten flour, clarified butter, and raw sugar), proportioned to their means, and send it, together with the articles above enumerated, to the place where the ceremony is to be performed. The sites usually selected are the Dharamsal (Sikh temples), a Marhi (or Asthan, dedicated to Mahadeva), or a Than (temple in which the River-god is worshipped); those that are built close to the sea or flowing water are preferred. The ceremony begins with a procession, consisting of all the friends and relations of the family, headed by the Brahmans and musicians. On arriving at the spot selected, the boy is seated upon the ground with a copper coin under his right foot; and in this position his head is shaved, a Choti[6] only being left. He is then bathed in a state of nudity if under thirteen years of age; when arrived at puberty, he wears a small Languti, or apology for an apron. He is afterwards seated upon a Mohri (wooden pestle), whilst the Brahmans recite Mantras (religious formulæ) over him, and the Jajak perform upon their cymbals. The Naugirhan ji Puja is then gone through in the following manner. The boy is presented with a quantity of rice in a large platter, and directed to divide it into nine little heaps, placing a betel nut and a dry date upon the top of each. A prayer is recited over these articles, and the boy is dressed in a new Languti and turban provided for the occasion. The Brahmans, after receiving Dakhna,[7] place the Janeo round the neck of the candidate, who performs Namiskar to the priest. His friends and relations then address Wadhai (congratulation) to the father in the following terms, "Baba! to khe Wadhai,"[8] and the latter distributes gifts to all the religious characters present. The boy then rises, takes a staff in one hand, a ladle in the other, and with a hatchet upon his shoulder, walks round the assembly. When he reaches his father, or the person superintending his investiture, he says to him, "Baba, baba! Gang wanyan," and receives the reply, "Baba! tu na wanyin; to ja parpota na wanyan."[9] The father then draws a thread from his turban, and presents it to his son as the sign of a covenant made between them that the boy shall be formally betrothed as soon as possible after investiture. This being done, the Brahmans instruct the boy in the respect due to the Janeo, and the way to dispose of it on certain occasions,[10] concluding with whispering a few unintelligible words in his ear.

The Janeo is composed of three cotton threads, each of which contains three small twists. Its length is about five feet; it is worn over the left shoulder, passes down the right side, and the knotted ends hang down below the waist. It is made and sold by the Sarsat Brahmans; the Pokarna clans prepare their own Janeo. This thread of many virtues is by no means an expensive article; at the fair of Lall Udhero, near Hyderabad, ten may be bought for one Pice. It is not changed every year. When broken or otherwise injured it is thrown into water, and the wearer goes to the priest for a new one. It is considered disrespectful to talk of *selling* a Janeo; when the Brahman is asked for it, he expects a moderate Dakhna, and in order to enhance the value of his merchandise, he seldom gives it without a number of questions and a little feigned unwillingness. The fresh string is put on either at home or at the priests house without any ceremony.

The marriages of the Lohana Amils are expensive, seldom costing less than five hundred Rupees; consequently many remain single till late in life. They seldom take more than one wife at a time, unless that one be barren. Divorces are rare, and there is no religious objection to marrying a widow.

Mangano, or betrothal, the ceremony preliminary to marriage, is managed by the mediation of a Sarsat Brahman, a Jajak, and their wives. The two males enter into a treaty with the father of the bride, whilst the females arrange matters between the women of the two families. When a match is intended, they await the first lucky day, and then send to the sister or sister-in-law of the bridegroom a Muro or dish of sweetmeats and cocoanuts, together with a few Rupees. The Sarsat and Jajak receive a small present of money. A dish of Jilebi (kind of sweetmeat), or something of the kind, is prepared in the Ghot's (bridegroom's) house, and distributed among the friends of the family. This concludes the preliminary rite, after which both parties patiently wait for the means of matrimony.

When the marriage day is fixed, the ceremony called Bukki is first performed. All the female relations and friends of the family assemble at the Ghot's house, where they find a heap of corn prepared for them. A few handfuls of the grain are thrown into a handmill, and the bridegroom is desired to touch its handle. The women then grind a small quantity of it. A Brahman, summoned for the occasion, puts a Tilak of vermillion upon the Ghot's forehead, and afterwards does the same to all the women present.

Dry dates and cocoanuts are distributed among the females; the priest's share is not forgotten, and a plateful of the same is sent to the Kunwari's (bride's) house. On the day after the Bukki, they prepare the Mahadew jo Rotu, or Mahadewa's bread.[11] This is taken to the Marhi, and offered to the Gosain in attendance. He retains about four pounds for his own use, and directs the remainder to be sent as a present to the caste brethren and friends of the future couple. Musicians are now summoned; they attend at the house day and night, and the melodious sounds which issue from it inform the world that a marriage is being performed.

Two or three days are allowed to elapse before the Majlis, or general entertainment, is prepared. A Yaddasht, or list of the names of all the near relations, male and female, is drawn up in the bridegroom's house; after which some members of the family call upon and personally invite them. The feast consists of meat pillaus and different kinds of flesh, with fruit, wine and sherbets; it is continued till the third, or more generally the fourth night. At the conclusion of it, sweetmeats are prepared by the Ghot's kinsmen, and sent out as presents. The bride receives every day six or seven Thali (large platters) full of this confectionery, together with some kind of Randiko (toy), as a painted wooden fruit or animal, placed upon the sweetmeats; the whole is covered with a handsome silk handkerchief.

The Jasraja jo Dinh,[12] is the ceremony that takes place two days before the nuptials. The Brahman, Jajak, and all the male kinsmen meet at the bridegroom's house, bathe and dress him. A woman's necklace is bound round his neck, and a gilt staff is placed in his hand. During the whole affair, some male relation, selected for the purpose, walks about with the Ghot, carrying a drawn sword. Music and different kinds of prayers are continued at intervals all that day, especially about the time of sunset.

The day before the nuptials is called Ghariya jo Dinh.[13] In the evening, the bridegroom's mother, or some near matronly relative, accompanied by fifteen or twenty women, and two or three men as a protection, goes to the nearest stream or well, fills an earthen vessel with water and decorates it with flowers. She then walks up and down a street or two, carrying the pot upon her head, and lastly returns home with it.

The marriage day is called Vihan, or Shadiya jo Dinh.[14] About sunset the Ghot is bathed and prepared for the ceremony called Dikh. His old clothes are torn to pieces by his friends, and he is dressed in a new suit; the last article of which is a woman's embroidered sheet thrown over his head. Above it a fillet of flowers and a paper cap about two feet long, covered with grotesque pictures of gods and idols, are placed. He is then seated upon a carpet spread upon the floor, whilst a mare[15] is being prepared for him to ride. At this period the assembly is feasted, and several dishes are sent as a present to the bride. The procession[16] now begins; the musicians lead the crowd, then come the male relations of both parties; behind them the bridegroom on his mare, and lastly the females in a compact body. They progress slowly through the streets, and at last reach the bride's house, though not by a direct road. There the Ghot dismounts to the sound of music, and enters, accompanied by his nearest relations. The women of the procession repair to the female apartments, where they find the bride sitting ready dressed to be harangued and consoled by her mother. The part of the procession not belonging to the family retire to a tent, or some place outside the house, and amuse themselves with talking, smoking, and drinking sherbet. Before the bridegroom enters the room, the lady is placed in a recumbent posture upon a carpet or mat, and is covered with a wadded quilt. The Brahman, Jajak, and two women hold two pieces of cloth, one over her and the other along the side towards the company, so as effectually to conceal her from prying eyes. The Ghot is then desired to sit at her feet upon the quilt; in this position some milk is poured over and money waved round his head. Finally, prayers are recited by the Brahman, and the bridegroom rises. Some female relation instantly raises the bride and huddles her, wadded quilt and all, into the next room. Presently the same female returns, and ties the end of the bride's veil to the bridegroom's shawl or girdle. The Kunwari is now brought back into the room, and seated by the side of the Ghot upon a small Sandal (a kind of chair). Then, in presence of the relations, a Brahman lays his hands upon the heads of the young couple, and recites the Vedi or nuptial form, together with a little of the peculiar poetry called Lavan.[17] The bridegroom's father fees[18] the Brahmans and Jajaks, and distributes alms and presents to religious characters and the poor. After this the bride's father, with a handkerchief wound round his neck, in token of supplication, advances and washes the bridegroom's feet in a large pot of milk; he then presents his son-in-law with a trifling sum of money,[19] gives over all his daughter's clothes and jewels, and with much and sententious good advice, solemnly commits her to his charge. To this the Ghot responds with sundry promises to love, cherish and protect her.

These preliminaries often last till the approach of dawn; when they are duly concluded, the Ghot again mounts his mare, and the Kunwari steps into a palanquin without untying the veil and shawl. They slowly advance towards the bridegroom's house, and when arrived there, dismount. Both pass the night together. At daybreak the parents and male relations of the bride go to the nearest river, plunge in and congratulate each other upon having got rid of the household calamity, namely, a daughter.

Early in the morning the Ghot rises and repairs to his bride's Peko,[20] or paternal home. He spends the day there, and sends for his wife in the evening. After passing three days together, the young couple separate, the bridegroom returning to his own home, till the Sataro, or seventh day, when he and his relations are invited to a grand feast by his father-in-law. Next day the separation concludes, the wife returning to her husband's house.

All the Hindoos in Sindh burn their dead. The sick man when near death[21] is bathed, covered with a shawl and placed upon a Chonko (*i. e.*, a spot smeared with cowdung, and sprinkled with a little barley or sesamum). If any one happen to expire in his bed, the male member of the family who attended the deceased becomes defiled, and cannot be visited by Brahmans till he has been purified at some well-known place of pilgrimage. Ganges water and sherbet made of Tulsi leaves, are poured into the dying man's mouth. If he be rich, alms of money, grain, fruit, and other articles are liberally distributed to the Brahmans and poor people; if not, a little wheat and clarified butter are considered sufficient.

Immediately after the death the mourners assemble, and Bhagats (a peculiar class of Banyan devotees) begin religious songs and prayers, recited to the sound of instruments. The Charni, or bier, is now prepared. It is composed of seven pieces, two long and five short, of some pure wood, as tamarisk, &c. Upon this framework the stalks and leaves of the Jowaree (*Holcus Sorghum*) are spread, above them a layer of cotton, and upon that a white sheet. The corpse is bathed and placed upon the sheet in its Kafan, a kind of shroud which covers the face, and is tacked together down one side of the body. Lastly, a piece of silk or gold cloth is tied over the bier with fine twine; perfumes and flowers are thrown upon it, and the corpse is considered ready for burning.

The bier is raised by three or four Kandhi, or pall-bearers, who are relieved of their burden by the other friends of the deceased at certain intervals. They are assisted by the head mourner, who is termed the Pinniyawaro.[22] On the road the relations throw up dry dates into the air over the corpse: these are considered as a kind of alms, and are left to the poor. Before arriving at the Masan, or burning place, the body is placed upon the ground, and the Pinniyawaro, holding in his hand a Paro, or earthen pot full of water, together with the three Kandhi, the Brahmans and the Jajak, stands at the head of the corpse. The priests now recite prayers over a little barley and Sesamum, which are wetted and placed in the head mourner's hand; after this the face of the deceased is uncovered, and the grain inserted into the shroud. The Pinniyawaro then walks round the corpse three times, sprinkling the ground with water, and breaks the pot which he carried, upon a pickaxe half buried in the earth at the corpse's head. The pall-bearers again raise the bier. When arrived at the Masan, they find a pyre of Babul wood, about four feet high, and six feet by five, ready prepared. A few pots full of cold water are thrown upon the body, its face is uncovered, and a piece of copper money is put into its mouth.[23] The Pinnyawaro then stands a little to the right of the corpse's head, and supported by the three Kandhi, lights the pyre at the four corners with bundles of wood. Oil or clarified butter is thrown upon the flame, after which the mourners retire about twenty or thirty paces and recite prayers till the body is consumed. The procession then returns to the spot and perambulates the pyre three times, performing the ceremony called Perinpe Karanu̱. This is a mark of respect to the ashes of the dead, it is done by raising the joined palms of the hands as high as the tip of the nose. All now proceed to the sea, a river or a well. On the way it is customary to sit down and for each individual to write upon the dust with a short bit of stick, in any character familiar to him, the words "Ram Ram Sat," (the Lord is Holy) either three or seven times, after each time carefully effacing them with the fingers. The mourners then bathe in their clothes, change their dress and when the Jajak addresses them with the phrase "Wiho Penchani ja Kalyan,"[24] retire a few paces, sit down and talk.

At this time the chief mourner, remaining with a Brahman upon the bank of the river, digs a hole there and buries some grain. This is called Pinni pa'anu. He then receives from the hand of the priest a pot containing water, a little sacred grass and an iron key, and is desired to keep it for twelve[25] days constantly near him.

When the Pinni is duly concluded, the chief mourner returns to the company, who, at the order of the Jajak,—Penchu warayo,—"twist their turbans" round their heads, and return home. Each person before entering his house makes the Nafar (cook) bring him a pot of water and a handful of ashes and salt mixed. After waving the former round his head as a kind of expiation, he pours it on the ground and throws the latter into the nearest corner.

The Pinniyawaro and Kandhi, instead of going to their houses repair to that of the deceased, which, during the funeral has been purified with cowdung by the servants. They first lead a female calf all round the rooms. Next, a small hole is dug where the owner died, and in it a lamp is so placed under an earthen pot cover and a blanket, that no one but the Pinniyawaro who trims it every morning, may see it.

It is kept burning till the dawn of the eleventh day[26] after the death; at which time it is carried away and thrown into the sea or river.

On the Chauntho, or fourth day after the funeral, a Jajak goes round to all the caste brethren inviting them to wash their heads. When they are assembled the Pinniyawaro accompanied by priests, relations and servants proceeds to the graveyard, collects the ashes of the dead in an earthen pot, returns to the mourners, and with them repairs to the river or sea side. He there embarks in a boat and casts the pot into the stream,[27] meanwhile the rest remain seated upon the bank, chatting and exchanging rough jests. When the Pinniyawaro returns all bathe, and with the exception of him, wash with clay and oil, amusing themselves with manual pleasantries and abundant facetiousness till it is time to return home. The pall bearers must go back with the chief mourner to the house of the deceased, where they eat a certain sweetmeat made of sugar, milk, clarified butter and grain. They are then permitted to visit their families for a few hours, but are obliged to return and feast with the Pinniyawaro, on buttermilk and a kind of bread, sweet and unleavened. After this they may return home, but are not allowed to eat anything there before the Jajak commands them to "twist their turbans." They have now finished their labours and are no longer accounted impure.

The Pinniyawaro continues to bathe every day and to perform the rite of Pinni in presence of a priest. He lives on grain and vegetables, dines, smokes and sleeps alone, as he is still in a state of defilement, and before each meal he must feed a cow with cooked grain, and persuade her to drink or pour the water upon her tail.

On the Yaraho, or eleventh day after the death, the soul of the deceased is supposed to leave his house. The chief mourner must first throw away the lamp; he afterwards returns to the river in company with Brahmans and a Karnigor.[28] There he performs various ceremonies, such as casting into the stream an earthen pot containing matches and short sticks of Bhan (a kind of poplar), presents an offering of dates, rice, milk, incense and other articles to the river-god, and after the priest has poured three hundred and sixty pots of water upon the roots of a Peepul (*Ficus Religiosa*),[29] bathes and returns home.

The first thing done on entering the house is to offer the couch, bedding and some clothes of the deceased to the Karnigor, provided he will eat some sweetmeat prepared for the occasion. As in case of his refusing the offer, the ghost of the dead man would haunt the house, he always rejects the first advance, and demands fees together with all the articles of dress left by the departed. He is sometimes very extortionate,[30] and not unfrequently violent disturbances ensue. The Karnigor, however, seldom fails to win the day. When his avarice is satisfied, he eats four or five mouthfuls of the sweetmeat, seldom more, for fear of the spirit. After this he carries off his plunder taking care not to look behind him, as the Pinniyawaro and the person who prepared the confectionery wait till he is fifteen or twenty paces off, break up all the earthern cooking pots that have been used, and throw three of the broken pieces at him in token of abhorrence.

On the twelfth day the Pinda (offerings to the manes of the dead) are made. The Pinniyawaro rises early in the morning, bathes in some river and returns home, carrying an earthen pitcher full of water. In the mean time twelve Brahmans meet at the house which has been previously purified with cowdung, and one of them, generally a Sarsat, acts as Guru (religious teacher). He recites prayers whilst the Pinniyawaro smears with cowdung a place in front of the Brahman, scatters barley and Sesame over it, moistens some raw rice and disposes it in nine little heaps upon the ground prepared for it. These are the Pinda. Some lines of thin string are spread over them and betel nuts are placed in order between the heaps. The Pinniyawaro then rubs some vermillion as a Tilak for the Pindu in the palm of his hand and scatters a little of it over each heap by sharply jerking the forefinger of the right hand.[31] Honey and milk, mixed together, are poured upon the rice, incense is lighted and its smoke directed towards the offering. Lastly, the Guru recites certain prayers, whilst the Pinniyawaro, holding his Janeo, takes water from a cup in the hollow of his joined hands, and scatters it over the offering by inverting the palms. This is repeated three times: the heaps of rice are then collected and put into the cup, which is carefully covered over with a cloth. Thus concludes the Kacho (raw) Pindu. It is succeeded by the Pakko (cooked) Pindu, a similar proceeding, except that this time boiled rice is taken from the food prepared for the Brahmans. When the ceremony is over, the Pinniyawaro takes up the cups containing both offerings and throws them into the river. He then returns to his guests and washes their feet, after which they all sit down to a feast of vegetables and different kinds of bread. If the Pinniyawaro be a rich man, he makes presents to all the Brahmans: if not, he merely gives a fee and some articles of clothing to the Guru. The feast seldom ends before the evening. About sunset a Jajak goes about the town, and warns all the relatives and friends that the Baraho[83] is come. They assemble at the house of the deceased, and at the order of the Jajak, remove the dirty skull caps, which they have worn as mourning since the death, and put on their turbans. At the end of this ceremony the Pinniyawaro stands at the door and replies "Sat Ram!" to "Ram, Ram!" the salutation with which he is addressed by each of his departing guests. When all are gone the Pinniyawaro, accompanied by a few relations, repairs to a river or well, and there eats a little of the sugar cake called Patasha,[83] and drinks some water. He then carries some of the same sweetmeat as an offering to the Gosain of the nearest Marhi, and afterwards returns home.

On this day ends the Garar, or reading of holy books, by a Pokarno Brahman, for about two hours every evening at the house of the deceased. This is only done by the wealthy, who give liberal presents of money and clothes to the officiating priest.

The list of ceremonies is not yet concluded. When a month has elapsed, another Pakko Pindu must be prepared, and at least one Brahman feasted: the same is done after three and after six months have passed, and on the anniversary of the death a greater number of priests must be entertained. Finally, ever afterwards in the month Baddu, on the day of the week when the individual died, a Kacho Pindu must be offered up.

These ceremonies vary much in different places. Their great number is of course intended to benefit the priestly order and other religious idlers;[34] at the same time the expense attending them serves forcibly to impress upon the minds of the people the solemn nature of such an event as the death of a relation.

Females do not attend at the funeral pyre, the Pinni or the Pinda. During those ceremonies they go to the river, bathe and lament. From the first to the twelfth day after a death, women visit each other and carry on a perpetual succession of weeping, shrieking, tearing hair and beating breasts. This is called Siyapo; it is kept up for twelve months when the head of a family dies. Their mourning is a dress of coarse cotton cloth dyed with madder;[35] for a husband it is worn a whole year. Twelve days is the shortest period for which it can be assumed, however distant the relationship of the deceased may be. The Sati rite appears now unknown to the Sindh Hindoos, though doubtlessly practised by them in the olden time. Young widows sometimes find second husbands, the latter, however, lose reputation by such a connexion. Of late years some castes have got into the habit of marrying a brother's widow: the purer families still view it in the light of an incestuous union.

The ceremony of female burial very much resembles that of males, except that the corpse is bathed by women, the Garar is not performed, and the wives of Brahmans are feasted instead of their husbands.

Wills are drawn up by the legator. When any one dies intestate, the Brahman divides his property according to the rules of Hindoo law.

Conversion of the Hindoos to Islam has sensibly diminished, as might be expected, since it ceased to be compulsory. Formerly it must have proceeded so rapidly as almost to threaten the very existence of Hinduism; at Mathara, Hala and other places, there are still whole streets full of Nau-Muslim (New Moslems), as the converted pagans are termed by the Faithful. The ceremony of conversion is as follows:—The Hindoo is bathed from head to foot, dressed in pure garments, generally of a black colour, and taken to the Mosque to listen to a Maulud,[36] of which he does not understand a word. He is then mounted upon a horse, or placed in a palanquin and carried round the town, accompanied by a crowd of people firing guns, performing on musical instruments, and displaying other signs of joy. When he dismounts, pieces of money are thrown upon his head, and are afterwards given to him as a present. He is then taken to the house of the Kazi, who chooses him a name.[37] Finally, he mentions some caste into which he wishes to be received, and is circumcised with all due solemnity. This last measure is omitted in the initiation of females; in all other points the ceremony is the same. It is presumed and believed that the proselytes are afterwards instructed in the rules of the strange religion; generally speaking, however, they are left in almost utter ignorance of them. They frequently retain their aversion to beef and other equally unmistakeable proofs of a heathen origin. The Moslems, here as elsewhere, honour new converts in theory and despise them in practice: for the advantage of their religion, however, they are careful not to make any display of contempt and seldom neglect to provide them with a wife and some kind of employment.

The exigencies of their peculiar position have compelled the Sindh Hindoos to relax one of their strictest rules and re-admit members of their own body whom force or persuasion separated from them. This, however, is confined to those places where the Hindoos are not sufficiently numerous to be able to reject such persons. As has been before mentioned, in some towns they are much more strict than in others. For instance, at Kurrachee, where the Moslems are in the minority, one of the richest merchants was not permitted to return to his caste. He was a Tohryal (circumcised), and had tasted impure meats; this was deemed a sufficient objection against him, and although he has for years conformed to the practice of his former faith, and has been most liberal in fees, donations and alms, he is still compelled to eat and drink alone. At Shikarpur, and other places, this would not have been the case.

During the native rule any attempt at apostatising from the Moslem faith would infallibly have incurred condign punishment. Under our government the candidate applies for a written permission, directed to the Kardar, or revenue officer, and a circular to the Mahajans (merchants), advising them that they may re-admit the applicant. The apostate Shaykh then applies to the Brahmans, and spends some time and a considerable sum of money in cajolery and bribery. At last the priest yields and asks the candidate three times in a set phrase whether he be willing and ready to return to the faith of his forefathers. This being duly answered in the affirmative, the candidate is desired to name his terms, which are raised by infinite haggling and chaffering to the utmost of his means, and he solemnly promises to obey the Brahmans in every thing. His head is then shaved and he is directed to feed cows in the jungle for about a week, during which time he wears a skull cap and cloth round the waist. A staff is placed in his hand, but no slippers are allowed. After this he returns home, his head is again shaved, and the place where the Choti ought to be is left untouched by the razor.

After the candidate's house has been purified by cowdung, Brahmans repair to it for the purpose of praying and performing some minor ceremonies. Again the candidate is asked if he be willing to return to Hinduism, and receives from the priests certain rules of conduct, which he is ordered strictly to follow. Presents of money, clothes, grain, clarified butter and other edibles are given to those who officiate; the latter then name some particular place of pilgrimage which the candidate must visit. This is imperative, but the distance of the holy spot, the time to be spent there, and the alms to be distributed, are proportioned to the pilgrim's means. When he returns, he must feast a number of Brahmans, and recommence a course of offerings; he is also expected to give small presents of sweetmeats to all his brotherhood. Thus concludes the ceremony; the candidate being now supposed to be restored to his former state of purity.

CONCLUDING REMARKS.

Having arrived at this point of my labours, it may be as well to offer a summary of the views proposed in the preceding pages.

Sindh, still a new country to us, is and will be an important portion of our Eastern empire, for two reasons. In the first place, it may be made the common commercial depot of Central Asia; and secondly, it is an advanced line of posts thrown out to protect India from her natural enemies, the turbulent, warlike and powerful trans-Indine nations.

The province is at present in an impoverished condition, requiring a large amount of expenditure, which future years may reimburse to us. It wants population to cultivate the land, and money to enable the agriculturist to thrive.

With respect to the people, one main difficulty appears to be that of adjusting the balance between two rival races. Under a rule of foreigners, the Moslem and Hindoo will ever be antagonists; and to judge from experience, the former must succumb to the superior craftiness and stricter combination of the latter. To maintain as much as possible the equality of these great divisions, is to serve our own interests.

The natives of Sindh complain at present of the depressed state of the country, and the want of facility for education; the former is a grievance, not an evil; the latter should be remedied as soon as possible.

As we effect with one, all that a native prince can do with a dozen officials, a large body of men have been temporarily thrown upon their own resources. This of course causes discontent. The substantial Jagirdar, or country gentleman, now complains that he receives neither pay nor presents from us; that he is disabled by poverty from procuring labourers for his estate, and that his younger brothers and children, who formerly supported themselves by the sword or the pen, are become mere burdens to him. The middle classes lament that they cannot find employment, and that when employed their emoluments are comparatively trifling. Those who live by commerce declare that as demand decreases their manufactures are ruined, and the wholesale shrinks rapidly into the retail trade. The Ryots complain of scarcity of money and the impossibility of procuring loans from Shroffs and Banyans.

But these are the necessary miseries of a transition state. Our policy is based upon the sound principle, that agriculture and commerce are the only sources of wealth to a country which does not, like Mexico and Southern India, spontaneously produce the material or the means of riches. The soldier and writer will become, as cultivator and merchant, so many labourers in the field of prosperity, instead of being what they are under native rule—mere channels down which the stream of pay flows.

As regards education, we have hitherto been somewhat inactive. The native universities and colleges have been allowed to fall to ruin, and we have not substituted others in their stead. The Sindhis require vernacular works to be prepared for them, grammars, vocabularies, and translations of our popular school books. That their wants will be eventually ministered to, there is no doubt; the sooner, however, we extend the helping hand to moral progress the better.

The language popularly called the Sindhi is an ancient, copious, grammatical, and, to a certain extent, a cultivated dialect. As it is universally understood throughout the province, it must be considered more suitable for official correspondence and the transaction of public business, than the solecistic Persian now in use. Nothing can be so well adapted practically to facilitate fraud and injustice, as the employment of two languages, one of them understood only by the educated classes.

The last point to be noticed with respect to the Sindhi dialect is, that it contains some old and popular compositions which should be collected and preserved as a standard of language, and as an aid to the European scholar. We are not likely to derive much amusement or improvement from the literary effusions of a semi-barbarous race, but as a means of power they are valuable weapons in our hands. The Russians, the craftiest, if not the most successful of

Oriental politicians, have long since printed and translated the vernacular works of the Affghans; we, on the contrary, scarcely took the trouble to ascertain the nature of a tongue spoken throughout a country with which we have had intimate relations for the last twenty, and where we reigned masters during five years.

APPENDIX I.

The following short list of words, denoting the sounds of different animals may suffice as a specimen of Scindee copiousness :—

Bánga[1] *s. f.* Lát[i] *s. f.* Salát[i] *s. f.*	the crowing of a cock

Bek[a] *s. f.*, the cry of a goat
Bekár[a] *s. f.*, an intensitive form of the same word
Bebrát[u] *s. m.*, the bleating of a lamb, sheep, &c., in fear or pain

Bhún *s. f.* Bhumbát[u] *s. m.*	the buzzing of bees, flies, &c.

Bhaunk[a] *s. f.*, the bark of a dog
Bokan[u] *inf.*, the noise of a he-goat
Búbár[u] *s. m.*, the baying of a dog

Charchát[u] *s. m.* Chíchát[u] *s. m.*	the buzzing of bees or flies, cry of a child

Dhik[a] *s. f.*, the grunting of a buffalo
Guran[u] *inf.*, the noise of a ram
Gájgar[u] *s. m.*, the roaring of lion, tiger, &c.

Háhur[a] *s. f.* Hánhur[a] *s. f.* Henkár[a] *s. f.*	the neighing of a horse

Hing[a] *s. f.*, the braying of an ass

Karko *s. m.* Karkan[u] *inf.*	cackling of a hen, &c.

1 The philologist will observe that some of these words are derived from other languages; others, being imitative sounds, owe their similarity to accident.

Katí *s. f.*, the sound made by the camel grinding his teeth
Kánwkánw[u] *s. m.*, the cawing of crows, yelping of a dog in pain
Kík[a] *s. f.*, the trumpeting of an elephant, any shrill cry of pain
Kunak[a] *s. f.*, the grunting of a buffalo
Kúk[a] *s. f.* }
Kúkát[u] *s. m.* } the bark of a dog
Miyáw *s. m.*, the mewing of a cat
Mek[a] *s. f.*, the bleating of sheep
Onáí *s. f.*, the howling of a jackal
Rambha *s. f.*, the roaring of a bull
Rar[i] *s. f.* }
Rarhát[u] *s. m.* } the cry of a camel, any unpleasant cry
Sít[a] *s. f.* }
Síndh[a] *s. f.* } the kind of whistle called by the Arabs Sifr
Yakhyakh[i] *s. f.*, the yelping or snarling of a dog

APPENDIX II.

LIST OF THE PRINCIPAL BELOCH CLANS SETTLED IN THE PLAINS OF SINDH.

Babur
Badání
Badrání
Bágrání
Baharání
Bahrání
Bangulání
Barphat
Bhúrgarí
Budhání
Bugtí (Boogties)
Buldí

Cháchar
Chándiyo
Cháng
Chángání
Chángiyá
Chhalgerí
Cholání

Dedo
Doomkí (Doomkies)
Dhonkái

Eesbání

Gaból
Gádhái
Giskorí
Gorchání
Gorphánd
Gopáng
Gungání

Holání

Jádání
Jakhar
Jakrání
Jalálání
Jalbání
Jamálí
Jarawár
Jat

Jatoi	Lurka	Omrání
Jiskání		Onar
Joyo	Magsí	
	Malik	Pogh
Kakání	Mánikání	
Kaloí	Marí (Murree)	Rájer
Kalphar	Mir-jat	Rakhsháni
Kaprí	Mondrání	Rind
Karmatí	Muzárí	
Khoso		Sajadi
	Nidámání	Salamání
Laghári	Nizamání	Sarkhání
Lajwání	Nodání	Shahwání
Lakókar	Nohání	
Lashárí	Notání	Tálpúr
Lúnd	Notkání	Thoro

APPENDIX III.

THE Sindhis, like their neighbours the Belochis and their conquerors the Arabs, are divided into a number of tribes, or rather clans. The Rasm or recognised practice of the country allows of intermarriage, but forbids the marriage of a female from a higher into a lower family. In some of the oldest tribes not a little of the true spirit of clanship as known to Europe, appears to exist. A Sindhi family, for instance, like the Abro have their own traditions preserved and frequently recited by their own minstrels: they firmly believe that no other clan is equal in valour or beauty, and despise all the rest merely because they do not belong to the same name:

The following is a list of the principal clans of pure Sindhís:—

Abro	Agím	Arisár
Abro Daoch	Ahmedání	
Achhro	Akro	Bádul
Agár	Amro	Bádí-poto

Baghdo
Bahár
Bahban
Bahman
Bákúr
Bakhiyár
Bákro
Bambho
Bandejo
Báran
Báú
Behan
Berand
Bhaláí
Bhambro
Bhánai
Bhand
Bhetro
Bhati
Bhinto
Bhiriyo
Bhojo
Bhopatani
Bhopat
Bhugiyo
Bodlu
Boro
Boraro
Bukiro
Burbuli
Burdi
Bútro
Buzdár

Chaghdo
Chahán
Cháran
Channo
Chániyo
Chandveno
Chauhán
Chhediyo
Chhoretho
Chhortiyo
Chhutto

Dachar
Dador
Dad-poto
Dadhar
Dagar
Dáheri
Dakak
Dakho
Dall
Dambhar
Daochh
Daraz
Dáro
Dars
Dáyo
Depar
Deto
Dero
Dhagar
Dhággar
Dháro
Dhoki
Dinejo
Domki
Dúákar
Dublo
Dunyo
Dudh
Dúdo

Gaddo
Gaggan
Gahlro
Gahelo
Gaícho
Gajan
Gambhir
Gánghro
Gand-Sághar
Gárái
Garmo
Gel
Giddar
Gidor
Guggo
Gungo

Hákit
Hále-poto
Hálo
Haliyo
Hamáti
Hamirako
Heláyo
Hingorjo
Huliyo

Isanpoto

Jagsi
Jagiyo
Jahejo
Jakhro
Jámot
Jebar
Jhabro
Jhangasiyal
Jokiyo

Juno
Junejo

Kachhelo
Káho
Káko
Kalhoro
Kamandiyo
Kán
Kánand
Kándro
Kánro
Kánth. Kas
Kathiyán
Katiyár
Karkuli
Kebar
Kháro
Kháwar
Khachar
Kháki-poto
Khalifo
Khokhar
Khushk
Kiryo
Kishmishi
Kiyan
Kodar
Kokar
Koryo
Kokáryo
Kongar
Kubbar

Labán
Ládo
Laddi
Lageto
Lákhiyo

Lákho
Lallang
Landri
Lángáh
Lándar
Logo
Loko
Lodhiyo
Long

Machhar
Machhi
Maháro
Mahmat
Mahmúd
Malár
Máliyo
Málú-poto
Máhiyún
Mahesar
Manáhi
Mandar
Mandhor
Mange-poto
Mangnejo
Mangriyo
Manguáno
Masháikh-poto
Mazdiyo
Meman
Mehar
Merí
Mindhro
Mirákhor
Mocho
Mor
Moháno
Multáni
Múso

Nágúo
Náich
Nárejo
Nahiyo
Nor
Notăni
Notiyár
Númryo

Othar

Pahwar
Pahor
Pallah
Palli
Parah
Parahár
Páran
Parbatiyo
Parrár
Páro
Parosar
Patáfi
Pussáyo
Pússiyo

Ráhú
Rájer
Rajero
Rájsí
Ramdeh
Ramzam-poto
Rangi
Rano
Raniyo
Ráthor
Rúnjho

Sadehar

Sadhúchyo	Sehro	Teno
Sagho	Sehto	Tháím
Sáhar	Siddik-poto	Tívno
Sáho	Siyál	Tunyo
Sáhim	Sipio	
Sakheráni	Sodhar	Udhejo
Sálár	Sodho	Unnar
Sammo	Soho	Utho
Samejo	Sopár	
Sámtiyo	Sorangi	Wahiro
Sánd	Sudar	Wangiyár
Sángi	Súfi	Wari-poto
Satpuryo	Súmro	Warso
Satthio		Wáyiro
Shaitáni	Tajujo	Widhrijo
Shodo	Táju	Wighyámal
Sholáni	Táro	Wikazo
Shoro	Tehbo	Wikyo.

APPENDIX IV.

It is difficult for a traveller, ignorant of the African languages, and possessing but slender means of obtaining information, to avoid errors in collecting specimens of the language used by these slaves. The following words were written down as pronounced by one of the most intelligent Africans, and afterwards other Sidis were consulted in order to insure as much accuracy as practicable. To the linguist they may possibly convey some idea of the class and nature of the dialect, and with this view they are offered to him.

Akánepá, give	Babayá, father
Akábijá, sell	Báredi, cold weather (Arabic)
Akáje, come	Bandúk, musket (Persian), &c.
Akánedá, go away	Begá, shoulder
Akáfengá, take	Benderá, a kind of cap
Akchukolá, carry away	Búrí, a hookah (Arabic)
Akúnah, (there) is none	Buzzí, a goat (Persian)

Chídore, a finger
Chhiní, earth, flat ground
Chinhándá, a couch
Choma, brass, copper
Chombo, a ship

Dámo, blood (Arabic)
Devo, the beard
Dibitá, a box (Indian)
Dimere, milk
Dizzí, a plantain
Druguángo, brother
Dupuko, a mouse

Fáká, a cat
Falási, a horse (Arabic)
Funnú, a jackal
Furá, the nose

Gáo, a shield
Gemá, good
Gerá or Gamirah, a camel (Arabic?)
Gopingá, bent, crooked
Guá, sugar cane
Gukú, a cock
Gurúe, a pig

Hí, this

Juwa, the sun; a day

Kaletá, come
Khánjo, a shirt
Khiriyál, tin
Khundoro, a sheep
Kisú, a knife
Kisumgurá, a hare

Kofiah, a cap (Arabic)
Komongo, iron
Kuná, beat

Lakáse, a wolf
Liyále, a real (the coin)
Lumbuángo, a sister

Máchho, an eye
Májí, water
Mákomo, the hand
Mámáyá, mother
Mánámukki, a woman
Márome, a man
Marimiye, my, mine
Mariyako, thy, thine
Mariyúre, his
Masekiro, the ear
Mazewá, the breast
Máwe, a hill, a stone
Mawingo, a cloud
Meso, the eye
Menú, a tooth
Mgongo, a back
Miye, I
Misare, an arrow
Moezí, a moon, a month
Moto, fire
Mromo, the mouth
Msetemi, a jungle
Mtoto, a child
Mtongi, an earthen pot
Muguru, a foot
Mukátí, bread
Mukokí, a spear
Mutámá Holcus Sorghum (the grain)
Mutomá, a slave

Ngombe, a cow
Nkúfá, a corpse
Nyátí, a buffalo
Nyámmá, flesh
Nyamkerá, a bear
Nyembe, a Mango (Indian?)
Nyoere, hair
Nyumbá, a house

Ogarí, rice, food
Okáre, sit.

P'háni, sea (Indian)
P'hep'ho, cold
Pinde, a bow

Rubo, half-rupee (½ real?)
Rupángá, a sword

Samorí, clarified butter
Sarawáli, trowsers (Arabic)
Sahni, a cup (Arabic)
Samági, a child
Siko, night
Simbah, a lion (Indian?)

Singo, the neck or throat
Sonbá, fish

Thembre, an elephant
Thende, dates
Thondua, stars

Uje, come
Umbúá, a dog
Ummeyye, strike,
Undoke, rise
Usmáme, stand
Usangeze, strike
Utanbo, stomach

Vidorí, finger
Viyakází, a daughter
Vukhe, hot weather
Vurá, rain

Wápí, where?
Weye, thou

Yure, he

Zahabo, gold (Arabic)
Zewá, a pigeon

The numerals are—

1. Moyà	6. Thandatú	11. Moyá Kummí; and so on
2. Perhí	7. Mfúngat	
3. Táhtú	8. Mnání	100. Kursh
4. Mme	9. Mpyá	1000. Kummí Kursh
5. Tháno	10. Kummí	

Very few Sidis can count more than six or seven in their own language, the deficiency is supplied by the use of Sindhi.

APPENDIX No. V.

Abstract showing the population of the Province of Sindh on the 1st February, 1851, as taken from the returns of the Collectors of the three principal divisions of the country, namely, Kurrachee, Hyderabad, and Shikarpur.

Collectorates.	Number of Towns and Villages.	Moslems.			Hindus.			Others.			Total.		
		Males.	Females.	Total.	Males.	Females.	Total.	Males.	Females.	Total.	Males.	Females.	Total.
Kurrachee . . .	1144	81,099	58,361	139,460	23,765	17,812	41,377	2,558	1,955	4,513	107,422	78,128	185,550
Hyderabad . . .	4977	227,751	182,443	410,194	61,593	47,143	108,736	18,254	14,627	32,881	307,598	244,213	551,811
Shikarpur . . .	1410	142,604	114,424	257,108	42,158	38,373	80,531	7,056	5,786	12,842	191,818	158,583	350,401
	7531	451,454	355,228	806,682	127,516	103,328	230,644	27,868	22,368	50,236	606,838	480,924	1,087,762

Kurrachee, May 1851.

NOTES.

CHAPTER I.

(1.) Kahgil; thick mud, mixed with chopped straw and other materials, used as plaster throughout Sindh and Central Asia.

(2.) Exactly resembling the Khamsin of Egypt. They are common throughout Persia, Affghanistan, the regions lying to the south and east of the Indus as far as Cutch; but, curious to say, they do not extend southwards of the latter province.

(3.) They did not, it may be urged, take the opportunity to attack us when the Kabul disaster presented the fittest opportunity. But their conduct on that occasion was no guarantee that they would not attempt to rid themselves of what they considered a "pestilence in the land," at some other seasonable conjuncture.

(4.) "Sind" is supposed to have been a brother of "Hind" (the populator of India), and a son of Noah.

(5.) Most geographers divide the country into two districts, Lar and Siro; a town called Halah, lying a little north of Hyderabad, forming the point where the frontiers unite.

(6.) The thermometer is seldom higher than 92° Fahrenheit; when at Sukkur it would not be lower than 112°.

(7.) The ancient Hindoo names of Hyderabad, are Nerun's Fort and Patolpur; this settles the disputed question at once. See Chap. II.

(8.) In July, 1839, a force of native troops, amounting to 1,600 men, in excellent condition, was stationed on the hills near Tattah; in November, the miasma of the inundation left fifty of them fit for duty.

(9.) The colleges for which Tatta was formerly celebrated; the Portuguese church at the east end, and the large citadel on the western extremity have long since been level with the ground. The splendid mosque erected by one of the deputies of the Emperor Aurungzeb, partially preserved, though deserted, is still the most conspicuous building in the town.

(10.) For an account of this worthy, see Chap. VIII.

(11.) Shikarpur, like Multan, was considered a gate of Khorasan, leading directly to Candahar by the Bolan Pass.

(12.) For full information respecting every question connected with the river in modern days, the reader may be referred to the Official Reports on the Indus, &c., &c., by Lieutenants Wood and Carless, of the Indian Navy, published by Captain Postans in his work on Sindh.

(13.) Anciently there were eleven large mouths to the Indus; three of them now suffice to discharge its waters in the dry season. The navigable course of the Indus is usually estimated at 900 miles. Its average breadth below Hyderabad is about three-quarters of a mile; higher up and lower down it is much wider. The maximum strength of the current is seven and one-sixteenth geographical miles an hour: the height of the inundation varies from thirteen to sixteen feet.

(14.) "Dandh," or "Kolab," is a tract of low land flooded by the inundation, partially or totally dry during the cold season, and at all times a hot-bed of miasma.

(15.) The Hindoos of Sindh have a tradition that Hiranyakasipu, the demon king of Multan, was powerful enough to draw down Megha Rasa, the Cloud-god, from heaven, and compel him to promise never to visit the Valley of the Indus. Besides the preternatural, there is an obvious natural cause for the almost total absence of rain in the want of trees, the destruction of which is one of the excesses to which the rancour of Asiatic warfare leads.

(16.) Captain James M'Murdo, a great authority in the historical, and all other subjects connected with our province, opines that the libraries and records of the old Mohammedan families of Bukkur and other cities, would, if laid open to us, considerably increase our stock of knowledge regarding ancient Sindh. I utterly failed to discover any of these treasures; the only Arabic chronicles shown to me, were recent translations of modern histories, probably from the Persian; and the value attached to them by their ignorant possessors was almost incredible.

(17.) As General Briggs, the learned translator of Ferishtah remarks, these books are not easily procurable. I doubt, however, whether, if procured, they or any other Moslem work would, as he thinks, throw light on the intercourse said to prevail between India and Egypt previous to Mohammedanism.

(18.) Nos. 3. and 4. were translated, or rather epitomised by the late Captain Postans.

(19.) The "Ex-political" author of "Dry Leaves from Young Egypt."

(20.) Rajput Rajahs or princes.

(21.) Alor, the ancient capital of Sindh, is supposed to have been situated about four miles from Rohri. See Chap. IV.

(22.) "Dewal was probably somewhere near Kurrachee, the present seaport of Sindh; it could not be at Tatta, as supposed by Ferishta." So says Elphinstone, "History of India," book 5, chap. 1.

In the second chapter, I have given my reasons for believing that Dewal and Tattah are the same place.

(23.) Kasim's romantic and tragical end is narrated at length by Elphinstone and Postans (Chap. IX).

(24.) Of this tribe, the native histories expressly say that its lineage is not clearly traced. Elphinstone calls them the "Sumera Rajputs," Postans "A clan of Arab extraction." The names of the earlier princes are Hindoo, those of the later ones Moslem, proving that they were originally idolators, afterwards converted to the faith of Mohammed.

(25.) The Sammahs were certainly Rajputs; for the present Jarejahs of Cutch still derive their origin from them.

(26.) This flight is celebrated in Oriental history, on account of the romantic circumstances which accompanied the birth of Akbar at Omerkot, the desert fort of Eastern Sindh.

(27.) This leader was the first whom history mentions as employing Arab and Portuguese mercenaries. His European soldiery fell into disgrace, in consequence of their burning and pillaging Tattah during the chief's absence from the city. Jani Beg had also 200 natives dressed as Europeans, who were therefore the first *Sepoys* used in India.

(28.) Not a Beloch, as is generally stated. The Kalhora family, as will afterwards be seen, claimed an Arab and a holy origin; the imposture was admitted because it was properly supported by sword and flame.

(29.) An Affghan of the venerated tribe called the Sadozai; he had been highly favoured by Nadir, who appointed him to one of the highest offices of the court. From some superstitious notion, he changed the name of his clan from Abdali to Durrani, and it has ever since retained the latter appellation.

(30.) In A.D. 1758, the Hon. E. I. Company's factories were established at Tatta and Shah Bunder.

(31.) Disappointed in a war with the Rajputs of Cutch, he returned to Sindh, and threw an embankment across the eastern bank of the Indus, which entirely cut off the sweet water of his enemy's country. The tract, once a rich and valuable rice-land, is now a salt and useless marsh.

(32.) The Belochis in Sindh owed their elevation entirely to their valour and conduct. A little before the subjugation of the province by Nadir Shah in the eighteenth century, Meer Shadad Khan, a Beloch noble, emigrated from his native hills in consequence of some dissension with his uncle, Meer Sobdar Khan, and took service under Miyar Nun Mohammed, the Kalhora. He raised himself to a high rank at the viceregal court of Sindh, and died about 1747, leaving four sons. Of them the third, Meer Bahram, succeeded him in as head of the tribe, took a prominent part in the tumults raised against the Kalhoras by their vassals, and fell a victim to the jealousy of Miyan Sarfaraz Khan.

(33.) Who, after vainly supporting the cause of the fugitive Abd el Nabi by two large armies, under Madad Khan and Ahmed Khan, conferred upon him the government of Leia as an indemnity. The Kalhora, true to his blood, had the folly and ingratitude to rebel against his powerful benefactor. He died in poverty and obscurity at Dehrah Ghazi Khan.

(34.) The bequest was in proportion of one-half to the senior surviving brother, Ghulam Ali, and one-fourth to each of the others.

(35.) Amounting to 130,000*l.* per annum. In A.D. 1833, the Talpurs were punished by Shah Shuja for failing to assist him when he attempted to recover his throne, and for neglecting to defray the portion of arrears of tribute accepted by that monarch in 1805. Until 1839, the usual evasions continued; at that time Shah Shuja agreed to receive 230,000*l.* in commutation of all arrears, and remission of all future payments on the same account.

(36.) Sher Mohammed of Mirpur, however, was most open and unguarded in his expressions of enmity.

The Ameers can scarcely be blamed for their double dealing; they individually desired to please the British Government, but they also feared to disgust the Belooch clans, to arouse the hostility of the Affghan nation, and to assist in placing one of their principal enemies, Shah Shuja, in a condition to be most formidable to themselves.

(37.) Amongst other things, they were accused of intriguing with the king of Persia, and a paper was intercepted which gave some little colour to the accusation.

(38) Mirs Nur Mohammed, Nasir Khan and Mir Mohammed. Mir Sobdar was exempted from the charge, in consequence of his undeviating attachment to the British interests.

(39.) A similar treaty, except that payment of subsidy was omitted, had been concluded with the Khairpur Ameers, by Sir Alexander Burnes. Mir Shir Mohammed, of Mirpur, had been admitted to a participation of the terms granted to his Hyderabad brethren, on the condition of his paying £5,000 per annum.

(40.) First, Mir Ali Mardan, the third son of Mir Rustam; secondly, Mir Rustam's other children, supported by Nasir Khan, the eldest son of his deceased brother, Mir Mubarak; and, thirdly, Mir Rustam's younger brother, Ali Murad.

(41.) The land was grudged much more than the towns, on account of the Shikargahs, or game preserves, which line the two margins of the stream.

(42.) Consisting of three hundred men of Her Majesty's 22nd foot, mounted on camels, one hundred Irregular Horse, and two guns.

(43.) For a detailed account of this brilliant affair, and the splendid victories of Meeanee and Dubba, the official despatches of Major Outram and Sir Charles Napier are all-sufficient. See Appendix to Captain Postan's "Personal Observations in Sindh."

(44.) These two princes, both of them firm friends to British interests, were involved in the common misfortune of their family.

CHAPTER II.

(1.) Who it must be observed have no proper name for the Indus in general and vulgar use; the Mitho Daryau, or "Sweet-water sea," is the vague expression commonly employed. They do not therefore much commit themselves when, pointing out a channel, they assert that the "Daryau" was there many generations ago.

(2.) So called probably from the huge Hindoo pagoda, which formed a prominent feature in the town. We are certain that the modern Tatta occupies the ground of the ancient Dewal, as the Arabs and Persians know it by no other name—Shal i Dibali still being used to mean a shawl of Tatta manufactory.

(3.) Translation. p. 102. Dr. Lee has, however, confounded Bukkur with the Bhagar creek of the Indus. Ibu Batuta's is simply a MS. error, for Bakar or Bukkur, the Arabic name of the place given to it by the early settlers, and meaning "the dawn."

It may not be considered inopportune here to observe that the "Itinerary of Hiuan Tsang" gives an accurate and evidently an authentic account of Sindh. I mention this because the antiquity and, consequently, the value of the work have been questioned in "an attempt to identify some of the places mentioned in the Itinerary of Hiuan Tsang," by Major W. Anderson, C.B., Bengal Artillery (Journal of the Bengal As. Soc., December, 1847.) The passage alluded to is the following:—

"De la retournant a Kiu-tche-lo (Cutch) au nord, traversant un desert (the Tharr, a sandy waste which separates Sindh from Cutch) passant le Sin-tou (the Sindhu or Indus) on arrive au royaume de Sintou (Sindh) 7,000 li de tour. La capitale Pi-tcheu-pho-pou-lo. Le roi est de le race Chou-to-lo. Asoka y a bâti beaucoup de stoupas."

Hiuan Tsang travelled in the seventh century of our era: in the early part of which, according to the native annalists, Chach the Braman usurped the throne after the death of Rahi Sahasi the second. That the Chinese travellers Chou-to-lo means the Chatur or Chitor tribe of Rajputs, we cannot doubt, as the author of the Tohfal el Kiram expressly mentions that the *Rana Mihrat Chituri* was slain in single combat by Chach, in an attempt to recover the kingdom after his kinsman's death.

The circumference of Sindh, as given by Hiuan Tsang, well accords with its traditional extent at the time of the Moslem invasion. The native annalists describe Sindh, in the days of the Rahis, or Hindoo rulers, as bounded by Candahar and Seistan on the north, by the port of Surat on the south, by Mekran west, and east by Cashmere. The latter country must not be confounded with the curtailed province which now bears the name.

Being ignorant of the Chinese language, I am unable even to offer a conjecture concerning the hopeless word Pi-tcheu-pho-po-lo. The metropolis of the Rahis was Alor or Aror.

(4.) From November to April, or at the farthest, May, as the Khamrya (excavators) could not work during the intense heat.

(5.) Of which there were about twelve varieties.

(6.) The "Wah," is a large canal excavated by Government; the Karriyo or Kassi, a smaller watercourse dug by the cultivator.

(7.) The instrument generally used was a stick, the length of which was fixed by means of a yard measure made of *paper*.

(8.) The Begar, or statute, was, however, generally speaking confined to upper Sindh.

(9.) Viz.—The slope from west to south, (or from Sukkur to the sea), and that from the river laterally from each bank towards the inland countries.

(10.) The names of two powerful Baloch clans, many of whom are landholders in Sindh. Jagirdars, or feoffees, generally managed to secure possessions near the heads of canals and the main trunks, leaving the land at the tail to the less fortunate subjects of Government. Thus the latter were, to a great extent, dependent upon the former for their supply of water during the inundation.

(11.) This is only done about the time when the Indus begins to fall; for the prosperity of the season depends much more upon the duration than upon the height of the inundation.

(12.) There is little danger of our losing much bullion by this proceeding, as the Cafila trade would not fail to restore it to us.

(13.) About one hundred and fifty feet square.

(14.) The Rabi is the vernal; the Kharif the autumnal crop. The former is sown in the three autumnal months, brought forward, as in India by the heavy dews and cool nights of that season, and reaped in the spring. The summer is the time for the latter, which is watered by the flooding of the river, and cut in the autumn, after the inundation subsides.

(15.) The principal kinds of land are three in number, viz. Sailabi, or ground watered by inundation: Charkhabi, that which requires waterwheels, and Barani, soil where rain falls.

(16.) A measure of grain. Sixty Kasa, in Sindh, make the well-known Kharwar (equivalent to about 850 lbs.)

(17.) Or Factotums, who, like the Fattori of Italy, generally throve by ruining their masters.

(18.) It was in this way that the rough census of the population, called "Khaneh-Shumari," was made under the native princes. We always find it difficult to arrive at any approximation to the numbers of the people in a newly conquered country, especially in the towns and cities. The dislike appears to arise from the necessity of mentioning their females, a vague fear that Government is plotting some mischief against them, and a superstitious aversion to assist in rousing Divine wrath by what they consider such a display of pride as that of numbering the people.

(19.) The Tahwildar, in such cases, would not respect even the protection of an independent territory.

(20.) As "intrusted" to the Kardars and others. Under native governments, as a general rule, Ijareh (or farming out taxes) is a fertile source of tyranny and oppression, and Amani of fraud and abundant peculation. No imposts afforded such facilities for roguery as the Sair.

(21.) The term Jeziat was changed into Peshkash, "a present," as more euphonious to Hindoo ears. Not less anxious were their masters the Ameers that the sum paid by them to the British Government should be called Kharj i Chaoni, or camp expenses, instead of the offensive appellation, Khiraj (tribute). The Beloch Sardars, or heads of clans, claimed Peshkash from Hindoos residing under their protection. When any one of the latter class married or remarried, the sum of five rupees was presented to the chief. On great occasions, such as the betrothal, nuptials or any member of the Sardar's family, the Hindoos were taxed for the feasts and entertainments.

(22.) Dr. Burnes, and the other travellers who visited Sindh during the rule of the elder Ameers, give many instances of their furious bigotry. The juniors, however, soon merged that feeling into one of utter inability to manage their kingdom without the aid of Hindoos.

(23.) The generic name for Persian wheels. The species are, first, Nar, the large or double wheel; second, Hurlo, the smaller one; third, Payrati, a foot wheel.

(24.) The Rhizome, seeds, pollen and other portions of many aquatic plants are eaten by the lower orders in Sindh.

(25.) Grass and vegetables brought to a town to be sold were not taxed, but the Seapoys at the gate were allowed to take a Chungi (handful) as the doorkeeper's perquisite.

(26.) The anchor being figuratively termed the ship's nosering.

(27.) The long slips of paper, which the Moonshees used for revenue accounts and other official documents were called Khasra when large, when of smaller size, Bandi.

(28.) The trial by ordeal, though forbidden by the Koran, is to be found in some form or other throughout the Moslem world. In Sindh it is called Toro: the following are the most popular of its many varieties:—

> First. They dig a trench about seven paces in length, and half that breadth, fill it with burning charcoal, and after fastening leaves over the feet of the accused party, desire him to walk leisurely along the whole length of the pit.

Second. A Kodar or pickaxe is heated to redness, and the defendant, after having his hands covered with green leaves is desired to take it up and step seven paces with it before he drops it.

Third. A Pice or other copper coin is put at the bottom of a large pot filled with fresh cowdung, and the latter is warmed till it boils up. The accused then plunges his hand in and draws out the coin.

Fourth. They plant a pole in deep water, and the defendant grasps it, keeping his head under the surface till an arrow shot by a vigorous arm is brought back to the place whence it was discharged.

None of these trials can be called too severe for the endurance of a stout ruffian determined to carry his point. It can scarcely be called a curious fact that this juggling is to be traced almost all over the world; men are so fond of calling in the preternatural and supernatural to settle and explain the natural.

CHAPTER III.

(1.) Which is among the Pubb Hills. The popular belief is, that no camel can approach the tomb, as the lady will not forgive those animals for carrying away her husband. A pilgrimage to the holy spot secures much happiness to the visitor, and many a devout believer has been fed with bread and milk by a hand stretched out of the tomb. These tales are considered sufficiently established to be chronicled in the historical works of Sindh; and we find in them, moreover, the physiological peculiarity common to visions in general, that the beautiful lady saint usually appears to the male, and her handsome husband to the female, pilgrims.

(2.) Most of these tales will be found translated or epitomised in the next chapter.

(3.) In grammar and structure resembling the Persian more than the Indian.

(4.) The late Sir A. Burnes studied the language, but did not write upon the subject. Lieutenant R. Leech, of the Bombay Engineers, printed a short grammar and dialect of Belochi, but condensed his labours so much that the work is of little or no use.

(5.) For instance, the modern Persian preserves the word Madiyan, a mare (derived from Madah, female); but, as the Belochi proves, has lost the corresponding vocable "Nariyan," a stallion, from Nar, a male.

(6.) The word "Játakí," spelt with the cerebral *T*, and the peculiar Sindh *J* or *Dy*, is an adjective formed from the proper noun Jat, the name of a people who were probably the aborigines of the Punjab. The author of the Dabistan applies the term "Jat dialect" to the language in which Nanak Shah composed his works.

The Journal of the Bombay Branch of the Asiatic Society, 1849, contains a short grammar, which may serve as a specimen of the Játakí tongue. The reader is referred to it for fuller information upon the subject of the following remarks.

(7.) Any Hindustani grammar will explain the Nastalik and Naskhi alphabets. For the Gurumukhi, Carey or Leech's grammar may be consulted; the latter also gives the common Lande characters. The Ochaki, and a variety of local alphabets, may be found in the Sindhi grammar published by Captain Stack, of the Bombay Army.

The Rev. Dr. Stevenson, arguing from the close similarity that exists between the initial letters of the number-names in the Sindhi language, and the numeral cyphers, considers the mercantile marts on the Indus as the origin of the system of notation now in use throughout the civilized world. But the Sindh characters, being all modern, cannot lay claim to the honour of the invention, which must be ascribed to India, the great arithmetician of eastern nations.

(8.) Hindoos as well as Mussulmans are included in this name. The following remarks are intended to apply to the Munshis and other educated classes, who studied Persian for either pleasure or profit. The reigning family in general, and a few of the courtiers who were always at the capital, had the advantage of learning the language from Persian masters.

(9.) In Arabic it appears to have but one sound, that of the "u" in "but," and it is not affected by the letters which follow it.

(10.) It is amusing to see such solecisms introduced into our own grammars; for instance, in the second edition of the Persian Moonshee, revised and corrected by W. C. Smyth, Esq.

(11.) A fair specimen of Indo-Persian style. The work is a collection of anecdotes written by a native of Hindostan, and as much admired there as it would be despised at Shiraz. These remarks refer to the language; as the book has been translated, the English reader can satisfy himself, if curious, about the value of the matter contained in it.

(12.) The remarks upon the Buhar i Danish also apply to this well-known work.

(13.) The Persian MSS. written in Sindh, add errors of copying to mistakes in spelling; the consequence is, that the most correct will offer an average of five or six blunders in each page, many of them unintelligible to the best Munshis.

(14.) Certainly as old as the Guzerattee tongue, which the Parsees in the eighth century of our era found very generally spoken in the country where they settled.

(15.) A few years ago, that distinguished Orientalist Major-General Vans Kennedy, when applied to for an examination in the Sindhi dialect, replied that he was not aware of the existence of any such language.

Since that time, public opinion has taken two courses; the first and general one being that Sindhi is a rude and unwritten form of Hindostani. Secondly, that Sindhi is a grammatical, copious and ancient dialect, derived from Sanscrit, but containing little or no literature, and, therefore, all but totally uncultivated.

Even the author of the Guzerattee Dictionary, a work published in 1846 asserts that "in the province of Cutch there is no written language except the Goojratee."

(16.) I state this on the authority of natives, having endeavoured in vain to procure a copy of the Pothis (or Scriptures) belonging to the Dedh (tanner) caste.

(17.) These short vowels are so rapidly pronounced that the student will find at first no small difficulty in learning to detect their presence and to distinguish one from another. Such as they are, however, they must be strictly attended to, otherwise the sound of the language is completely changed, and the distinctions between case and number done away with.

(18.) And therefore require a postposition at all times, whereas in Sindhi that inelegant appendage can be elided in poetry and measured prose. For instance Wakhar^{a} (jún) wíhún; "scores of merchandise;" Mihrade (jo) put^{u} "the son of Mihráda."

(19.) The language being also written in the Nashki character with, generally speaking, an Arabic preface and always the initial formula of the Moslem faith, Hindoos were not allowed, under pain of circumcision, to read these compositions. To the present day, although all of them can speak, few or none can read, the language; nor do they possess in it, I believe, a single work. The traders and shopkeepers, however, always keep their accounts and write their Hundis, or letters of credit, in the Sindhi language, using the alphabet peculiar to their caste.

The spoken dialect of the Hindoo in Sindh, as in India generally, differs from that of the Moslems in its greater admixture of Sanscrit, and in avoiding Arabic words.

(20.) These are very numerous, and some Polyglott specimens are to be met with, intended to teach Arabic, Persian, Sindhi, Belochi and Pushtu. It is said that translations of the celebrated Lexicons, such as the Kamus and Burhan i Kati, are to be found, but my efforts to procure them were unavailable.

(21.) Among which, curious to say, is the famous or infamous Koka Pandit's work, "De modis coeundi aliis que rebus veneris." There is no book in Eastern literature, except the Hitopadesa, which is to be found in such variety of languages. In Persian, Hindostani, and Panjabi it is called Lizzat El Nisa: in Arabic the Marifat El Nayk: in Sindhi the Farhat El Ashikin. The original is in Sanscrit verse, and numerous translations are to be found in the vernacular dialects of India, as the Maharatti, Teloogoo, &c.

(22.) Namely the Baits, or couplets, whose peculiarity will be explained and illustrated in the next chapter.

(23.) A poetical ornament particularly calculated to please the taste of a semi-barbarous people, who are willing to sacrifice sense to sound. The alliteration of the poems composed by the celebrated Abd el Latif is quite as artfully and successfully managed as in any of the productions of our Anglo-Saxon ancestors.

(24.) The war song or that sung in battle like the Arabic Rajaz is called "Shair" in Sindh, and is performed by the Mirasi, or bard, who accompanies the chief, during the combat.

(25.) And I may add by no means unpleasant to the European ear, when it becomes accustomed to the grotesqueness of the strange metre.

(26.) "Bait" in Arabic means a couplet: the Sindhis, however, apply the word to their peculiar triplets.

CHAPTER IV.

(1.) "Tarik," one who abandons the cares of life and sensual pleasures.

(2.) This is the popular belief. They say that he began to learn the alphabet, and when, after reading Alif, he arrived at Ba, the second letter, he refused to proceed saying "Alif is Alif," (*i. e.* there is only Alif, unity or One God) "and to know more than this much is vanity." It is, however, manifest, from the Sayyid's works that he knew Arabic and Persian well, had studied deeply and was master of much secular knowledge. Some Sindhis confess that their favourite poet was a disciple of the learned Abd el Baki, who taught at Matara.

(3.) They are so still. His Fakirs are known by their black or dark blue turbans, and are fond of carrying about a Tambur or guitar and reciting the saint's verses. The Fakiranis (female Fakirs) wear a sheet over the head and a cholo, or bodice, dyed with Chhodi (pomegranate rind).

(4.) Bhit[a] is a place near Matara. The word literally means "a pile," and it alludes to the Sayyid's having ordered his Murids and Fakirs to throw up a mound of earth sufficient to bear a village, a Khanikah (hermitage), and a Kubbo (domed tomb). Hence the Sayyid is popularly termed Shah Bhetai.

(5.) Fame, however, gives rather a scandalous account of the way in which this wealth was first acquired. When Jama, the wife of Abd el Nabi, the Kalhora prince, was beseiged in Hyderabad, she sent all her treasure to Bhit, in charge of these holy men. The Kalhora dynasty was soon after destroyed, and the wealth appropriated by Abd el Latif's descendants.

(6.) Shah is the title of Sayyids in Sindh. In the seventh chapter, some notice will be taken of this celebrated book.

(7.) Here called Khoinbria-waro from the town of Khoinbri, near Mirpur Khas. This man was a Laghari Beloch, and was raised by Mir Mohammed Talpur, from a low condition to that of a Sardar. He is the person who, a few days before the battle of Meeanee, went with his followers to Nasir Khan's Darbar, where all the Ameers were collected, and holding in one hand a sword, turban, and a suit of men's clothes, with a woman's "Paro" (petticoat) and Choli (bodice) in the other, told the chief to choose one or the other attire and behave himself accordingly. The unhappy Nasir Khan was thus forced to attack Sir Charles Napier at Meeanee. During the battle, when the Sardar saw that the day was going against his master, he requested the latter to send him with a select body of cavalry to fall upon the rear of the British. Nasir Khan, guessing his intentions, refused: upon this he ran away without any attempt at concealment, and never halted till he reached his own village. Hence his fellow-countrymen call him to this day the Lonbri (vixen fox), or Khobli (courtesan), and his name is seldom heard without one of these flattering appendages.

(8.) This of course is a mere invention; the catastrophe was caused by a chance shell.

(9.) The Orientalist will understand the contemptuous innuendo contained in the word "Gandu," but I dare not translate it by any expression that approaches the meaning of the original nearer than that of "scoundrel."

(10.) Shaykh Baha el din Zakariya was a Sohrehwardi Sufi of great eminence, by birth a Koraysbi, whose family emigrated from Mecca to Kharezm, and finally to Multan. He was born A.H. 578 (A.D. 1182), and died in the odour of sanctity, literally as well as figuratively, on the 17th Safar, A.H. 666 (A.D. 1267). The story of his studies, travels, pilgrimages, miracles, virtues and holy posterity is too long to be related here, but may be found detailed in the second volume of Ferishtah's History.

(11.) A curious way one might suppose of propitiating a saint. But popular superstition ascribes such surpassing virtues to the tomb of a holy man, and the journey to Multan was so long and troublesome, that casuists must make some allowances for the crime of the Murids.

Strange as it may appear to the European reader, the event alluded to in the text is by no means without examples. The people of Multan murdered Shams of Tabriz, the celebrated Murshid, or spiritual teacher, and the more celebrated Hafiz, in order to bury him in their town. The Affghan Hazarehs make a point of killing and burying in their own country any stranger who is indiscreet enough to commit a miracle, or show any particular sign of sanctity.

(12.) Tasting the flesh or blood of Auliya (holy men) is considered by ignorant mystics an act of peculiar religious efficacy.

(13.) Samoi, from the Sammani jo Gothu or the remains of ancient Tatta, near Lake Kinjur, generally called the "Samoi (or Sammani) jo diro or padu," Anglicè, the ruined heaps of the Sammah clan. The word Mamoi is translated either by "Cannibals" or "revealers of hidden things," and Haft-tan alludes to the seven headless trunks.

(14.) Tamachi was the third prince of the house of Sammah, a clan which governed Sindh for more than two centuries. He and his family were taken prisoners and confined at Delhi by the Mogul.

(15.) This curiously resembles the Delhi tradition respecting the Khilli, or metal pillar, which Prithwi Rajah drew forth from the snake's head; and thereby lost his crown. In Sindh, however, some few Mussulmans have acquired a faint knowledge of Hindoo traditions, religion and sciences, by studying Persian analyses of Sanscrit works; and possibly this circumstance may account for the garbled similarity of the two traditions.

(16.) Captain Del Hoste, of the Bombay Army, some years ago published one of these rhymes, but sadly disguised, in the Transactions of the Bombay Geographical Society. I heard them in 1844, and I think it impossible that in so short a time after the battles to which they are referred, any forgery could have become so generally known to, and firmly believed in, by the people.

(17.) The original being written in a peculiarly rough and rugged style, a literal translation will not be attempted. The verses are given as usually quoted by the people, though to all appearance many of them are in a mutilated state.

(18.) The admirer of Oriental legendary lore may find the whole tale of the Dyke of Aror, in the translation of the Tohfat El Kiram, by Lieutenant Postans.

(19.) Such prophecies being in fact mere efforts of memory, causality, and comparison, or as the metaphysician expresses it "the operation of a sound and combining judgment."

(20.) The Dirhem is a nominal sum in Sindh, valued at about four Annas.

(21.) Equally happy is the prophecy in Panjabi, which is current among the Hindoos, and ascribed by them to the Gurus or holy men of the Sikhs:—

"1. Satánawwe sat chádiye, athanawwe hatta tár;
2. Nananawwe nar jágsi, púre sau je je kár."

1. In '97, they (the Ameers) shall lose all power, in '98 the shops shall be shut (*i. e.* the wars and riots begin).

2. In '99, men of might will awake (arise or appear on the stage) and in the full hundred each will attend to his own business (in quiet and order).

The Hindoo date here alluded to is the Sambat year, as it is commonly called. Now A.S. 1897 = A.D. 1841, when the Ameers began to lose power; in the next year their troubles commenced; in A.D. 1843, they were conquered and dethroned, and in A.S. 1900=A.D. 1844, Sir Charles Napier announced that not another shot would be fired in Sindh.

(22.) In fact exactly performed the part attributed by Burnet to "Lilliburlero."

(23.) The prophecy was that Bhurtpore was impregnable to every invader, except an alligator: "Kumbheer-meer" would mean the "Lord alligator," and the similarity of sound to "Combermere" was sufficient to dishearten the defenders.

(24.) My MS. is a small one of about thirty pages composed in excellent Sindhi and occasionally in execrable Persian. When the original presents any peculiarities of sound, metre or construction it is given in Roman characters with a translation subjoined. I have attempted to render each word as literally as possible into English. Some of the verses are quoted from well-known bardic effusions, as those of Mir Bahar, and others.

(25.) The ruins of Bambhora lie on a hill almost surrounded by a plain of sand a little to the right of the road from Wuttajee to Gharra in Lower Sindh. The town is supposed to have been built upon the plain and was destroyed by divine wrath in one night in consequence of its ruler's sins. To judge from appearances the place must at one time have been rich and populous: even now after heavy rains the people find coins, ornaments and broken pieces of metal amongst the ruins of the Fort.

(26.) Different kinds of perfume.

(27.) In other words, "chez vous," "in your own house," as it were.

(28.) This is a specimen of the affixed pronoun, which, however, is here unusually used together with the separate form. The result is additional emphasis.

(29.) The diminutive form of Bábiho. So also Punhal is affectionately used for Punhú.

(30.) The Hindoos admire this bird's song as much as Persians do the bulbul's, and Europeans the nightingale's notes. Its cry always appeared to me harsh and monotonous, but this was probably caused by the want of pleasant associations or agreeable recollections attached to it. A Pundit on the contrary will manifest most acute gratification at the sound, testifying the same by ample quotations of Gitas and Shlokas.

(31.) This is an instance of love, not at first sight, but caused by simply hearing the name of another. Oriental poets are full of allusions to this peculiar way of propagating the tender passion. So the Arabs say—

"And the ear becometh enamoured before the eye at times."

And the Persians often quote these lines,

> "Not merely by the eye is fancy bred
> It frequently ariseth from the ear as well."

Tales and stories in the East abound in examples of passion produced by the mere sound of a name; and every day life affords occasional instances of it. Besides this the reader must bear in mind that these verses are all susceptible of a Sufi, or mystic interpretation and must be understood metaphorically as well as literally. A Sindhi would consider Punhu as a type of the immortal spark in the breast of man, which by the influence of some exciting cause is suddenly inflamed and burns to unite itself with the source of light. Thus the Beloch becomes a kind of pilgrim who in his progress towards eternity leaves behind him the world and its connexions, its pleasures and its pains. The classical scholar will recollect the speech of the "philosophic goddess" of Boethius, in which the legend of Orpheus and Eurydice is, with some little ingenuity, made to convey a similar moral lesson.

(32.) Meaning the joys of society and friendly intercourse. Music (if it may be called such) is here a *sine quâ non* in social meetings.

(33.) Alluding to the Son̤ or Sugún, a kind of divination by means of the position of birds and beasts, their cry, the direction of their flight, and other such particulars.

(34.) This is still the usual practice in all these countries. It is not, however, more common than in Naples, and other parts of Southern Europe.

(35.) "With my eyes," as the Persians say "Chasm," *i. e.* "your order be upon my eyes," the most precious part of the body.

The reader must not think that the bard has violated the poetical precept "*Nec Deus intersit, &c,*" without full and sufficient reason to produce his *speciosa miracula*. The incident is introduced to contrast the virgin purity of Sassui with the loose conduct of Sehjan, and give an instance of the power of intercession with Heaven.

(36.) To impress the people of Bambhora with a high sense of their wealth and importance.

(37.) Meaning what fine bird art thou—a robber on a large scale or a petty thief? The old lady saw that Punhu was a Beloch, and addressed him accordingly.

(38.) A class of people celebrated throughout this part of the world for the rascality of the males and the unchastity of the females.

(39.) Literally "in his pit." The Adano, in Persian "páchâh," is the little pit in which the weaver places his feet when sitting at the loom.

The next verse is a very insulting one, accusing as it does a respectable female of intriguing with the Thori or inhabitants of the Tharr (the sandy desert on the eastern frontier of Sindh), who are of the most impure caste, and considered the scum and refuse of society.

(40.) The reader must bear in mind the peculiarities of Mussulman society. Amongst us it might be considered an effectual antidote to romance for the author to inform his readers that his hero has left two wives at home and set out in quest of a third. So also in the present instance, the husband's peccadilloes are recited without a word of blame or reproach. The sketch, however, is very true to life in Sindh, and as has before been remarked, there is an inner meaning to all the scenes.

(41.) A red coloured fluid used by Hindoos on certain festivals as a sign of joy. Here, however, it is employed as a token of grief.

(42.) The "Nai" in Sindhi exactly corresponds with the Italian "*fiumara;*" being the bed of a mountain stream, generally dry but converted by a few hours rain into a raging torrent. Arrian mentions the loss incurred by Alexander's army in consequence of encamping too close to one of these channels.

(43.) The Korar and Luhar are well known kinds of snakes.

(44.) It is difficult, properly to translate this couplet, which, to judge from the terseness of the language and the beauty of the sentiment, belongs to the Shah jo Risalo.

(45.) The Lorh is a peculiar kind of tomb: the Manah is a place to sit in and watch the country around.

(46.) These verses allude to the popular Moslem idea concerning those who die in the odour of sanctity. Their graves are wide and light, so as to form rather a pleasant abode than otherwise: and their corpses, if they can be called so, are merely sleeping, not liable to death or decay, as is the case with ordinary sinners. No true Mussulman doubts for a moment that if his Prophet's tomb were opened, the body within would appear exactly as it did in life.

(47.) This story being a very long one will necessarily be much abridged. It is, however, one of the prettiest of the legends of Sindh, and many of the sentiments and expressions put into the mouth of Marui by the Sufi poet are not inferior in beauty and pathos to the charming verses attributed to Maisunah of the Beni Kalab.

The Sangi is a Sindhi clan living near Omerkot. The word Marui means the girl belonging to the Maru tribe, a semi-nomadic race inhabiting Malir and the regions about the Tharr.

(48.) It is customary among the people of the Tharr, to send for an astrologer and give the child a name on the sixth night after its birth.

(49.) These lines are not without humour, and a pleasant touch of feeling, contrasting the grotesque image of a Sindhi shepherd and his rude occupations with the beautiful Marui. The picture too is very true to nature. One of the common *passetemps* of the country people in this province is to spin coarse thread, which is afterwards sold to the weaver for rough blankets and other such articles. In the verse just quoted the shepherd is represented with a twist of wool round his wrist, and in his hand a little pebble or clod attached to the end of the yarn to make it twist and facilitate the spinning.

(50.) Dodo was a Sumra prince celebrated for his valour and generosity in the annals of the province.

(51.) This is a figure of speech, not to be literally understood.

(52.) *i. e.* a nose beautiful among noses, as the waterlily is among the wild flowers of the lake.

(53.) Mocharo Malir—"the charming Malir"—is a district near Omerkot, celebrated in Sindhi pastoral poetry as the Arcadia of that ill-favoured land.

(54.) The Kungu is a peculiar kind of rouge in great request among the ladies and kept in a little ornamented box. The poet compares the daughter with the dye itself as being the more brilliant of the two.

(55.) Literally, "mother," an affectionate style of address to a daughter, but sounding very uncouth to our ears.

(56.) On account of the bravery of his attire.

(57.) The lady shrinks backwards and saves her fair form from the defilement of being touched by a stranger and one of the ruder sex; thereby evincing much modesty and sense of decorum. The word "Hamir" is probably a corruption of "Amir," and is always applied in Sindhi poetry to the princes of the Sumra dynasty. Ghotio literally means a little bridegroom and is here used as an affectionate epithet. The last verse shows that Umar was so much delighted by Marui's giving him water to drink that he poured it out as an oblation to Heaven for her welfare and happiness. It may be taken figuratively and understood of his blessing her, it being a custom in Central Asia, when one person brings water to another, especially if the former be a woman or child, for the drinker to utter a benediction.

(58.) These Pirs were some holy men buried at Panwar (a district in the Tharr), and invoked by its shepherd population.

(59.) These lines are a fair specimen of the alliteration and peculiar rhyme of the Sindhi "Baita" the final syllables of the first and second lines corresponding with "bari" the cæsura of the third verse.

(60.) The Mujawir is the person who attends the tomb, hermitage or spot consecrated to a favourite saint.

(61.) Ladies of even the most "uneasy virtue" in Sindh allow themselves some latitude in speaking of and to these holy men, looking upon them pretty much in the same light as the fair ones of Mediæval Europe regarded their father confessors. Marui tells her companions in sportive mood to join the Fakir in his ramblings, and calls him her brother the more effectually to prove that he is not her lover. The pernicious practice of taking unto oneself what is called in Hindostani a "Munh-bolá bhái," or "a strange man dubbed a brother" is unfortunately as prevalent in Sindh as it is in India.

(62.) The word "Niwari," here translated "free," is synonymous with the Arabic "Mujarrad," and bears the double signification of a latitudinarian, and one effectually detached from the pomps and vanities of this world.

(63.) This violent instance of Platonic affection may sound uncouth to an European ear, but is not less true to human nature in the East.

CHAPTER V.

(1.) Professor H. H. Wilson has illustrated the difference, in his Treatise on the Dramatic System of the Hindoos.

(2.) Belonging to the Rajput Rathors. Rano also was of that race, and belonged to the Sodho clan, which is numerous about Omerkot and the Tharr, where they are the hereditary Sardars of the country. Under the Ameers, their head man levied Pannacheri from the graziers around, and was never interfered with in his prerogatives. Although Hindoos, they intermarry with Moslems, and do not refuse to eat with them.

(3.) Hindoo religious mendicants are called "Sami," and politely addressed as "Babu."

(4.) Kak is the name of a river which once flowed near Omerkot, but is now dried up. Upon its banks there are the ruins of an old town, and some traces of Mumal's Mahaling, or Mari (a house with an upper story).

(5.) The name of the bard.

(6.) The Sari or Sarri is a necklace of gold beads worn by Hindoo mendicants. The next line alludes to the tasteful custom of "gilding refined gold," by means of certain minerals which deepen its colour. The Bhonwr is the large black bee who figures so often in Hindi poetry, and he is here described as so enamoured of the blossom in question that he is willing to pay for permission to alight upon it, though a thousand gardens are open to him gratis;—a conceit perhaps a little too far fetched to be commendable.

(7.) Ludrano was a town near Omerkot, now in ruins.

(8.) The beggars of Kashmir are justly celebrated in this country for audacity and importunity.

(9.) Exaggeration in Sindh, as well as in many other countries, is considered the soul of sublimity.

The picture of the wandering mendicant is a very correct and natural one. He is taken in and stripped by the fair Corinthian, and compelled to become a beggar; it is even hinted that he lost his religion and turned Hindoo, in despair of doing anything by being a Mussulman. This, however, is a mere figure of speech, a poetical ornament. Shikarpore, in Upper Sindh, had a bad renown for similar displays of guile in the fairer, and weakness in the rougher, sex. In 1845, I saw one, and heard of several, Affghan and other traders, who had come down from their own country with horses and merchandise, and were so effectually ruined by the sirens of Sindh, that, driven to assume the Fakir's garb, they were wandering about the place in a state of half idiotcy.

(10.) The names of the fairest of the frail sisterhood.

(11.) The Otak in Sindh is a place where men only dwell: it has no Zenanah or private rooms.

(12.) Meaning to inform her that he was no Patholi or silk weaver, a race of men who are about as much abused in the East as the tailor is among us. He gave the grain to his horse to show how superior he was to his comrades.

(13.) These verses are extremely idiomatic, and not without difficulty. My Moonshee says that "Kám^{a} hall^{i}" is the poetical form for Káman^{i} hallandar, "a walking woman," opposed to those who ride in litters or on camels, the final syllables being elided by Tarkhim or Apocope.

(14.) A bedstead with a carpet thrown over it, and with or without pillows to recline upon, is the seat appropriated to the chief man of an assembly in Sindh.

(15.) Attracted by its peculiar fragrance.

(16.) "Sat bhatiro," literally, "One having seven ways, manners or colours;" hence it comes to signify variegated, beautiful.

(17.) Dhat^{u} is the name of a province near Omerkot. The people are called Dhátí.

(18.) In this verse "Kawát^{u}" or "Kanwánt^{u}" is a young camel; "Gonro" a colt, and "Chatt^{u}" one that has just been weaned. "Mayyo" and "Dágo" are full-grown camels; "Khíro" one under three years; "Donk^{u}" when between three and six years old; when full grown, viz., after the sixth year, it becomes "Uth^{u}."

(19.) In this instance the final consonants of "Hall^{u}" "Karahall^{a}" "Tarahall^{a}" and "Múmall^{a}" are reduplicated by paragoge. "Karahall^{u}" is the affectionate or diminutive form of "Karaho," a camel. "Tarahall^{u}" is synonymous with "Koláb^{u}"—low land where rich vegetation abounds. The "Nángel^{a}" or "Nágelí" is a creeper of which camels are very fond.

My Moonshee says that "Chandan^{u}" is either the name of a kind of tree, or may mean sandal wood, in which case it would be a poetical exaggeration.

(20.) A sign of most humble supplication.

(21.) Hence the tale is known by the title of Sohni and the Mehar; the name of the latter being unknown to fame. This class of people are here what the Arcadians are in our pastoral poetry; they are also celebrated for their skill in playing upon the Bansli or Nar. This "Doric reed" of Sindh is a "Scrannel pipe" about two feet long, furnished with four stop holes; the player accompanies it with a droning sound, like that of the worst description of bagpipe. The people, however, are so fond of it, that many of them will pass hours in listening to the performance, which, when heard from some distance and in the stillness of the night, has a plaintive sound which is not disagreeable.

(22.) Because as long and only as long as her affection continued in all its intensity, she would be preserved from all hidden dangers by the power of heavenly love. The same mysterious agency seems, in Horace's opinion, to have saved him from the wolf's fangs, when, singing the praises of his Lalage, he was wandering through his Sabine grounds.

It is a melancholy fact, however, as many legends prove, that this protection seems to be extended to amours which are far more remarkable for intensity than for morality.

(23.) In the original, "Tanạ Manạ Sohní," a play upon the lady's name. "Sohno" is synonymous with, and no doubt formed from, the Sanscrit "Sobhána," beautiful.

(24.) The "honour," *i. e.*, the wives and families of the chiefs.

(25.) A short account of these events is given in the Tohfat el Kiram, page 40. The bardic chronicles of course deal more in detail, and are by no means scrupulous in adhering to historic fact.

(26.) In Mr. Shakespeare's Dictionary, the names of the lovers are explained as "Hero and Leander." Beyond the slight similarity of sound, there does not appear to be any resemblance between the legends. Ranjha is also called Vedan; and, as well as his innamorata, rejoices in a variety of names and surnames. The story also is told very differently in different parts of the country. I have given it as it was recited to me by the Langha of Sindh.

(27.) Being insensible to all earthly joy or pain, except love.

(28.) A mark of passion on the part of the lady. So in Persia the note on red paper prepares the lover for approaching success.

(29.) The name of Hir's husband.

(30.) Called in Persian "Gil i Sarshui," in Sindhi "Metụ." It is mixed with oil and perfume, and used to wash the hair and body. Saadi has an elegant allusion to it in the Gulistan.

The lady here means that she will collect the clay where Ranjha bathed, and apply the same to her fair locks,—a high compliment.

(31.) Near Tatta. Remains of solid edifices are still to be traced along its banks.

(32.) These wells still remain; they are popularly supposed to have been sunk in the rock by demon hands.

The Tanda or little village called Shah Makkai, close to the fort of Hyderabad, contains, I believe, the tomb of Mall Mahmud.

CHAPTER VI.

(1.) Generally at the age of four years and four months, as it is supposed that, before that time, the memory is not sufficiently developed.

(2.) Boarding schools being, fortunately for the boys, unknown. None but the wealthiest classes keep private tutors; the expense, however, is not more than from thirty to sixty rupees per mensem.

(3.) Except on Fridays and other holidays.

(4.) Such as a Pag (turban), with the Pirhan (shirt), Sutthan (drawers), Lungi (waist cloth), and Rumal (handkerchief). These five articles of clothing made up the Khilat or dress of honour.

(5.) This system of perquisites is decidedly bad, as the Akhund always refuses to commence anything new, book or study, without his fee. So, if on Friday the customary Nazzaranah (present) of a few pice is not offered, the boy loses his holiday. On the three great Eeds or fetes of Bakar, Fitr and Barat, the pedagogue writes two or three couplets upon rudely ornamented paper, and receives from four annas to a rupee for the same. These specimens of art are called Eedi, and are usually hung against the wall, as samplers would be in England. At the same time it must be recollected that the teacher seldom receives more from each pupil than half a rupee per mensem, and is therefore compelled to make up the rest by presents.

(6.) Such as the short chapters of the Koran, which are used in daily prayer, together with easy mnemonical lines upon different subjects. Some of these are sufficiently ingenious, but trifling and ill-selected in point of subject. For instance, one couplet describes the five Sin of a good Kani, or reed pen:—1st. It must be Sanhi (fine); 2nd. Sallira (well pierced); 3rd. Surkha (red); 4th. Sain (straight); and lastly, Supaka (ripe and well grown).

(7.) Or Farahi; a thin board made of some hard and fine-grained wood. It is sometimes stained red, black, green, or yellow. The ink contains no mineral substance, and is therefore easily washed off; the board being smeared with a thin layer of clay and water. Metal plates are sometimes used. When the pupil has become somewhat skilful in the management of his pen, he lays aside the board and uses a material called Daftari. It is made of several sheets of writing paper pasted together, smeared with a composition of verdigris, and glossed with a Mohro (polishing instrument made of steel), so that it may be washed when dirty.

(8.) Such puerilities, however, must not be charged upon the Sindhis; they generally originate with the Arabs, who, as a nation, have suffered from the abuse of veneration probably more than any other race. Whenever the subject of religion is brought forward, reason seems to leave them in a state of thorough destitution. At other times their minds display considerable discernment, energy and originality.'

(9.) See Chapter III.

(10.) A work which may be recommended to the European scholar when beginning to read Sindhi. The Arabic and Persian vocables in which it abounds will facilitate the study; the style is pure, copious, and not too much laboured.

(11.) Such stories are so similar throughout the world, the reader may easily guess that all the suitors who were unable to reply properly, suffered instant death. The invariable simplicity of the questions thus proposed, from the time of the Sphinx downwards, is intended, I presume, to diminish any feeling of pity or regret one might be disposed to entertain for the fate of individuals that possessed so small a share of intelligence.

(12.) Even in Persia, the people seldom peruse the pages of Jami or Nizami without a Sharh (commentary). Hafiz is the household poet of Persia, and they hear and read his verses too often to require any other aid.

(13.) This account of the Madrassa is derived from the information of a native who studied at Matalawi in his youth. I have no reason to doubt his words. Captain Hamilton (the traveller in A.D. 1744) says of Lower Sindh, "The city of Tatta is famous for learning in theology, philology and politics, and they have above *four hundred* colleges for training up youth in those parts of learning."

(14.) Many of whom exist, half blinded by reading all night with a dim oil lamp, and stupified by logic and theology; occasionally perhaps by more natural means.

(15.) Every pupil, however, began his studies with the Makhdum, for the sake of Tabarruk, or good omen.

(16.) That at Matari contained, I am told, about twenty cells, in each of which three or four scholars might be accommodated; the gates were locked at night, and no strangers, male or female, were permitted to remain. The more advanced students were allowed to live in the town Musjid (mosque), and this was the less dangerous, as the feelings of the "town and gown" towards each other were even more decidedly hostile than at our universities.

(17.) This being a religious punishment, boasting the authority of the Koran, no disgrace was incurred by the infliction. The fanatic Wahabis used regularly to flog every member of their society, male and female, for such a light offence as coming late to the five daily prayers. At every blow the fustigator exclaimed, Taubah (repentance!); the fustigated, Y'allah (Yes, by God!)

(18.) No critique upon the merits of these books will be offered, as I hope at some future time to finish a detailed account of the principal works on the study of language and scholastic science in use throughout the tribes of Islam.

(19.) Opposed to Sarf i Kabir, or the conjugation of the verb through its several voices, moods and tenses.

(20.) The two elementary treatises published by Captain Lockett. Calcutta, 1814.

(21.) The equally well known book of syntax by the same author is very seldom read.

(22.) Who composed the soundest standard works upon the subjects of grammar, syntax, logic and metaphysics, before, it is said, the age of ten.

(23.) Also by Ibn Hajib. There is a translation of this into Persian verse, which is sometimes used.

(24.) So called because the quotations from the text-book are always prefaced with a Kala (he said), and the annotation begins with Akulu (I say).

(25.) The "half-day" and the "whole day's" work.

(26.) As formerly the case in Europe. The Moslem theologian holds the dogma of the three moral certainties, viz.:—

1. The Koran, or Revelation.
2. Sunnat, the known practice of the inspired and infallible Prophet.
3. Ijma, the universal consent of all God's people, or Islam.

Now to these three the logician has the impertinence to add a fourth certainty, known to be of Pagan origin, viz., the Kiyas, or syllogism. The theologian very properly conceives this to be a most diabolical idea.

Some learned divines have gone so far as to assert that Lucifer was the inventor of the syllogism; he having been the first to dispute the propriety of bowing down to Adam. His argument, they gravely state, was as follows:—

My nature is fiery, man's earthy;
Fire is better than earth;
Ergo, my nature is better than man's.

This fact, however, did not prevent some of the most orthodox and celebrated churchmen from venturing upon the task of purifying logic by diluting the wisdom of the Greeks with some very heterogeneous additions. The effect produced upon the reader, is precisely that usually experienced when perusing Watt's Logic after Aldrich.

(27.) Affghanistan and Persia. In Arabia, especially the southern parts, the style called Warsh, a branch of the Nafi system, is more common than that of Hafs.

(28.) The profession is considered a very creditable one in a religious sense, and many sayings of the prophet inculcate its excellence. It is not, however, considered at all necessary to understand the words repeated.

(29.) In the Persian language. It has been translated into the vernacular.

(30.) In the East, every gentleman necessarily knows something of the healing art. The medical profession, therefore, ranks next to the clerical in point of respectability; and so highly is the study thought of, that even royalty itself will occasionally condescend to dose its subjects.

(31.) The standard works are about seventeen or eighteen. I do not quote their names, as I have not read them, and can offer no information upon the subject of their contents.

(32.) The Ameers, therefore, always made either the prescriber, or a confidential servant, take the first dose intended for themselves. When the servant was made the victim, he always took care to exact a fair portion of the fee from the physician, under pain of misrepresenting the effects of the medicine, pretending great suffering, or declaring that he was poisoned. The medical man was careful not to refuse a share of his gains, or his head would probably have left his shoulders.

(33.) Not neglecting, however, to make up the prescription himself, and to charge at least a rupee for every pice paid to the druggist.

(34.) The Persian women have the name of a Jinn, to whose malevolence they attribute the disasters of parturient ladies. The ill-omened word is, I believe, Al.

(35.) As, for instance, Nadir darak raft, ("Nadir is gone to hell,") to remember the date of the death of Nadir Shah, whom I would willingly call the Great, had not an authority in such matters given him the character of a "Persian Robber." The complimentary nature of the chronogram arises from the religious prejudices of his countrymen.

The Persian student should remember that it is not customary to employ insignificant words to express dates, especially in verse; the two couplets in Jones' Grammar are poor specimens of this use of the Abjad.

(36.) It is by means of its peculiar rhythm that the Koran is so easily learned by heart, and probably it was composed in this form partly in order to assist the memory.

(37.) For the practical purpose of compiling the Janam Patri and Tripno. The former is indispensable to every Hindoo child, being at once his horoscope and guide throughout life. The price is from eight to twenty rupees, and the document is drawn up in the form of a long slip of paper, or rather papers pasted together, in a fair, bold, Devangari hand, illumined with grotesque sketches of the conjunctions and aspects of the planets, eclipses, and other such important events. The duration of life, habits, tastes, dispositions, and often the future fate of the individual are so carefully described, that nothing can occur to him throughout life that is not (after the event) discoverable in the Janam Patri.

The Tripno in form resembles the horoscope. It is a species of almanac, somewhat resembling the Moslem "Takwim." The subject is the duration of the Yoga, Nakshatra, Tithi, Wara and other astronomical divisions of time. The object of it is of course devotional.

(38.) With very little knowledge of Cocker's art. The only rules regularly learned are those of Jama (addition), and Khora or Zarb (multiplication). In this latter they are generally able to multiply 24 by 24 at least, and thus make up in some degree for their deficiency in the other branches.

(39.) At the same time it is only fair to state that the Sindh Hindoo possesses apparently great and even unusual capability for the mere acquisition of language. Next to arithmetic and intrigue, it is his forte.

(40.) As opposed to the Sindh Moslem. Islam in India is not so scrupulous as in our newly-conquered countries; and whenever in this province one of the Faithful proved himself peculiarly unprejudiced, I have observed that he was some emigrant in search of fortune.

(41.) Injudicious, as our name and fame throughout the East have been gained and are to be preserved by avoiding this and other dangerous errors of the Portuguese. In Persia, the Russians, by their early acts of bigotry, have secured for themselves the jealousy and mistrust of the bulk of the nation—the populace. And though Russia has now so far altered her tactics that her representative has, it is said, erected at Teheran a Taziyah-khaneh, or building devoted to commemmorate the Hasan and Hosayn tragedy, still the suspicions of the vulgar once well aroused, pursue the track of her policy with unremitting attention. We, on the contrary, as a nation unknown except by report, would be welcomed by the mass of the Persian population.

(42.) Literal quotations of certain very unsupported assertions.

(43.) An alphabet much used in the Punjaub, as we are informed by Lieutenant Leech (Introduction to Panjabi Grammar) for accounts and book-keeping.

(44.) For purposes of concealment, as cypher is used amongst us. Moreover, the people of India generally consider a distinct "Kalam," or alphabet, as a necessary appendage to language, and are far from admiring the ingenuity of Europe when informed that one character is used for a dozen different tongues.

(45.) The initial vowels only being expressed.

(46.) Namely the six peculiarly Sindhi, and the fourteen Arabic and Persian letters. It may be objected that words derived from the two latter dialects are used without points in some of the Indian alphabets (as in Guzerattee, &c.) and require no mark of distinction. This certainly is the case, but the Sindhi borrows a dozen foreign words where the Indian appropriates one.

(47.) When the Maharattas found themselves obliged to transact extensive public business, they invented a running hand, the Mori. We must teach the Sindhis two instead of one character—a Herculean task.

(48.) Commonly and erroneously called the Sindhi. There is no one alphabet peculiar to, or generally known throughout the province.

(49.) Many of the consonants as well as the vowels would require alteration, as, generally speaking, there is no distinction between the symbols denoting the aspirated and unaspirated.

(50.) This respect for the Naskhi increases in proportion as it diverges from Mecca, the fountain head of Islam. The wild Affghans, for instance, will often salam, bless and almost pray to the holy handwriting.

(51.) A cognate dialect to Sindhi. The alphabet, however, is much less complicated, as it rejects five of the Sindhi letters. The present system of writing Panjabi like Hindostani was, I am told, generally adopted about twenty or thirty years ago. Before that time, it was confined to the learned and polite; and the generality of writers were unaccustomed to distinguish the cerebrals by means of diacritical marks, and ignorant of the many improvements now known to all.

CHAPTER VII.

(1.) As opposed to the other Lizzat El Nisa.

(2.) As imitation of the prophet in every respect, from the most trifling gesture to the weightiest duty, is strictly enjoined on all Moslems; this is, indeed, thorough practical conservatism, with all its advantages and disadvantages. It is needless to state that, although practicable, it is not practised.

(3.) The European reader must not suppose that there is any impiety or depreciation of worship intended by this remark of the Sayyid's; celibacy in the East has always been considered what it is—an unmitigated evil, and the practical good sense of the founder of Islam induced him to declaim against it in his code of laws.

(4.) Even, says the Sayyid, if he "order her to cut off her breasts, and fry them in oil!"

(5.) What palatable advice for polite Europe!

(6.) Personalities being considered disrespectful.

(7.) Chamberlains, carpet-spreaders or executioners.

(8.) All classes in Sindh, from Mir to Ryot, testify excitement by loudness and shrillness of voice; even when the princes held "privy councils," and closed the doors to their most confidential servants, the voices of the debators could be heard at the distance of twenty yards.

(9.) The forest or wild man.

(10.) Sir prince or sire.

(11.) The "greater palace," as opposed to Khurd, the lesser.

(12.) In this they resemble the Affghans, Persians and other nations of Central Asia, who live in lands where grapes are plentiful, and the climate cold. They are not habituated to early drinking, and can therefore get through immense quantities of liquor in their own countries; in India, they often suffer, like Europeans, from complaints brought on by their excesses.

Few Affghans will object to taste English spirits as a tonic or medicine when sick or wounded: unlike the Indians and Sindhis, they prefer brandy to liqueurs.

(13.) The Persian word "Sabzeh"—verdure, contains a double entendre, as it also means hemp (Bhang).

(14.) Or twisted coil of Munj, the leaves of the Sarr (*Arundo karka ?*). The use of this tinder is supposed to increase the intoxication.

(15.) The Persians are much addicted to the use of Charas; the Affghans still more. At Candahar, they have certain places outside the town in which they meet, with a headman to direct the proceedings, and a guard for the protection of the revellers. The Mullas sometimes attempt to put a stop to this recreation, but their attempts are always futile, and often cause much bloodshed, as the sword is always drawn on such occasions. The scene of smoking is a very ludicrous one. The smokers sit in a long line, each man facing his neighbour's back, and whenever a laugh or a cough (produced by the contraction of the nerves of the throat) is heard to proceed from one person, it runs through the whole assembly, without any man being able to say what he is amused by.

(16.) The Orientalist will understand the meaning of the latter term, which is quite untranslateable.

(17.) Near every large town there are sometimes as many as fifty or sixty of these places, called after the name of the owner, as Nanga Shaha-jo-Dairo. The keepers receive from the habitués small presents of money and clothes. They are accused of inducing young men to drink Bhang, by offering it to them gratis at first, till the habit becomes a confirmed one; the juvenile drunkard is then turned out till he can pay for the indulgence, and thereby induced to rob his parents or friends.

(18.) Pir Mangho was the original inhabitant of the spot. On one occasion, when visited by four celebrated Fakirs and friends, he caused water to issue from the lower part of a rock. Another holy man made the spring a hot one. Shaykh Farid threw a flower into the water, and metamorphosed it into a monstrous alligator. A third stuck his tooth brush into the ground, and caused it to become a lofty palm; while the fourth made honey and butter drop from the tree.

Pir Mangho died, and was buried by his four friends at this spot. His tomb is still a place of pilgrimage.

(19.) So the Yezidis, Shaitan-parasts, or devil worshippers of Kurdistan, term Satan "Melek-Taus," the "Peacock king."

(20.) The religion of the Sindhi is almost universally the Hanafi form of Islam. A few belong to the Shieh sect, but the numbers are too inconsiderable to be troublesome. There is little religious hatred between the sects, a fact to be accounted for by the great numerical superiority on the part of Tasannum. Among the Shiehs, the concealment of their tenets, technically called Takiyyeh, is universally practised, and a member of that sect would no more venture to curse Omar or Usman in Sindh, than he would in Mecca or Bokhara. As many of the Talpurs were Shiehs, their protegés were of the same way of thinking; but the tenets of Tashayyu suffered considerably as usual by constant collision with a more powerful rival.

(21.) Herklots. Qanoon e Islam, Chapter 27.

(22.) Herklots, Chapter 35.

(23.) In no Oriental language, except the Panjabi, have I ever met with the word Para, a masculine form of this vocable. In Arabic, the Peri is called a Jinnyat, and therefore made the feminine form of a Jinn, or being created from fire. The "fairy," as the word proves, is of Persian origin, and it is not uninteresting to trace the gradations through which the beautiful sylphs of Guebrism dwindled down into the pigmy green folk of northern Europe.

(24.) Mr. Lane (translator of Arabian Nights) mentions this practice in Egypt, but does not account for it.

(25.) The books principally studied are the Fal-nameh, the Tali-nameh, the Nadir el fawaid, the Miat el fawaid, and the Hasan el Hasin.

(26.) Anciently in England called Carecte, Carrecte, Charecte, Chareot or Characte (Character), meaning certain charms or spells in the form of prayers written in scrolls, and hung about the neck.

(27.) So in Persia there are many of these formulæ, composed in corrupted Hindi or Sanscrit, and consequently recited without the reciter understanding a word of his prayer.

(28.) See Herklots, Chapter 30.

The practices to which he alludes, though, generally speaking, they exist unknown to Europeans, are prevalent throughout the East. In Persia, no man would drink a drop of sherbet in his bride's house, unless he saw her father take some before him. As a rule, these things are seldom done except between the sexes, and to cause love.

(29.) The branch of magic set apart to the recovery of stolen goods, is called in Sindhi "Vinyano" or "Gahno."

(30.) A fair anticipation of the doctrine of "development." Gold by the Arabs is defined to consist of Ziba (quicksilver), and Kibrit (sulphur), intimately mixed and cooked by the vapours and genial warmth of the earth.

(31.) Amongst all native states, from China to Algiers, there is great danger in being even suspected of possessing such a secret. It would expose the savan to persecution and torture, for the purpose of extorting it from him, as infallibly as if he had been a rich Jew, accused of magic before the Holy Tribunal.

(32.) Called Kushto; they are used as tonics, and considered very invigorating.

(33.) San, the Crotalaria Juncea.

(34.) By the mountaineers of Scotland it was called Sleina-nachd, or, "reading the speal-bone," or the blade-bone of a shoulder of mutton. The poet Drayton alludes to the practice of this "divination strange" amongst the "Dutch made English," settled about Pembrokeshire, in his Polyolbion, Song 5. Camden notices the same superstition in Ireland.

(35.) By learned soothsayers only, as such a flight of science would, of course, be far beyond the powers of the rustic prophets who usually practise this art.

With Moslem diviners, however, the Ilm El Aktaf is not much in favour; they consider it one of the "Matruk" or obsolete studies, which belonged to the Age of Ignorance. Still, very few of them would venture to doubt its present, and none its former, efficacy.

(35[2].) The little work to which I refer had the honour of a reprint at Bombay, and many native gentlemen who know English have had an opportunity of learning that "it was held by Napoleon Buonaparte as a sacred treasure," &c.

(36.) Some knowledge of this "ridiculous trade" is necessary to the Orientalist, on account of the allusions to it which abound in the works of the Persian and other poets. During Fath Ali's reign, a humorous bard, when neglected by one of the young princes, begged permission to recite in his presence a panegyric ode which he had composed. One of the couplets was,

"Whoever seeth thy face in his dreams,
Shall roll on heaps of gold and silver."

The prince pretended not to understand the allusion, and dismissed the wit with an ample present. The following rule of Ibn Sirin's will explain the lines: "Cuicumque in somniis excrementum humanum appareat, vastus auri et argenti cumulus illi continget.",

(37.) "Son[u]," probably a corruption of the old Persian word "Sugun," an omen.

(38.) Stated to be as much as rupees 2000.

(39.) At the same time unhappily common. Very few Sindhis would be restrained from theft by a feeling of honesty, or sense of duty; though at the same time, the name of thief is offensive to them. This is not always the case among uncivilized tribes.

Some of the chiefs of clans did not object to order robbery, and divide the spoils with the thieves. Many took a pride in this procedure, as the non-interference of the native governments was considered to be a tacit admission of their being superior to the laws. The robber chiefs on the frontier were paid by the Ameers, and yet levied black mail from travellers, and on occasions robbed them also. The people of the plains erected Thulls or Martello towers, capable of containing from twenty to fifty men, or built mud forts, with ramparts and battlements, surrounding a space of level ground, where their cattle might be placed in safety when a raid was expected. Towards Kusmore, on the north-west frontier, the traveller will immediately remark the number of maimed and wounded cultivators. Before we took possession of the country, this was one of the points which the hill robbers often attacked.

(40.) The Affghans and Persians are, probably, more formidable liars than the Sindhis, both on account of superior intellect, more stubborn obstinacy, and greater daring in supporting the falsehood.

CHAPTER VIII.

(1.) The great linguist, however, translates Alastu bi rabbi-kum, "Art *thou* not with *the* Lord;" that is, "Art thou not bound by a solemn compact with Him!" Well might Leyden assert, that he would surpass Sir William Jones "A hundred fold in Oriental learning."

(2.) See in Chapter 26, a most garbled account of the discipline and religious exercises of the order.

(3.) For we read of no psychology, spiritualism, or mysticism in Jewish history before the return from the Babylonish captivity.

(4.) Taken from a work upon the subject of practical Tasawwuf, by one Mahmud of Shahr Karriyah, a disciple of the celebrated saint, Pir Ali Gauhar. In the following pages, I have borrowed much from this book.

(5.) And might not the Eleusinian mysteries have diffused throughout Greece and Rome the Oriental opinions concerning the existence of spirit (αυτμη) and matter? Otherwise whence did Virgil, to mention no others, derive the Spinozism expressed in the 4th Georgic?

(6.) Europeans frequently complain of the exaggeration and want of order in Persian poetical ideas. They do not sufficiently consider the difference between the European's and the Asiatic's powers of Imagination and Comparison. Not unfrequently the criticism is that of ignorance of the true nature of the idea, as, for instance, when Carlyle (Specimens of Arabic poetry, p. 14,) attributes to Hafiz an allusion to certain opinions of the Pagan Arabs.

(7.) Hence Monotheistic poets continually borrow from their Pantheistic brethren. Who has not observed the Platonism of our bards, from Spenser down to Wordsworth?

(8.) The breath of life breathed into man's nostrils. The Rauch of the Hebrews, the Ruh of Arabia, πνεῦμα among the Greeks, and Animus, Anima and Spiritus among the Romans. In all cases, ideas are limited to words, and the latter so explain the former, that the history of language is, in fact, the history of man's ideas, opinions and belief.

(9.) Evidences of its antiquity may be found in the annals of almost every ancient and civilized race. Sufis were called by the Guebres, Wizhah-darun, Raushan-dil, &c.; by the Hindoos, Gnaneshwar and Atma-gnani. Among the Greeks they became Platonists, and have continued up to the present time, under divers mystic appellations, with tenets modified by the ages in which they lived.

Tasawwuf, again, has perpetuated an idea, which may be considered an Asiatic form of the doctrine of development. Probably deriving the dogma from Socrates and Plato (their favourite philosophers), they formed from the "archetypes" of existence, a regular system of spiritual creation anterior to the material. So much doubt hangs over the authenticity of the Koran and its authorship, and so many traces of palpable deception may be observed in the Ahadis of the prophet, that it is very doubtful whether the doctrine of pre-existence is a fundamental one of Islam, or the introduction of a later age.

(10.) Or Sayyid Abd el Latif. See Chapter IV.

(11.) Hence it is that Hafiz has probably driven more readers mad than Thomas Aquinas.

(12.) As, for instance, in the verses upon the subject of Marui.

(13.) Not including the second rate saints, who probably would be upwards of a hundred.

(14.) Some of the chief Pirs are so ignorant that they will write Yhangal for Yangal, Mashud for Mashud, and so on.

(15.) There is an old Joe Miller told in Affghanistan;—for aught I know, throughout Central Asia,—that a Murid once boasted of his Pir's habit of going every night to heaven like the Prophet. As the story was doubted, the disciple applied to his master for a confirmation of its truth in presence of the sceptics, and when the Pir denied the assertion, beat him into asserting it.

(16.) Hence it is that Hindoos will sometimes become the disciples of Moslems; not, however, that they abandon the religion of their forefathers, but because, like such religionists in general, they consider it safer to believe too much than too little. In Sindh they always visit the superior by night. In Affghanistan, where they are half Mohammedans, they act more publicly, having no Brahmans to correct their evil practices of paying strangers, and besides, being glad to secure some kind of religious protection without completely compromising themselves.

(17.) So different in this point from the Italians, as their proverb proves,—"Passato il pericolo, gabbato il santo."

(18.) Mohammed humbles himself by owning to the imperfection of man, himself included; Junayd exalts himself. The Sufi explains the difficulty thus:—The saint, being of a lower capacity than the Prophet, spoke as one filled with divine love; the Prophet's superior capability showed him how much more was to be attained by man.

(19.) A Jelali is not necessarily a Moslem. When an infidel, it is concluded that on the Yaum el Misak—the day of covenant between the created or separated spirit and the Supreme Soul—he either refused to enter into, or broke the express compact to believe in his Creator.

(20.) A Kalandar is defined to be a Sufi, who has no Murshid or religious teacher, but works out his salvation by himself. The orthodox Sufis blame the order, but cannot help owning that it has produced some very distinguished saints.

The Kalandar does not, however, refuse to take Murids, or followers, as is proved by the case of Lal Shah-Baz.

(21.) "Dread," as it was heard from the distance of six miles. Kutb el Zaman (pivot of the age) is one of the prophet's innumerable *noms de guerre.*

(22.) Called Lall, or "Red," because, on one occasion, to imitate Abraham, he sat a whole year in a Kanai (iron pot), covered with a lid, and placed over a roaring fire. As might be expected, when he came forth his colour was rubicund.

He is termed the Shah-Baz, or "falcon," because he assumed that shape in order to release a distinguished saint and friend, Shaykh Sadr, who had been impaled by an infidel king on suspicion of magical practices.

(23.) The first and second are the most common in Sindh; the third and fourth are numerous in India. For an account of them, see Ferishtah, vol. 2, p. 711, 786, Bombay edition.

D'Ohsson says nothing of the Chishti order; the other three are not described, as they have been noticed by many authors.

(24.) Or "Kursi-namah," the line of investiture from the Prophet downwards. It is in this sense opposed to the Shajarah, or Nasab Namah, the genealogical tree or line of descent.

(25.) Rug for kneeling upon in prayer.

(26.) The words are, I believe, "God bless and save Mohammed and his descendants."

(27.) The feet are drawn up, so that the heels touch the hams, and the individual "sits at squat," with the arms placed across the knees, and the head resting upon the former. A sheet is sometimes thrown over the head. This position finds great favour with the Sufis.

(28.) A formula repeated aloud, as opposed to "Fikr" (a meditation). The Kadiri order affects the Zikr, and never regards the presence of infidels. As loudness of voice is considered a kind of semi-religious merit, it is by no means pleasant to live in their neighbourhood.

(29.) Called Habs el Nafas. The origin of this practice may be traced to India and Persia. I have never, however, heard of the Sufis performing the hypnotic exercise of fixing the eyes on the tip of the nose, or trying to look upwards between the eyebrows, as practised by the Hindoos and Guebres.

(30.) About two fingers' breadth below the left nipple.

(31.) The idea is the same as the Haft-payeh of the Guebres. The Hindoos probably produced the germ of it in their system of the Dasadwar (the ten passages in the human body for the action of the faculties).

(32.) The Murid is the pupil, as opposed to the Murshid, Pir or Shaykh (the instructor). Sufis in general are called Salik, "wayfarers," as being travellers (on the road to heaven, salvation, &c.)

(33.) Some conclude each formula with the phrase "Ilahi anta maksudi wa rizaka matlubi." "O Lord, Thee I search, and thy daily bread I desire."

(34.) As regards all these numbers it must be recollected that the point is settled by the Murshid, who in the case of a rich or great Murid, would have sense enough to suit the number of prayers to the energy or faith of his pupil.

(35.) Herklots (pp. 296-7) and Mrs. Mir Hasan Ali (vol. ii. p. 248) give an imperfect idea of these nice distinctions.

(36.) Opposed to the Nakshbandi, who believe in Wahdat el Shuhud, and consider the recognising a distinction between Creator and creature a step above the opinion that identifies them.

(37.) The Khalifeh is of two kinds :—

First. Jaddi, hereditary, a blood relation.
Second. Khulfai, one selected by or adopted by a Pir.

(38.) The list of several degrees given in the work of Firuz i Sufi is as follows :—

1. Mukallid or Talib, a pupil, apprentice.
2. Kamil, perfect, a master.
3. Mukammal, more perfect, one who has instructed many masters.
4. Akmal, most perfect, the highest class of such devotees.

Besides which there are always 356 Auliyae Din or great saints, most of whom are Sufis, viz. :—

300 Abtal, the lowest class of the order Wali, or holy man.	Different grades of dignity, the last being the highest.
40 Abdal.	
7 Sayyah.	
5 Autad.	
3 Kutb el Autad.	
1 Kutb el Aktab.	

(39.) Meaning "one of negative actions," *i. e.* whose actions do not proceed from himself.

(40.) Most sects, however, allow a Murid to choose another Murshid when one departs this life: comparing such case to the succession of the prophets.

(41.) Particularly the exalted action of the faculties under the influence of modified mania.

(42.) A Persian book composed by one Mohammed Aazam bin Shaykh Mohammed in A.H. 1194 (A.D.) 1780). It is one of many written upon the subject of the multitudinous Pirs of Sindh.

(43.) Or Mekkali, "Mecca-like," (in sanctity, &c.). Jam Tamachi built a mosque on these hills by order of the holy Shaykh Hammad, and ordered that people should be buried round it, instead of being carried for sepulture to Pir Patta.

(44.) The Langotu, in the Sindhi language, meaning a suspender. Scantiness of habiliments is peculiar to the Kalandar and Jelali Fakirs.

(45.) See Chapter III. for a short account of this individual.

(46.) An especial mark of favour. Both holy men had probably performed their ablutions before going to prayer, and even passing by carrion would have been extremely offensive to them.

(47.) A Hadis declares that no Sayyid is ever black, one eyed, a coward, a miser, a man with a thin beard, &c. &c..

(48.) Some approved hagiologists relate this story about Shaykh Hasan Safai, another very venerable person.

(49.) Mister Sweet and Mister Dyed.

(50.) Very similar is the Irish legend of St. Kevin and the seven churches.

(51.) Hasan and Hosayn. These appearances, however, are not always material, though, at the same time, not completely spiritual. They may be called semi-material, as the visions appear material to spiritual persons only: the vulgar herd of historians and annalists cannot hope to be so favoured by Heaven.

CHAPTER IX.

(1.) Probably because the celebrated saint and scholar, Shaykh Abd el Kadir Gilani, popularly called "Pir i dastgir," belonged to this family. This Abd el Kadir's name is, perhaps, greater in Sindh than in any other Moslem country.

(2.) Whereas the Kalhoras claimed descent from Abbas. They were originally Channa Sindhis, and therefore converted Hindoos. When the family rose to distinction, it asserted a right to be called Beni Abbas; but their Shajaro or genealogical tree was pronounced by the learned to be a complete failure. Upon this, they sent a messenger to copy the documents in the possession of the holy men of Sehrah Khatibah, and when the latter offered some objection, the Kalhoras confiscated their feofs, attacked and destroyed their villages, carried off the copper plates upon which the Shajaro was delineated, and thus became undoubted descendants from Abbas and Murshids.

(3.) Whereas in Arabia generally, if the father be a Sayyid, the sons would take his rank, whatever that of their mother might have been; and also the daughters, who would be styled Sharifeh. On the other hand, the offspring of Sayyid mothers by common Moslems would merely be Arabs.

(4.) The word is generally corrupted into "Buzrig."

(5.) Both of them Talpurs, an inferior hill clan. Even when they became rulers of Sindh, Mahmud Khan, the lord of Kelat, was ready to go to war with Amir Ghulam Ali Talpur, because the latter had the audacity to propose to a female of his family (the Kambarani).

(6.) The Dheri is a bit of stone or other such material, round which the raw wool thread is twisted. The Kambo is a long cloth thrown over the right shoulder, and so fastened round the waist as to leave a place for the lambs and kids that are too young to walk.

(7.) He was cut down by Ismail Mombiyani, a Sindhi, who immediately struck his head off. The Kalhora had previously ordered one Shah Baharo to do the deed: he refused, but offered to fight Mir Bahram single-handed. The event is still celebrated in Sindh, and is a kind of common place with the bards and singers.

(8.) Whence they emigrated under a leader called Kambar. Hence it is that the chief clan is called Kambarani. They own, however, two distinct families of Belochis, namely, the aborigines of Mekran, whom some call the Kuch Belochis, and those Arabs who emigrate from Arabia with Hajjaj, the son of Yusuf, and settled in the conquered provinces of Mekran and Belochistan, whilst the rest of the invading army marched into Sindh.

(9.) Moreover, he can honour and confide in a brave man, even though that man be an enemy—a rare thing among Eastern nations!

(10.) Especially drinking. The younger members of the court used to set their followers a very bad example by indulging to excess in champagne, curaçoa and other liqueurs. Thus, intoxication became a fashionable vice among the sons and grandsons of the old Ameers, to whose ears the name of a spirituous liquor was an abomination. Of course, the people soon learned to imitate their princes.

(11.) Whence they also imported the Shieh tenets, so extensively adopted by the juniors of the ruling family. The Belochis in Sindh are almost universally Hanafi Moslems.

(12.) The blades are of two shapes, curved and straight: the best specimens of the former came from Khorasan and Persia, the latter from India. Inferior swords are made in Cutch and Guzerat, and the worst of all is the Sindhi blade, its price being usually from five to six rupees.

The Belochi is ignorant of the complicated and grotesque Indian style of sword play, which presents such a contrast to the graceful and scientific practice of our schools. His fighting is a simple exchange of cuts, to be received upon the shield, or to be avoided by retreating.

(13.) Where it is said a skilful archer can sometimes pierce an iron spade at the distance of fifty or sixty yards.

(14.) Who set a very bad example to their inferiors by being perpetually in the company of panders and prostitutes. By this conduct, they lost to a great extent the respect of their brave and hardy followers.

(15.) As a discipline to secure her chastity.

(16.) Not all children, as has been erroneously stated.

(17.) Hence the popular expression, "Mai di dhi khir pi mui;" Anglicè, "The lady's daughter died drinking milk."

(18.) In a short description of this extraordinary people, see "Goa and the Blue Mountains," &c. Bentley.

(19.) The Ameers preferred the Arab, Persian and Khorasan breeds.

(20.) Two Persian treatises on Farriery and Falconry.

(21.) Jat^u in the Sindhi dialect means, 1, a camel driver or breeder of camels; 2, the name of a Beloch clan.

Jat^u, or, written as it is pronounced, "Dyat^u," has three significations:—1. The name of a tribe (the Jats); 2. A Sindhi, as opposed to a Beloch—in this sense an insulting expression. So the Belochis and Brahuis of the hills call the Sindhi language "Jathki." 3. A word of insult, a "barbarian," as in the expression, do-dasto Jat^u, "an utter savage."

(22.) Lieutenant Wood's work shows that the Jats are still found in the Panjab, and all along the banks of the Indus, from its mouth to the Attock.

(23.) Under the name Jat no less than four distinct races are comprised. For a short account of them, see the preface to a grammar of the Jataki dialect, published by the Bombay branch of the Asiatic Society, 1849.

It appears probable, from the appearance and other peculiarities of the race, that the Jats are connected by consanguinity with that peculiar race the Gypsies. Of one hundred and thirty words (as used by the Gypsies in Syria), no less than one hundred and four belong to the Indo-Persian class of language. The rest may either be the remains of one of the barbarous tongues spoken by the aboriginal mountaineers who inhabited the tract between the Indus and Eastern Persia, or the invention of a subsequent age, when their diffusion throughout hostile tribes rendered a thieves' language necessary. The numerals are almost all pure Persian. There are two words, "Kuri" (a house), and "Psik" (a cat), probably corrupted from the Pushtu, "Kor" and "Pishu." Two words are Sindhi, "Manna" (S. Mani), bread, and "Hui" (S. Hu), he. As might be expected from a tribe inhabiting Syria, Arabic and Turkish words occasionally occur, but they form no part of the ground-work of the language.

(24.) Alluding to the colour of their clothes.

(25.) The Meman in Sindh has his own handwriting: in Cutch, he uses the Guzerattee character.

(26.) The word Khwajeh seems to be a titular appellation of the race: in Persian, it signifies a bard, a teacher, and a merchant; it is sometimes prefixed to an individual's name, as our Mister, or addressed to a person, as we should say Sir. The general reader will detect in the "Coyia" of the "Arabian Nights," a French attempt at the orthography of Khwajeh.

(27.) Sir Erskine Perry's remarks upon the origin of this strange tribe are, I believe, inaccurate. He says, "The Kojahs are a small caste in West India, who appear to have originally come from Sindh or Cutch, and who, by their own traditions, which are probably correct, were converted from Hindooism about 400 years ago by a Pir named Sudr Din. * * * * Although they call themselves Mussulmans, they evidently know but little of their prophet and of the Koran, and their chief reverence at the present time is reserved for Agha Khan, a Persian nobleman well known in contemporaneous Indian history, and whom they believe to be a descendant of the Pir who converted them to Islam."

It must be remembered that the Shieh branch of the Moslem creed, whenever settled amongst anti-religionists, always holds as a tenet, and rigidly adheres to the practice called Takiyyah, *i. e.* the systematic concealment of everything that concerns their faith, history, customs, and, in a word, any peculiarities the disclosure of which might be attended with unpleasant consequences.

(28.) He was driven out of Persia after a most ridiculons attempt at rebellion against the reigning sovereign, Mohammed Shah. His claim to the throne is based upon his religious position as head of the Ismailiyeh heresy.

For a popular account of the sect which gave origin to the once dreaded assassins, see "W. C. Taylor's History of Mohammedanism and its sects."

(29.) In Bombay they have now split into two classes, one party still acknowledging the Agha's authority; the other setting up a person named Nur Mohammed, as their superior. A bloody feud was lately the result of the dissension.

(30.) Literally "handless" or "maimed."

(31.) The legend of the flying carpet probably gave rise to these numerous tales about Sulayman and his wanderings. In Affghanistan, Luristan and Kurdistan, there are all kinds of traditions and descriptions of that prophet's adventures. No eastern Moslem doubts that he visited Cashmir, and some assert that he reigned over it for some time.

(32.) They are the worst clothed class in Sindh. A Mohano is scarcely ever seen with slippers; but this may be a custom among them.

(33.) Sometimes a Georgian was brought down, but only on private order; their price being too high to admit of much speculation.

(34.) As the Sirdar of Nooshky said to Captain Christie, "The severest punishment we can inflict on one of them is to turn him about his business."

(35.) All the African blacks in Sindh are of the Moslem persuasion.

(36.) Similar to that called "Kil" in Persia.

(37.) I never heard of a book amongst them.

(38.) All rules of grammar are of course unknown to them.

CHAPTER X.

(1.) See Chapter III., where Babbur ("Mimosa tree") is the name given to a slave.

(2.) In Sindh, Akiko includes the ceremonies of the sacrifice, and the shaving of the child's head. Not so in Hindostan, especially the Deccan. See Herklot's Qanoon e Islam. Chapter 3, Sect. 2, Note.

(3.) No evil results are expected from the circumcision of adults; it has often been tried in the cases of African slaves. The cure, however, is generally protracted for the period of at least six weeks.

(4.) As the holy law of the Koran is, like many other sacred compilations, utterly inadequate to provide for the legislative wants of the remote lands and times, which it accidentally reached, throughout Islam the Rasm or ancient practice of the country is held sacred by the people, always when not in direct opposition to revelation, sometimes even when it is so.

It is a mistake not unfrequently made by Europeans to suppose that the law of the Koran necessarily settles a disputed point between Moslems. And it is by no means an easy operation to adjust the balance between the good sense of the ancient practice, and the discrepant decrees of the inspired volume.

(5.) Colonel Sleeman considers "this squandering of large sums in marriage ceremonies" to be "one of the evils which press most upon Indian society."

(6.) The same vile practice prevails among some of the lowest castes of Hindoos in India.

(7.) The Var is a ring made of several circles of plain metal. The Khirol is a single circle with a flat surface like a seal ring, but containing no stone.

(8.) Considered a beauty in Sindh.

(9.) These, however, as well as shaving are seldom used in Sindh. Vellication is the prevailing method; it is extremely painful at first, but the skin soon loses its great sensibility.

(10.) Surma (antimony) is more frequently used on ordinary occasions than Kajjal.

(11.) Generally made from the Sarih (*Sinapis glauca*), perfumed with ottar of Roses, Chambeli (a kind of jasmin), or some other popular scent, and coloured red with madder.

(12.) A composition called Eriyo or Kinkino.

(13.) Among the highest classes as long as six weeks.

(14.) Generally a Nath or large gold or silver ring worn by married women only in the right or left nostril. Secondly, a Bulo or small ring inserted in the cartilage between the nostrils, and allowed to hang over the upper lip. Among the wealthy it is set with coral, pearls or precious stones. The poor content themselves with a bit of silver made in the form of a drop, and called a "Paro." Thirdly, a Mundhi, or finger ring of gold, with a ruby, turquoise or diamond inserted into it. The less expensive ones are enamelled; the cheapest are of plain metal.

The number of jewels depends, of course, upon the wealth of the parties; among the very rich, large sums of money are thus expended.

(15.) The highest classes do not send witnesses: the father, or some other near relative, constitutes himself the wakil. Also when the bride is very young, she is not consulted.

(16.) Presents of dress sent before marriage among the respectable natives are considered the wife's property.

(17.) A corruption of the Persian "Sargasht."

(18.) A "happy woman," *i. e.* one happily married to her first husband Properly speaking, the parents of both parties should be alive, but this condition is sometimes dispensed with.

(19.) The verses are, as usual, enigmatical.

By the moon, the bridegroom is intended: the bride is called a Hur, or virgin of Paradise. She is also termed a "Sister," on account of the tie of brotherhood which unites all the Faithful. And the hope that she may use her anklets means, "May she never be a widow;" as the use of that ornament is, or ought to be, interdicted to relicts.

(20.) A certain omen of approaching death, according to the most approved Arabian Oneirocritics.

(21.) This part of the subject is too generally known to Europeans to require any details.

(22.) So, and sufficiently incorrectly, the author of the Kanz el Ibrat defines Sijjin. His account of the pains of the tomb is not nearly so long as that of many learned men, some of whom enumerate not less than ninety-nine varieties, a few of them borrowed from the Ahadis, and many more of their own invention.

(23.) He was afterwards obliged to leave the city. A very similar case occurred a few years ago at Naples. Some freethinker acquainted with chemistry thought proper to show how blood could be made to effervesce; and the government, out of compliment to San Gennaro, the city's patron saint, banished him immediately.

(24.) There is a popular idea in many parts of the East, that during the death-throe, when agony induces violent thirst, the Father of Sin appears to the dying man and offers him a cup of pure water in exchange for his precious soul. Hence, probably, the custom of moistening the lips.

In cold climates the idea would scarcely take root.

(25.) Hence it is that aged Moslems are fond of staining the beard. In facetious tales, it is not uncommon for young maidens insultingly to compare the hoary honours of their old admirers' chins to cotton in the mouth of a corpse.

Throughout Islam generally the people dislike the odour of camphor, connecting it naturally with its use amongst them. I have heard Persians, when speaking of a dismal or dreary book, say, "it has the Bue Kafur" (smell of camphor).

(26.) Herklots. Qanoon-E-Islam. Glossary, p. 60, "Abeer."

(27.) The reason of which is the popular belief, that the sooner the corpse is buried, the better it is for all parties.

Within and near the tropics, there is good sense in the ordinance.

(28.) As in Sindh, Mecca is supposed to lie in a due south direction, the direction of the corpse is N. and S.

(29.) According to the law of Abu Hanifah. The works called Siraji and Mir Sharif, together with other commentaries on the Ruku (paragraph) of the Koran, which treats of legacy, are those generally studied.

The Iddat, or stated period of widowhood, is also settled according to the Hanafi law.

(30.) Corresponding with our mourning.

The Sindhis rarely wear black clothes as a sign of grief, though sometimes a male will put on a turban of that colour.

The Arabs of the present day, as well as the ancient, consider the practice to be an innovation, and certainly, it was not known in the time of the Prophet. Probably the Moslems of Central Asia derived it from the Guebres, amongst whom it may be traced up to the time of Siyawush.

(31.) The religious reason of which is, that on the Last Day such pebbles, it is asserted, will pray for the forgiveness of the dead man.

The tree Arak, a species of Salvadora, has a kind of sanctity among Moslems generally, as being a native of W. Arabia, and having been esteemed by the Prophet. In Sindh, it is considered the best for Miswak (sticks to clean the teeth).

(32.) Or make a solemn promise to the dying man. This is called "Umanat Karanu."

CHAPTER XI.

(1.) Meaning those settled in the plains. The nomadic tribes of Sindhis, and those inhabiting the hills, like the Jokiya near Kurrachee, are scarcely to be distinguished from the Belochis.

(2.) The lower the caste is, the blacker its colour. Fairness distinguishes the higher classes, particularly the females, among whom it is possible to find individuals very little darker than the Spaniards or the Portuguese.

(3.) That is to say, the head entirely shaven, as in Arabia, not partially, as in India, Persia and Affghanistan. Some Sindhis, however, and many of the Belochis, allow a long lock of hair to grow at the poll of the head.

(4.) Principally by old men and prostitutes.

(5.) Different kinds of toasted pulses and grains.

(6.) Chashm e Murwarid ("the pearl eye"), as it is called in Persian.

(7.) Of Fitr and Bakar. Herklots, page 268. The Eedgah is the place where prayers are read.

(8.) A very violent exercise intended to strengthen the arms, and muscles of the chest and back. The athlete lies flat upon his stomach, raises himself from the ground upon his hands, and then sinks down again. This is repeated as often as possible.

(9.) Who consider that gambling during the month of Sawan is a species of religious exercise. The Hindoos do not, however, limit play to that small portion of the year.

(10.) Exactly resembling the way in which we do it.

(11.) It exactly resembles the game played in Europe. Its Persian origin is very probable, as it appears to have been known there in very ancient times, and was more likely to travel westward from that country, than to have been imported into it.

(12.) See Herklots. Appendix, p. 52, "Pucheesee."

(13.) A man who killed his wife under such circumstances was always applauded for the deed. If the husband chose to overlook his wife's offence, a fine was taken from the detected paramour and paid to government, besides which he was flogged and otherwise punished if of low rank. When the adultress was put to death, her lover was required to give his sister, daughter, or some other female relation, in marriage to the injured husband. This was always exacted by the Belochis, in the rare cases when they refrained from killing both parties.

(14.) As, for instance, Mazenderan in Persia, and Tehamah in Arabia, both of which localities have as bad a celebrity as Sindh.

(15.) As the Zenani boli, or female dialect, of Hindostan.

(16.) A new class has lately appeared, composed of women who are half respectable, half prostitutes; they devote themselves to Europeans and the Seapoys. At Hyderabad, the courtesans have complained that their occupation was gone, in consequence of the loose conduct of the married women.

(17.) The former is the polite, the latter the rude, generic name of the caste. It is also used insultingly to any description of female.

(18.) Instead of the Cholo, Belochi women generally wear the Gaghgho, a long shift resembling our night shirts, but opening behind between the shoulders, and with half arms. It is generally made of red or white stuff, and reaches almost down to the ancles. Among the lowest orders of that people, no trowsers or drawers are worn under it.

(19.) The working classes, such as the fishermen's wives and others, always wear the Gaj without any shift over it.

(20.) Perhaps there may be some physiological reason for this peculiarity. It is observable among the nations living between the Caspian and India, as the Persians, Affghans, Belochis and Sindhis. It is found in Cashmir, but it is not general in Hindostan.

(21.) For instance, Herklots. Appendix, p. xvii.

(22.) "Langho" is an uncivil, "Manganharu" a polite name for these people: they are also called "Bhanu" and "Mangato" in Sindh, and "Mirasi" towards the north.

(23.) In honour of Mohammud, the celebrated ode called, from its first words, "Banat Suad," was composed; the reward was a Khelat or robe, given by the Prophet to the poet. In several parts of the Moslem world there is a popular superstition about this ode, that if recited in presence of a superior, it will infallibly have the effect of procuring a present of clothing.

(24.) Being compelled by sickness to leave the country, I was unable to procure any information about the Kalwat, or to observe the instruments used by them and the Langha.

(25.) "Shisho" means "glass;" and "basho" is that kind of insignificant reduplicative noun called "Muhmilah" in Arabic grammar.

(26.) So the Musalli (sweeper) in Affghanistan calls his clan the "Shah-Khel," or "royal tribe."

(27.) In many parts of Sindh there are Mussulman sweepers, who must not be confounded with the Bali-Shahi.

(28.) The word being composed of "Dah" (ten), and "Pher" (a difference or change). Among the Affghans there is a similar pun made upon the word "Panj-abi" (one of "five waters," *i. e.* the child of "five fathers").

CHAPTER XII.

(1.) In Sindh, the worshippers of Vishnu are called Vishanvohu, (a corruption of "Vaishnava"). They are forbidden to drink spirituous liquors, or to eat meat, fish, onions, eggs and other irregular kinds of food. Any Brahman, Banyan or Shudra may become a Vishanvohu, by first going to some well-known Tirth (place of pilgrimage), and afterwards paying due attention to his diet.

(2.) Like the Banyans. The words do not, as in India, denote any difference of caste; for instance, the son of a "Ram" or "Das" may be called "Chand," or "Rae," and *vice versâ*.

(3.) There are three years in Sindh, as in India generally. 1st. The Arabic Hijri or Lunar. 2nd. The Indian, or Luni-solar; and, 3rd. The Fasli or official year, determined by the seasons. Vikramaditya's Æra (the Sanbat) is commonly used by the Hindoos here; that of Shalivahan is known to the Brahmans only. The ancient Indians had six seasons; their modern descendants have three; the Arabs and Persians four, and the Sindhis generally, like the Portuguese of Goa, reckon only two, namely, the Siyaro, or cold weather, and the Unhalo or Arhar (hot half of year). At the same time, as some words for spring and autumn are required, especially in poetry, "Buhar" and "Sawan" are borrowed from the Persian and Sanscrit.

The names of the days of the week and months in Sindh are evidently corrupted Sanscrit. The Moslems borrow from the Arabic words to denote Wednesday, Thursday and Friday (Arba, Khamis and Jummo). Hindoo names of months are known to Mussulmans as far north as Peshawar. The Affghans have terms derived from their own language to express them.

Among the Sindhis, Saturday and Sunday are unlucky days: Tuesday is praised by the Hindoos, and deemed unfortunate by the Moslems. The Brahmans are aware of the existence of the several Yugas, but never assume the commencement of the last one as a date. Their minor subdivisions of time are exactly similar to those known in India. Many Brahmans can calculate the intercalation of the month (called Adhaku), but they appear to insert it into any part of the year indifferently.

(4.) "Red lead." Mlenchha means a "Gentile," *i. e.* one not a Hindoo.

(5.) In Sindh, the "Pujaro" is the worshipper of the River-god; "Shewak," one that adores the Hindoo triad; and "Trahlio," the follower of some religious mendicant.

(6.) Different kinds of fairs and pilgrimages.

(7.) At such times the Chuna, or side locks, are also removed.

(8.) These books in India are usually produced and received as testimony in a court of law. This should not be generally allowed in Sindh, as few men can currently read their own handwriting a month after it was written, and thus numerous errors creep in.

(9.) The newly married man was expected to stay at home till the birth of his first child. After that, he might set out on his travels as soon as he pleased.

(10.) Of which, as great a variety is found in Sindh as in any part of India.

(11.) Called also the Japamala. It consists of twenty-seven beads, which are told over four times; the number of one hundred and eight being the most proper for the repetition of such forms as "Ram, Ram, Ram;" "Wah Guru ji ki Fath!" "Shri Ganesaya Namaha," &c.

(12.) Of the two Granths (Scriptures), viz., the Adi Granth, and the Dashema Granth, the former is the more respected, the latter the more obeyed, because the easier to obey. The Panja Granth is a collection of five short poems, as its name denotes; they are called, 1. Jap; 2 Sandar; 3. Sukhmani; 4. Bawan-akhri; 5. Sidha-gosht. Interspersed among these are many of the peculiar kinds of hymns called Bani and Gita.

(13.) Nanak, like all eastern prophets, was a poet of no mean celebrity. In early times, prophecy and poetry seem to have gone together in passing for supernatural productions. So the ancients could not account for Homer's powers of versification, except by deriving them from the Muses and Apollo.

(14.) The polite and reverential way of speaking of the inspired Book.

(15.) A wooden stick, forked at the top, to enable the devotee to rest his forehead upon it.

(16.) From the Sindhi verb "Bhabakanu," to boil up.

(17.) The polite appellation of the caste.

(18.) I have given these words as a specimen of their peculiar dialect. The word Dand properly means anything mixed and spoiled, as grain with mud, &c.

The Ameer, Fath Ali, is said to be a man of "half family," because he was ruler of the country.

(19.) Its votaries, however, are quite as bigoted as in Western India generally; this has been proved by their systematic opposition to the introduction of vaccination, because, as they alleged, it was impious to interfere with the operations of the Goddess Devi, to whom the origin of the disease is ascribed.

(20.) Their ideas on this point, however, are not strictly defined; Venkunth (as they call it) is another Paradise with them, and not a few cling to a confused system of metempsychosis.

(21). A large dish composed of cooked rice or fine flour, sugar and clarified butter.

(22.) Called "Panjara," because consisting of stanzas of five lines. The hymn addressed to Uddhero Lall (quoted below), is a sample of this kind of composition.

(23.) The meaning of the Persian and Arabic Khwajah Khizr, which in Sindhi is translated by Sanwal Shah, the "green king." The Spaniards also have their Rio verde,—verdant river.

(24.) The name of the Banyan poet. The original hymn contains one hundred verses. Many of them have been omitted; tautology and repetition are easily pardoned in Sindh.

(25.) It is in the Sindhi language, apparently a translation from the Persian, and yet a great favourite with the educated Hindoo. The Orientalist will not fail to remark how it abounds in the common places of Eastern devotional poetry.

(26.) The sheet thrown over the shoulder by the poorer classes in Sindh.

(27.) A pun upon the saint's name, "Lal" here meaning "a ruby."

(28.) Ardas, a religious offering. Vriddhi, increase (of wealth, happiness, &c.). Siddhi, accomplishment (of all designs, temporal and eternal).

(29.) The province that had the honour of producing Lal Shah-Baz.

(30.) "Book of Omens." See Chapter 7.

CHAPTER XIII.

(1.) A kind of head Moonshee, who acts as accountant, &c.

(2.) As the Wejhan-waro was obliged to keep an impression of every seal that he cut, stamped upon a piece of paper, he was always able, if willing, to lend himself to the fraud.

(3.) Certain manuscript directions issued to the native officials.

(4.) Hence it is called "Janeo ji Shadi:" It is invariably performed as soon after a boy has reached his fifth year as the means of a family will permit; and never is delayed beyond the twenty-fifth.

(5.) A kind of necklace worn by women. It is also called Dusri or Dohri, and is made of two lines of little gold beads, threaded on silk. This, together with the boy's clothes, is considered as a perquisite belonging to his female relations.

(6.) The knot of hair worn by Hindoos on the poll of the head.

(7.) "Dakhna," the technical name for a present to a Brahman. "Namishkar," the reverence made to the priestly tribe.

(8.) "Father, thou art congratulated."

(9.) The first sentence means, "Father, father, I am about to die!" It is, however, enigmatical, although generally understood as above translated. The father replies, "Son, thou goest not (to death), nor do thy grandchildren go." These are set forms of words.

(10.) For instance, when bathing, after water has been poured over the body, the Janeo is cleaned before the limbs are washed.

(11.) Of flour, clarified butter, and raw sugar, varying in quantity from ten to fifty pounds.

(12.) "The day of Jasraj." Many trifling explanations of the word are given. Jasraj is the name of a popular Hindoo saint.

(13.) "The day of the water-pot."

(14.) "The day of joy." "Mahurat," which properly means, the nuptial procession, is also used to denote the marriage day.

(15.) Popular superstition never allows a horse to be ridden on such occasions.

(16.) The part of the procession that accompanies the bridegroom is called "Jani," opposed to "Mani," those who attend upon the bride.

(17.) Both the Vedi and the Lavan are in Sanscrit.

(18.) A hundred Rupees is the sum usually given.

(19.) From one to two hundred Rupees. If the present be too small, the Ghotapiu (bridegroom's father) objects to it, and the sum to be paid is settled by the Brahmans.

(20.) "Peko" (*i. e.* Piyajo), or "Pekano ghar," is the father's house (speaking relatively to the bride); opposed to "Sahorano ghar," the house of her father-in-law.

(21.) Strange to say, the fine distinction drawn by the Brahmans in India between death during the Uttarayan (northing of the sun), and Dakhshanayan, is not recognised by the Sindh Hindoos.

(22.) The Pinniyawaro is so called from the rite "Pinni." He is generally the eldest son, nephew, or near relation of the deceased.

(23.) This is done by the Pinniyawaro. In some places, at this stage of the proceedings the chief mourner removes and presents to the Jajak a gold ring, which is purposely left on one of the dead man's fingers. Various articles, such as a little clarified butter, sandal-wood, &c. are placed in the corpse's mouth; but in this, as in other parts of the ceremony, the local customs differ greatly.

(24.) "Sit ye down, may the company be happy!"

(25.) The water is changed every day.

(26.) Called the "Yaraho;" the ceremonies performed on that day are described below.

(27.) If the deceased be rich, his ashes and the remains of his bones, reduced to a fine powder, are mixed with milk, made up into a ball, covered with deerskin, gold cloth, and other materials, and given either to a servant or to some religious mendicant, to be cast into the Ganges. The expense of this luxury varies from fifty to three hundred rupees.

(28.) The Karnigor, according to some, is a Banyan; others say he is a mixed breed between a Brahman father and a Shudra mother. North of Hyderabad, his appearance and conduct resemble those of the servile; south of the same place, those of the priestly order. He will eat meat and fish, but takes nothing from the hand of a Moslem.

As there are very few families of this class in remote places, Brahmans act as Karnigors at funerals. Their peculiar duties appear to result rather from the practice of the country, than to originate from the written authority of the Shastras.

(29.) This accounts for the presence of this tree at wells, on the banks of rivers and other such places.

(30.) At female burials, the Karnigor's wife attends, and she is generally even more exorbitant in her demands than her husband is.

(31.) An action called "Patashtha.'

(32.) The twelfth day, or its ceremony.

(33.) Herklots. Appendix, p. 42. He calls it Butasha.

(34.) From eighty to two hundred rupees would be the general range of the expense. This is rather a long "undertaker's bill," but more civilized people than the Hindoos allow themselves to be imposed upon in as barefaced a manner.

(35.) The head of a widow (even of a Brahman) is either shaved only once, or not at all, unless she visit some place of pilgrimage. The latter is an optional act of devotion. She removes all her ornaments, except the nose ring, for a few days, and uses no oil or perfumes during that period.

It is evident from these proceedings, that Sindhi Hinduism in some essential points is lax in the extreme.

(36.) "Sermon," generally in Arabic, upon the subject of Mohammed's birth, &c.

(37.) Which, as in India, has always the prefix of Shaykh.